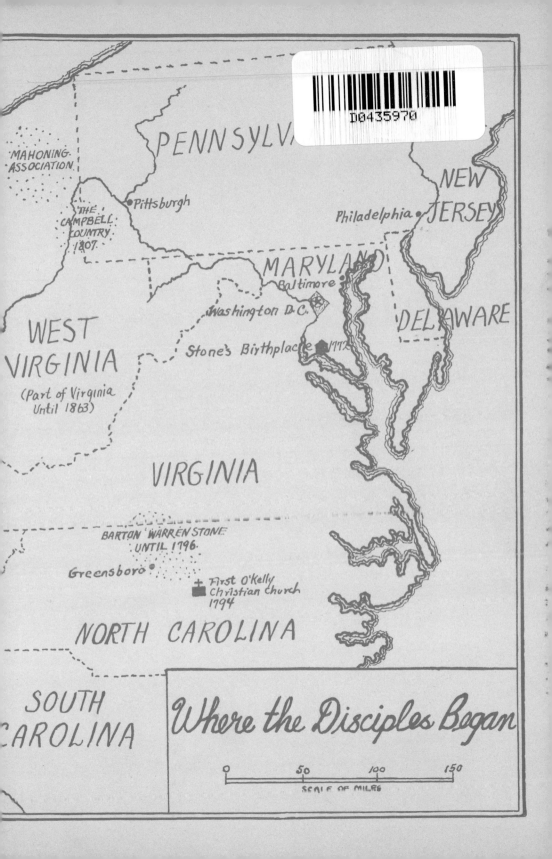

PENNSYLVA...

NEW JERSEY

MAHONING ASSOCIATION

•Pittsburgh

THE CAMPBELL COUNTRY 1807

Philadelphia•

MARYLAND

Baltimore

Washington D.C.

DELAWARE

WEST VIRGINIA

(Part of Virginia Until 1863)

Stone's Birthplace 1772

VIRGINIA

BARTON WARREN STONE UNTIL 1796

Greensboro•

First O'Kelly Christian Church 1794

NORTH CAROLINA

SOUTH CAROLINA

Where the Disciples Began

0   50   100   150

SCALE OF MILES

Journey in Faith

**A HISTORY
OF THE CHRISTIAN CHURCH
(DISCIPLES
OF CHRIST)**

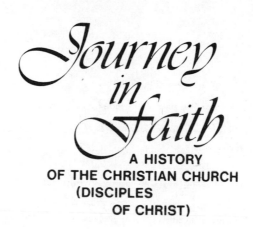

Journey in Faith

**A HISTORY
OF THE CHRISTIAN CHURCH
(DISCIPLES
OF CHRIST)**

by
**Lester G. McAllister
William E. Tucker**

The Bethany Press

Saint Louis   **Missouri**

Second Printing, 1977

Library of Congress Cataloging in Publication Data

McAllister, Lester
   Journey in faith.

   Bibliography: p.
   Includes index.
   1. Christian Church (Disciples of Christ)—History.
I. Tucker, William Edward, 1932-   joint author.
II. Title
BX7315.M3   286'.6   75-11738
ISBN 0-8272-1703-X

Jacket by Dorothy J. Eicks

Manufactured in the United States of America

Foreword

Where does the Christian Church (Disciples of Christ) stand in the North American social and religious scene at the end of the twentieth century? Such a question can be answered only by a careful look at our history. A reexamination is in order. The heritage, the roots of the movement must be looked at again. The eras of expansion and enthusiasm should be charted. Strife and division, cooperation and unity have played their parts in bringing this religious body to its current status.

Specifically, there is need for another look at the early Disciples on the American frontier, at the beginning of the nineteenth century. What happened to the dreams of those days? Is there yet occasion to rejoice in hope?

Historical research in the past quarter century affords much new grist for the writer's mill. A new, interpretative history that not only tells whence we have come and where we are now but also gives some indication of how we might yet become what we ought to be, is now possible and highly desirable.

Writers, in the recent past have justified their efforts in various ways. A half century ago, B.A. Abbott wrote in a "Prefatory" to his book, *The Disciples: An Interpretation* (Christian Board of Publication, 1924) that "no one can write an authoritative book for the Disciples of Christ." He went on to say that "it is not necessary and it is not desirable . . . but books of interpretation and information are needed."

More recently, in 1973, George G. Beazley, Jr., edited a work on the Disciples of Christ for a German series on American churches, *Die Kirchen der Welt* (Evangelisches Verlagswerk, Stuttgart). An English edition was published, *The Christian Church (Disciples of Christ): An Interpretative Examination in the Cultural Context* (The Bethany Press). In a foreword, Dr. Beazley speaks of the standard, general history:

5

The Disciples of Christ: A History (The Bethany Press, 1948). He considers the authors and feels that "certain hard questions" need to be asked "in the context of a world church and the present cultural climate" which did not concern the earlier writers. This Dr. Beazley seeks to do in the opening and closing chapters of this book.

As for Garrison and DeGroot themselves, they displayed the plan in their foreword to write "a more comprehensive history of the Disciples than any now in existence." They expressed the hope that "it may be the means to a clearer understanding and a deeper appreciation" of the Disciples of Christ.

Considering all of the above viewpoints, and after consulting with various leaders of the church, in 1970 Orville W. Wake, who was serving as the president of the Christian Board of Publication, and I, serving as editor of The Bethany Press, decided that a new history should be undertaken. The result of this decision is now history itself, in the form of this book.

The project called for writers who could be comprehensive and interpretative without being pedantic. We found them in the persons of Lester G. McAllister, Jr., and William E. Tucker. Their doctorates were attained in American Church History with concentrations on the Disciples of Christ. They occupy chairs of church history in leading theological seminaries. Both are trustees of the Disciples of Christ Historical Society and respected by their colleagues in the American Society of Church History. Their previous writing shows them to be careful scholars who write so that one can understand what they are saying.

This is a history of the Christian Church (Disciples of Christ). Hence, no attempt is made at a full assessment of the activities and current status of two other denominations which designate themselves as the Churches of Christ, and the undenominational fellowship of Christian Churches and Churches of Christ. Both of these groups share their early history with the Christian Church (Disciples of Christ). Where the story is parallel, or impinges, it is told in an accurate and unemotional tone.

The time chart at the beginning will be of great help to all readers who need to get their perspective with a few dates.

6

The bibliography is the most complete and usable one in print. Dates of birth and death of persons mentioned in the text, if known, are given in the Index.

We have had the critical assistance of such scholars as Dwight E. Stevenson, Ronald E. Osborn, and Claude E. Spencer. Their comments and advice have made this a better book.

We are glad to present this book to the church and to all who like to read history. It is fascinating and forcible, a very readable book. Christian homes; church and ministers' libraries; church school, college, and seminary classrooms will all find this history highly desirable. It tells our story as it is, and gives us new hope and courage.

Howard E. Short
Distinguished Editor Emeritus
of the
Christian Board of Publication

Preface

The opportunity to write a comprehensive history of a religious denomination occurs only once in a generation or so. Over a quarter of a century has passed since the appearance of *The Disciples of Christ: A History* by Winfred E. Garrison and Alfred T. DeGroot. Their widely read volume, written shortly after the end of World War II, reflects the milieu of the 1940s and the state of historical research at that time. The intervening years have been unusually eventful and tumultuous. A collision of values and viewpoints, especially in the 1960s, shook the foundations of church and society in North America and shattered the triumphalism inherited from former eras.

Like other religious communions, Disciples groped their way toward a reshaping of their priorities. Their sustained effort to develop a more viable church structure led to the adoption of the "Provisional Design of the Christian Church (Disciples of Christ)" in 1968. They chose to participate in the Consultation of Church Union and in other ecumenical ventures at home and abroad. Meanwhile, a surge of interest in Disciples history resulted in a considerable number of important articles and monographs. All of these developments, no doubt, figured in the decision of the Christian Board of Publication under the leadership of Orville Wake to publish a new history of the Christian Church (Disciples of Christ).

Howard E. Short, editor of The Bethany Press at the time, set in motion a long and involved process when he approached the authors at the 1971 General Assembly of Disciples in Louisville and invited us to write a volume on the Stone-Campbell movement from its beginnings on the American frontier to the present. Responding favorably, we proceeded almost immediately to deal with a myriad of

9

details. For the last three years work on the project has continued at a determined and sometimes hectic pace.

Although one of the authors resided in Indiana and the other in Texas, we decided to collaborate as much as possible at every stage in the development of the manuscript. We relied heavily upon correspondence and met now and then in Fort Worth or in Indianapolis or somewhere in between. After the outline had been prepared and revised five times, we accepted individual assignments for the various chapters. McAllister wrote Chapters 2, 4, 5, 7, 11, 12, 14, 16, 17, and 18; he also made the Index. Tucker prepared the timeline and wrote Chapters 1, 3, 6, 8, 9, 10, 13, 15 and the bibliographical essay. We exchanged first drafts of all material; each author criticized the other's work. Howard E. Short served as project coordinator. He advised and encouraged us throughout the period of planning and writing.

The purpose of this volume is to provide a balanced and scholarly history of the Disciples. Instead of viewing the Stone-Campbell movement in isolation, we endeavored to see it within the context of Christianity in North America. Combining chronological and thematic approaches, we aimed to relate the life and thought of a church in process of developing. Perhaps the most difficult chapters to write were those dealing with the recent past. Time is needed to gain perspective. No attempt was made to present in detail the programs and policies of agencies and divisions of the church. Limitations of space dictated other omissions which are all too glaring to the authors. In any event, we trust that our book will encourage the scholarly community to respond to the need for specialized studies treating important but overlooked or misunderstood aspects of Disciples history and thought.

Both of us welcome the opportunity to acknowledge assistance from many quarters. A few individuals were especially helpful. The crucial roles of Howard E. Short and Orville Wake already have been mentioned. Howard Short, Dwight E. Stevenson, Ronald E. Osborn, and Claude E. Spencer read the final manuscript in its entirety. We are grateful to them for saving us from a number of factual errors, misjudgments, and infelicities. Marvin D. Williams, Jr., librarian and archivist of the Disciples of Christ Historical

Society, selected the photographs in the book and responded to our inquiries with dispatch and great care. Our debt to him is large. Other friends and colleagues of the authors deserve recognition for assisting us in a variety of ways. They include Harold E. Fey, Clark M. Williamson, Albert A. Hofrichter, Leslie R. Galbraith, David McWhirter, Thelma Hodges, Harold L. Lunger, Elizabeth Enix, J. Cy Rowell, M. Jack Suggs, Robert A. Olsen, Jr., Mary Maddux, Roscoe Pierson, William Martin Smith, William L. Miller, Jr., James Sugioka, David Moreno, Gertrude Dimke, Howard Dentler, and Kenneth L. Teegarden. Roland K. Huff and the entire staff of the Disciples of Christ Historical Society served us faithfully and well. W. A. Welsh, now president of the Christian Board of Publication, took a personal interest in the book and rarely missed the chance to remind us of approaching deadlines. Sherman R. Hanson, editor of The Bethany Press, combined patience with diligence in fulfilling his responsibilities. It was our privilege and good fortune to work with him and with Dorothy Eicks as copy editor. A special word of thanks is due Christian Theological Seminary and Texas Christian University for relieving us of many routine tasks so that we could devote large blocks of time to sustained research and writing.

In the mid-1970s the Christian Church (Disciples of Christ) is reexamining its heritage and searching for its identity. We hope that this volume will be useful both in the reexamination and in the search.

Lester G. McAllister
William E. Tucker

Contents

TIMELINE OF THE CHRISTIAN CHURCH
(DISCIPLES OF CHRIST)

Christians in the West		Reformers or Disciples	
1796	Barton W. Stone became regular supply preacher at Cane Ridge and Concord in Ky.		
1798	Ordination of Stone by Transylvania Presbytery	1798	Thomas Campbell became settled minister of Ahorey Church in Ireland
1801	Cane Ridge Camp Meeting		
1803	Formation of Springfield Presbytery		
1804	"The Last Will and Testament of the Springfield Presbytery"; adoption of the name, "Christian"		
		1807	Arrival of Thomas Campbell in the United States
		1809	"Declaration and Address"; organization of Christian Association of Washington; arrival of Alexander Campbell in the United States
		1811	Organization of Brush Run Church
		1812	Ordination of Alexander Campbell
		1815	Acceptance of Brush Run Church into Redstone Baptist Association
		1823	Beginning of *The Christian Baptist*

1824	First meeting of Barton W. Stone and Alexander Campbell
1826	Beginning of *The Christian Messenger*

1827	Appointment of Walter Scott as evangelist of Mahoning (Baptist) Association
1830	Dissolution of Mahoning Association; beginning of *The Millennial Harbinger*

Christian Church (Disciples of Christ)

1832	Union of Christians and Disciples at Lexington, Ky.
1836	Founding of Bacon College
1840	Founding of Bethany College
1849	First national convention at Cincinnati, Ohio; organization of American Christian Missionary Society
1851	First missionary, Dr. James T. Barclay, arrived in Jerusalem
1855	Beginning of *Gospel Advocate*
1856	Beginning of *American Christian Review*
1863	Beginning of *Gospel Echo* (later *The Christian-Evangelist*)
1866	Beginning of *Christian Standard;* death of Alexander Campbell
1874	Organization of Christian Woman's Board of Missions
1875	Organization of Foreign Christian Missionary Society
1883	Organization of Board of Church Extension
1887	Chartering of National Benevolent Association (later Division of Social and Health Services)
1895	Organization of Board of Ministerial Relief (later the Pension Fund)
1906	Acknowledgment of Churches of Christ as religious communion
1907	Formation of Federal Council of Churches (later National Council of Churches) with Disciples as one of the charter members
1909	Centennial Convention at Pittsburgh, Pa.

1910	Establishment of the Council on Christian Union (later the Council on Christian Unity)
1911	Chartering of Christian Board of Publication
1913	Launching of Men and Millions Movement
1914	Formation of Board of Education (later the Board of Higher Education)
1917	Organization of International Convention of Disciples of Christ and National Christian Missionary Convention; "Heresy Trial" at The College of the Bible (renamed Lexington Theological Seminary)
1918	Beginning of *World Call*
1919	Creation of United Christian Missionary Society
1921	Formation of All-Canada Committee
1927	First meeting of North American Christian Convention
1930	First World Convention of Churches of Christ
1935	Beginning of Unified Promotion; organization of Disciples Peace Fellowship
1938	Formation of Home and State Missions Planning Council
1941	Establishment of Disciples of Christ Historical Society
1944	First observance of Week of Compassion
1946	Launching of Crusade for a Christian World
1948	Establishment of World Council of Churches
1950	Formation of Council of Agencies
1960	Authorization of Commission on Brotherhood Restructure
1962	Entrance of Disciples into Consultation on Church Union
1963	Publication of The Panel of Scholars Reports
1968	Adoption of Provisional Design for the Christian Church (Disciples of Christ)
	RECONCILIATION: Urban Emergency Program of the Christian Church (Disciples of Christ)
1971	Separate listing of "Christian Churches and Churches of Christ" as a religious communion in *Yearbook of American Churches;* formation of Committee on Black Church Work; United Christian Missionary Society restructured into Division of Homeland Ministries and Division of Overseas Ministries.
1974	Implementation of Church Finance Council

1

FROM CAMP MEETING TO GENERAL ASSEMBLY: AN OVERVIEW

If the past and present give any solid clues as to the shape of the future, believers who pale at the prospect of a superchurch—encompassing *all* variations of Christian life and thought—have little reason to grow apprehensive in the United States of America. "It has been granted to the Americans less than any other nation of the earth to realize . . . the visible unity of the church of God," observed Dietrich Bonhoeffer following his final visit to the United States. "It has been granted to the Americans more than any other nation of the earth," he continued, "to have before their eyes the multiplicity of Christian insights and communities."[1] Written in 1939, Bonhoeffer's remark remains an apt and useful generalization in our time.

There is growing evidence, to be sure, indicating that denominational peculiarities no longer capture and hold the

---

1. Dietrich Bonhoeffer, *No Rusty Swords: Letters, Lectures and Notes, 1928-1936, from the Collected Works of Dietrich Bonhoeffer*, vol. 1, ed. by Edwin H. Robertson (New York: Harper and Row, 1965), p. 94.

undivided attention of church people. In significant numbers they attend the suburban sanctuary nearest them and move without pangs of conscience from one denomination to another with a different heritage in polity and doctrine.

Even so, Protestants in America belong to more than 220 separate religious bodies, ranging in size from the Southern Baptist Convention with over 35,000 congregations to the little known Church of Daniel's Band which claims an inclusive membership of 200. An additional and undetermined number of sects and dissident groups like The Church of God Incorporated moves through the full cycle of birth to death without coming to the attention of those who compile statistics on religion in America. In sum, diversity is a distinctive mark of the church in American society.

Of all these religious bodies, one of the largest to have originated on American soil is the Christian Church (Disciples of Christ). Beginning as a handful of believers in the early nineteenth century, Disciples placed heavy emphasis on evangelism and expanded rapidly until about 1900. The heart of their numerical and financial strength lies in the Midwest and the Southwest. Slightly more than one-third of all Disciples in the United States and Canada can be found in Indiana, Missouri, Ohio, and Texas. Another third of the participating membership is located in the six states of California, Illinois, Iowa, Kansas, Kentucky, and Oklahoma.[2]

The overwhelming majority of Disciples reside in the continental United States as would be expected of a communion which is widely recognized as an "American religious movement." But there are thousands of members in countries, far and near, around the world. Many of this far-flung group have joined other Protestant bodies in forming united churches to minister more effectively in the name of Christ; others are involved in the process of negotiation with a view to union.

The growth of Disciples from obscurity to prominence on the religious scene in the nineteenth and twentieth centuries gives substance to Alexander Campbell's reflection in 1848:

---

2. For a compendium of information on Disciples, SEE the *Year Book and Directory of the Christian Church (Disciples of Christ)*. Published annually as the title indicates, the *Year Book* contains reports of the church's units and divisions, statistical reports of congregations in the United States and Canada, and a ministers' directory.

"The beginnings of all things are both small and weak. Yes, the oak is in the acorn, the giant in the embryo, and the destinies of the world in the fortunes of an individual."[3]

As is the case in other segments of mainstream American Protestantism, vast differences in thought and practice characterize Disciples. Except for the explicit commands and proscriptions of the New Testament, they never have sensed any compelling need to accept uniformity as a cardinal virtue. The name, Rupertus Meldenius, is familiar only to history buffs among them, but they made a slogan of his classic phrase: "In essentials, unity; in nonessentials, liberty; in all things, charity."

Some Disciples worship in cathedral-like sanctuaries and are accustomed to formality in worship; others "go to preaching" in simple frame structures and treasure the informality of worship. Some Disciples believe in the trinitarian nature of God and question the faith of those who deny the virgin birth of Jesus. To others, the trinitarian formula makes no sense, and the doctrine of the virgin birth is irrelevant save as a symbol of God's amazing grace. Some Disciples hold firmly to the conviction that the church's mission is to "preach the Word" and scrupulously avoid involvement in the massive social and political problems which wrench society; others know with absolute certainty that the Body of Christ is under mandate to promote justice and dignity for all peoples, "to afflict the comfortable as well as to comfort the afflicted." Some Disciples ministers follow the Christian year in developing their sermons and find the *Book of Common Prayer* to be helpful in preparing for corporate worship; others are queasy about any prayer book and always "pray from the heart." Disciples, in short, prize freedom and are not of a mind to feel guilty about their diversity. But their companionship with Christ has constrained them to be companions with one another, to use a phrase of H. Richard Niebuhr's, and has welded them into a brotherhood with a tradition and a purpose to fulfill.

Like other denominations Disciples are indebted to certain key leaders whose witness gave birth to the movement. An art medal, struck in 1972 and devoted to the Christian Church (Disciples of Christ), bears the likenesses of Alexander

---

3. Alexander Campbell, *Millennial Harbinger*, May 1848, p. 279.

FOUR FOUNDING FATHERS

Alexander Campbell

Thomas Campbell

Walter Scott

Barton Warren Stone

Four men are generally considered "founding fathers" of the Christian Church (Disciples of Christ). Each made significant, unique, and enduring contributions to the emerging movement.

Campbell and Barton Warren Stone. Two others, Thomas Campbell and Walter Scott, might also have been depicted. These four deserve to be regarded as founding fathers and are so recognized.

Of the four, priority in time belongs to Stone. A native American frontiersman, Barton W. Stone was born in 1772 near Port Tobacco, Maryland, and was educated at David Caldwell's Academy in North Carolina. He enrolled in Caldwell's "log college" with the intention of pursuing a career in law but changed his mind and entered the Christian ministry. After teaching in Georgia and preaching in North Carolina, he moved to Kentucky and requested ordination from the Transylvania Presbytery. Presbyterians subscribed to a creed, the Westminster Confession of Faith, and required their ministers to accept it as containing the system of doctrine taught in the Bible. Stone hedged, agreeing to regard it as normative only insofar as it was "consistent with the Word of God." Ordained in spite of this qualified endorsement, he became pastor of two small Presbyterian churches at Cane Ridge and Concord in Kentucky.

During Stone's ministry the Cane Ridge Camp Meeting attracted thousands to one of his little churches. As host minister he played a prominent role in this revival but was overshadowed by Richard McNemar, another Presbyterian minister in Kentucky. Disapproving of the acrobatic Christianity so much in evidence at Cane Ridge and in other frontier camp meetings, orthodox Presbyterians brought formal charges against McNemar for deviating from the Westminster Confession and violating church discipline. Before he could be exonerated or found guilty as charged, he withdrew from the jurisdiction of the Synod of Kentucky.

Stone and three other dissenters accepted McNemar's decision as their own, and the five of them in 1803 formed the independent Springfield Presbytery which answered to no synod or to any other ecclesiastical body. Within a year they and David Purviance dissolved the presbytery and published *The Last Will and Testament of The Springfield Presbytery.* In this extraordinary document they insisted that each congregation should govern itself, argued that the Bible is the "only sure guide to heaven," and expressed a desire to "sink into union with the Body of Christ at large." Having renounced the name "Presbyterian" as sectarian, they agreed henceforth to call themselves Christians. Over the next quarter of a century this loose association of Christians gained several thousand converts but lost four of the six signers of *The Last Will and Testament.* Two returned to the Presbyterians; two became Shakers. Only David Purviance stood firm with Stone, who earned the right to serve as spokesman for a majority of Christians in the West.

Similar in many respects to Stone's Christians was a small band of self-styled "Reformers" or "Disciples" led by two onetime Presbyterians, Thomas Campbell and his son, Alexander. An Old Light Anti-Burgher Seceder Presbyterian minister in Ireland, Thomas emigrated to the United States in 1807 and became minister of several churches within the jurisdiction of the Chartiers Presbytery in southwestern Pennsylvania. Very few months passed by before he found himself at odds with the presbytery's leadership over the issues of the nature of faith and the authority of creeds. He renounced creedal statements as terms of communion and denied that a rise in one's emotional temperature is essential to "saving faith." Offended if not dismayed, several members of the presbytery brought charges against Campbell for teaching contrary to accepted Presbyterian standards of doctrine. No longer at home in the Chartiers Presbytery, he withdrew and, together with a small group of sympathizers, formed the Christian Association of Washington in 1809. They agreed to speak where the Scriptures speak and to remain silent where the Scriptures are silent.

To summarize the group's thinking and to provide a basis for reform, Campbell wrote the *Declaration and Address.* Clearly the most influential document in Disciples history, the *Declaration and Address* has been called "one of the great milestones on the path of Christian unity in America."[4] "Tired and sick of the bitter jarrings and janglings of a party spirit," Campbell argued that the church of Christ on earth is "essentially, intentionally, and constitutionally one." To achieve unity, he added, the church had no alternative but to restore the Christianity of the New Testament. Precisely at this point Campbell sounded a theme familiar to

---

4. Donald H. Yoder, "Christian Unity in Nineteenth-Century America," in *A History of the Ecumenical Movement, 1517-1948,* ed. by Ruth Rouse and Stephen C. Neill (London: Society for Promoting Christian Knowledge, 1954), p. 237.

knowledgeable church people across the land. As Professor Sidney Mead has noted, each American denomination sought "to justify its peculiar interpretations and practices as more closely conforming to those of the early church as pictured in the New Testament than the views and policies of its rivals."[5] From 1809 into the twentieth century, in any event, the thinking of Disciples focused on the concepts of Christian unity and the restoration of primitive Christianity.

In the meantime Alexander spent almost a year in study at the University of Glasgow in Scotland. There he met Greville Ewing who introduced him to the works of John Glas and Robert Sandeman, thoroughgoing advocates of a return to New Testament Christianity. The thought of these men stirred Alexander so profoundly that he withdrew from the Seceder Presbyterian Church. The son's experience and decision paralleled his father's, although they were thousands of miles apart and neither knew of the decisive step taken by the other.

When in 1809 Alexander Campbell arrived in America, he found himself in complete agreement with the *Declaration and Address.* Notwithstanding Thomas' disavowal of the intention to "make a new party," the Christian Association of Washington in 1811 constituted itself into the Brush Run Church and licensed Alexander Campbell to preach. Under his direction the congregation rejected infant baptism on the ground that Christians in the New Testament period baptized only adults and by immersion. The practice of believer's baptism paved the way for the Brush Run Church to become associated with the Redstone Baptist Association.

While the tenuous relationship between Reformers and Baptists lasted for around fifteen years (from 1815 to 1830), the two groups never really enjoyed harmony. Crucial differences on matters of faith and practice spelled trouble from the outset. The Baptists had to contend not only with an obstreperous (to their way of thinking) Alexander Campbell but also with Walter Scott, another immigrant and Presbyterian-turned-Reformer. Scott's search for "the ancient order of things" led him to the conviction that the New Testament contained a sharply defined plan of salvation. If

5. Sidney E. Mead, *The Lively Experiment* (New York: Harper and Row, 1963), p. 108.

man would confess his faith, repent of his sins and be baptized, God would respond by remitting man's sins and granting him the gifts of the Holy Spirit and eternal life. Expounding his simple formula and using the "five-finger exercise" to maximum advantage, Scott attracted extraordinary interest among frontier people in the Western Reserve. As a result, there came to be many Baptists who in effect were followers of the Campbells and Scott. No wonder dissatisfaction increased and ended the short-lived relationship between Baptists and Disciples.

This turn of events freed the Campbell movement to come together with the Christians of Stone's persuasion in an informal union. Both groups regarded the fragmentation of the Body of Christ as an unmistakable indication of a disobedient and ineffective church. They rejected "man-made creeds" as tests of fellowship, insisting that the New Testament was the only foundation for firm and lasting unity among Christians. In view of their striking similarities, about 12,000 Disciples and 10,000 Christians united in the 1830s. Although Stone played the major role in bringing Disciples and Christians together and regarded the union as the "noblest act" of his life, Alexander Campbell became the dominant figure in the movement. A scholar of the first rank, a proud and aggressive leader, and a forceful spokesman, he guided Disciples through the backwaters of American religious life; his home in Bethany, Virginia (now West Virginia) doubled as the "headquarters" of the growing movement.

Strange as it may seem, there was no firm agreement at the point of choosing a name for the new fellowship. Peter Cartwright, a volatile and outspoken Methodist circuit rider on the American frontier, was one of many detractors to refer to Disciples as Campbellites.[6] This nickname was used as a means of poking fun at the upstart Disciples, and they resented it. Although Alexander Campbell never won a medal for his humility, he certainly had no intention of seeing the movement saddled with his name. He took seriously the precept to *"Call no man on earth Father, or Leader, or Master"* and chided those who "were proud of the livery they wear, and would have us to be like themselves—the followers

---

6. SEE *Autobiography of Peter Cartwright* with an introduction, bibliography and index by Charles L. Wallis (New York: Abingdon Press, 1956), pp. 234-235, 262-264.

of a fallible earthly leader."[7] Designations such as "Campbellites" and "Stoneites" were inappropriate for a reformation movement which aimed to unite the church by restoring New Testament Christianity. Only a biblical and nonsectarian name would be acceptable. Two terms, "Disciples" and "Christians," met the proposed standards and gained solid support.

Alexander Campbell preferred "Disciples" or "Disciples of Christ" and cited four reasons for his preference: (1) The name was more ancient than "Christians." Prior to being called Christians at Antioch, followers of Christ were disciples. (2) The name was more scriptural than "Christians," or so Campbell argued. By actual count the term "Christians" occurs but twice in the Book of Acts whereas "Disciples" appears more than thirty times. (3) The name was more descriptive than "Christians." As a term of identification, "Christians" was lacking in precision and distinctness. (4) Finally, the name was more unappropriated than "Christians." Other groups identified themselves as Christians, argued Campbell, "while we are the only people on earth fairly and indisputably in the use of the title *Disciples of Christ.*"[8]

Stone disagreed. His group had been known as Christians for over twenty-five years; the term seemed exactly right. In response to one of Campbell's articles on "Our Name," Stone replied with an uncharacteristic note of bitterness: "You well knew the great attachment thousands of us had to the name *Christians.* . . . Brother Campbell, ought you not to have respected the feelings of so many, who united their energies with *yours* in promoting the common cause?"[9] Walter Scott sided with Stone even though his personal relationship with Alexander Campbell was much closer and warmer. So did Thomas Campbell. Admitting his own attachment to the term, "Christians," he wrote: "It is, without exception, the most exalting, the most honorable, and distinguishing title under heaven. Excited, therefore, by these considerations, let us hold it fast, and endeavor to walk worthy of it."[10]

In spite of his great respect for his father and the appeals of

7. Alexander Campbell, *Millennial Harbinger,* August 1839, p. 338.
8. SEE Alexander Campbell, *Millennial Harbinger,* September 1839, pp. 401-403.
9. Barton W. Stone, *Millennial Harbinger,* January 1840, p. 21.
10. Thomas Campbell, *Millennial Harbinger,* January 1840, p. 21.

Scott and Stone, Alexander Campbell refused to budge. Consequently, there was no resolution to the controversy. Both "Christians" and "Disciples" or "Disciples of Christ" came to be regarded as appropriate designations for the Campbell-Stone movement.

The inability of the group to settle on one name has caused much confusion and some frustration over the years. Those who followed in the train of Alexander Campbell and Barton Warren Stone have asked time and again: "What shall we call ourselves? Can we not have a name that doesn't need to be explained and defended among people who have little or no understanding of Disciples and their tradition?" To cite but one example of this sense of frustration, a number of Disciples women presented the following petition to the Cleveland Association of Disciple Ministers in 1884:

We ask for a name, a denominational name by which we may be known as one people. We labor under embarrassment constantly because of this. We co-operate with other churches in Christian and charitable work. And why not have a name by which we may be known as our people. We therefore ask your most worthy body to decide on a name, for this city. We feel this will aid us in our work and give us better standing in this community.[11]

In responding the ministers encouraged the use of "Disciples." Their judgment reflected the opinion of many Disciples at the time and anticipated a government decision some years later. When an official religious census of the United States listed the movement as "Disciples of Christ" in 1906, the fellowship had a corporate name. Had Alexander Campbell been alive, he could not have claimed a clear-cut victory. "Christian" remained the most widely used name for *local congregations* across the land. To this day the typical designation of a congregation is First (or some comparable term) Christian Church. Frequently "Disciples of Christ" is added parenthetically.

As if they were bent on perpetuating confusion in the public mind, Disciples changed their corporate name to the Christian Churches (Disciples of Christ) in 1957. Little more than a decade later, in 1968, the present name—Christian

---

11. Quoted in Henry K. Shaw, *Buckeye Disciples* (St. Louis: Christian Board of Publication, 1952), p. 118.

Church (Disciples of Christ)—was adopted. Yet the Disciples of Christ Historical Society is responsible for maintaining and building the archives of the communion; and the principal journal of the Christian Church was named *The Disciple* in 1974. The pattern of ambivalence continues.

To complicate matters still more, there are two other religious bodies in the United States which share a common heritage with Disciples but are otherwise unrelated to them. The first of the two is known as the Churches of Christ. Even so, a number of local congregations of Disciples retain the name, Church of Christ, for their origin antedates the division which resulted in the formation of the Churches of Christ. Moreover, Disciples in other parts of the world (Great Britain, New Zealand, and Australia, for example) also refer to themselves as Churches of Christ. The second group prefers to be called "Christian Churches and Churches of Christ" and is so designated in the recognized listing of American churches.

All in all, the situation today is one of bewildering confusion. A local Church of Christ may be related to the Churches of Christ or to the Christian Churches and Churches of Christ or even to the Christian Church (Disciples of Christ). A local Christian Church may support either the Christian Church (Disciples of Christ) or the Christian Churches and Churches of Christ. If anything, the question of a name has grown more complicated with the passing of the years.

In the 1830s followers of Campbell and Stone refused to permit disagreements on the name and other differences to keep them apart. Discussion was heated but not divisive, for both groups aimed to give expression to the essential unity of the church.

Disciples increased from 22,000 to almost 200,000 between 1832 and 1860. Membership quadrupled in the 1830s and then doubled in the next two decades. Some overly optimistic members of the movement read the evidence as an indication that in time Disciples would conquer the nation if not the world. They did not seem to realize that the growth rate would decrease as the base broadened. In any event, their own sense of mission contributed to this remarkable growth. Protestantism had gone astray, they felt, and the "denominations" must be led back to the primitive pattern of the church. In final analysis, there was no distinction between the primitive pattern and the Disciples plea. By virtue of their self-assumed role in American religious pluralism, they understood themselves as participants in a nineteenth-century reformation of global significance.

This rapid growth made it necessary for Disciples to develop some means of cooperating beyond the local congregation. Their seriousness of purpose and commitment to evangelism prompted them to establish relationships at county, district, and state levels. Cooperative programs developed rapidly in Ohio, Kentucky, Illinois, Indiana, and other states. Then in 1849 the first national convention of Disciples met in Cincinnati and approved a constitution for the American Christian Missionary Society. More than any other leader, David Staats Burnet prodded Disciples to organize for action.

The evolving connectionalism among Disciples cannot be understood fully without taking into account a basic change in Alexander Campbell's thinking. Through *The Christian Baptist,* a monthly paper he edited and published from 1823 to 1830, he attempted to expose the pretensions of the clergy, to attack unscriptural organizations of the church, and to destroy all confidence in creeds as tests of Christian fellowship. He accused ministers of avarice because they received salaries; he loathed ministerial titles, and opposed formal education for ministry on the ground that it tended to elevate the clergyman above the layperson. The editor of *The Christian Baptist* was an iconoclast. He urged the church to return from Babylon and Mammon to Jerusalem and justice. In later years as he dealt with the responsibilities of leadership his distinctions between Babylon and Jerusalem became blurred. Founder of Bethany College in 1840, Alexander Campbell consented to become first president of the American Christian Missionary Society in 1849 and held the position until his death.

Throughout the 1840s and the 1850s a gathering storm over slavery threatened to spend its fury on all Americans, regardless of color or class or denominational affiliation. After Lincoln was elected President of the United States, the secession of the South divided the nation. The Civil War cast a long, dark shadow over the churches. Baptists, Presbyterians, and Methodists split, and of the three only the Methodists have reunited. Although the sentiment of most Disciples reflected the dominant thinking of the region in which they lived, their church's national convention was in effect an assembly of individuals rather than local churches and hence lacked the authority to disfellowship congregations for any reason. A loose and weak national structure enabled Disciples to avoid official if not actual division. In any event, seeds of discord had been sown and in time grew to full bloom.

Rapid change and continuing growth marked the post-Civil War era of Disciples history. A grateful communion mourned the passing of Alexander Campbell in 1866; preceding him in death were Barton W. Stone in 1844, Thomas Campbell in 1854, and Walter Scott in 1861. Inspired by the vision and work of the four founders, Isaac Errett, Archibald McLean, J. H. Garrison, and a host of others led the "Restoration Movement of the Nineteenth Century" into a new day. Two journals, the *Christian Standard* and *The Christian-Evangelist*, grew into powerful mediums of expression and exerted influence far beyond their subscribers. Disciples established new agencies (for example, the National Benevolent Association, the Board of Ministerial Relief, and the Board of Church Extension) and founded more colleges than they needed or could possibly support. Whereas their modest efforts in overseas missions floundered and failed prior to the Civil War, they began to succeed in the 1870s and thereafter. Responsible in large measure for the growth in missionary interest and financial support were the women of the communion under the strong and persuasive leadership of Mrs. Caroline Neville Pearre. Her work gave birth to the Christian Woman's Board of Missions in 1874. Within a few decades Disciples had both the structure and the commitment to support men and women in mission around the world. Demonstrating their concern for cooperation at the interdenominational level, some of them joined with other Protestant bodies in forming the Federal Council of Churches (now the National Council), and their representatives attended ecumenical conferences in North America and abroad. By the turn of the twentieth century the movement claimed more than a million members; thirty years later membership had risen to over a million and a half. Without question, the post-Civil War era was a period of advance for Disciples—advance through storm.

In transit and tension, Disciples were plagued by what J. H. Garrison called "a morbid fondness of controversy." Disciple scholasticism gained a large following among laypersons and ministers alike.[12] Emphasizing the relevance of Alexander Campbell's biblicism for their generation, they created an orthodoxy as precise and as rigid as any in American Protestantism. Lost in a maze of legalism was the great slogan of the first generation: "We are not the only Christians; we are Christians only." Yet another group of Disciples expressed alarm over the move toward scholasticism and attempted to keep in mind the magnanimous impulses of Campbell and Stone.

A principal source of discord was the statement: "Where the Scriptures speak, we speak; where the Scriptures are silent, we are silent." Strict restorationists or scholastics argued that the New Testament provided an exact pattern for the faith and practice of the church in every age. Any deviations amounted to rejecting the Word of God and could not be tolerated. Since the early Christians organized no missionary societies and worshiped without the aid of organs, Disciples should do likewise. Moderate Disciples disagreed, insisting that Christians should resort to "sanctified common sense" in those matters where the Scriptures are silent. To restore New Testament Christianity, they saw no need to disband missionary societies and to oppose instrumental music in worship. Both scholastics and moderates accepted the principle: "In essentials, unity; in nonessentials, liberty; in all things, charity." But they did not specify the same essentials. Debate led to discord, and discord to separation. A sizable group formed the now distinct Churches of Christ. This division among Disciples became apparent as early as the 1880s; for the next twenty years autonomous congregations either split or joined one of the contesting parties. The schism was recognized officially in 1906, for in that year the United States Religious Census listed the Churches of Christ as a separate religious body.

---

12. SEE George G. Beazley, Jr., "Who Are the Disciples?" in *The Christian Church (Disciples of Christ): An Interpretative Examination in the Cultural Context,* ed. by George G. Beazley, Jr. (St. Louis: The Bethany Press, 1973).

The ill will generated in the Civil War found expression in this division. It is no mere coincidence that two-thirds of those who chose to affiliate with the Churches of Christ lived in the eleven states of the former Confederacy. "If Disciples had not disagreed over instrumental music and missionary societies," David E. Harrell, Jr. remarked, "they would have divided over something else."[13] The Civil War unquestionably was one of the dominant factors leading to a major split in the ranks of Disciples.

A significant number of scholastics remained within the parent body. Aiming to defend their interpretation of restorationism at all costs even if it meant cultural and religious isolation, they resisted all efforts to strengthen and unify the national agencies of Disciples. As theological conservatives, they detected evidences of liberalism in the organizational structure of Disciples and became convinced that the movement had veered far off the course charted by Stone and the Campbells. Disenchanted and unwilling to compromise their convictions, many of them gradually abandoned the historic missionary and benevolent institutions. Now they attend their own conventions, publish their own journals, support their own colleges, identify their own ministry, and refuse to cooperate with regional and international manifestations of the church among Disciples.

For many years these believers denied that they constituted a separate communion, and Disciples were reluctant to read them out of the brotherhood. A few people attempted to maintain lines of communication between the disputants, but little dialogue took place. The publication of *A Directory of the Ministry of the undenominational fellowship of Christian Churches and Churches of Christ* in 1955 prompted one observer to write: "The die is cast—there is to be a second division in the ranks of the Disciples of Christ, a second falling away from the 'Reformation for Christian Unity.' "[14] Adopting the name, Christian Churches and Churches of Christ, the fellowship of loosely related congregations has been listed in the *Yearbook of American Churches* since 1971. So Disciples pursued the grand objective of uniting the

13. David E. Harrell, Jr., "The Sectional Origins of the Churches of Christ," *Journal of Southern History*, August 1964, p. 262.
14. Alfred T. DeGroot, *Church of Christ Number Two* (privately printed, 1956), p. 1.

church but contributed still another name to the long list of Protestant bodies in America.

Taking into account the entire course of Disciples history, it is easy to conclude—as has Alfred T. DeGroot—that "the principle of restoring a fixed pattern of a primitive Christian church is divisive and not unitive."[15] The fracturing experience of Disciples suggests that the church must seek ways to be informed by and bear witness to the Scriptures without opting for biblical literalism and yielding to the simplism of an inflexible restorationism.

In the middle decades of the twentieth century, Disciples shared the strengths and weaknesses, the successes and failures, of mainstream American Protestantism. They survived the Great Crash of 1929 and endured its aftermath only to be caught up in the suffering and ambiguity of World War II. Following the war there was an extraordinary upswing of interest in piety and in organized religion throughout the United States. This pervasive religious revival, which crested in the late 1950s, brought about dramatic increases in church participation and in monetary support. If the postwar boom in religion lulled Disciples into complacency, the widespread religious disillusionment of the 1960s surprised and shocked them. Chastened by the severe criticisms leveled at the institution of the church and all other symbols of "The Establishment," they entered the 1970s in a less defensive mood and more willing to fulfill their ministry within a society that some thinkers regarded as post-Christian as well as post-Protestant.

Disciples have given major attention to their own heritage and structure throughout the radical shifts of the post-World War II era. They belatedly came to sense the vitality of the theological renaissance identified with Karl Barth's thundering affirmations in Switzerland and with the Christian realism of Reinhold and Richard Niebuhr in the United States. In 1956 the United Christian Missionary Society and the Board of Higher Education created and appointed a fifteen-member Panel of Scholars to reexamine the doctrines and beliefs of Disciples "in a scholarly way." "The tenets held by our fathers in the faith needed to be restudied and

---

15. Alfred T. DeGroot, *The Grounds of Divisions Among the Disciples of Christ* (privately printed, 1940), p. 220.

validated or modified in the light of modern scholarship," wrote Willard M. Wickizer on behalf of the sponsoring agencies. He continued: "New light and understanding should be sought. A new and firmer base of Christian doctrine should be laid. A new certainty concerning what we believe and why we believe it should be achieved."[16] The Panel's three-volume report, entitled *The Renewal of Church* and published in 1963, gave Disciples fresh understanding in their search for a viable and biblically grounded theology.

A Commisson on Brotherhood Restructure, established in 1960 and chaired by Granville T. Walker, was charged with the responsibility of recommending an organizational structure for Disciples which would reflect the wholeness of the church. The Commission's work resulted in "A Provisional Design for the Christian Church (Disciples of Christ)." Acceptance of this document made possible the reconstitution of Disciples in 1968 and gave full recognition to national and regional as well as local manifestations of the church. A General Assembly of the Christian Church (Disciples of Christ) in the United States and Canada, comprised of official delegates, replaced the International Convention which until 1967 had permitted everyone in attendance to vote on business items. Finally, after more than a century of compromised and eventually unsuccessful efforts, Disciples had felt their way to a form of church government which provided for representative democracy. It was a major accomplishment.

The exhaustive and exhausting search for adequacy in thought and structure did not keep Disciples from full participation in ecumenical Christianity. The Council on Christian Unity reminded Disciples of their basic commitment to the unity of the church and encouraged them to take care lest they fall victim to denominational provincialism. In addition to maintaining strong relationships with both National and World Councils of Churches, Disciples became fully involved in the Consultation on Church Union. A Disciple, Paul A. Crow, Jr., was named the first general secretary of the Consultation; his fellow Disciple, George G. Beazley, Jr., served as chairman from 1970 to 1972. Although long-range ac-

16. Willard M. Wickizer, "A Statement Concerning the Panel of Scholars," in *The Reformation of Tradition*, ed. by Ronald E. Osborn (St. Louis: The Bethany Press, 1963), p. 8.

complishments remain to be seen, the Consultation is surely the most ambitious and striking Christian unity venture in the history of American Christianity. As for the witness of Disciples in both overseas and homeland ministries, their strategy of mission is clearly ecumenical; most of their missionaries and fraternal workers around the world, for example, are active in national union churches. It is true that Disciples in the United States and Canada have not participated in a single union since the followers of Stone and the Campbells came together around 1832. Their interest in the oneness of the church, however, is deeply rooted; and their ecumenical involvements—especially in the twentieth century—have been extensive.

The focus of attention thus far has been on the Christian Church (Disciples of Christ) in the United States and Canada. The movement was confined to the boundaries of North America for only a brief period of time. As early as 1835 William Jones was an advocate of Alexander Campbell's thought in England, and by 1847 the Churches of Christ (Disciples) in Great Britain claimed a membership in excess of 2,000. The Associated Churches of Christ (Disciples) in New Zealand trace their origin to 1843 when Thomas Jackson inspired a few believers to form a small "congregation according to the Apostolic order." Thomas Magarey, a member of this congregation in Nelson, New Zealand, moved to Adelaide in 1845 and wasted little time in helping to organize the first of the Churches of Christ (Disciples) in Australia. The numerical growth of Disciples in Great Britain, New Zealand, and Australia has been quite modest indeed. Even so, they constitute important and valued segments of the world fellowship as do Disciples in the Republic of Zaire, in Puerto Rico, and elsewhere.

Gripped by the conviction that the sun never set on Disciples, Jesse Bader conceived of an organization to sponsor worldwide meetings of members of the communion. His dream turned into reality with the formation of the World Convention of Churches of Christ in 1930. Designed to promote fellowship and to provide inspiration, the first gathering met in Washington, D.C., and was attended by over 8,000 people. Successive conventions have been held at intervals of about five years.

To indicate the sweep and direction of Disciples history from Cane Ridge to the present, several influential leaders have been mentioned by name. Reference has been made to a number of important events and pivotal issues. A few statistics have been cited. It would be sheer nonsense, however, to suppose that any genuine understanding of Disciples is possible without recognizing the inestimable significance of the rank and file—ministers and laypersons alike—who never made the headlines or attracted widespread public attention.

The history of Disciples is the history of untold believers gathering around the Lord's Table each week in remembrance and in thanksgiving, giving of their substance to support the mission of the church at home and abroad, and living out the Gospel with varying degrees of success and failure from day to day. The history of Disciples is the history of thousands of congregations calling pastors, approving and subscribing budgets, ordering their priorities, confronting or avoiding controversial issues, responding to human needs close at hand and far away, and attempting to be church in communities—large and small—around the globe. Disciples history is far more than the sum of the separate life stories of individuals and congregations, however; it is the record of *a people,* past and present, related to each other in purpose and program and structure. Notwithstanding their separateness, Disciples have a lively and growing sense of corporate identity, for they share a common heritage, affirm a basic faith in Jesus as Christ, and bear witness to Thomas Campbell's conviction that "the church of Christ on earth is essentially, intentionally, and constitutionally one."

This chapter is intended only as an overview of Disciples history. Now we turn to a substantive and detailed account of the background and development of the Christian Church (Disciples of Christ).

2

AMERICAN BACKGROUNDS

The highly favorable setting for the emergence of a significant new Christian movement was to be the United States of America newly formed from virgin land by immigrant people. The American experience to 1800 had affected the religious development of the people in ways which later would influence directly the beginning of a unique "American religious movement," the Christian Church (Disciples of Christ). Those hearty and adventurous persons who had come to America's shores in the colonial period had discovered that large areas of land, sparsely inhabited, made possible religious diversity and experimentation scarcely imagined before. They could dream of a new beginning, free from the traditions, prejudices, and persecutions of the Europe they had left behind. In church, as well as in public affairs, they planned so that the laity increasingly could demand and get a greater share in decision-making and authority.

DEVELOPMENTS IN AMERICAN CHRISTIANITY TO 1800

Beginning with the first settlement in America space always played an important role in the evolving culture, politics, and religion of the settlers. From the religious viewpoint space and the availability of land insured a freedom to worship and to develop church life independently. If there was disagreement with religious neighbors, one simply moved on. The settlement of the Connecticut River valley after the Puritans quarreled in early Massachusetts followed this pattern. Space and isolation practically assured religious diversity for America. Beyond the older settlements of the original thirteen colonies the country opened out toward the West with illimitable space for expansion. Drawn by the opportunities of a virgin land, a steady stream of settlers from the earliest days of colonization moved in waves toward the western frontier.[1]

The American religious experience prior to 1800 had led the people to believe that in this land mankind truly had the opportunity for a new beginning. Life here could attain the potential which God had intended it to have. This view was particularly strong among the Puritans of New England. In this new land men and women could escape the poverty, wars, social stratification, and lack of opportunity which they believed were the fate of Europeans. Many of those persons who immigrated to America believed in the possibility of a thoroughgoing reform for society. As a consequence, many new experiments in Christian organization arose across the years. Applying this principle, Thomas Campbell was later to reason that if diverse colonies could create a new form of government, the United States of America, certainly a new form of the church could be devised, leaving behind the conflicting parties of European Christianity. Why not a united Church of Christ?

America was far removed from the seats of ecclesiastical power. With few exceptions the only power possessed by the clergy was the authority inherent in their strength of will and character. Under these conditions the laity developed an increasingly strong influence in church affairs. They thought this development was not merely a practical accommodation to their situation. Many literate Britishers had been taught

---

1. Mead, *The Lively Experiment,* Chapters I and II.

from childhood to view the course of history as predetermined by God's overruling providence. Since most of those persons who settled the land at this time were of British background, many colonists regarded the settlement of America as no ordinary venture. In the view of many of the colonists they were doing God's will and work.

Furthermore, men who had gained independent status as property holders by clearing their own lands with guns and rifles close at hand were not the type to be unduly submissive to authority. Their independence soon asserted itself. The development of the lay vestry in Virginia and congregational polity in New England set examples for the other colonies. This gave the laity increased control over the churches. An immediate consequence of this lay predominance in the affairs of the churches was the emergence of what would later be described as "local autonomy."[2] With single congregations beginning of necessity as independent self-governing units, resistance developed when attempts later were made to regularize their status by subordinating them to larger units of ecclesiastical control. Men who were building a new country with days and weeks of unremitting toil, their own resources, and their own unconquerable determination, were not apt to respond positively to preaching stressing dependence and authority.

THE GREAT AWAKENING

By 1800 certain characteristics of American Christianity had become clearly identifiable as a result of the colonists' experience. These characteristics were religious diversity, voluntary support of a church or religious organization, and the assertion of complete religious freedom. Left unanswered was the question as to how the church is to increase if it is not to have a favored position before the law. In the early colonial period religion played a major role, both as a motive for colonization and as a determining force in the daily life of the individual and community. Then ensued a serious decline of religious interest. By the third and fourth generations strict religious observance was less appealing than the secular

---

2. Winthrop S. Hudson, *Religion in America* (New York: Scribner's, 1965), p. 12ff. Hudson's book is a good short study of American religion.

process of earning a living. As the principles of diversity and religious freedom were being worked out in the experience of the people, the colonies, especially where there were established churches, found fewer and fewer persons to support the church or to take an active interest in it.

The reaction to this decline came in the revival in Christian faith called "the Great Awakening."[3] Although usually dated from 1740, the Great Awakening was part of a series of revivals that commenced as early as 1727. Its theological basis was thoroughly Calvinistic but extreme Calvinistic doctrines were modified somewhat in the middle and southern colonies. The notable figures in this wave of evangelical interest were Jonathan Edwards (1703-1758) of Massachusetts and George Whitefield (1714-1770), an associate of John Wesley (1703-1791) in England. While preaching in America, Whitefield did not establish a separate religious movement, but his flaming zeal and eloquence kindled the fires of devotion in lukewarm saints and stirred thousands of sinners to penitence. His work, especially in the central and southern colonies, reinforced the evangelical efforts of a succession of pioneer preachers of all persuasions. Together they set going a revival movement which continued to the end of the eighteenth century. Crossing the mountains to the frontier of Kentucky and Tennessee in the early nineteenth century, it became known as the Second Great Awakening (or Great Western Revival).[4]

It was from this experience that the church found the answer to the compulsory membership of state churches. If church membership could not be established by law, it would be necessary to persuade individuals to receive salvation and enter the church voluntarily. Still another characteristic of American Christianity had been formed; that of revivalism and personal evangelism.

The churches were frequently divided on the question of

3. SEE Hudson, Chapter III, for a full and detailed discussion of this event and its importance to American Christianity.
4. The actual continuity between the First and Second Great Awakenings in the South can be traced by the succession of leaders and preachers of evangelical bent who learned from one another and carried the movement forward. Jonathan Edwards (1703-1758), George Whitefield (1714-1770), William Tennent (1673-1746), Samuel Blair (1716-1751), Samuel Davies (1723-1761), David Caldwell (1725-1824), James McGready (1758?-1817) and Barton W. Stone (1772-1844), in succession, either taught or learned from one another.

revivalism. Some pastors and people accepted the evangelical resurgence while others deplored it. At the same time a climate of readiness for limited cooperation transcending denominational lines came both directly and indirectly from the Great Awakening.[5] The American people found, in the revival, a common theological and emotional interest. A new understanding of mutual problems was brought about. As it swept through the various colonies the Great Awakening provided the first great common event experienced among Americans from New England to the South and into the back country. It thus contributed to an emerging sense of nationality. By bringing thousands of ordinary folk into churches long dominated by more aristocratic elements in society it intensified the democratic spirit of American religious and political life. It added strong impetus to the demand for religious liberty. The leaders in the revival often were the advocates of cooperation and union, jointly developing benevolent institutions such as orphanages. The whole movement diluted and by-passed denominational prejudice and sectarianism. Interest in the Great Awakening diminished, however, as in the 1770s the colonists prepared to defend their rights as citizens. The American Revolution was to affect the churches profoundly.

THE CHURCHES AND THE REVOLUTIONARY ERA

The significance of the Revolutionary era for the churches is not difficult to discover. First, it is clear that the churches experienced a prolonged period of disruption and decline. The reasons are many but among them would be the inevitable spiritual distractions brought on by war, with their accompanying physical sufferings, injustice, and divided loyalties. Second, the extended political crisis lasting from 1783 to the election of Thomas Jefferson (1743-1826) as President in 1801, accelerated the advancement of rationalist philosophy, natural theology, and secularization. The age introduced new forms of thought which in turn contributed to theological change. Third, the emergence of a new nation forced the churches to organize themselves more in accord-

---

5. C. C. Goen, *Revivalism and Separation in New England* (New Haven: Yale University Press), 1962. pp. 63-85.

ance with the reality of the American situation. Churches with close ties to Great Britain or to Europe found it necessary to sever those relationships.[6]

Christianity in America actually declined during the Revolutionary era. The two decades after the war, 1783-1803, brought the churches to a lower state of vitality than at any other time in American history. The process of decline which had begun earlier was hastened by the war itself. During and after the war there was a large-scale flight from the new nation of English sympathizers, clergy and laity alike. Scores of congregations and churches were divided over the support of the war. Many ministers were drawn into the chaplaincy of the revolutionary forces, while some pastors found themselves in actual combat. In addition to these losses of leadership, the more generalized disruption, impoverishment and occasional devastation wrought by the war left the churches disorganized and their members preoccupied with the more urgent questions of survival.

After 1783 the churches continued under less than favorable conditions. There was widespread apathy in regard to the Christian faith. For several decades after the end of hostilities, the people were involved in the many-faceted problems of politics and government. When independence was achieved a long-submerged social struggle surfaced. The underprivileged sought better material advantages for themselves and their families, usually by moving toward the West. By the end of the period church membership had dropped both relatively and absolutely. It is estimated by most historians that not more than ten percent, and possibly as few as five percent, of the population were affiliated with a church. For many churchmen membership itself became increasingly nominal. Most of the college faculties were scattered and the facilities of the colleges were appropriated for military use. These developments adversely affected the recruitment and training of a clergy. An emotional expression of faith was frowned upon and revivalism came to a tem-

---

6. Sydney E. Ahlstrom, *A Religious History of the American People* (New Haven and London: Yale University Press, 1972). Chapter 23 has a full discussion of the churches and the period of the American Revolution. Ahlstrom's book is the most definitive history of American religion yet written and is highly recommended for all aspects of the study of religion in America.

porary halt everywhere except in the remoter parts of the South.

One intellectual movement which influenced many persons and enjoyed great prestige during this era was that of rationalism. Rational religion, or Deism, was accepted by more and more thinkers. It assumed that reason and scientific knowledge could supply all the necessary elements of religion and ethics, though many of the upper classes might concede that revelation was still needed by the masses.[7] Ethan Allen (1738-1789), Thomas Paine (1737-1809), Elihu Palmer (1764-1806), Joel Barlow (1754-1812), and others launched a frontal attack upon the whole concept of revealed religion. The intellectual leaders of this period were Deists.

The writings of John Locke (1632-1704) provided a connection between the rationalist view of religion and the political ideas which found expression in the American Revolution. Among the nation's early leaders Locke's prestige was high. His *Essay Concerning Human Understanding* (1690) had exalted man's rational powers by asserting that knowledge comes from the senses as a result of experience and reflection. His *Reasonableness of Christianity* (1695) argued that the essence of Christianity is to be found in its ethics (the practice of virtue) and that its excellence consists in the fact that it is fully in accord with the dictates of human reason.

More moderate than the Deists, Locke did not suggest that revelation was superfluous, nor did he doubt the inspiration of the Bible or the messiahship of Jesus. He held that these were means by which essential truths beyond the grasp of common people were made known to the mass of mankind. The writings of Locke were read widely in America. Many of the leaders in the struggle for independence were deeply influenced by his religious and his political views. His religious views were to affect directly many of the religious developments on the frontier in the early nineteenth century. Locke's political views were little more than a distillation of concepts that had long been current in Calvinist doctrine.

Thomas Jefferson was unquestionably the most significant

---

7. SEE Smith, Handy, and Loetscher, *American Christianity,* Vol. I (New York: Scribner's, 1960), Chapter VII, for illustrations of attacks on traditional Christian doctrine by American writers of the Enlightenment.

of the American rationalists, and his place in the history of American religion is important because of his leadership in intellectual affairs as well as in politics.[8] His philosophy of religion and his political theory form a thoughtfully unified whole based upon his interpretation of Locke's thought. Thomas and Alexander Campbell were to make a religious application of many of Locke's ideas even as Jefferson made a mainly political application of them.[9] Jefferson planted, cultivated, and brought to full growth the fruits of rationalism. Those fruits were a belief in progress, confidence in man and in his capacities as developed in education and in political institutions. Americans uncritically appropriated and zealously promoted all of these throughout the nineteenth century.

It is ironic that the Revolutionary era, which produced a time of difficulty and decline for the church, would provide the conditions for a new surge of Christian faith such as had not been known in America for several generations. The great growth and development of the American churches in the nineteenth century depended mainly upon 1) the reality of religious freedom, 2) the growing acceptance of the idea of denominationalism, and 3) the rapid growth in favor of the voluntary principle in matters pertaining to church membership and support—all of which came out of the eighteenth century.

SEPARATION OF CHURCH AND STATE

In America the people were accustomed to free and open debate on all religious questions. Within a large segment of the population there was little regard for clergy, councils, or creeds. On the whole, their church organizations were as simple and democratic as the congregations of the Baptists, or were as republican as the Presbyterians. Under both forms of church government members were permitted to elect and dismiss their own religious leaders. In short, America at the end of the Revolutionary era enjoyed a larger degree of religious liberty than was to be found in most other nations.

---

8. Robert Healey, *Jefferson on Religion in Public Education* (New Haven: Yale University Press), 1962. Especially p. 45 ff.
9. Locke's influence on early leaders of the Christian Church (Disciples of Christ) will be developed more fully in later sections of this book.

However, increased agitation for the separation of church and state, the corollary of religious freedom, had accompanied the opening of the American Revolution, especially in New England and Virginia. Today it is generally agreed that religious freedom was not so much the result of the winning of the war as simply a confirmation of liberty achieved before the Revolution, at least in a majority of the colonies. Religious diversity, together with a certain amount of freedom, had been realized prior to 1776 in most of the colonies, and was actually responsible at times for agitation for political freedom.

The final struggle over the principle of separation of church and state actually came between the years 1779 and 1785. In the former year several bills pertaining to religious liberty were offered the legislative body in Virginia. Among them was one prepared by Thomas Jefferson. It was written into the laws of the newly established state as the "Bill for Establishing Religious Freedom." The road to the acceptance of this famous measure was long and painful but finally passage took place in 1785. Religious liberty had triumphed in Virginia and was soon to spread throughout the nation. The fight for religious freedom and separation of church and state was not led entirely by Virginia and Thomas Jefferson, however. Success was due also to the example of Rhode Island and to the perseverance of the Baptists in Virginia and throughout the land.

A few years later, in the form of the first amendment to the Federal Constitution, separation of church and state was to become a part of the fundamental law of the land. This charter freed the churches from the control of civil authority and, in effect, licensed them to compete with each other, and with no religion at all, on equal terms. A principle now identified as "pluralism" had been established in the new nation's religious life.[10] In the future, all religions, not just Christianity, would be on an equal footing. A principle had been evoked which would have long-reaching effects on the future of American Christianity.

---

10. The principle of pluralism in recent years has attracted increasing attention from historians. SEE, for example, Franklin H. Littell, *From State Church to Pluralism* (Garden City: Doubleday and Company, 1962), or Paul Kauper, *Religion and the Constitution* (Baton Rouge: Louisiana State University, 1964).

DENOMINATIONAL DEVELOPMENT AFTER THE REVOLUTION

After the Revolution, it took the major Protestant churches until about 1800 to regroup and reorder their forces. In a nation committed to religious freedom, and especially to the voluntary principle of church support, the most natural form of church organization would be denominational. The principle of "denominationalism" (that is, each church tradition considering itself but a part of the whole and yet each having complete autonomy and sovereignty) would guide the churches in their future growth and development in the United States of America.[11]

By 1800 the churches had become acutely aware that the nation which had won a war for liberty, for religion as well as for politics, had forgotten once cherished spiritual values. Christian leaders believed that the health of any society was dependent upon the moral principles and virtuous habits taught by true religion. In short, the goal of the churches in the early days of independence and on into the nineteenth century became the creation of a Christian nation.[12] Despite the slow growth of church membership during this period, there can be little doubt that by the early nineteenth century the Protestant denominations had well begun the process of dominating the new nation's cultural life.

The years immediately following the close of the American Revolution became a period of constitution-making, both within the states and in the church bodies. Prior to the Revolution several of the American churches had ties with Great Britain and Europe. Thus the Anglicans had been subject to the bishop of London and the Methodists were under the direction of John Wesley, the English founder of the movement. The Presbyterians, Quakers, and Lutherans were related culturally, but not specifically tied to Europe organizationally. The Congregationalists and Baptists had developed in America with each congregation theoretically independent.

---

11. SEE H. Richard Niebuhr, *The Social Sources of Denominationalism* (New York: Meridian Books, 1957). See also, Hudson, Chapters II and V.
12. SEE Martin E. Marty, *Righteous Empire: The Protestant Experience in America* (New York: The Dial Press, 1970), or Robert T. Handy, *A Christian America* (New York: Oxford University Press, 1971). For a treatment of the same subject from the viewpoint of Disciples history SEE David E. Harrell, Jr., *A Quest for a Christian America*, Vol. I (Nashville, DCHS), 1966.

The Methodists were the first American religious body to form a national organization. Their priority in this respect is due to the fact that their structure was largely worked out for them by John Wesley. At the close of the Revolution the Methodists in America, as well as those in Great Britain, were still a part of the Church of England. When peace came in 1783, Wesley immediately turned his attention to the needs of his American followers. He decided to ordain clergy and reduced the Thirty-nine Articles of the Church of England to twenty-four, leaving out all reference to Calvinistic teaching. He also prepared a "Sunday Service" which was an abridged form of the English liturgy, and compiled a hymnbook.

Proceeding with orderly dispatch the Methodists called a conference to meet in Baltimore, December 24, 1784. There Wesley's proposals to the churches were read and received with respect by the more than fifty preachers present. Francis Asbury (1745-1816), Thomas Coke (1747-1814) and Thomas Vasey were elected by the conference as superintendents. Wesley's other suggestions were acted upon and the Methodist Episcopal Church was formed. Coke soon returned to England. Though Wesley remained in nominal control of the American Methodists until his death, the work of the "Christmas Conference" was the last effective connection of the American Methodists with their founder.

Of all the American churches the Episcopalians suffered most as a result of the Revolution. Theirs had been the established church in five of the nine colonies with establishments. When hostilities ceased the church practically disappeared. Its clergy was dispersed, its buildings gone, and its people demoralized. Everywhere also the church had suffered in public estimation. It had been the church of the English royal officials and this fact alone was a severe blow to its popularity. The first step in the formation of an American organization was the calling of a convention to be held in New York, October 1784. In this and succeeding meetings work was done on a new constitution which was finally adopted in 1789. This constitution called for the formation of a Protestant Episcopal Church in the United States, to be governed by clerical and lay representatives from each state. The liturgy and doctrines of the Church of England were adopted so far as they were consistent with the American form of government.

The Presbyterians were well fitted to meet the new problems of an independent America. They had given unlimited support to the Revolution. They had an American-educated and able leadership, imbued with the American spirit. For these reasons the task of forming a national organization was comparatively simple. There was to be a reorganized General Assembly and synodical plan, a Directory of Public Worship, and a slightly revised version of the Westminster Confession of Faith along with other necessary changes. In spite of the difficulties the churches faced, no other church had grown more rapidly. Between 1758 and 1789 two hundred and thirty new ministers had been ordained and new presbyteries were formed in the West and South. Redstone Presbytery in southwestern Pennsylvania was founded in 1781. At the close of the war two presbyteries were organized in Kentucky—Transylvania and Lexington. The Synod of New York and Philadelphia was the most important Presbyterian body in the country, though there were several other Presbyterian bodies, such as the Associate and Associate Reformed synods, and two conservative bodies representing the Covenanters and the Seceders. The constitution-making period which created the Presbyterian Church in the United States of America was between 1785 and 1788.

Other churches, small in constituency and influence, included the Lutherans, the Dutch and German Reformed Churches, the Moravians, the Mennonites, and the Society of Friends (Quakers). Roman Catholics were to remain few in number until the large immigrations which were to come later in the nineteenth century.

Strange to say, New England Congregationalism seemed to be little affected by the nationalizing tendencies and centralizing influences of the period. The Congregational leaders emphasized the pure democracy of Congregationalism. In Massachusetts particularly, the tendency was to reassert the old emphasis upon the independence of each congregation. Even in Connecticut the decentralizing tendency was abroad, so that in 1784 the law establishing the state association of Congregational Churches was repealed. This failure on the part of Congregationalism to unite effectively in these years of national expansion slowed down the growth of the denomination. Congregationalists did join with Presbyterians in the 1801 "Plan of Union" to evangelize in the West. The arrangement did not work very well, however, and later voluntary missionary societies were created to establish congregations. Such organizations, however, were no match for the more highly developed denominational machinery of the Presbyterians, the Methodists, or even of the Baptists.

The Baptists of the early period of independence had evolved a distinct national spirit and to a certain degree a national organization. This had come about, in spite of Baptist theory of the complete independence of each congregation, because of their leadership in the fight for religious liberty and the separation of church and state. In order to carry out this fight effectively, organizations that were strong enough to bring pressure to bear upon the new state governments were found to be necessary. Thus there arose the Warren Association made up of the Baptist churches in New England. In Virginia a General Committee, made up of delegates from the several Baptist associations, maintained an existence from 1784 to 1799. This General Committee carried on an extensive correspondence with other Baptist associations and congregations in the several states. In the early national period Baptists continued to profit from the revivalistic fervor of the Great Awakening. In the South, where revivalism had continued even through the Revolution, Baptists made larger and more important advances than in New England and the middle Atlantic states. The union of Separate and Regular Baptists in 1787 left them poised to capitalize on the westward movement into Kentucky and Tennessee.

Thus, by 1800 the traditional American churches had well-developed national and regional organizations. The denominations were formed and beginning to function fairly well just as the leaders became aware of another problem that was to be of serious and continuing concern. This was the problem presented by the flow of population into the fertile valleys beyond the mountains. Establishing churches and providing a ministry in the new settlements was to be a task of considerable magnitude. Discipline of these freedom-loving frontier groups was to be even more difficult.

EMERGING NEW CHRISTIAN GROUPS

In 1800 a large proportion of the American people were attached to no church. Those persons for whom the established church had never meant more than nominal commitment found it easy to drop out when there was no compulsion. Everywhere, in the long-established communities of the seacoast as well as in the newer western settlements, there was a limitless opportunity for evangelization, innovation, and religious experimentation. There were still vestiges of religious establishment in a few states (Connecticut until 1818, New Hampshire until 1819, and Massachusetts until 1833), but churches were now mostly supported by voluntary gifts, not by taxation, and there were few endowments. No church had legal or official advantage over any other. Every person was free to practice and propagate the religion of his or her choice, to start a new religious organization if desired, or to stand aloof from all the churches, depending on his or her own understanding of truth. Never before had such conditions of religious freedom existed. These conditions were to be of great importance in the development of the Christian Church (Disciples of Christ).

The complete and unprecedented religious freedom and the spirit of individual independence account in large measure for the rise of many new Christian movements in America at this time. Other factors in such developments were the large proportion of the population outside the membership of the churches and the disinterest in, and revolt against, many of the orthodox doctrines of Calvinism. The widespread reading of, and interest in, the writings of the Deists and rationalists played its part too. The influence and example of many small independent evangelical groups such as the Scotch Baptists, the Glasites, the Sandemanians and the Haldanes, which had arisen only recently in Great Britain, contributed to these developments. Strict obedience to religious authority lessened as the rising sense of the common man's competence to do his own thinking and make his own decisions grew. Finally, the rapid movement of the population toward the frontier, where all these impulses to independence had opportunity for full growth, provided the environment for new movements to develop without fear of discipline from ecclesiastical authorities.

Many of these tendencies had been developing before the American Revolution and were ready for full development after the Revolutionary era. They manifested themselves in innovation and experimentation in biblical interpretation, in Christian doctrine, and in church government, affecting all the churches to a greater or lesser degree. However, one direct and far-reaching result of the American spirit of freedom and independence was the birth of several movements which rested upon what they believed to be a new approach to the Scriptures, particularly the New Testament, as a source of fresh insight into religion.

To those Americans moving westward who had an interest in religion and were evangelical-minded, freedom of the will was more than a deeply held theological belief. It meant also the freedom of the individual to accept the gospel and to read and interpret the New Testament for himself. Among early Kentucky Baptists there was an element strongly opposed to creeds and denominational names. It stressed the idea of a "simple gospel" long before either Stone or the Campbells appeared on the scene. The South Kentucky Association of Separate Baptists in 1787 was formed of eleven congregations which were "constituted on the Bible." In North Carolina and in southern Indiana (to which state many individuals migrated from North Carolina) some Baptist churches later became "Churches of Christ" without being conscious of any great change. The oldest Baptist Church in Indiana, established in Knox County in 1798, took as its name "the Church of Christ on Owen's Creek." It later followed Alexander Campbell's teaching and was known as the Stoney Point Christian Church. The Cumberland Presbyterian Church was formed in 1810 because of disagreements with other Presbyterians, supposedly over questions of theology and government, but fundamentally from the desire for a type of religion at once more simple and more free.

In addition to those movements in which the desire to establish a simple biblical faith formed at least an important part of the motive, there is evidence that many individuals, quite independently of each other and of all these, made almost identical discoveries of what they considered "original ground." By 1800 seemingly spontaneously in New England, in Virginia and North Carolina, and in Kentucky, individuals and informally gathered congregations were experimenting with literal interpretation of the New Testament and calling themselves Christians, Christian Churches, Churches of Christ, and Churches of God.

One such group, formed in New England, developed from the independent reactions of two young men, Elias Smith [1769-1846] and Abner Jones [1772-1841], against the Calvinistic doctrines which prevailed in the Baptist churches of which they were members and for which they were beginning to preach. Many years later, after Alexander Campbell had discovered the existence of the New England Christians, he entered into a correspondence with the leaders of this group. He soon became convinced that his movement and theirs had little in common. This development in New England, as well as those elsewhere, illustrates the great amount of experimentation which took place several years before either the Stone or Campbell movement came into being. They all pointed toward a simple and scriptural religion and came from currents of thought originating among independent and dissenting preachers in Great Britain adapted to American needs and usage.

THE O'KELLY MOVEMENT

The largest of these early independent Christian movements, and the one most directly affecting the history of the Christian Church (Disciples of Christ), arose in Virginia and North Carolina in 1794. In that year a break in the fellowship of the Methodist Episcopal Church was made final. The specific issue which brought about the rupture was the question of episcopacy versus congregational polity, but this question led ultimately to larger issues of biblical interpretation and doctrine. The forces for simplicity in doctrine and freedom in church government were at work.

When the Methodist Episcopal Church was formed at the famous Christmas Conference of 1784, an important decision was made when it was agreed that they would constitute themselves an "episcopal" church. There were some preachers who opposed that decision. Though still without bishops, the conference ordained Francis Asbury on successive days as deacon, elder, and "superintendent." Asbury promptly changed his title to "bishop" and proceeded to exercise ecclesiastical powers with a strong hand. Among other things, he assigned every presiding elder to his district, every preacher to his circuit, and from his decisions there was no appeal.

By virtue of his strong will and dominant personality such powers came naturally to Asbury. His many excellent qualities, his tireless energy, his complete devotion to his work, and perhaps above all, the success of his methods, ultimately won approval from the great majority of Methodists, preachers and people alike. There were some, however, who were restless under Asbury's leadership. Some of the preachers looked upon Asbury's assumption of power as contrary to the Scriptures. One of these men was James O'Kelly (1735?-1826). O'Kelly was a man of commanding personality and more than average ability, and he became the popular hero of his followers.[13] He possessed strong likes and dislikes. Being thoroughly impregnated with the ideals of liberty and pioneer freedom, he wanted these ideals applied in church government.

O'Kelly had become a Methodist lay preacher in 1778 and was active in the evangelistic endeavors which led to early Methodist growth in Virginia and North Carolina. He attended the Christmas Conference of 1784 where he was ordained.[14] As early as 1790 O'Kelly raised questions as to the propriety of having bishops and led a minority of preachers in a futile protest against Asbury's assumption of episcopal powers. Asbury made O'Kelly a presiding elder, but, even then, O'Kelly continued to head the group of the discontented who opposed what seemed to them an unscriptural assertion of authority.

At the Methodist General Conference in 1792 O'Kelly introduced a resolution permitting a preacher the right of appeal to the conference if he did not like the appointment he received from the bishop. After three days of heated debate

---

13. Milo T. Merrill, *A History of the Christian Denomination in America* (Dayton, Ohio, 1912). pp. 32-40.

14. Wade Crawford Barclay, *Early American Methodism*, Vol. I (New York: The Board of Missions and Church Extension of the Methodist Church, 1949), pp. 161-162. SEE, also, Charles F. Kilgore, *The James O'Kelly Schism in the Methodist Episcopal Church* (Mexico City: Casa Unita de Publicationes, 1963).

the resolution was voted down. Thereupon O'Kelly and a number of other preachers withdrew from the conference. Later many of those who had joined O'Kelly in his earlier protests yielded to Asbury and the majority, leaving O'Kelly and Rice Haggard, a lay preacher and longtime supporter of O'Kelly in his campaign against autocratic control, to carry through with their principles of reform. This break in the Methodist ranks is commonly referred to as the "O'Kelly Secession."

In August 1793 O'Kelly and Haggard petitioned Asbury to meet them in a conference to examine church government by the Scriptures. Asbury refused. The following December those who had seceded decided to sever all relations with the Methodist Episcopal Church and to take the name Republican Methodists. They were said to have had, at this time, fewer than 1,000 members. The movement remained in this transitional stage, as a group of separated Methodists, only about seven months.

Then a conference was held at Old Lebanon Church, in Surry County, Virginia, just across the James River from Williamsburg, on August 4, 1794. There the Republican Methodists adopted as their new name the "Christian Church" and declared that the Bible should be their only guide. O'Kelly devised what became known as the "Five Cardinal Principles of the Christian Church." These resolved 1) that there should be complete equality among all the preachers; 2) there should be no bishops, superintendents, or presiding elders in the Methodist fashion; 3) ministers and laypeople alike were to enjoy the fullest liberty in interpreting Scripture; 4) the principle of congregational independence was to be applied; and 5) conferences would be advisory and every church would "call its own pastor and enjoy the greatest freedom."

Within a few years the O'Kelly movement discovered the existence of the New England Christians and found their thinking to be congenial to their own. The two movements ultimately joined forces. Still later they aligned themselves with Christian groups in Ohio and Indiana to form the Christian Convention in the United States. This church united with the Congregational Church to become the Congregational Christian Churches in 1931.

THE NAME "CHRISTIAN"

The adoption of the name "Christian" by the O'Kelly group was suggested by Rice Haggard. It is well to note here, though it will be discussed more fully in the next chapter, that this same Rice Haggard was the man, who, ten years later, suggested to the Springfield Presbytery in Kentucky that it take the name "Christian." At no time, however, did Haggard claim to have been the first to suggest such a name. In all probability Haggard had been introduced to such concerns as name and scriptural authority by a reading of the sermons of the Presbyterian revivalist and educator Samuel Davies (1723-1761). Davies was widely read at the time and had a great influence on the area where Haggard lived and preached.[15] Many other religious leaders in Virginia and North Carolina were teaching and preaching similar ideas.

In Virginia and North Carolina, as has been noted, the influence of the Great Awakening continued to the close of the eighteenth century and beyond. This continuing revival movement in which the most prominent figures were "New Light" (i.e., revivalist and evangelical) Presbyterians was to have its influence in several ways on the history of the Christian Church (Disciples of Christ). William Tennent (1673-1746), one of the secondary leaders of the Great Awakening, had founded a "Log College" in 1720 for the training of ministers. Samuel Blair (1716-1751), trained by Tennent, established another such college at Fagg's Manor in Pennsylvania.

Among Blair's students was Samuel Davies, who became the acknowledged evangelical leader of the southeastern states. Davies was a tower of strength for the revival movement. His spirit lived on in the work of David Caldwell, Henry Pattillo, and other evangelical Presbyterians. These influences later made themselves felt on Barton W. Stone and other early leaders in Kentucky as well as as on evangelical leaders in Virginia and North Carolina. This

---

15. For the origin of the name "Christian" in connection with American church groups SEE Robert William Gates, "Samuel Davies to Barton W. Stone: A Study in Antecedents" (unpublished B.D. thesis, Lexington Theological Seminary, 1964). The use of the name is traced to a series of sermons published in London in 1728. SEE B. Grosvenor, *An Essay on the Name Christian* (London: Clark and Hett, M.DCC.XXVIII).

strain of revivalistic Presbyterians tended toward loose views of the Calvinistic doctrines. They collaborated on friendly terms with the Methodists. It was in this manner that Samuel Davies, through Rice Haggard, had influence on the O'Kelly movement in such matters as the form of church government and the name "Christian." Through Rice Haggard a separating Methodist movement in Virginia and North Carolina and a separating Presbyterian movement in Kentucky would both be deeply influenced.

PRELUDE TO REVIVAL

Geography and development of the West were to play their part in the further unfolding of American Christianity. A look at population and the frontier as it existed at the end of the eighteenth and the beginning of the nineteenth centuries proves instructive. In the first general census taken in 1790 it was found that there were in round numbers 4,000,000 people in the United States, and the enumeration revealed that population was moving rapidly westward. The census showed that five percent of the total population was already living west of the mountains, in southwestern Pennsylvania, in western Virginia, and in the present states of Kentucky and Tennessee. These were the exact areas which were to see the rise of the Stone and Campbell movements.

This western movement, noted in the first census, continued with increasing momentum for the next four decades. Previous to 1795 the largest percentage of population was going into the region south of the Ohio River. The general economic distress along the eastern seaboard following the Revolution accelerated this westward movement. In the northern and middle states the movement was soon checked by the return of better times but in the South hard times persisted with a consequent continuation of migration into Kentucky and Tennessee.

Until 1803 the young nation extended only to the Mississippi River and after that only to the vaguely defined limits of the Louisiana Purchase. By modern standards even the Eastern cities were small in 1800: Philadelphia had a population of 41,220, while Boston could boast of only 24,937 citizens.[16] New York City was the largest with 60,489 persons, including the metropolitan area. In the West there were only villages. Pittsburgh with a population of 1,565 was strategically located at the head of the Ohio River. Cincinnati, settled in 1789, had a population of 2,540 persons by 1810. The Northwest Territory had been organized under the Ordinance of 1787 and comprised the area now occupied by Ohio, Indiana, Illinois, and parts of Michigan and Wisconsin. The immorality of slavery was already disturbing some leaders of the new nation who were able to secure its prohibition within the limits of the Northwest Territory. Marietta, founded in 1788, was the territory's first settlement and capital. The Indians had been moved out of the eastern and southern parts of the territory in 1796 after Anthony Wayne's expedition against them. By 1800, even as settlers began to arrive in increasing numbers, the whole Northwest Territory had a total of only 51,000 inhabitants.

Kentucky, enjoying a prosperity based upon slave labor and good cash crops, could boast a somewhat more cultivated society than that of the free territory north and west of the Ohio River. It had an older culture than any other state so far West, and was practically a generation ahead of its neighbors. In 1800 Kentucky had 221,000 inhabitants. Lexington, its cultural center, had a population of only 1,795, of whom 439 were slaves. Slavery in states south of the Ohio River was to affect the way in which many of the churches developed, including the Christian Church (Disciples of Christ).

Most of what is now the United States was frontier at the beginning of the nineteenth century. Only after the American Revolution and the establishment of the new nation with a constitution in 1789 was it possible for numbers of people to move across the barrier of the Appalachians which separated the coastal areas of the original colonies from the inland West. As pioneers moved over the mountains and were thrown more and more on their own resources, the frontiersman cherished simplicity, practiced direct action, and was suspicious of complicated systems imposed by authority.

As the nineteenth century began, the most conspicuous

---

16. All population figures in this section are taken from *Report of United States Census Bureau*, Second and Third Census (Washington, D.C.: William Duane, publisher, Apollo Press, 1802 and 1811).

feature of American Christianity, after its freedom and diversity, continued to be its divided state. There were several large denominations of about equal size and an even greater number of smaller ones, but most persons were outside the church. The evangelistic task facing the church was of awesome proportions. The disunion of the Christian forces on the often uncouth and raw frontier was therefore most distressing, and the need for its correction was urgent. The church's historic concern for unity had entered upon a new phase. Because of the growing acceptance of the principle of separation of church and state, unity was no longer, as it had been in the European countries, a political matter. It was becoming a purely religious problem, to be solved, if it could be solved at all, by biblical study, by theological discussion, by persuasion, and by voluntary action.

Now that Christians knew religious liberty they were for the first time in a position to seek a kind of unity built upon that freedom. It was under these conditions that the pioneers of the Christian Church (Disciples of Christ) began their movement for the unity of all Christians on the basis of the restoration of a simple and noncreedal Christianity grounded in the New Testament.

The frontier rapidly receded, and the new settlements quickly assumed the characteristics of those areas from which the settlers had come. It was chiefly a rural society both East and West. Moral and religious conditions on the whole were at low ebb along the Eastern seaboard. They were even more deplorable in the new West. Not all settlers were honest, hard-working, God-fearing individuals. Peter Cartwright (1785-1872), the frontier Methodist circuit-rider, reported that Logan County, Kentucky (on the border of Tennessee where a new religious fervor was soon to appear) was called "Rogues Harbor." The area was a refuge for escaped murderers, horse thieves, highway robbers, and counterfeiters. People from the East who visited the West were shocked by the swearing, fighting, gouging, Sabbath-breaking, and general lawlessness which prevailed. A revival of religion and the Christian faith in America and in the West would not be long delayed.

The Second Great Awakening (or Great Western Revival) began during the 1790s in New England with scattered renewals of piety in various towns. It then gathered momentum in the early years of the new century. In the southern back country "New Light" Presbyterians, Methodists, and Baptists had kept the first Great Awakening alive and carried the seeds of the Second Great Awakening over the mountains to the new settlements in Kentucky and Tennessee. The most cataclysmic outbreaks of religious enthusiasm occurred in Kentucky at the great camp meetings of 1800 and 1801, most memorably at Cane Ridge, in Bourbon County, Kentucky. It is that event and its consequences that set the stage for the next developments.

3

STONE AND THE CHRISTIANS
IN THE WEST

The sparks of revivalism burst into a roaring flame on the American frontier in the early nineteenth century. The Great Awakening of New England, said Ralph H. Gabriel, "was a backyard bonfire in comparison with the religious conflagration lighted by the Revival of 1800."[1] Extraordinary excitement and emotional upheaval marked this Second Awakening or Great Revival of the West. Evangelical preachers seized the opportunity to press for an acceptance of the Gospel, and their striking success enabled the church to become firmly planted in the expanding raw provinces of the new nation.

Of the innumerable religious happenings in the Second Awakening, none attracted as much attention and generated as much enthusiasm as the Cane Ridge Camp Meeting of 1801 in Bourbon County, Kentucky. The surge of piety at Cane Ridge and at other camp meetings prompted many of the faithful to take heart and to thank God for the outpouring of his spirit among a pioneer people engaged in a daily struggle for survival. "I saw the religion of Jesus more clearly exhibited in the lives of Christians then than I had ever seen

---

1. Ralph H. Gabriel, *The Course of American Democratic Thought,* second edition (New York: The Ronald Press Company, 1956), p. 35.

before or since to the same extent."[2] Thus wrote Barton Warren Stone (1772-1844) in 1831 as he remembered "with a mournful pleasure" the widespread kindling of religious affections thirty years earlier.

Stone did not form his impression of the Second Awakening on the basis of secondhand information. He had the good fortune, to his way of thinking, of participating in the Cane Ridge Camp Meeting. A Presbyterian minister at the time, he subsequently withdrew from the denomination and became the most respected and honored leader of the Christian movement in the West.

By common consent Barton W. Stone is recognized as one of the founding fathers of the Christian Church (Disciples of Christ). Without intending to detract from the others, it is worth noting that before they even emigrated to the United States he was sounding the themes that became central in the tradition of Disciples. When Stone renounced the Presbyterian name in 1804 and agreed henceforth to call himself a Christian only, Thomas Campbell (1763-1854) was serving as minister of an Old Light Anti-burgher Seceder Presbyterian church in northern Ireland. Alexander Campbell (1788-1866), the son of Thomas, was a precocious youth of fifteen. Walter Scott (1796-1861) had yet to celebrate his eighth birthday in Scotland. Without any question, the life and witness of Stone was of pivotal significance in the origin and the formative period of the Christian Church (Disciples of Christ).[3]

THE ROAD TO MINISTRY

A fifth generation American, Barton Warren Stone was born near Port Tobacco in southern Maryland on December 24, 1772. Several of his forebears had figured prominently in the early history of Maryland. William Stone, his great-great-great-grandfather, was the first Protestant governor of

---

2. Barton W. Stone, *Christian Messenger*, July 1831, p. 165.
3. SEE the following for details of the life and thought of Stone: John Rogers, *The Biography of Elder Barton Warren Stone, Written by Himself: With Additions and Reflections by Elder John Rogers* (Cincinnati: J. A. and U. P. James, 1847); Charles C. Ware, *Barton Warren Stone: Pathfinder of Christian Union* (St. Louis: The Bethany Press, 1932); and William G. West, *Barton Warren Stone: Early American Advocate of Christian Unity* (Nashville: The Disciples of Christ Historical Society, 1954).

Maryland. Thomas Stone, another relative, was a member of the Second Continental Congress and one of four from Maryland to sign the Declaration of Independence. Shortly before the outbreak of the Revolutionary War, Barton's father died. Mrs. Stone was left with a large family of seven sons, one daughter, and one grandson. Barring economic disaster, the family property—including a plantation and fifteen slaves—appeared adequate to support the large number of dependents. For some reason Mrs. Stone sold the family holdings near Port Tobacco and moved with her children to Pittsylvania County, Virginia, in 1779. Perhaps economic considerations prompted the decision. Maybe family acquaintances had moved to the frontier of Virginia and encouraged her to do the same. We have no way of knowing. In his autobiography Stone dismissed the first seven years of his life in three short sentences.

The new home of the Stones was on the Virginia-North Carolina border and only thirty miles from David Caldwell's academy. After exhausting the meager educational resources of his immediate vicinity, Stone used his part of the family inheritance to finance his education. "Having determined on my future course," he wrote, "I bade farewell to my mother, brothers, companions and neighbors, and directed my way to a noted Academy in Guilford, North Carolina, under the direction of Doc. David Caldwell. Here I commenced the Latin Grammar the first day of February, 1790."[4] The decision to enter this academy was more far-reaching than Stone could possibly have imagined at the time.

Until they moved to Virginia, the Stones were affiliated with the Church of England. Now Stone entered a "log college" of a Presbyterian minister. David Caldwell (1725-1824), a native of Pennsylvania, had been educated in William Tennent's Log College (later Princeton) in New Jersey. Caldwell moved to North Carolina in 1765, founded a school, and served as minister of two Presbyterian churches. He was as versatile a man as any who lived in the area. In addition to teaching and preaching, he farmed and practiced medicine. Caldwell was not the only Presbyterian to found a

---

4. Rogers, *The Biography of Elder Barton Warren Stone,* p. 6. Unless otherwise indicated, all quotations from Stone in this chapter are taken from the volume by Rogers. For Stone's autobiography, SEE pp. 1-79.

log college in North Carolina. But his school was the most famous of them and deservedly so, for he educated a number of men who gave strong leadership in the political and religious arenas of the South. Five of his students served as state governors; fifty entered the ministry.[5] In selecting a school, Barton W. Stone chose well.

When Stone began his course of study under David Caldwell, the academy was in the midst of a period of religious excitement. The fiery James McGready (1760-1817), a Presbyterian minister in Guilford County, had visited the school and thundered his message of judgment with telling effect. Many of the students had experienced conversion and were meeting daily for prayer and worship. Stone rebelled and decided to go to another school for no other reason than "to get away from the constant sight of religion." Prevented by bad weather from leaving on the appointed day, he remained and soon found himself listening to Mr. McGready. As he pleaded with sinners to flee from the wrath to come, McGready made a lasting impression on Stone. "Such earnestness—such zeal—such powerful persuasion, enforced by the joys of heaven and miseries of hell, I had never witnessed before," confessed Stone. "Such was my excitement, that had I been standing, I should have probably sunk to the floor under the impression."

A vigorous Calvinist, McGready helped Stone to sense the gravity of sin and the depravity of the human spirit, but his insistence that man must wait for God to grant the gift of salvation left Stone puzzled and confused. Stone availed himself of the means of grace, but nothing seemed to happen. Looking back on this period in his life, he wrote: "For one year I was tossed on the waves of uncertainty—laboring, praying, and striving to obtain saving faith—sometimes desponding, and almost despairing of ever getting it." Then Stone heard William Hodge, a former student of Caldwell's. A "son of consolation," Hodge emphasized the love of God instead of describing the horrors of hell in lurid detail. Stone responded. It became clear to him that the Gospel really was good news, good news for him. He was converted.

---

5. For an uncritical biography of David Caldwell, SEE E. W. Caruthers, *A Sketch of the Life and Character of the Rev. David Caldwell, D. D.* (Greensborough, N. C.: Printed by Swaim and Sherwood, 1842).

Stone had entered Caldwell's academy with his mind set on a career in law. Following his conversion he became a candidate for the Presbyterian ministry. Encouraged by David Caldwell, he applied for a license to preach and was requested to prepare a discourse on the doctrine of the Trinity for the next meeting of the Orange Presbytery. Stone was apprehensive. Indeed, he had been a reader of the Bible for years; it was about the only "decent" literature available to a youngster on the Virginia frontier. He was not aware of a single book on the Trinity, however, and could not recall having heard a sermon on the topic. William Hodge proved to be helpful to Stone as did a volume by Isaac Watts entitled *Glories of Christ.* The presbytery accepted Stone's theological statement. His examination completed, Stone was promised his license to preach at the next session of the presbytery six months later.

Another problem troubled Stone. In debt, he decided to visit two of his brothers in Georgia with the hope of finding work. Shortly after arriving, he accepted a position as "professor of languages" in Succoth Academy, a Methodist school founded by Hope Hull (1763-1818) in Washington, Georgia. Hull was well known as a powerful preacher and had many contacts among Methodists in the South. Still vivid in his mind was the Baltimore conference of Methodists in 1792 at which time James O'Kelly and several other preachers expressed keen dissatisfaction with the autocratic style of Bishop Asbury. Hull wanted to make the Methodist system more democratic, but he refused to join the O'Kelly secession. In the light of his wide experience in the church, Hull spoke frequently with Stone and made a strong impression on him.

Stone also came to know John Springer (1744-1798) in Georgia. A warm and tolerant person, Springer was minister to a Presbyterian parish near Succoth Academy. Stone prized Springer's friendship and counsel. "I constantly attended on the ministrations of Mr. Springer," Stone wrote in his autobiography. "With him I became intimate, and to him I was warmly attached. By his discourse I was always profited, and began to feel a very strong desire again to preach the gospel." The concern and encouragement of

Springer helped Stone immensely as he pondered his future and felt his way toward ministry.

In the spring of 1796 Stone returned to North Carolina and received his license to preach from the Orange Presbytery on the sixth of April. Henry Pattillo (1726-1801) addressed the candidates for license—Stone and two other men—and presented a Bible to each of them. The seventy-year-old Pattillo had studied theology under Samuel Davies, leader of the Great Awakening in Virginia, and had served as chaplain of the first Provincial Congress of North Carolina in 1775. A book of Pattillo's sermons, published in 1788, makes it clear that he can hardly be described as a crusty sectarian who saw little if any difference between the Presbyterian Church and the kingdom of God. He lamented the presence of bigots in all churches and asked: "Of how many spiritual meals does this contracted temper of soul deprive the Christian world?" "I fear," he continued, "we have many such in our own church, who miss having their souls quickened by the preaching of an honest *Baptist,* or a warm *Methodist,* because they have different views, of some Christian doctrines, from the system embraced among us." At the very heart of his witness was the conviction that a faithful life is more to be desired than soundness in theology. To use his own words:

An error in judgment, where all honest pains for information have been taken, cannot be ranked among the vices. In such a case, guilt can have no place, for the will is not concerned. One evil word; one wicked action; one harsh censure, as they proceed from the heart, and are the choice of the will, have infinitely more of evil in them, than a mistaken judgment has. Thou who judgest, and condemnest thy brother, for unfound opinions, *shalt thou escape the judgment of God?* The better life of thy brother shall rise up against thee, and condemn thy better faith, that did not *work by love.*[6]

Pattillo's witness reflected the same spirit of tolerance that Stone had sensed in David Caldwell, William Hodge, Hope Hull, and John Springer. The piety and dedication of these men, all of them Presbyterians except Hull, took deep root in the heart and mind of Barton W. Stone.

When Stone received his license to preach, he and Robert Foster were appointed "to ride and preach in the lower parts of the state." Presbyterians were very weak in these coastal

6. Henry Pattillo, *Sermons* (Wilmington, N.C.: Printed by James Adams. 1788), pp. ix and xi.

counties. Stone and Foster failed to arouse much interest and were discouraged at the results of their missionary endeavors. Foster wondered if he had made a mistake in choosing the ministry for his vocation. Stone though despondent was not to the point of giving up. He decided to leave North Carolina and selected Florida as his destination. At least he would be a stranger there and would not feel obliged to live up to the expectations of those who knew him.

The very next Sunday he stopped to worship and discovered that an "old lady" of his acquaintance was in the congregation. Upon hearing his story she asked whether he might be a latter-day Jonah and suggested that he consider moving to the frontier beyond the Appalachian Mountains. Troubled and perplexed, Stone accepted her advice and started a long and eventful trip to the West. This abrupt change of mind, brought about by a chance conversation with a woman whose name is not even remembered, was to be of decisive importance to Stone and, for that matter, surely helped to shape the course of Disciples history. On his way through Virginia, Stone met a friend who insisted that he preach at Grime's Meeting House the following Sunday because no other Presbyterian minister was available. Stone hesitated. Looking back upon the experience, he wrote: "With great difficulty I was prevailed on to ascend the pulpit. While singing and praying, my mind was happily relieved, and I was enabled to speak with boldness, and with profit to the people." The response heartened Stone and removed some of his doubts concerning his fitness for ministry. According to Charles C. Ware, Stone "knew that this was his call" to be a minister.[7]

Stone remained in Virginia for a couple of months and preached frequently before moving on through Tennessee to Kentucky. The journey was difficult. He stopped for extended periods in various places, including Knoxville and Nashville. In October 1796 he became the regular supply minister of two Presbyterian churches, Cane Ridge and Concord, in Bourbon County, Kentucky. Cane Ridge was seven miles east of Paris; Concord (now in Nicholas County) was ten miles northeast of Cane Ridge. Stone's predecessor, Robert Finley, had been deposed on account of "habitual inebriety" and "insubordination."

---

7. Ware, *Barton Warren Stone*, p. 56.

During Finley's six years at Cane Ridge he—like many Presbyterian ministers—educated several men for the ministry. Among them were Richard McNemar (1770-1839), John Thompson, and John Dunlavy (1769-1826)—three prominent leaders associated with Stone in giving birth to the Christian movement in the West.

There was a good response to Stone's ministry at Cane Ridge and Concord. The two congregations requested him to become their "settled and permanent pastor." He accepted the call with the understanding that, according to Presbyterian practice, he now would have to seek ordination from the Transylvania Presbytery. To prepare for his ordination examination, he turned again to the study of theology and tried to come to terms with Presbyterian doctrines. "This was to me almost the beginning of sorrows," he wrote later.

I stumbled at the doctrine of Trinity as taught in the Confession; I labored to believe it, but could not conscientiously subscribe to it. Doubts, too, arose in my mind on the doctrines of election, reprobation, and predestination, as there taught.

The practice of piety in daily life made sense to Stone, but the fine points of Calvinistic theology left him dazed. Even though two members of the presbytery, Dr. James Blythe (1765-1842) and Robert Marshall (1760-1832), tried without success to help Stone resolve his theological problems, they persuaded him not to postpone the date of his ordination. The Transylvania Presbytery met at Cane Ridge in 1798. In the examination of Stone prior to his ordination, he was asked: "Do you receive and adopt the Confession of Faith, as containing the system of doctrine taught in the Bible?" Stone replied: "I do, as far as I see it consistent with the word of God." In spite of his honest hedging, the presbytery raised no objection. He became an ordained minister of the Transylvania Presbytery on October 4, 1798.

CAMP MEETING CHRISTIANITY

Newcomers were pouring into Kentucky in record numbers when Stone began his ministry at Cane Ridge and Concord. The trickle of Americans advancing into the great West swelled virtually into a flood after the Revolutionary War. The population of Kentucky, which was admitted to statehood on June 1, 1792, increased from less than 75,000 in

1790 to over 220,000 at the turn of the century. Although precise statistics are not available, it is probable that in 1800 not more than four to five percent of all Kentuckians claimed membership in some church. "The population of the State," wrote one nineteenth-century historian, "advanced with incredible rapidity, and soon outstripped the supply of the means of grace. Worldy-mindedness, infidelity, and dissipation threatened to deluge the land, and sweep away all vestiges of piety and morality."[8]

The lack of vitality in Stone's congregations became a matter of great concern to him. Referring to the apathy in the Cane Ridge and Concord churches, he wrote in his autobiography: "Things moved on quietly in my congregations, and in the country generally." As he wrestled with the growing problem of indifference, he heard about an outbreak of religious excitement in Tennessee and in southwestern Kentucky. The Second Awakening was under way.

The revival began under the leadership of James McGready, the Presbyterian preacher whose witness had quickened interest in religion at Caldwell's log college during Stone's student days. In pronouncing the judgment of God on gambling and other forms of immorality, McGready aroused strong opposition in Orange County, North Carolina. "Certain lewd fellows of the baser sort" burned his pulpit and left a threatening letter written in blood. McGready moved to Tennessee and then on to southwestern Kentucky, where he became pastor of the Gaspar, Muddy, and Red River congregations in Logan County. There he gave highest priority to the task of campaigning for revival. Joining him in the effort were William Hodge and the brothers McGee, who also had moved to the West from North Carolina. Their unremitting attacks on sin and their urgent pleadings for sinners to experience the new birth touched exposed nerves. To capitalize on the wave of enthusiasm, McGready and the others began to hold preaching meetings in the back country. In time these outdoor meetings attracted hundreds of people who came in wagons with sufficient provisions to camp on the ground for

---

8. Robert Davidson, *History of the Presbyterian Church in the State of Kentucky* (New York: Robert Carter, 1847), p. 131. Quoted in Ernest T. Thompson, *Presbyterians in the South, 1607-1861* (Richmond: John Knox Press, 1963), p. 125.

This sketch by a modern artist recreates an opening phase of the Cane Ridge Revival in August 1801.

The Cane Ridge Meetinghouse near Paris, Kentucky, where Barton Warren Stone was minister.

several days. A unique American approach to evangelism was born. The first planned camp meeting in the United States was held under McGready's direction at the Gaspar River Church in July 1800.

Barton W. Stone decided to attend a camp meeting in Logan County in the spring of 1801. The extraordinary response of the people astounded him. He saw religion at fever pitch; many people "got religion" on the spot. Stone carefully observed the physical demonstrations that accompanied the conversion experience. A number of the affected fell to the ground, as if dead, and lay motionless for several hours before regaining full consciousness. As they shouted with joy for their deliverance from the devil, others were caught up in the frenzy and praised God for the gift of salvation. Although Stone saw much in Logan County which he regarded as fanaticism, he became convinced that on balance the good far outweighed the bad.

Certain that a new day had arrived for Christianity on the frontier, Stone returned to Cane Ridge and Concord renewed in spirit and determined to plant the seeds of revival among his people. His congregations promptly showed signs of new life. Like fire in "dry stubble driven by a strong wind," the Second Awakening moved across the Kentucky frontier. The full range of religious expressions which Stone had observed in Logan County jarred central Kentucky as thousands participated in camp meetings at Concord, Point Pleasant, and Indian Creek in May and June of 1801.

The Second Awakening reached its climax at the Cane Ridge Camp Meeting on August 7-12, 1801. A social event of great magnitude as well as a religious happening, Cane Ridge attracted a cross section of the population. The pious were there, to be sure. So were the curious and the lonely who lived day by day in isolation on the frontier and welcomed the chance to socialize. Estimates of attendance ranged from ten thousand to thirty thousand. Although Presbyterians sponsored the meeting, a number of Methodist and Baptist preachers mounted stumps and from these wilderness pulpits proclaimed God's love for sinners. The Cane Ridge Camp Meeting was a remarkable demonstration of Christian unity, for denominational loyalties melted in the heat of revival.

Emotion ran high at Cane Ridge and resulted in a baffling display of acrobatic Christianity. As had been the case in previous camp meetings, sinners awakened to the Gospel fell victim to a variety of bizarre physical exercises. Shouts and shrieks of joy mounted into a dissonant crescendo that one witness likened to the roar of Niagara. The falling exercise affected all kinds of people "from the philosopher to the clown." Some caught the jerks and began to dance or to bark. Stone commented on the barking exercise:

A person affected with the jerks, especially in his head, would often make a grunt, or bark, if you please, from the suddenness of the jerk. This name of barking seems to have had its origin from an old Presbyterian preacher of East Tennessee. He had gone into the woods for private devotion, and was seized with the jerks. Standing near a sapling, he caught hold of it, to prevent his falling, and as his head jerked back, he uttered a grunt or kind of noise similar to a bark, his face being turned upward. Some wag discovered him in this position, and reported that he found him barking up a tree.

Still others ran as if from the devil to the point of exhaustion, "laughed" with indescribable solemnity, and sang "not from the mouth or nose but entirely in the breast." This unrestrained behavior was characteristic of camp meeting religion throughout Kentucky and Tennessee. Even so, the intensity of enthusiasm, the degree of tumult, and the size of the crowd made Cane Ridge unique and prompted eastern newspapers to give it extended attention. As Charles M. Johnson has written, "Cane Ridge was, in all probability, the most disorderly, the most hysterical, and the largest revival ever held in early-day America."[9]

In Stone's judgment, the hysteria and the moral irregularities on the campground did not discredit Cane Ridge. Surely a large group of people was led to give more than passing thought to the religious dimensions of life. It is impossible to determine how many converts were added to the churches, but those who ventured an estimate suggested a number between one thousand and two thousand. Even if the conservative figure is accepted as more likely to be accurate, church membership in Kentucky increased dramatically as a result of

---

9. Charles M. Johnson, *The Frontier Camp Meeting: Religion's Harvest Time* (Dallas: Southern Methodist University Press, 1955), pp. 62-63.

Cane Ridge, not to mention the impact of other camp meetings across the state. Moreover, the absence of sectarian rivalry at Cane Ridge was especially impressive to Stone. He recalled: "We all engaged in singing the same songs of praise—all united in prayer—all preached the same things— free salvation urged upon all by faith and repentance."

THE BEGINNING OF CONTROVERSY

If revivalism has tended to obscure denominational distinctions and to promote unity among Christians, it has also been a disruptive influence in the American church over the years. In fact, one historian has argued that "revivalism has been one of the most divisive forces in American religion."[10] The Second Awakening is a case in point.

A significant group of Presbyterian ministers in Kentucky regarded the revival more as an irritating problem, perhaps even a curse, than as a blessing. Ministers were not obliged to present their credentials before receiving permission to preach the Gospel in a camp meeting. What really mattered was a man's power of persuasion, not his educational and theological qualifications. The unordained and the ordained labored side by side, proclaiming salvation for all in utter disregard of the Calvinistic doctrine that Christ died only for the elect, and exciting the crowds to activity that bordered on the ridiculous. At stake were Presbyterian approaches to ordination, theology, and order and decency.

About three months after the last amen had been spoken at the Cane Ridge Camp Meeting, dispute arose within the Presbytery of Washington, which included churches in Kentucky and Ohio. Three elders in the Cabin Creek Church in Kentucky accused their pastor, Richard McNemar, of advocating doctrines that contradicted the Bible and the Westminster Confession of Faith. He had "expressly declared," they reported, "that a sinner has power to believe in Christ at any time," and "that Christ has purchased salvation for all the human race, without distinction." A member of the revival or New Light party in the Presbyterian Church, McNemar had been a prominent preacher at Cane Ridge and

10. William Warren Sweet, *The American Churches: An Interpretation* (New York: Abingdon-Cokesbury Press, 1947), p. 71.

at other camp meetings in Kentucky. He regarded physical agitations on the campgrounds as sure signs of God's presence. An invasion of the spirit brought about high voltage religion, to his way of thinking. An antinomian, McNemar accepted the Holy Spirit rather than the Bible as the central source of revelation. Church order and orthodoxy were of little concern to him. Without doubt, he was guilty as charged. No one appeared at the appointed time to substantiate the case against him, however, and the Presbytery of Washington refused to consider it. Subsequently, the pastor and elders at Cabin Creek resolved their differences and agreed to "pass over all past altercations."

When McNemar became minister of the Turtle Creek, Kentucky, church shortly thereafter, he promptly aroused the ire of an elder in the congregation. His heretical preaching kept him in trouble and the presbytery in turmoil. After questioning McNemar on one occasion, the presbytery declared that his ideas on particular election, human depravity, the atonement, and the nature of faith were "essentially different from that sense in which Calvinists generally believe them" and were "strictly Arminian." He was allowed, nevertheless, to continue preaching.

Other "revival men" among the Presbyterians shared McNemar's general theological position except for his antinomianism. John Thompson, minister of the Springfield (now Springdale) church in Ohio, also aroused solid opposition. Eighty petitioners, for example, requested a reexamination of McNemar and urged that Thompson be questioned on the fundamental doctrines of religion. The presbytery's refusal prompted a lively protest. The two parties in the church, revivalists and antirevivalists, were on a collision course.

The Synod of Kentucky, meeting in the fall of 1803, censured the Washington Presbytery for mishandling the McNemar-Thompson case and received a resolution to "enter on the trial or examination" of the two men. While the resolution was being debated, McNemar and Thompson withdrew with three others and returned to protest the proceedings and to renounce the jurisdiction of the Synod of Kentucky. In the document which was read to the synod, they wrote: "We declare ourselves no longer members of your reverend body, or under your jurisdiction, or that of your Presbyteries."

They cited three reasons for their action: (1) The minutes of the Washington Presbytery, which the synod sanctioned, misrepresented McNemar's position. (2) The synod would not permit the interpretation of Scripture by itself and refused to admit that "the Holy Spirit speaking in the Scriptures" is "the Supreme Judge by which all controversies in religion are to be determined." (3) Some statements in the Confession of Faith stood in sharp contrast to the "doctrines of grace, which, through God, have been mighty in every revival of true religion since the reformation." In the light of these considerations, they concluded: "We bid you adieu, until, through the providence of God, it seem good to your reverend body to adopt a more liberal plan, respecting human Creeds and Confessions." Dated on September 10, 1803, in Lexington, Kentucky, the document was signed by the five men in the following order: Robert Marshall, John Dunlavy, R. M'Nemar, Barton W. Stone, John Thompson.[11]

Shocked and dismayed by this turn of events, the synod appointed several of its members to counsel with the protesters and urge them to reconsider. They would not budge, so the synod had no alternative but to suspend them from "the exercise of all the functions of the gospel ministry" and to declare their pulpits vacant.

THE SPRINGFIELD PRESBYTERY

Although the dissenters repudiated the authority of the Synod of Kentucky, they still considered themselves to be Presbyterians. Consequently, they organized the Springfield Presbytery in the fall of 1803. To explain their actions and to interest others in joining them, they published a lengthy *Apology* of 141 pages on January 31, 1804. In common usage today an apology is an expression of regret and an admission of error, but they certainly were not feeling sorry or having second thoughts. Quite the contrary, they apologized in the historic sense of justifying and defending their position. Each

---

11. The full text of the document is quoted in William Warren Sweet, *Religion on the American Frontier:* vol. 2, *The Presbyterians* (New York: Harper and Brothers, 1936), pp. 318-319. SEE also Rogers, *The Biography of Elder Barton Warren Stone*, pp. 169-171.

of them signed the document which was entitled *An Apology for renouncing the jurisdiction of the synod of Kentucky, a compendious view of the Gospel and a few remarks on the confession of Faith.*[12]

The work was divided into three sections. Robert Marshall described the events which led to a withdrawal from the synod. In his detailed account, written from the point of view of one who had been mistreated, he quoted extensively from the minutes of both the presbytery and the synod. Barton W. Stone wrote the second section on "A Compendious View of the Gospel." After dealing with several theological topics including the nature of faith and the meaning of the Gospel, he anticipated objections and proceeded to answer them "for the satisfaction of honest inquirers." John Thompson concluded the *Apology* with "REMARKS ON THE CONFESSION OF FAITH." He argued against creeds as terms of communion and insisted that Scripture alone is the perfect standard for the life and thought of the church. "Is it not better," he asked, "to clear away all the rubbish, of human opinions, and build the church immediately on the rock of ages, the sure foundation which God has laid in Zion?" As for the Westminster Confession, he predicted that in time it would be given "to the moles, and to the bats."

Reprinted in Georgia and Virginia, the strongly worded *Apology* attracted attention. The Synod of Kentucky reaffirmed its stand in a *Circular Letter* written by John Lyle. Robert Hamilton Bishop countered Stone's approach to the Gospel with an *Apology for Calvinism.* The pamphlet warfare, as one might suspect, added another layer of tension to the theological dispute and widened the gap between the orthodox and the heretics.

Fifteen "regular societies" or congregations were related to the Springfield Presbytery in 1804. Seven of the congregations were in Ohio and the other eight in Kentucky. Among them were Cane Ridge and Concord. Many others had been caught up in the Second Awakening and were sympathetic to Stone and his associates. It would be a mistake, however, to presume that the Springfield Presbytery—described by Peter Cartwright as a "trash trap"—grew into a

---

12. The text of the *Apology* is reprinted in John Rogers, *The Biography of Elder Barton Warren Stone*, pp. 147-247.

sizable and structured body. Unlike other presbyteries, it elected no officers and exercised no control over member congregations. Essentially the Springfield Presbytery was a loose and informal association of five ministers who shared a common point of view and maintained their relationship, forged in the crucible of controversy, without developing a form of church organization.

The five increased to six when David Purviance (1766-1847) joined the group. A former member of the Kentucky legislature and a ruling elder in the Cane Ridge church, he was especially close to Stone. Around 1801 he decided to give up his political career and devote the remainder of his life to ministry. In preparation for the theological examination leading to ordination, Purviance asked Stone what books to read. Stone replied: "Read the Bible."[13] He followed Stone's advice, but the West Lexington Presbytery refused to act on his application for ordination. The presbytery stalled on the ground that his theology did not conform to the Westminster Confession. Stone and his associates raised no questions as to Purviance's doctrinal soundness and ordained him gladly. In David Purviance the Springfield Presbytery gained a strong advocate and a staunch opponent of creeds as tests of Christian fellowship.

Less than ten months after the Springfield Presbytery had been formed, it was dissolved in a meeting at Cane Ridge on June 28, 1804. Why did the six men take such an abrupt and decisive step? Stone suggested in his *Autobiography* that they reached the decision to disband the Springfield Presbytery when they became convinced it was a sectarian movement. The explanation is plausible. To formalize the act of dissolution and publicize it, they wrote *The Last Will and Testament of the Springfield Presbytery*. One of the most important documents in the entire course of Disciples history, it is brief enough to be quoted in its entirety:

"The Last Will and Testament of the Springfield Presbytery"

The Presbytery of Springfield, sitting at Cane-ridge, in the county of Bourbon, being, through a gracious Providence, in more than ordinary bodily health, growing in strength and size daily; and in

13. Levi Purviance, *The Biography of Elder David Purviance, Written by Himself: With an Appendix by Elder Levi Purviance* (Dayton: B. F. and G. W. Ells, 1848), p. 139.

perfect soundness and composure of mind; but knowing that it is appointed for all delegated bodies once to die; and considering that the life of every such body is very uncertain, do make, and ordain this our last Will and Testament, in manner and form following, viz.:

Imprimis. We *will,* that this body die, be dissolved, and sink into union with the Body of Christ at large; for there is but one Body, and one Spirit, even as we are called in one hope of our calling.

Item. We *will,* that our name of distinction, with its *Reverend* title, be forgotten, that there be but one Lord over God's heritage and his name One.

Item. We *will,* that our power of making laws for the government of the church, and executing them by delegated authority, forever cease; that the people may have free course to the Bible, and adopt *the law of the Spirit of life in Christ Jesus.*

Item. We *will,* that candidates for the Gospel ministry henceforth study the Holy Scriptures with fervent prayer, and obtain license from God to preach the simple Gospel, *with the Holy Ghost sent down from heaven,* without any mixture of philosophy, vain deceit, traditions of men, or the rudiments of the world. And let none henceforth take *this honor to himself, but he that is called of God, as was Aaron.*

Item. We *will,* that the church of Christ resume her native right of internal government—try her candidates for the ministry, as to their soundness in the faith, acquaintance with experimental religion, gravity and aptness to teach; and admit no other proof of their authority but Christ speaking in them. We will, that the church of Christ look to the Lord of the harvest to send forth laborers into his harvest; and that she resume her primitive right of trying those *who say they are apostles, and are not.*

Item. We *will,* that each particular church, as a body, actuated by the same spirit, choose her own preacher, and support him by a free will offering, without a written *call* or *subscription*—admit members—remove offences; and never henceforth *delegate* her right of government to any man or set of men whatever.

Item. We *will,* that the people henceforth take the Bible as the only sure guide to heaven; and as many as are offended with other books, which stand in competition with it, may cast them into the fire if they choose; for it is better to enter into life having one book, than having many to be cast into hell.

Item. We *will,* that preachers and people, cultivate a spirit of mutual forbearance; pray more and dispute less; and while they behold the signs of the times, look up, and confidently expect that redemption draweth nigh.

Item. We *will,* that our weak brethren, who may have been wishing to make the Presbytery of Springfield their king, and wot not what is now become of it, betake themselves to the Rock of Ages, and follow Jesus for the future.

Item. We *will,* that the Synod of Kentucky examine every member, who may be *suspected* of having departed from the Confession of Faith, and suspend every such suspected heretic immediately; in order that the oppressed may go free, and taste the sweets of gospel liberty.

Item. We *will,* that Ja___ ___, the author of two letters lately published in Lexington, be encouraged in his zeal to destroy *party-ism.* We will, moreover, that our past conduct be examined into by all who may have correct information; but let foreigners beware of speaking evil of things which they know not.

Item. Finally we *will,* that all our *sister bodies* read their Bibles carefully, that they may see their fate there determined, and prepare for death before it is too late.

Springfield Presbytery,}
June 28th, 1804 } L.S.

Robert Marshall, }
John Dunlavy, }
Richard M'Nemar, } *Witnesses*
B. W. Stone, }
John Thompson, }
David Purviance. }

Dismissed by one nineteenth-century historian as a "sorry attempt at wit" and by another as "nonsensical and profane," "The Last Will and Testament" is far more than a humorous and sarcastic document. The witnesses expressed a strong desire for Christian union, affirmed the right of each congregation to govern itself, singled out the Bible as the only standard of Christian faith and life, and repudiated the Westminster Confession because it was both useless and harmful. Not to be overlooked is the deep sense of evangelical piety which is reflected throughout the statement.

The witnesses appended an "Address" to "The Last Will and Testament." This address reiterated their concern for Christian union and reported their discovery "that there was neither precept nor example in the New Testament for such confederacies as modern Church Sessions, Presbyteries, Synods, General Assemblies, etc." In referring with approval to "the beautiful simplicity of Christian church government, stript of human inventions and lordly traditions," they came close to advocating the restoration of primitive Christianity.

The authorship of "The Last Will and Testament" has been a debated subject for many years. One historian, highly regarded for his careful scholarship, pointed to Stone as the author of the document. A more recent study has argued persuasively that the evidence, although not decisive, favors McNemar rather than Stone. Whether or not authorship is attributed to McNemar, "there is not the slightest evidence that Stone wrote, or suggested the writing of 'Last Will and Testament.' "[14] Stone agreed with the document in any case. Otherwise he never would have joined the others in signing it.

EMERGENCE OF THE CHRISTIAN CHURCH

During the final meeting of the Springfield Presbytery on June 28, 1804, the signers of "The Last Will and Testament" faced the issue of naming their movement. They were no longer Presbyterians and needed to identify themselves in such manner as to avoid sectarian overtones. Rice Haggard, a new member of the group, proposed the name "Christian." It was accepted at once. The death of the Springfield Presbytery marked the birth of the Christian Church in the West.

A Virginian, Haggard had been ordained as a Methodist minister in the early 1790s. He stood shoulder to shoulder with James O'Kelly in resisting Bishop Asbury, and the two had joined together in forming the Republican Methodist Church. When the Republican Methodists changed their name to the "Christian Church" at a conference in Surry County, Virginia, on August 4, 1794, it was at Haggard's suggestion. Obviously, the one-time associate of O'Kelly was well prepared for the discussion with Stone and his colleagues in 1804. He had rehearsed his speech ten years earlier.

The Christians in the West, according to Stone, "published a pamphlet on the name, written by Elder Rice Haggard, who had lately united with us." Lost for scores of years, the document was rediscovered in 1953 by John W. Neth, Jr. Entitled *An Address to the Different Religious Societies on the Sacred*

---

14. William G. West, *Barton Warren Stone*, p. 77.

Import of the Christian Name and published anonymously, it bears the same title as a sermon preached many years earlier by Samuel Davies. Although there are a number of differences between the two pieces, their similarity in phraseology and content is striking and hardly coincidental.[15] In addition to arguing that "followers of Christ should be called Christians and nothing else," Haggard scored the "religious societies" for departing from the Bible and elevating nonessentials to terms of communion. "One thing I know, that wherever nonessentials are made terms of communion, it will never fail to have a tendency to disunite and scatter the church of Christ," he wrote. An outspoken Christian primitivist, Haggard singled out divisions in the church for stinging criticism. "To me it appears," he wrote, "that if the wisdom and subtilty of all the devils in hell had been engaged in ceaseless counsels from eternity, they could not have devised a more complete plan to advance their kingdom than to divide the members of Christ's body."[16] Regardless of the degree of his reliance upon Samuel Davies, Haggard deserves more attention from historians of the Disciples than he has received.

Besides Haggard, several other preachers quickly joined the new fellowship. Among them were Malcolm Worley, an elder in McNemar's church, and Matthew Houston, the "hot gospeler" and Presbyterian pastor of the Silver Creek and Paint Lick churches. Another was Reuben Dooly (1773-1822), who attended the Cane Ridge Camp Meeting and in time came to know Stone and David Purviance well. Clement Nance (1756-1828) was the most important early convert. Like Haggard he had quit the Methodist ministry in Virginia to work with James O'Kelly. After an eighteen-month stay in Kentucky, Nance moved to Indiana in 1805 and became the pioneer preacher of the Christians in that state.

---

15. For an analysis of the similarities between the sermon by Davies and Haggard's *Address*, SEE Robert William Gates, "Samuel Davies to Barton W. Stone: A Study of Antecedents" (unpublished B. D. thesis, Lexington Theological Seminary, 1964), pp. 145-150; SEE also Colby D. Hall, *Rice Haggard: The American Frontier Evangelist Who Revived the Name Christian* (Published by University Christian Church in Fort Worth, Texas, 1957), pp. 51-53.
16. Rice Haggard, *An Address to the Different Religious Societies, on the Sacred Import of the Christian Name,* reprinted in Footnotes to Disciple History, no. 4 (Nashville: The Disciples of Christ Historical Society, 1954), pp. 15-17, 18, 20-24.

The Christians began with a group of churches as well as ministers. This nucleus consisted of the congregations which retained the Springfield renegades as their pastors. As ministerial converts joined the movement and began to preach, new churches, of course, were formed. Referring to this period, Stone wrote: "The churches and preachers grew and were multiplied; we began to be puffed up at our prosperity." There is no evidence that the Christians benefited from a ground swell of support and interest, but by the close of 1804 they could claim at least fifteen churches (including Cane Ridge and Concord) in Kentucky and southwestern Ohio.

The movement faced its first severe challenge in 1805. Three strangers—Issachar Bates, John Meacham, and Benjamin Seth Youngs—arrived in Bourbon County. They represented the United Society of Believers in Christ's Second Appearing and had been sent down from New Lebanon, New York, to evangelize in the heartland of the Second Awakening. Founded by Ann Lee Stanley (1736-1784), the Shakers—to use their popular name—testified that Christ already had made a second appearance on earth in the life and witness of "Mother Ann." Following their leader, they opposed the institution of marriage and forbade all sexual activity. Convinced that the spirit of God was directly accessible to all believers, they lived together in highly regulated and extraordinarily successful communities. The positive response to their message enabled the Shakers to establish a village near Harrodsburg. Malcolm Worley and Matthew Houston were two early converts. Moreover, Richard McNemar and John Dunlavy, joined by several families in their congregations, transferred their allegiance to the Shakers.

A plague had descended upon the Christians, threatening their very existence. Aghast at first, Stone and others reacted vigorously to prevent a further thinning of their ranks. "Never did I exert myself more than at this time, to save the people from this vortex of ruin," Stone wrote. "I yielded to no discouragement, but labored night and day, far and near, among the churches where the Shakers went."

Their growth interrupted for a brief period by the Shakers, the Christians survived with modest losses only to lose Robert

Marshall and John Thompson in 1811. They publicly retracted their errors and returned to the Presbyterians. Of the five founders of the Springfield Presbytery, Barton W. Stone alone remained with the Christian Church.

Stone carried on. In addition to David Purviance and Clement Nance, a number of other preachers continued to be strongly committed to the movement; from year to year the ministerial fellowship expanded as more and more men "received the call" and began to learn ministry by engaging in it. Throughout the 1810s and 1820s the Christians gained in momentum and in strength. Their growth was no more striking than that of the Baptists and Methodists in the Middle West, to be sure, but it was impressive. Even though statistics for the period are incomplete and probably inflated, it is reasonable to conclude that membership exceeded 12,000 by the late 1820s. Christians in the West had spread from their base in the Kentucky-Ohio region to Tennessee, Indiana, Missouri, Illinois, Alabama, Iowa, and other states.

Farmer-preachers and preaching laymen complemented the work of traveling evangelists in extending the witness of the Christian Church. Typical of many was the brother who preached regularly at "four stated places of religious worship"; he began a note to Stone as follows: "Dear Brother—I have just left my plough a few minutes to inform you how I am doing."[17] Another thought to send Stone a report of his previous year's work.

Brother Stone: I have not been altogether idle. Since I have been here, I will give you an account of the last year. On last Christmas day I constituted a church. Since that time I have constituted two others, and attended with Brother J. B. Thompson in constituting two more—making 5 in all. I have preached on an average five times a week; and have received into the church of Christ more than one hundred members, and have immersed 50: and in the same time I have cleared 5 acres of woodland, and raised 500 bushels of corn, with my own hands, and no other help than two little boys about 12 years old, and one horse. While I was gone abroad to preach, the plough must stand. Yet blessed be God, my health and spirits are good, and my family is healthy: and what is better than all, the good cause of the Master is prospering, and prospects

---

17. *Christian Messenger,* August 1831, p. 186.

look much brighter for the coming year, than they have for the past.[18]

Many Christian preachers felt the continuing tug between pulpit and plow.

An independent attitude characterized the western Christians. Outspoken in their opposition to ecclesiasticism, they kept alive the spirit of "The Last Will and Testament" and its insistence on the right of each congregation to self-government. In spite of their strong leaning toward localism, they nevertheless made sporadic attempts to relate to each other across congregational lines. As early as 1804 Stone and his associates announced "a general meeting of Christians at Bethel, seven miles below Lexington, on Thursday before the second Sabbath of October next." The purpose of the meeting, however, was not to develop an organization but "to celebrate the feast of love, and unite in prayer to God for the outpouring of his Spirit." In 1810 a group of ministers met in Kentucky and agreed to "unite themselves formally," but they failed to carry out their resolve. Conferences multiplied and began to meet with greater regularity as the years passed, but they remained by design nothing more than regional rallies. In the main, the business of such conferences was to hear reports from the various congregations and to decide on a place and time for the next meeting.

On rare occasions the western Christians showed signs of moving toward a sense of corporate responsibility. For example, a Christian conference convened in Fayette County, Kentucky, on August 31, 1827. The report of the meeting includes this note: "By request of the church at Round top meeting house, Brother Wm. Reid was ordained to the ministry of the Gospel and its ordinances."[19]

In the absence of organization, the *Christian Messenger* provided a means by which western Christians could communicate with each other and gain an appreciation of the wholeness of their movement. Stone founded the monthly journal in November 1826. As editor and publisher, he used his paper to state his own theological position and to take a stand on critical issues facing the church. News from congregations and preachers, especially their achievements in

18. *Christian Messenger*, January 1832, p. 28.
19. *Christian Messenger*, September 1827, p. 255.

evangelism, appeared regularly. Apologizing for his failure to include reports of revivals in one particular issue, Stone noted: "Revivals continue among us as stated in former numbers."[20] In addition to publicizing forthcoming meetings, Stone printed many conference minutes. "We have received for publication several minutes of different conferences," he wrote in 1830. "Our work is too limited to give them all a place in our columns. We can only give the substance of them."[21] A newspaper for the Christians, the *Christian Messenger* sheds more light on their activities than any other single source.

Given the limited number of Christians in the late 1820s, Stone's monthly had a good circulation. Writing in 1829, he commented: "My friends, trusting in your goodness, I have sent the *Christian Messenger* to nearly 2000 subscribers for almost three years." He added that he "was greatly in arrears" and pleaded with readers to pay for their subscriptions.[22] Regardless of the size of the subscription list, the *Christian Messenger* increased the visibility of Stone and strengthened the movement which came to be associated with his name.

Throughout his years of service to the Christian Church in the West, Stone reserved little time for leisure. Added to his ever-growing responsibilities in the life of the movement was the necessity of providing for a large family. He married Eliza Campbell (1784-1810) on July 2, 1801—about a month before the Cane Ridge Camp Meeting. They lived together at Cane Ridge for almost nine years until her death on May 30, 1810. Their only son died in infancy. Left with four young daughters, he found homes for them and spent more than a year as an itinerant evangelist. Stone remarried on October 31, 1811. His second wife, Celia Wilson Bowen (1792-1857), gave birth to four sons and two daughters. At the persuasion of her relatives, the Stones moved from Cane Ridge to Tennessee in 1812. Two years later they returned to Kentucky, living first in Lexington and then in Georgetown.

To support his family, Stone had to divide his time between service to the church and more remunerative work.

---

20. *Christian Messenger*, July 1828, p. 216.
21. *Christian Messenger*, December 1830, p. 286.
22. *Christian Messenger*, May 1829, p. 186.

He conducted a school in Lexington and served as principal of Rittenhouse Academy in Georgetown. He sold his Bourbon County farm before moving to Tennessee but in 1819 purchased 123 acres near Georgetown; he took care of the land while teaching and preaching at the same time. Barton W. Stone was no stranger to hard work. Referring to himself, he wrote in 1829: "To make bread, I know one who has labored by night in his field, with his hoe, while others were reposing in sleep. But, brethren, let us not be discouraged."[23]

Forced to spend long hours farming, Stone converted his fields into a makeshift study. He wrote: "My opportunity to read was very limited, being compelled to manual labor daily on my farm; but so intently engaged was my mind . . . that I always took with me in my cornfield my pen and ink, and as thoughts worthy of note occurred, I would cease from my labor, and commit them to paper." On many occasions he was absorbed in thinking through some theological issue. Try as he might, he could not ignore the responsibility of seeking to understand and interpret the faith he practiced. He generally arrived at positions which amounted to attacks on orthodoxy and embroiled him in controversy. Although Stone is remembered as a man of sweet reasonableness, he moved from one theological dispute to another. On the first page of the *Christian Messenger* in 1831, for example, he felt obliged to state: "The same course will be pursued in this, as in the former volumes, except that useless controversy shall not be attended to, and practical religion more zealously enforced."[24] Like most New Year's resolutions, the promise was made but not kept.

Stone struggled especially with the nature of Christ and the relationship between Father and Son. He could not bring himself to accept the affirmation in the Westminster Confession that Christ as the second person in the Trinity is "very and eternal God, of one substance and equal with the Father." It was beyond him to fathom how "two whole, perfect, and distinct natures, the Godhood and the manhood" could be "inseparably joined together in one per-

---

23. *Christian Messenger*, April 1829, p. 133.
24. *Christian Messenger*, January 1831, p. 1.

son, without conversion, composition, or confusion."[25] The doctrine of the Trinity, to Stone's way of thinking, was neither sensible nor biblical. Perhaps God's threeness might be understood as a trinity of modes or functions in the sense that one person could be father, son, and husband. Stone was disinclined to regard modalism as a final answer, however. In sum, he argued that Christ was the Son of God, not "very God." Clearly he placed the Son in a subordinate role to the Father, but he refused to admit that in so doing he detracted from the divinity of Christ.

In interpreting the work of Christ, Stone rejected the doctrine of limited atonement because God surely would not play favorites with the human race by saving only the elect. Moreover, he convinced himself that Christ died on the cross to reconcile man to God, not God to man. The concept that a sacrificial Son appeased a vindictive Father made a mockery of the love of God. In Stone's judgment, God's attitude toward mankind remained constant; mankind's attitude toward God needed changing, and for that purpose Christ lived and died. Although Stone went to great lengths to argue his case, he recognized that in final analysis a believer could receive the grace of God in Christ without fully or even correctly understanding the doctrine of the atonement. To make his point, he used an analogy:

A father provides plentifully for a large family of children. Some of them may know the means by which the father got the provisions—others may not so well know, and the youngest may scarcely know any thing more than that the father's love provided these things. Yet they all eat and thrive, without quarreling about the means by which the provisions were obtained.

"O that Christians would do likewise," he concluded.[26]

As regards the evolving tradition of Christians in the West, Stone's emphasis on the necessity of union among followers of Christ was vastly more consequential and far-reaching than his Christology. His practical concerns and his theological interests converged into a clear focus in his unwavering ad-

---

25. For the text of the Westminster Confession, SEE *The Creeds of the Evangelical Protestant Churches with Translations,* ed. by Philip Schaff (London: Hodder and Stoughton, 1877), pp. 600-673. SEE especially pp. 619-620.
26. James M. Mathes, *Works of Elder B. W. Stone, to Which Is Added a Few Discourses and Sermons,* second edition (Cincinnati: Moore, Wilstach, Keys and Co., 1859), p. 117.

vocacy of Christian union. He used the very first issue of the *Christian Messenger* to express his ecumenical conviction with precision and forcefulness. In an article entitled "Of the Family of God on Earth," he wrote:

It is frequently asked, Why so much zeal in the present day against authoritative creeds, party names, and party spirits? I answer for myself: because I am assured they stand in the way of Christian union, and are contrary to the will of God.

It is again asked, Why so zealous for Christian union? I answer, because I firmly believe that Jesus fervently prayed to his Father that believers might all be one—that the world might believe in him as sent by the Father.

If we oppose the union of believers, we oppose directly the will of God, the prayer of Jesus, the spirit of piety, and the salvation of the world.[27]

Barton Warren Stone had not forgotten "The Last Will and Testament." His burning desire to heal divisions in the body of Christ caused him to pay special attention to a group of Reformers led by two Scotch-Irish immigrants, Thomas and Alexander Campbell.

---

27. *Christian Messenger*, November 1826, pp. 15-16.

4

BRITISH BACKGROUNDS

While the developments in the foregoing chapters were unfolding on the American frontier, certain events taking place
in northern Ireland, Scotland, and England were destined to
affect the history of the Christian Church (Disciples of
Christ). It has been seen how distinctive American
developments at the turn of the nineteenth century led to the
emergence in Kentucky of a new Christian movement which
later joined with other churches and leaders to become the
Christian Church (Disciples of Christ). The European
backgrounds of the Disciples are found in northern Ireland,
Scotland, and England. These backgrounds were shaped by
nonconformist and free-church movements in the last part of
the eighteenth century. Through them Disciples relate
directly to the full history of Christianity.

The Christian Church (Disciples of Christ) throughout its
history has advocated a united church. It should be
remembered that for Christianity's first ten centuries almost
everyone thought of the church as united. Perfect as it was in
theory, the unity of the church was never completely realized
in fact. Even before the claims for the supremacy of the
bishop of Rome in the Western church had reached their full
development, the Eastern church resisted the papacy's

claims. In 1054 the separation between the Greek and the Latin branches of the church became complete.

In Western Christianity the same qualities which gave the medieval church its power provoked revolt against it. A combination of ecclesiastical and political power was sufficient to suppress dissenters or drive them into hiding. However, beneath the seemingly solid structure of the church there was an underground current of dissent. Occasionally this dissent came to the surface as in the attempted reforms of John Wyclif (c.1330-1384) of England, and of John Huss (c.1373-1415) of Bohemia, each of whom had a sizable popular following. Such approaches to dissent and reformation from the twelfth through the fifteenth centuries were symptomatic of forces which later found more effective expression in the Protestant movement.

THE PROTESTANT REFORMATION

The Protestant Reformation of the sixteenth century was a complex of many independent movements.[1] Most of its basic ideas had found expression among earlier reformers and dissenters, but the time came when political and cultural conditions gave them more effective support. These changed conditions included the decline of feudalism with the corresponding growth of nation-states, the invention of the printing press, a new prosperity brought on in part by the voyages of discovery, the rise of a banking and merchant class, and the growth of cities. All contributed to the creation of a climate in which reform could take place. Another important aspect was the coming of the Renaissance and the blossoming of Christian humanism. These altered the intellectual and cultural atmosphere of Europe, so that the spirit of inquiry and individualism could prevail.

The Protestant Reformation was a revolt against the abuses and misuse of ecclesiastical power. It was a protest against some practices within the church but not against the church as such. It was an attempt not to defeat the church, but to free it from the corruptions which had invaded it. By recovering the New Testament understanding of the doctrine

---

1. *Harold Grimm, The Reformation Era* (revised ed.) (New York: Macmillan, 1973). This is a good, short, comprehensive study of the Protestant Reformation.

of the church the reformers aimed to restore the church to its original and essential purity.

The Protestant Reformation was composed of five main movements. These five originated separately and never succeeded in unifying, though there were many efforts to unite them. Some of these movements produced churches with distinctive identities, theologies and polities. The following distinctive church groups can be identified:

1) The movement of Martin Luther (1483-1546) in Germany and Scandinavia.

2) The movement of Ulrich Zwingli (1484-1531), originating in Zurich, in the German-speaking part of Switzerland.

3) The Reformed churches which followed the teachings of John Calvin (1509-1564). Their original influence was in Switzerland but Calvinism became dominant in Scotland, the Netherlands, and certain parts of France. It was also strongly represented in western Germany and in the countries east of Germany, and furnished the background for the Puritanism of England.

4) The Anglican movement in England and Ireland, which maintained a Catholic form of worship but separated itself from the ecclesiastical structures in Rome.

5) A number of separate movements such as the Anabaptists, the Moravians, and the Mennonites.

The Protestant Reformation by the nature of its development remained incomplete. It began with an attempt to go back of the complex and elaborate traditions of the medieval church to the more fundamental authority of the early church. While not opposed to tradition, the Reformation went behind tradition to the New Testament, but before its reform was complete it bogged down in biblical literalism and legalism. No agreement could be reached on a correct interpretation of the Scriptures. As a result, the medieval synthesis was cut asunder with a resulting chaos of conflicting viewpoints.

The reasons why the Protestant churches could not be united were not insignificant. Churches were politically divided because of an intense, newly emerging nationalism. Each church was linked in a close relationship to the government of its own country. A united church would have had to cross national boundaries. They were divided further, as has been seen, because they grew out of separate reform movements, each with its own theological presuppositions. It was not that the reformers of the sixteenth century were indifferent to union. The colloquy at Marburg in 1529 was one attempt to unite. They clung to union as an ideal, and some of them tried hard to realize it, but the forces contributing to division were too strong for them.[2] By the end of the century the church had fallen into a tragically divided state.

SOME SEEKERS OF CHURCH UNITY

Even in the period of the most violent conflict among intolerant parties seeking to compel conformity, or to drive each other out of the church, there were prophetic voices urging the possibility and the rightness of church union with freedom of conscience. The question was how to have diversity and unity. A writing of "Rupertus Meldenius" (probably Peter Meiderlin, a Lutheran theologian of whom little is known) appeared in Germany in 1626. In this writing appears the classic slogan: "In essentials, unity; in nonessentials, liberty; in all things, charity."

John Bergius [1587-1658], a liberal Calvinist of Frankfort-on-Oder, quoted this from Meldenius; Richard Baxter [1615-1691], of England, quoted it from Bergius. The Lutheran theologian, George Calixtus [1586-1656], of Helmstadt, spent much of his life trying to prove that the differences between Lutherans and Calvinists ought not to divide them.[3]
He was even willing to unite with a reformed Roman Catholic church if union could be accomplished no other way.

John Dury (1595-1680), born in Scotland but educated for the ministry in Holland, was the hardest worker for unity of the seventeenth century. For nearly fifty years he traveled unceasingly throughout Europe trying to bring about religious harmony. His platform for unity included agreeing upon a body of "practical divinity" in place of creeds, abolishing all sectarian names (using instead "Reformed Christians"), and allowing individual freedom in nonessen-

---

2. John T. McNeil, *Unitive Protestantism* (Richmond: John Knox Press, 1964). A splendid exposition of the history of early efforts toward church union.
3. Winfred E. Garrison and Alfred T. DeGroot, *The Disciples of Christ: A History* (St. Louis: Bethany Press, 1948; revised ed., 1958), p. 41.

tials. Hugo Grotius (1583-1645), a Dutch Arminian and the father of international law, wrote two books on ways to establish church unity.

John Locke, referred to in Chapter 2, sought to work toward Christian unity in the publication of his *Letters Concerning Toleration.* The year 1689, which saw the publication of Locke's first *Letter Concerning Toleration* in Holland, where he was living in exile, was also the year which ended Stuart intolerance in Britain. The new regime of William and Mary put an end to anything that could be called persecution in England and opened the door to the possibility of dissent from the established church.

Benjamin Grosvenor (1676-1758), a former Presbyterian minister, became a spokesman for the Independents (i.e. Congregationalists) in London. In 1728 he published a book of sermons entitled *An Essay on the Name Christian,* the main import of which was the necessity for Christians to cease using denominational names and to use only scriptural terms in describing themselves. This book of sermons had wide circulation not only in Great Britain but also on the frontier in America where it influenced Rice Haggard, Barton W. Stone, and other church leaders.

RESTORATION MOVEMENTS IN GREAT BRITAIN

In the late eighteenth and early nineteenth centuries, Great Britain saw the emergence of a considerable number of small and independent movements which used the "restoration" phraseology and which aimed, in a more literal and precise way than any of the preceding movements, to return to the exact practice of the apostolic churches with reference to doctrine, ordinances, methods of worship, forms of organization, and the name of the church itself. All these groups remained small, and many of them soon vanished, but in the long run their influence was considerable.[4]

Their common idea was that the existing churches were cluttered with human additions to divine revelation; that the creeds were too complicated and speculative; that worship was too formal and the clergy too eager for worldly advantage.

---

4. Alfred T. DeGroot, *The Restoration Principle* (St. Louis: Bethany Press, 1960). Chapter VI.

They stressed the independence of the local congregation and the importance of lay leaders. There is no indication that church unity played a part in the program of any of these groups. It should be noted, however, that their platforms contained many ideas congenial to the spirit of the American frontier. Many of their ideas did, in fact, circulate freely in the backwoods of North Carolina, Virginia, Kentucky, and Tennessee.

GLAS AND SANDEMAN

One movement of special interest to Disciples because of certain similarities of practice is that of John Glas (1695-1773) and his son-in-law, Robert Sandeman (1718-1771). John Glas had been one of the first of the Scottish Independents (i.e. Congregationalists). He had left the established church in Scotland in 1728, adopted Independent views, and formed churches in most of the large towns in Scotland, where his followers were called "Glasites." Glas distinguished between the Old and New Testaments; in the former he held the state and the church to be identical, while in the latter he saw the church as purely a spiritual community. The aim of his movement was to restore primitive New Testament practices. About 1755 Robert Sandeman developed and enlarged these views into a more precisely stated position.

Sandeman gave the movement its theological content. He upheld the doctrine of justification by faith, but he thought of faith as limited largely to its intellectual content. Sandeman believed that faith is simple assent to the New Testament testimony concerning Christ. He advocated the weekly observance of the Lord's Supper, the "holy kiss" between Christians, love feasts, weekly contributions for the poor, mutual exhortation of members, and a claim of the Christian community on private goods. He would place church government in the hands of bishops, elders, and teachers. He afterward came to America, founded a congregation at Danbury, Connecticut, in 1763, and remained there the rest of his life. This congregation affiliated with the Disciples shortly after 1840. There were probably never more than twenty to thirty churches of this order in Great Britain or America, but Sandeman's works were read and highly regarded by many leaders who had no commitment to the peculiarities of his sect.

Early in Alexander Campbell's leadership of the Disciples the charge was made that he was a "Sandemanian." Campbell answered by saying that he had studied Sandeman's ideas and that he would acknowledge himself debtor to Glas and Sandeman, but he did not believe they "had clear and consistent views of the Christian religion *as a whole.*"[5]

THE HALDANES

The movement initiated by James Alexander Haldane (1768-1851) and his older brother, Robert (1764-1842), two wealthy laymen of the Church of Scotland, was similar in many ways to that of Glas and Sandeman. The Haldanes were concerned over the formalism and sterility of the established church and alarmed by the rationalistic theology current in their day. After a profound religious experience they broke with the established church in 1799. They spent their money freely in promoting an evangelistic revival in Scotland and in building tabernacles in Edinburgh and Glasgow. They encouraged lay preaching and established institutes to train young men from families of the poor to preach.[6]

The Haldanes brought the famous English evangelist Rowland Hill (1744-1833) from London to hold meetings in Scotland and later financed a visit by Hill to Ireland. Rowland Hill represented something of what the Haldanes hoped to accomplish. Hill, also a man of some means, became an ardent participant in the evangelical movement while a student at Cambridge University. In disfavor with the Church of England because of evangelical activities, he participated in the organization of the British and Foreign Bible Society and the London Missionary Society. It was as a traveling evangelist, however, that his influence was greatest.

The Haldanes, like Rowland Hill, were zealous for the extension of Christianity in Scotland and elsewhere. In 1797

---

5. *The Christian Baptist,* May, 1826, pp. 202 ff.
6. Alexander Haldane, *Memoirs of the Lives of Robert Haldane of Airthrey, and of His Brother, James Alexander Haldane* (New York: Carter and Brothers, 1857).

James A. Haldane organized the Society for Propagating the Gospel at Home, which was a general agency for the promoting of the evangelical cause.

On the recommendation of Mr. Greville Ewing [1767-1841], a former Church of Scotland minister who was in charge of the Haldanes' seminary in Glasgow, they adopted congregational independency as being the order of the New Testament churches and introduced the weekly observance of the Lord's Supper. . . .They moved rapidly toward . . . the conviction that any true reformation of the church required exact conformity to apostolic teaching and practice.[7]

In 1807 the Haldanes became convinced that the scriptural form of baptism was immersion and abandoned the practice of baptizing infants. Ewing could not follow them in this change, and, for this and other reasons, relations between them became strained. The Haldane influence is seen in the Campbells' later position in regard to church organization and practice. Also Walter Scott was associated with a Haldane congregation when he just arrived in Pittsburgh. The restorationist proposals of the Haldane brothers were to alter the religious thinking of persons not only in Scotland and Ireland but also on the American frontier. The Scottish Independents were never a large movement but had a lasting influence.

NORTHERN IRELAND AND THE CAMPBELLS

The scene now shifts to Ulster, the counties of northern Ireland. Settled largely by Scots during the preceding century or two, Ulster at the end of the eighteenth century was largely Presbyterian and, therefore, Calvinistic. The greater part of Ireland was Roman Catholic, and all the more solidly so because of resentment toward the Anglican church, which was established in all of Ireland as the church of the English overlords. The Presbyterians of Scotland and northern Ireland were divided into several bodies. In the life and ministry of a particular Presbyterian pastor, Thomas Campbell, and of his eldest son, Alexander, are to be found the specific British backgrounds of the Christian Church (Disciples of Christ).

---

7. Garrison and De Groot, *The Disciples of Christ*, pp. 51-52.

Thomas Campbell was born February 1, 1763, in County Down, Ireland. His father, Archibald Campbell, was in early life a Roman Catholic, but he rejected this church as being out of harmony with the teaching of the Bible and later became a member of the Church of Ireland (Anglican). The formality of the worship of that church and its apparent want of piety and evangelical zeal led Thomas Campbell as a young man to the fellowship of the Seceder branch of the Presbyterian Church in Ireland. The church of the Seceders had been created by men determined to preserve a congregation's right to select its own ministers.

At first Thomas Campbell turned to schoolteaching for a living. A good school was obtained for him at Sheepbridge, near Newry, County Down, through the influence of a fellow Seceder, John Kinley. Apparently a man of prominence and means, Kinley was so impressed with Thomas' ability and promise that he offered to finance his education if Thomas would carry out an earlier intention to enter the ministry. Campbell thereupon enrolled as a student at Glasgow University where he studied from 1783 to 1786.[8]

About 1786 Campbell completed his literary course with honors and the next year attended the theological school maintained by the Anti-Burgher branch of the Seceder Church at Whitburn in Scotland. The Anti-Burghers opposed the requirement that the burgesses of the Scottish cities swear to support the established church. These quarrels continued in northern Ireland and young Thomas Campbell took the Anti-Burgher position. The Reverend Archibald Bruce (d.1816) was at this time the professor of the Anti-Burgher seminary. A highly qualified and popular instructor, he held the post for twenty years. He was an orthodox Calvinist in theology but tended toward belief in a congregational polity.

Teaching school and preaching occasionally at Ballymena, in County Antrim, while completing the five-year theological course, Thomas met Jane Corneigle (1764-1835), of French Huguenot heritage. The exact date of their marriage is unknown as family records were later lost, but the date usually accepted is sometime in June 1787. When their first child, a

8. Robert Richardson, *Memoirs of Alexander Campbell*, I (Philadelphia: Lippincott, 1868), p. 21-25. SEE Lester G. McAllister, *Thomas Campbell—Man of the Book* (St. Louis: Bethany Press, 1954), for a definitive biography of Thomas Campbell.

son named Alexander, was born, September 12, 1788, Thomas and Jane Campbell were still living near Ballymena in the parish of Broughshane. Shortly after 1791 Campbell and his family moved to Sheepbridge where he resumed teaching and preaching for Seceder congregations nearby. The Campbells later moved to Market Hill, in County Armagh, not far from Newry. Still a probationer in the Seceder Church, he apparently made the move to supply the needs of the weaker churches of the district.

About 1798 Campbell accepted a call to become the pastor of a congregation recently established at Ahorey, in the open country four miles from the town of Armagh in County Armagh. He and his family moved to a small farm near Rich Hill, a rather substantial village only a few miles from the church. From a high hill near his farm Campbell would have been able to see several counties, and in the distance Loch Neagh. After settling into his new home and becoming acquainted with his new field of work, he was ordained as the pastor of the church. The family was happy at last to be established on a fairly permanent basis.

Thomas Campbell was determined that his eldest child should have the advantage of a good education. Alexander was enrolled in an elementary school at Market Hill, where he boarded with the family of a local merchant, when the family moved to Ahorey. Later Alexander spent two or three years in the academy which his uncles, Archibald and Enos Campbell, had opened at Newry.

The time came when Campbell decided to continue his son's education under his personal supervision. He found Alexander more devoted to sport and physical exercises than to anything else, but finally the young man turned back to studies again. As Alexander grew older his father introduced him to the works of John Locke, whose *Letters Concerning Toleration* made a lasting impression on him and whose *Essay Concerning Human Understanding* was read under the father's direction. Thomas was anxious that his son should be prepared to enter the university if ever an opportunity should present itself. To this end he instructed Alexander in Latin and Greek and, as time went on, even anticipated the usual college course.

Thomas Campbell's ministry in Ireland extended through

troubled years of civil commotion. The first regular lodges of the Society of Orangemen were founded in 1795 in County Armagh, although the order had existed earlier. This organization had as its object the driving of all Roman Catholics from Ulster. Unidentified individuals went about in the night searching houses for arms. This practice was taken advantage of by common robbers who plundered the people and their property. Another group whose purpose was to "protect" the Protestants was the "Peep-o'Day Boys" who gained their name from the dawn hours chosen for their raids on Catholic villages. The Roman Catholics in return formed the society of "The Defenders."

All these disturbances culminated in the rebellion of the Irish against the English in 1798 with great discontent all over northern Ireland. After 1801 peace was partially restored by a new agreement with England, but many Irishmen were still restive. In all this Thomas Campbell took a position opposing all secret societies and the use of violence toward persons of differing views. Shortly after 1804 Campbell moved his growing family (now composed of seven living children: three sons and four daughters) to nearby Rich Hill so that he might open an academy, thus augmenting his meagre income.

INFLUENCES AT RICH HILL

There were not only political and economic disturbances in Ireland at the beginning of the nineteenth century, but religious ones as well. In 1795 a question arose among Burgher Presbyterians over the power of civil magistrates in religion. This had the effect of producing two parties, distinguished from each other by the terms "Old Light" Burghers and "New Light" Burghers. The same controversy spread among the Anti-Burghers. The "Old Light" party was headed by Archibald Bruce, Thomas Campbell's former seminary teacher. In August 1806, Bruce organized a new presbytery. When Thomas Campbell joined the Seceder church as a youth, he had become affiliated with the Anti-Burgher sect of the Seceders. When in 1806 the Anti-Burghers divided, Campbell found himself a member and minister of the Old Light Anti-Burgher Seceder Presbyterian Church.

Even though he was a member of a strict Seceder sect, Campbell always displayed a surprising independence of mind, balanced by a catholicity of spirit. A man of a quiet peaceful nature, he was disturbed by the bitterness of sectarian strife and bothered by the triviality of the differences over which men quarreled. In consequence three influences began to move Thomas Campbell and he came to represent a new and different type of Scotch-Irish Presbyterian preacher.[9]

The first influence, and probably the most important, was that of the congregation of Independents which he found when he moved his residence to Rich Hill. He was on friendly terms with the pastor, a Mr. Gibson, and many members of the congregation. It was not unusual for Campbell after his return from the services of the church at Ahorey, two miles distant, to attend the evening meeting of this Independent (i.e. Congregational) fellowship.

The Independent congregation was liberal in granting the use of their meetinghouse to preachers representing differing points of view. This provided an opportunity for the residents of Rich Hill from time to time to hear persons distinguished in the religious world. On such occasions Campbell was one of the most attentive listeners. In this way his thinking on the religious questions of his day was tremendously stimulated. During this period he heard and had conversation with James A. Haldane and Rowland Hill as well as Alexander Carson (1776-1844) and John Walker (1768-1833), leading Irish evangelicals. The Independents of Rich Hill, however, were mainly Haldanean in sentiment. Coming as he did from the strictest body of Anti-Burghers, Campbell was much impressed by the tolerant attitude of the Rich Hill Independents.

The second influence operating at this time in the life of Campbell was that of the "evangelical" style of preaching. Introduced by Whitefield and Wesley earlier in the eighteenth century, the evangelical spirit was carried forward by Hill, Carson, Walker and others. Thomas Campbell warmly sympathized with the objects of the Society for the Propagation of the Gospel at Home, founded by James A. Haldane. He became a member and took great pleasure in aiding its operations in northern Ireland. These different movements, by their emphasis on simple New Testament

---

9. McAllister, *Thomas Campbell—Man of the Book*. pp. 44-56.

Christianity, increased Campbell's reverence for the Scriptures as the basis for church organization. They also deepened his conviction that the existence of sects and parties was a hindrance to the success of the gospel.

The third influence on Campbell was the very pronounced sectarian spirit in Ireland at this time. Not only was there a bitter feeling among the different denominations, but also there was a spirit of factionalism leading to conflict among the various branches of the Presbyterian Church. The differences which had occasioned the divisions were magnified, and all the branches were characterized by a spirit of bitterness and a narrow outlook. Campbell sincerely felt that such a spirit kept many individuals from accepting the gospel. His study and ministry thus far had presented him with the picture of a divided church. He was all too keenly aware of how trivial were the differences existing between the Burgher and Anti-Burgher churches in Ireland. The disputed oath was not required in Ireland, thus the original reason for the division did not exist. This so concerned Thomas Campbell that he resolved to seek reunion between the Burgher and Anti-Burgher Seceders in northern Ireland.

Under his leadership an effort was made to bring together those who felt as he did about the matter. A "Committee on Consultation" met at Rich Hill in October 1804 to discuss the possibility of uniting the Burgher and Anti-Burgher groups in Ireland. A report, with propositions of union, was prepared by Thomas Campbell and presented to the Anti-Burgher Synod of Ireland when it met at Belfast sometime after October 1804. It was favorably received. In March of the following year representatives of the Burghers and Anti-Burghers met at Lurgan, in County Armagh. There was a unanimous desire on both sides for a union. Meanwhile, the General Associate Synod in Scotland, hearing of a movement toward uniting the two denominations, expressed disapproval even before any application for union was received. Consequently, the effort failed for the time being.[10]

In 1805 the Synod of Ulster in Ireland applied to the General Associate Synod in Scotland for the right to transact its own business. Thomas Campbell was selected as the

---

10. Alexander Campbell, *Memoirs of Elder Thomas Campbell* (Cincinnati: H. S. Bosworth, 1861), pp. 210-213.

spokesman for the Irish ministers and journeyed to Scotland to lay the matter before the higher court. The General Synod decided there was nothing to be gained by such a proposal, and matters were left very much as they were before. His effort in 1805 failed, but his experience with this specific manifestation of the sectarian spirit made him more conscious than ever before of the need for a basis on which the church could unite.

REMOVAL TO AMERICA

After these experiences Thomas Campbell decided to migrate to the New World. With what mixed motives the decision to journey to America was made will never be known fully. The excessive strain of Campbell's labors as both preacher and teacher began to impair his health. He was afflicted increasingly by a stomach ailment, and his physician had prescribed a sea voyage. Undoubtedly his concern over the political troubles and the excessive sectarianism of the day played their part. Some of his friends urged a trip to America. Friends and neighbors had been migrating overseas. If he went, he could visit them and see the new country. Apparently there were family discussions as to the possibility of joining the steady stream of migrants to the New World. Furthermore, Alexander told his father that it was his intention to go to the United States as soon as he came of age. If they should consider seriously removing to America, the father's trip would make it possible to seek a suitable location for the family.

There were many reasons why Thomas Campbell might wish to consider moving to America. At this time there was a large and constant migration of Scotch-Irish families to the United States. The political troubles, the religious dissensions, the oppressive tyranny of landed proprietors over tenants, and the almost hopeless prospects of those with large families for success in life, led great numbers to seek a happier home in America. Several families of Campbell's acquaintance in the vicinity of Rich Hill had made their arrangements to set out for the United States. Others had left already. It was with high hope, therefore, that Thomas decided to visit the New World from which he would either return to Ireland or write the family to join him.

Among those who urged the American visit was the Acheson family. Members of the family had already gone to America and others were planning to leave. A young lady of Campbell's Ahorey congregation, Hannah Acheson, wished to go to her relatives who had migrated previously and had settled at Washington, Pennsylvania, on the Western frontier. Campbell agreed to escort her to her destination. He could thus perform a useful service and at the same time become acquainted with the country.

It was so arranged. Thomas Campbell left for Londonderry on April 1, 1807, after bidding his congregation, family, and friends farewell. He was accompanied by Hannah Acheson. The family and school were left in charge of Alexander, now a promising youth of eighteen. At Londonderry arrangements were completed for passage to Philadelphia on the sailing vessel *Brutus,* Captain Craig, master. On April 8, 1807, the wind being favorable, the ship *Brutus* set sail toward the West.[11] Thomas Campbell carried with him only a statement of his ministerial standing, his Bible, and possibly a few books and personal possessions. As he sailed from Londonderry, Thomas gazed for the last time on his native land. Ireland was behind him. Before him were a voyage of many days, and, then, the relatively new nation, the United States of America, and a frontier experience of considerable significance.

---

11. Richardson, I, p. 81 ff.

5

THE CAMPBELLS LAUNCH
A MOVEMENT

During Thomas Campbell's years in northern Ireland, a nation had come into being on the opposite side of the Atlantic. Something new in political and social life was developing in the vast expanse of land which lay west of the Allegheny mountains. There the common man saw unlimited opportunity, especially as Indian resistance crumbled. Only about five percent of the white population, approximately 200,000 persons, was living west of the mountains. Those persons moving into Kentucky and Tennessee through Cumberland Gap came mainly from areas of Virginia and North Carolina which had suffered economic depression following the Revolution. Farther north, the Ohio River, formed at Pittsburgh by the joining of the Monongahela and Allegheny Rivers, led from the Pennsylvania gateway to the West. The road across the Alleghenies extending westward from Philadelphia and Cumberland to Washington, Pennsylvania, swarmed with wagonloads of settlers and their livestock.

THE FRONTIER OF WESTERN PENNSYLVANIA

Cheap land was the main motivation for the westward movement. Incessant physical labor, however, was the price demanded of every member of a family in order to pay for a newly purchased farm or to extend the limits of an older one. The newness of the country and the feeling that men could there make a fresh start gave the church an opportunity to become a part of the new communities emerging on the frontier.

It was natural that Presbyterians of all persuasions would settle in Pennsylvania because of that state's policy of welcoming all denominations. The Treaty of Paris, which concluded the war between France and England in 1763, the same year in which Thomas Campbell was born, opened the western part of Pennsylvania to settlement by the British. Scotch-Irish immigrants poured across the Alleghenies into this new section. They were largely Presbyterians who quickly established churches as they arrived. The Redstone Presbytery, in western Pennsylvania, was established by the Synod of New York and Philadelphia in 1781. The first Presbyterian house of worship was erected in 1790, the meetings having been held in groves and private houses before that time.

The Presbyterians were a particularly rigid body in both doctrine and polity. They characteristically opposed every innovation designed to meet the peculiar needs or problems of the new country. Unlike the Methodist circuit rider and the Baptist farmer-preacher, who served all frontier communities equally, the Presbyterian preacher ministered primarily to people of his own background. Usually he sought out other Presbyterians and their settlements. This was the pattern followed by Thomas Campbell on his arrival in America. There were, in fact, so many Scotch-Irish Presbyterians in western Pennsylvania that it was called "an American Ulster." Most of those who came had been members of the established church in Scotland or in northern Ireland. However, some of those who came were from the Seceder churches. In addition to the General Assembly of the Presbyterian Church there was the Associate Synod of North America. This was in reality the organization of the Anti-

Burgher Seceder Presbyterians as the Burghers never had a distinct organization in America.

THOMAS CAMPBELL'S ARRIVAL AND SETTLEMENT

The annual meeting of the Associate Synod was in session in May 1807 when Thomas Campbell and Hannah Acheson arrived in Philadelphia. Shortly after his arrival Campbell sought the fellowship of his religious brethren and presented his credentials and letters of introduction brought from Ireland. Cordially received by the Anti-Burghers, Campbell accepted appointment for a year and requested assignment to Chartiers Presbytery since it included Washington, Pennsylvania, where many of his friends and acquaintances, including the Achesons, were located.[1]

On his arrival at Washington, Thomas Campbell was welcomed by a number of old friends and acquaintances who had known him in Ireland. Recognizing his worth and greatly respecting his ministerial standing, they were anxious to have him lead them and were quick to tell others their high estimate of him. Campbell became increasingly popular, especially as his ability and relatively tolerant spirit became known. The Seceder congregations, not very numerous in the area, were pleased to have such a man as their pastor.

TROUBLE IN THE CHARTIERS PRESBYTERY

Campbell was soon disturbed by and disappointed in the religious conditions he found in southwestern Pennsylvania. He had been troubled over the divisions of the church in northern Ireland, but if he had hoped that the spirit of liberty in America would cultivate a closer fellowship among the churches, he was quickly disillusioned. The church in the western wilderness had become more exclusive and intolerant than were the churches in either Ireland or Scotland.

The members of the Seceder church were widely scattered in this newly settled country, and in their midst were members of other denominations currently without affiliation. There were members of other branches of the Presbyterian church without pastoral oversight. Usually they did not seek membership in the Anti-Burgher congregations,

---

1. McAllister, *Thomas Campbell—Man of the Book.* Material on Thomas Campbell is from this book.

but unless they did and were formally admitted to membership, they were treated as outsiders. Campbell, however, welcomed them and extended to them the ministries of the church, even though they did not take formal membership. Soon suspicions began to arise in the minds of some of his fellow ministers; they wondered whether Campbell was as sound in doctrine and polity as he should be. Perhaps these ministers were jealous or envious of his leadership and his ability as a scholar and preacher. Whatever the reason, evidence that all was not harmonious in Chartiers Presbytery soon appeared.

Not long after his arrival, Campbell was asked to visit a few scattered Anti-Burgher Presbyterians at a community named Cannamaugh, and to hold a "sacramental" celebration among them. He was accompanied by William Wilson, a student minister of the Seceder church. Thomas was concerned for the many persons in other branches of the Presbyterian family who had not received the Lord's Supper for a long time, and who were in attendance at this service. Campbell proposed that all persons present were free to partake of the elements when they were offered, regardless of presbyterial connection. Wilson, Campbell's fellow minister, said nothing at the time but was shocked that Campbell would do this. The story of this heresy circulated rapidly. Not long afterward Rev. John Anderson refused to keep an appointment assigned by the presbytery for Anderson and Campbell jointly. He gave as his excuse Campbell's supposed deviation from orthodoxy. At the next meeting of the presbytery trouble began for Thomas Campbell.

Campbell was present for the session of the presbytery held in October 1807. It was charged that he had "publicly taught . . . that we have nothing but human authority or agreement for confessions of faith, testimonies, covenanting and fast days." When the vote was taken Campbell was convicted of deviation from Anti-Burgher doctrine. In this manner, within five months after his arrival in this country, Thomas Campbell was involved in controversy with his fellow Seceder ministers over questions of doctrine.

The opposition which he encountered in the presbytery seems to have removed any doubt left in his mind as to whether he would stay in America. In a letter dated January

1, 1808, written at Washington, Pennsylvania, Campbell urged his family to make preparations for immediate departure for the New World. On the evening of January 6 at a meeting of Chartiers Presbytery, Campbell heard the report of a committee appointed at the October meeting to investigate his public declarations. The committee presented its report in the form of seven charges. Campbell asked for opportunity to write his answers to the charges and present them later. At a meeting of the presbytery, February 1808, the charges and Campbell's written answers were read.[2]

In general, Campbell's replies to the charges revealed orthodoxy in most matters of doctrine and theology. On the whole, however, his answers were not satisfactory to the presbytery, as it censured him for not adhering to "secession testimony." The main differences between Campbell and the presbytery were really matters of church order and government. Campbell was actually in revolt against the authority of the presbytery and impatient with its limitations of fellowship. At the March meeting of the presbytery, Campbell asked the presbytery to reconsider its action but was refused. At a session held after adjournment, and after Campbell had left, action was taken suspending him from preaching "indefinitely, *sine die*." The April 1808, meeting of the presbytery was given over to preparation for the annual meeting of the Associate Synod of North America. It was to the synod Thomas Campbell now decided to take his case.

APPEAL TO THE ASSOCIATE SYNOD

Campbell was present when the Associate Synod was called to order on Wednesday, May 18, 1808, at Philadelphia. Campbell's case was put on the agenda together with petitions in his favor from many of his friends. At the third day's meeting the synod entered into a discussion of the dispute between Campbell and the Chartiers Presbytery. The minutes of the presbytery which related to the case and Campbell's written replies were read. The synod next read a statement of Campbell's entitled "Reasons for Protest and Appeal," in which he set forth in clear and sincere words his

---

2. William H. Hanna, *Thomas Campbell, Seceder and Christian Union Advocate* (Cincinnati: The Standard Publishing Company, 1935). The Minutes of the Chartiers Presbytery have been lost but have survived in great part in this work.

determination to accept the Bible as the basis for all his beliefs and practices. From this time forward Campbell defended the thesis that the union of all Christians should rest on the authority of the Scriptures alone.

In the following sessions it was evident that the synod, while it could not justify the method of the presbytery, felt called upon to censure Campbell's actions, and so virtually sustained the spirit and purpose of the charges originally brought against him. It is just as obvious that Campbell must have been somewhat outraged. The synod seemed to be doing its best to reach a decision satisfactory to all parties. At the same time the synod was quite justly suspicious of Campbell's views. Its analysis of his position was, in the main, correct.[3]

WITHDRAWAL FROM PRESBYTERY AND SYNOD

Even after the stormy sessions of the synod, Campbell still desired friendly relations between himself and the other members of the Chartiers Presbytery. He wanted to work among the churches in peace, but his hopes were not to be realized. Returning to Washington from Philadelphia, Campbell found that the presbytery had made no assignments for him to preach. At the meeting of the presbytery in September 1808, he asked the reason why but did not get a satisfactory reply. This was the beginning of further controversy between Campbell and the members of the presbytery which lasted throughout the year. Action was taken to suspend him immediately from ministerial office. Moreover, all congregations belonging to the presbytery were to be informed of his suspension, along with all the other presbyteries belonging to the synod. Campbell ignored all such suspensions and communications; both he and the presbytery waited for the annual meeting of the synod.

At the meeting of the synod in Philadelphia in May 1809 a paper prepared by Thomas Campbell, entitled "Declaration and Address to the Associate Synod," was received. A committee appointed to deal with the matter suggested that Campbell be permitted to withdraw his paper since in it he declined subjection to the synod, reflected on the presbytery

---

3. *Minutes of the Synod of the Associate Churches,* quoted in Hanna, p. 68 ff.

of Chartiers, and offered proposals inconsistent with Seceder doctrine. The paper was read, however, and the report of the committee that he be suspended permanently was accepted. Later a letter enclosing a fifty-dollar note was received from Campbell. In returning money advanced to him on his arrival two years before, Thomas Campbell brought to an end his relations with the Associate Synod of North America.

FORMATION OF THE CHRISTIAN ASSOCIATION OF WASHINGTON

Campbell's withdrawal from the presbytery and synod, however, brought no interruption in his ministerial labors. He continued to meet groups of friends and acquaintances in religious services and administered the Lord's Supper regularly. Those who heard him preach were intrigued by the constantly recurring theme of his sermons, a plea for the union of the divided church on the basis of the Bible. After several months of such meetings it became apparent that a permanent organization should be developed.

A group of earnest Christians gathered to discuss plans for the future in the home of Abraham Altars in the early summer of 1809. Thomas Campbell led the meeting in prayer and proceeded to review their reasons for the gathering. He dwelt at length on the evils resulting from divisions within the church and insisted on a return to the simple teachings of the Scriptures. Everything in religion not found in the Bible was to be abandoned so that a basis for Christian union could be formed. Bringing his message to a close, he put into simple terms the principle he understood the group to be acting on. "That rule, my highly respected hearers," said he," is this, that where the Scriptures speak, we speak; and where the Scriptures are silent, we are silent."[4] This dictum was to have many interpretations.

From this meeting Campbell conceived the idea of forming a Christian Association, which would be not a church but an agency for helping propagate the ideas of Christian cooperation. At a second meeting held August 17, 1809, it was decided to organize "The Christian Association of Washington," after

---

4. Richardson, *Memoirs of Alexander Campbell.* See I, pp. 236 ff.

the county in which the association proposed to be active. A committee of twenty-one members was appointed whose first action was to agree on the need for a published statement of the purposes and objectives of the organization. Campbell agreed to write such a statement.

Another decision involved building a meetinghouse for worship and preaching. The neighbors, in frontier fashion, assembled and erected a log building on the Sinclair farm, about three miles from Mt. Pleasant, on the road from Mt. Pleasant to Washington at the point where it was crossed by the road from Middletown to Cannonsburg. After it was completed the building was also to be used as a community school. Campbell preached there regularly. During this time Thomas was busy writing the statement of principles and objectives requested by the Christian Association. When it was completed, he read what he called a *Declaration and Address* at a special meeting of the association held September 7, 1809, where it was unanimously approved.

THE DECLARATION AND ADDRESS

The *Declaration and Address* is an unpretentious document, the work of a man who wrote down in honest words the thoughts important to him. The sentences are unnecessarily long, the thought is often too involved, but its presupposition was that the Christian faith of various denominations was valid enough. The objection was that the different parties held as essential many features of the church which were nonessential and that these nonessentials caused divisions.

Issued sometime during the last two weeks of 1809, the full title of the document was *Declaration and Address of the Christian Association of Washington.*[5] Printed at the office of the Washington newspaper, it was a booklet of fifty-six closely spaced pages containing four sections: a "Declaration" (three pages) giving the reasons, purposes, and

---

5. *Declaration and Address of the Christian Association of Washington County, Washington, Pa.* (Washington, Pa.: Brown and Sample, 1809). The full text of the *Declaration and Address* may be found also in Peter Ainslie, *The Message of the Disciples for the Union of the Church* (New York: Fleming H. Revell Co., 1913); William Robinson, *Declaration and Address with an Introduction,* (Birmingham, England: Berean Press, 1951); and *Declaration and Address* with *The Last Will and Testament of the Springfield Presbytery* (St. Louis: Bethany Press, 1955).

organization of the Christian Association; an "Address" (eighteen pages) amplifying the argument for the unity of all Christians; an "Appendix" (thirty pages) answering actual or anticipated criticisms; and a "Postscript" (three pages) suggesting two steps to be taken immediately. Aside from the main divisions, the book is without subheadings or topical arrangement, and the paragraphs are long and complicated.

The brief but important *Declaration* sets forth at least four principles underlying the Christian Association. They are:

First, the right of private judgment.

Second, the sole authority of the Scriptures.

Third, the evil of sectarianism.

Fourth, the basis for Christian unity in exact conformity to the Bible.

Immediately following the introduction, nine resolutions, intended to be a constitution for the association, were presented. The resolutions made provision for the promotion of simple evangelical Christianity, the voluntary support of a ministry, and the encouragement of the formation of similar associations. The organization was pledged to support such ministers, and such only, as sought to conform to the New Testament pattern. A standing committee of twenty-one members, to be chosen annually, was to guide the work of the association. The entire society was to meet twice a year, each meeting to be opened by a sermon, followed by a reading of the constitution, an offering, and the transaction of necessary business.

The program presented in the *Declaration* is that of an organization hopeful of attracting ministers and people committed to its purposes. The association was to be disappointed in all of its aims. The assumption underlying and harmonizing the proposals of the *Declaration* as well as the *Address*, is that it is possible to define a simple evangelical Christianity, with a definite body of doctrines and a definite program of ordinances, worship, and government for the church, all derived from the Scriptures and without the "inventions of men."

The *Address* amplifies the argument for unity of all Christians on the basis of scriptural authority and develops in detail the proposals for attaining such a goal. It is, for the most part, a tract on Christian unity. The first ten pages and the last five pages are devoted to a discussion of Christian union and the three between are devoted to the presentation of thirteen propositions, all concerned with the subject of Christian unity. The propositions are presented to stimulate thinking about common ground on which to build a united church.

After his experience with the presbytery and synod, Campbell was most careful to insist that these propositions were not to be used as a term of communion. All the other propositions seek to expand and implement the first one, perhaps the most famous sentence about unity Campbell ever wrote:

Prop. 1. That the church of Christ upon earth is essentially, intentionally, and constitutionally one; consisting of all those in every place that profess their faith in Christ and give obedience to him in all things according to the scriptures, and that manifest the same by their tempers and conduct, and of none else, as none else can be truly and properly called christians.

Campbell's thirteen propositions identify specific principles and may be summarized as follows:

First, the essential unity of the Church of Christ.
Second, the supreme authority of the scriptures.
Third, the special authority of the New Testament.
Fourth, the fallacy of human creeds.
Fifth, the essential brotherhood of all who love Christ and try to follow him.
Sixth, that if human innovations can be removed from the church, the followers of Christ will unite upon the scriptural platform.[6]

Campbell exhorts, appeals, quotes Scripture, and beseeches those who read to join the cause.

The *Appendix* contains some interesting passages, but is, in the main, a reiteration and extension of the ideas expressed in the *Declaration* and in the *Address.* The *Postscript,* written three months after the main body of the document had been submitted to the printer, contained two proposals, one for the preparation of a "catechetical exhibition" (for-

---

6. Frederick D. Kershner, *The Christian Union Overture* (St. Louis: Bethany Press, 1923), p. 26.

tunately never written) and a second proposing a monthly magazine to begin in 1810 and to be named *The Christian Monitor*. This project also was dropped, but it indicated a recognition of the need for some means of promoting the program.

In order to understand more fully the *Declaration and Address* a brief review of Thomas Campbell's philosophical background is in order. The philosophy of John Locke is most apparent in the document. More than likely Campbell was introduced to a form of Locke's thought at Glasgow University. Without question, Campbell was familiar with Locke's *Essay Concerning Human Understanding* and his first *Letter Concerning Toleration,* and guided his son, Alexander, in the study of these writings. Portions of the *Declaration and Address* could be almost direct quotations from John Locke.

The *Essay Concerning Human Understanding* quite clearly provided the basic ideas of Thomas Campbell concerning reason and faith. Locke's ideas on the function of the church are reflected in the *Declaration and Address* in Campbell's concept of a voluntary association of those interested in Christian union and in his assumption that individuals have the right to organize a church to worship God as they think proper. Before Campbell, Locke emphasized the sole authority of the Scriptures, the needless divisions of the church, and the essential requirements for church membership.

The *Declaration and Address* merits particular attention not only on its own account but also because, next to *The Last Will and Testament of the Springfield Presbytery,* it is the second oldest document of the Christian Church (Disciples of Christ). Two other movements, the Churches of Christ and the undenominational fellowship of Christian Churches and Churches of Christ, also trace their origins to this document. Scarcely noticed by the religious leaders of Pennsylvania on its publication, the document has had great significance in the development and promotion of Christian unity and is considered an important document in the history of the ecumenical movement.[7]

---

7. Rouse and Neill, *A History of the Ecumenical Movement, 1517-1948,* p.237.

THE FAMILY ARRIVES IN AMERICA

During the first days of October 1809 in the midst of editing and proofreading the *Declaration and Address,* Thomas received word that his family had arrived safely in New York from Scotland, had proceeded by stagecoach to Philadelphia and had made arrangements with a wagoner to be conveyed to Washington. On October 19 on the road from Philadelphia, about three days out of Washington, Thomas and a friend met the wagon with his wife, Jane, and the family. Having been separated for over two years, they were now united on the American frontier. Jane and the children related to Thomas the various incidents of the two years since his departure from Ireland. First, illness delayed their departure until late summer. At Londonderry they had taken passage on an ill-fated ship which was wrecked off the coast of Scotland. For various reasons, but especially because it would permit Alexander to take courses at the university, the family decided to winter in Glasgow. They had stayed in Glasgow until August 1809 when they had taken ship for New York.[8]

Thomas, in turn, gave the family a detailed account of what had happened to him in America, and especially his difficulties with the presbytery and synod. Alexander was particularly interested when his father told him that all his ties with the Seceder church were broken. By a somewhat different route the twenty-one-year-old Alexander had been brought to practically the same conclusions as his father. While in Glasgow he had come under the influence of Greville Ewing, the colaborer with the Haldanes. In an unsettled state of mind when the semiannual communion of the Seceders came around, he felt he could not partake. At the last minute he threw his communion token on the table, and in this symbolic act broke with the Seceder church. In addition, Alexander had decided finally to dedicate his life to the Christian ministry. Thus, father and son, miles apart, with no knowledge of what the other was doing, had come to similar decisions.

Alexander read and studied the *Declaration and Address* with interest and gave hearty approval to its propositions and

---

8. McAllister, *Thomas Campbell—Man of the Book,* pp. 101-104; pp. 139-174.

purposes. Impressed by the example of the Haldanes in Scotland, Alexander further stated that he had resolved never to receive any compensation for his ministerial labors. At the father's insistence Alexander gave himself at once to six months' disciplined study of the Scriptures. While his son studied, Thomas Campbell went forth from their Washington, Pennsylvania, home to preach to groups of interested persons.

By the spring of 1810 it became evident to Thomas Campbell that their cause was not progressing as he had hoped. The proposals of the *Declaration and Address* were not widely accepted, and no apparent effort was being made to form other Christian Associations. In fact, the association itself was slowly taking on the characteristics of a church. To avoid this Thomas finally decided to apply to the Synod of Pittsburgh for membership of the association in the regular Presbyterian church. The synod, meeting October 2, 1810, was quick in its response saying: "the Synod are constrained by the most solemn considerations to disapprove the plan (of the association) . . . and farther . . . Mr. Campbell's request to be received into christian and ministerial communion cannot be granted."[9]

In the first months after his arrival in America, Alexander attended his father's meetings, and studied long hours under his father's direction but remained in the background. At last, however, Thomas asked his son to speak at a public meeting held at Jacob Donaldson's home in the spring of 1810. His first sermon, preached on July 15, 1810, was received enthusiastically by a large congregation. Alexander himself realized that he had found his true vocation. From that day forward his services were in continual demand; the first year he preached no less than 106 sermons.

After the synod's rejection Thomas Campbell, still opposed to religious controversy, was willing to let matters rest as they were. Alexander, however, soon convinced the members of the Christian Association that some answer would have to be made to the synod. He decided to make the next meeting of the association, scheduled for November, the occasion for a public reply. From Alexander's address it is clear that the son

9. *Records of the Synod of Pittsburgh* (Pittsburgh: Luke Loomis, 1852), p. 75.

and father were in agreement that: 1) they regarded the denominations around them as having the substance of Christianity, but not its original nature; therefore the chief object of the proposed reformation was to restore the primitive church, 2) they regarded each congregation as independent, 3) they considered "lay preaching" as authorized and denied any distinction between clergy and laity, 4) they looked on infant baptism as without scriptural authority, 5) they anticipated the probability of the association's becoming a church in order to obey the Scriptures, and 6) in depending on scriptural authority they foresaw that some things, considered important to others, must be excluded.

In the fall of 1810 Alexander returned some books to the household of John Brown, who lived on a farm on Buffalo Creek about sixteen miles west of Washington but only eight miles from Wellsburg, in Brooke County, Virginia (now West Virginia). On this occasion Alexander Campbell first met eighteen-year-old Margaret Brown. The friendship ripened into love throughout the winter months, and on March 12, 1811, Alexander and Margaret were married. It was an event of considerable significance for the future. Bethany, as Alexander later called the place, was to be home for the rest of his life and the location from which he gave direction to a growing movement.

THE ASSOCIATION BECOMES A CHURCH

The Christian Association, meeting on May 4, 1811, constituted itself a church with a congregational form of government. At this same meeting, Thomas was chosen elder and Alexander was licensed to preach; ordination to Christian ministry came January 1, 1812. Following Haldanean practice, it was decided to observe the Lord's Supper weekly. The Christian Association had been meeting in the log building at "crossroads," but the newly organized congregation decided to build another meetinghouse. The site selected was on the farm of William Gilcrist, in the valley of Brush Run, about two miles above the junction of that stream with Buffalo Creek. Known as Brush Run Church, the building was a simple frame structure, eighteen by thirty-six feet with rough seats provided for the congregation. The first service was held in it on June 16, 1811, with the interior still unfinished.

After the formation of Brush Run Church, it was noticed that two or three of the members did not partake of the Lord's Supper with the rest. On being questioned they replied that they did not consider themselves authorized to partake since they had never been baptized. This raised the question of baptism in a most practical way. After due consideration Thomas Campbell agreed to immerse those wishing it, stating that he believed immersion was the New Testament practice. The baptism took place on July 4, 1811, in Buffalo Creek with Thomas Campbell officiating.

On March 13, 1812, Alexander's first child, Jane, was born, and with her birth he began to restudy the whole question of baptism. Up to this point the unity of the church and the restoration of the authority of the Bible had been the principal concerns of Thomas and his son, and neither of them had given baptism much attention. Now Alexander began to wonder if baptism was not a matter of more importance than they had supposed. Painstakingly he sought out the meaning of the word "baptize" in Greek and became convinced it means "to immerse." He became certain that the sprinkling to which he had been subjected in infancy was unauthorized by Scripture, and that he was consequently an unbaptized person. Furthermore, he could not consistently preach immersion and remain unimmersed.

Alexander made his final decision in June, 1812, and prepared to act at once. He knew a Baptist preacher, Matthias Luce (1764?-1831) of nearby Amity, Pennsylvania, and decided to ask Luce to immerse him. On his way to visit Luce he stopped to see his father and family who were then living on a farm between Washington and Mt. Pleasant. It was decided the service would be held Wednesday, June 12. On the day before, Luce and another man called on Thomas Campbell on their way to the baptismal site, the spot used by Thomas for the first immersion. Thomas decided to be immersed also.

The next day in a very long address Thomas reviewed the entire history of his thought on baptism and his determination to settle the matter on the basis of Scripture. Alexander then spoke on his reasons for immersion. Between them father and son spoke for nearly seven hours. When the speeches were over, Alexander Campbell and his wife, Thomas Campbell and his wife, and their daughter, Dorothea, with two other persons were immersed in Buffalo Creek. They first made a simple confession that "Jesus is the Son of God" with no account of a "religious experience" or other formality.

There had been no formal declaration of, no discussion of, the purpose of baptism. By common consent they came to believe baptism by immersion was the teaching of the New Testament and, therefore, not a matter of opinion. The adoption of immersion as an essential item in the Campbells' plan of Christian union radically changed the direction which they were to take from this time forward. No longer was it simply a matter of persuading churches to unite on the beliefs which Christians already held. It would be felt necessary to persuade them also to accept immersion which at that time only the Baptists believed to be commanded. It now seemed more important to seek first the restoration of the New Testament church and *then* to work for Christian unity.

FELLOWSHIP WITH THE BAPTISTS

The adoption of immersion by the "reformers," as they were soon called, erected a barrier between them and the other churches, especially the Presbyterians. The Presbyterian clergy were alarmed at the rejection of infant baptism. The bitter prejudice against Brush Run Church showed itself in many ways: in private conversation, in the pulpit, and in some instances in the economic boycott of members. Meanwhile, throughout the winter of 1812-13, the members of Brush Run Church met regularly for worship and preaching.

One result of the adoption of immersion was to bring Brush Run Church into more friendly relations with the Baptists. Although at this time there were few Baptists in the vicinity of Washington, they were quite numerous in the area just east of Washington and had formed the Redstone Baptist Association for the purpose of fellowship. In their preaching and visiting across the countryside, Thomas and Alexander Campbell became acquainted with the various Baptist congregations and their ministers who often urged them to join their association.

The Campbells, however, had several objections to such a union. Brush Run Church did, of course, follow the practice of immersion, but that was about the only respect in which it could qualify as a Baptist church. It did not accept the strongly Calvinist Philadelphia Confession of Faith; it differed on the place of the New Testament in relation to the Bible; on the qualifications necessary for baptism; on the purpose of baptism; and on the frequency of communion. The many invitations to join with the Redstone Association were discussed at length. Alexander had formed a less than favorable opinion of the Baptist preachers he knew, but he was better pleased with the Baptists as a group than with any other denomination. Some of the Baptist congregations began to send for Thomas and Alexander to preach for them. In the fall of 1812 Alexander attended a meeting of the association at Uniontown, Pennsylvania, but was not impressed. Meanwhile, the Baptists continued to ask the Campbells to visit their congregations and to preach.

Late in 1814 or early in 1815 the question of applying for membership in the Redstone Baptist Association was discussed seriously by the members of Brush Run Church. Their decision was to make application for membership and, at the same time, to write out a full statement of their beliefs. On eight or nine large pages they restated their protest against creeds and expressed a willingness to join the association only "provided always that we should be allowed to teach and preach whatever we learned from the Holy Scriptures, regardless of any creed or formula in Christendom." After much debate the association finally decided to admit Brush Run Church despite a small minority who objected and later caused trouble.[10] It was an exceptional case for which there was no precedent among the Baptists.

With their admission into fellowship with the Redstone Baptist Association in September 1815, the reformers were again part of a larger fellowship. Their hope was renewed that they might carry on their work, not as a sect, but within one of the major denominations. The relationship thus established was to continue for a number of years, though with

---

10. In *Minutes of the Redstone Baptist Association* (Pittsburgh: S. Engles, 1815), p. 5.

mounting tension. From the beginning it was evident that the Campbells and their followers did not regard themselves as merged indistinguishably into the Baptist denomination. Their sense of distinctive mission did not diminish.

ALEXANDER EMERGES AS LEADER

The adoption of immersion brought Alexander Campbell into a position of leadership in Brush Run Church and in the religious community as a whole. His leadership in forming the relationship with the Baptists strengthened this position. From this time forward, Alexander became definitely the leader, and his father the follower, in the advocacy of the principles for which they stood. Father and son, however, worked together for nearly forty years in the development of their program. Over an increasingly wide area the community became aware of Alexander's dynamic personality, his aggressiveness and burning certainty that what he believed was right.

In 1814 some members of Brush Run Church decided to join the westward migration and move as a body to a site near Zanesville, Ohio, where they could establish a religious colony. Plans for the move were formulated under the direction of Alexander Campbell, who was enthusiastic about the subject. John Brown, however, objected to having his daughter and son-in-law go away so far from him. In order to induce them to remain at Bethany he drew up papers turning over his farm to Alexander. Young Campbell agreed to this and, without his leadership, the others decided not to make the move. By this action Alexander's financial independence was established.

When the Redstone Baptist Association met at Cross Creek Baptist Church in 1816, Thomas Campbell presented the application for the admission of a small congregation organized at Pittsburgh. The group practiced immersion and each week observed the Lord's Supper followed by a sermon and instruction. The application was denied because its letter was "not presented according to the constitution of the Association" which required an acceptance of the Philadelphia Confession or its equivalent. This was but an indication of the troubled years ahead.

At this same meeting of the association Thomas also read a paper, called a "circular letter," which he had been asked to prepare on the subject of the Trinity. The Baptists were anxious to hear what the Campbells thought. In developing his topic Thomas reviewed what he felt could be learned from Scripture and concluded that the Father, the Son, and Holy Spirit coexist under relations which suppose their essential unity and that each of the divine characters has a power peculiar to himself. The elder Campbell did not use the word "Trinity" once in the document. Nevertheless, the association accepted his paper without amendment.

Alexander was asked to preach for the same meeting and chose as his topic a "Sermon on the Law." He had been studying the subject for some time, as there is evidence he preached a sermon with the same content as early as 1813.[11] He based his argument on Romans 8:3, with its emphasis on the distinction between the Old and the New Testament law and ordinances. Baptists had tended to accept all Scripture without this distinction. During the time the Campbells had been in the Redstone Association there had been some opposition to them but, in general, there had been cooperation. After the delivery of this sermon the opposition became and remained more pronounced.

These were days of discouragement for the Campbells over the direction the movement was taking. In the seven years since the publication of the *Declaration and Address* they had won few advocates to their cause. There were still only scattered individuals among the Baptist churches of eastern Ohio, western Pennsylvania, and Virginia, who believed as the Campbells did. Thomas and Alexander Campbell alone were preaching in behalf of the movement among the various churches.

BUFFALO SEMINARY

At the beginning of 1818 Alexander decided to open a school in his home at Bethany, for the purpose of educating

---

11. Alexander Campbell, *Early Manuscripts Discovered in Australia*, 1964. Microfilm, DCHS, Nashville, Tennessee. SEE also "Sermon on the Law" in Charles A. Young, ed., *Historical Documents Advocating Christian Union* (Chicago: The Christian Century Company, 1904), pp. 217-282.

young men for the ministry. This academy, known as "Buffalo Seminary," soon attracted not only a large number of young men who wished to study with Campbell but also young people of both sexes who wanted simply to receive a good basic education and who attended as day students. His father assisted in running the school. The seminary, failing to attract a significant number of students for the ministry, was closed in 1823. After five years as schoolmaster Alexander had decided on other approaches to the dissemination of his views.

ALEXANDER CAMPBELL AS DEBATER

In the hope that unpleasant argument might be avoided, Thomas Campbell had stated in the *Declaration and Address* that verbal controversy formed no part of his plan and would not be allowed. Principally because of his father's objections, Alexander at first refused to engage in an oral debate with John Walker, a Seceder Presbyterian minister of Mt. Pleasant, Ohio. However, debating was such an established practice throughout religious and civil society that it was hard for Campbell to resist. The occasion for the debate was a challenge from Walker to a Baptist minister, John Birch, or any other Baptist preacher of good standing whom Birch might choose to debate with him the question of baptism. Birch readily accepted the challenge and immediately urged Alexander Campbell to meet Walker. Twice Alexander refused the invitation, but at the insistence of his friends and many of the Baptist preachers he finally accepted only after having succeeded in convincing his father that there could be no valid objection to a public defense of revealed truth.

The debate was held June 19-20, 1820, at Mt. Pleasant, Ohio, about twenty-three miles from Bethany. The issue under discussion was the proper subject and means of baptism. Walker argued that baptism was the symbol of membership in the Christian church just as the practice of circumcision was a badge of membership in the Jewish faith. Young Campbell's reply was that circumcision required only racial descent from Abraham, whereas baptism demanded faith in Christ. Walker was inclined to repeat himself, so Alexander used his time during the debate to speak of the principles of

EARLY SCENES IN CHRISTIAN CHURCH HISTORY

The Campbell home in the 1860s. A photographic reproduction of a
water color made by Sarah Barclay Johnson probably in 1863.

Alexander Campbell's Study   Early sketch of Bethany College campus

the reformers; namely, the supreme authority of Scripture and the necessity of scriptural authority for every practice of the church. As to the correct form of baptism, Campbell tried to show that immersion was the teaching of the New Testament. Upon their return to Bethany, Thomas and Alexander Campbell edited and published the debate as taken from Alexander's notes.[12]

From this time forward it was felt by the two that orderly discussion on clearly stated propositions was one of the ways by which biblical truth might be advanced. Alexander recognized that here was a means of securing a wider audience for his views. Over the next twenty-three years he was to engage in four additional debates in Ohio and Kentucky which, along with his preaching and publishing, were to help make his name a household word in hundreds of pioneer homes.

At the close of the Walker debate, Alexander had issued a challenge to any reputable Presbyterian minister to continue the debate on baptism. In May 1823 he received a letter from Rev. William L. Maccalla (1788-1859) accepting the challenge. They decided to have the debate at Washington, near Maysville, Kentucky, beginning on October 15. Alexander presented what he and his father believed were the true and obvious teachings of the Bible, quoting the various passages of the New Testament which deal with the purpose of baptism as the "evidence" on which a Christian should base his beliefs. His was unquestionably a rational approach to religion.[13] Following this debate Campbell made his first visit to central Kentucky and became acquainted with the Christian movement led by Barton W. Stone and others.

In the spring of 1829 arrangements were completed for Alexander's widely known debate with Robert Owen (1771-1858), famous nineteenth-century social reformer and philanthropist of New Lanark, Scotland, and New Harmony, Indiana. The debate was held at Cincinnati, Ohio, April 13-21, on the question of Owen's "Social System" as against Alexander's defense of the Christian religion.[14] The prestige

---

12. *Campbell-Walker Debate* (Steubenville, Ohio: James Wilson, 1820).
13. *Campbell-Maccalla* Debate (Buffaloe, Va., Campbell and Sala, 1824).
14. *Campbell-Owen* Debate (Bethany, Va.: A. Campbell, 1829).

and renown of Alexander Campbell were increased by his
defense of Christianity against Owen's "Social System."
Campbell's defense of Protestantism in his debate with the
Roman Catholic archbishop of Cincinnati, John B. Purcell
(1800-1883), added luster to his name. Protestants were
alarmed at the growth of Catholic influence and power. The
subject was timely. Held in 1837 and lasting eight days, the
debate attracted wide attention. Campbell mainly affirmed a
series of negative propositions: that the Roman Catholic
Church is not catholic, apostolic, or holy, but a sect; that
apostolic succession has no foundation in Scripture, history,
or reason; that the doctrines of purgatory, indulgences,
private confession, and transubstantiation are false and in-
jurious.[15]

The fifth and last of Campbell's debates was held at Lexington, Kentucky, in 1843. The Presbyterians had lost many
members to the Christian movement of Stone and Campbell.
Campbell in a visit to Kentucky in 1842 learned that a public
"discussion of certain points at issue between Presbyterians
and those Christians called Reformers" was desired by some
of the Presbyterians. For more than a year letters were exchanged between the two parties arranging terms and the
propositions to be discussed. The Rev. Nathan L. Rice (1807-
1877), minister at Paris, Kentucky, was selected by the
Synod of Kentucky to be the Presbyterian advocate and the
illustrious Henry Clay was obtained as moderator. The
debate, held in the Main Street Christian Church between
November 15 and December 1, 1843, resulted in a published
volume of 912 pages. Such questions as immersion versus
sprinkling, infant versus believer's baptism, baptism for the
remission of sins, and the divisiveness of creeds were debated
at length. Dramatic oratory enlivened the sessions and the
public loved it.[16]

On the whole the five debates were to result in bitter
relations between the debaters and often between their
followers. It may well be argued that, while the debates did
much to promote a knowledge of Alexander Campbell as a
brilliant forensic master, they did little to further the aims of a
united church. However, there was wide dissemination of

15. *Campbell-Purcell* Debate (Cincinnati, O.: J. A. James & Co., 1837).
16. *Campbell-Rice* Debate (Lexington, Ky.: A. T. Skillman and Son, 1844).

Old church at Bethany where Alexander Campbell preached

Campbell's views on immersion and his defense of a return to New Testament practice.[17]

ALEXANDER CAMPBELL AS PUBLISHER

Alexander, in publishing the debate with Walker in 1820, soon realized the power of the press and the eagerness of the frontier people for religious literature. The first edition of 1,000 copies was quickly followed by a second of 3,000. Immediately after the debate he received correspondence from a large number of interested individuals. Campbell began to think seriously of issuing a monthly magazine especially devoted to the proposed reformation of the churches. The Campbells had discovered a way to carry their views to a larger constituency than they could reach personally.

In the spring of 1823 Alexander circulated the prospectus of a magazine to be called *The Christian Baptist,* a title adopted with some misgivings since the term "Baptist" was thought to be sectarian. The first issue was published August 3, 1823, and appeared monthly thereafter. The tone of the magazine was extremely critical of the clergy of the period. The articles and essays were frequently sarcastic and iconoclastic. The elder Campbell was aroused thoroughly by his son's boldness and sought to induce Alexander to adopt a

17. Garrison and DeGroot, *The Disciples of Christ: A History,* See pp 168-171; 171-174; 197-199; 228; and 231-234 for a detailed discussion of these debates.

milder policy. In time the younger Campbell apparently agreed with his father, for beginning in 1830 Alexander began circulation of another, more irenic, journal, *The Millennial Harbinger,* which continued publication for forty years. In the same year *The Christian Baptist* was discontinued.

Due mainly to *The Christian Baptist* and Alexander's preaching tours among the Baptist churches, the tensions between the Campbells and certain leaders and ministers of the Baptist associations continued to grow. Alexander created further tension in the spring of 1826 when he published a modern language version of the New Testament translated by British scholars a half century before.[18] He sought to present the New Testament in simple and understandable language which the reader could interpret for himself. Together with a preface, Campbell made "various emendations" in the text, added 100 pages of critical notes and appendixes, and published the whole from his printing office at Bethany. The major change was to write "immerse" wherever the older versions had "baptize"; thus John the Baptist became "John the Immerser." Modern diction was substituted for archaic forms. These changes gave great offense to all nonimmersionists, and, strangely enough, to most of the Baptists also. Nevertheless, the new version had wide circulation.

In 1835 Alexander Campbell edited a hymnal supposedly in cooperation with Barton W. Stone and other leaders of the Stone-Campbell movement. Stone was consulted only indirectly about the content and not at all as to title. It appeared as *The Disciples' Hymn Book* but on Stone's protest it was changed to *The Christian Hymn Book.* Campbell made substantial profits from the book but shared them with the churches in states where sales were made. The hymnal was published well into the last quarter of the nineteenth century. Other books were published from Campbell's press from time to time, among them *The Christian System* also in 1835.

---

18. *The Sacred Writings of the Apostles and the Evangelists of Jesus Christ, Comonly Styled the New Testament* (Bethany, Brooke Co., Va.: A. Campbell, 1826). SEE also, Cecil K. Thomas, *Alexander Campbell and His New Version* (St. Louis: The Bethany Press, 1958).

CAMPBELL AND THE VIRGINIA
CONSTITUTIONAL CONVENTION

Upon notice that a convention would be held in 1829 to rewrite the state constitution of Virginia (in which Brooke County was then located), Campbell announced his candidacy for election as a delegate. Criticized for turning from spiritual matters to follow the path of worldly ambition in politics, his defense was that he wanted to seek an end to slavery in Virginia. He was elected, served in the convention, and took a prominent part in the proceedings. Campbell led the fight to democratize the government, but against him was a great array of political talent. James Madison and James Monroe, both former Presidents of the United States, were there; John Marshall, chief justice of the United States, was there; and John Randolph of Roanoke was president of the convention. They were on the side of the wealthy landowners. Campbell crossed swords with them and lost. Slavery was to continue in Virginia for a while longer.

While in Richmond for the constitutional convention Campbell did not neglect his preaching. He preached every Sunday in one of the churches of the city with many of his fellow delegates in attendance. Former President Madison said later that he regarded Campbell "as the ablest and most original expounder of the Scriptures" he had ever heard.[19] The seeds of future Disciples congregations in Virginia were sown as Campbell gained wider recognition.

WALTER SCOTT AND THE MAHONING ASSOCIATION

On a visit to Pittsburgh in the winter of 1821-22 Alexander Campbell met for the first time a young Presbyterian recently arrived from Scotland. Walter Scott had arrived in Pittsburgh May 7, 1819, from New York. He soon met both Thomas and Alexander Campbell and discovered that he agreed with them on the main features of their program for Christian union. Prepared by education, natural ability, and religious devotion to become a fellow worker with them, Scott was able to work out in a systematized statement and to apply an effective evangelistic method for the reformers.

---

19. Richardson, *Memoirs of A. Campbell*, II, p. 313.

Such a means had been lacking in the Campbells' program.

Scott was born in Moffatt, Scotland, October 31, 1796. The family was large, but in spite of financial limitations Walter was helped to secure a good education. He later attended the University of Edinburgh. At the suggestion of an uncle, already in New York, he came to America in 1818. He spent nearly a year teaching Latin in an academy on Long Island before he joined the westward trek. Arriving in Pittsburgh, he found employment as an instructor in the school of George Forrester (d.1820). Forrester was also the leader of a small congregation of "primitive Christians" similar to those of the Haldanes in Scotland and to the many such groups which had sprung up on the frontier. The congregation practiced immersion and also followed the custom of footwashing and the "holy kiss." Forrester's piety and interest in the Bible as the basis of religious truth greatly impressed Scott. He became a member of the congregation.[20]

Before long Forrester withdrew from the school. Within a few months he accidentally drowned, leaving Scott the responsibility for the school and the church. In Forrester's library Scott found and began to study several of the writings of Glas, Sandeman, the Haldanes, and John Locke. Scott also came upon a pamphlet written by Henry Errett, father of Isaac Errett (1820-1888). Published by a New York City congregation of "Scotch Baptists," the tract was on the purpose and the meaning of baptism. Stirred by the ideas expressed in the tract, Scott closed the school and went to New York to seek out its author. Apparently disappointed in what he found there, Scott returned to Pittsburgh and resumed the care of the church while carrying on the teaching by which he earned his living.

Continuing his religious studies, Scott reached the conviction that the central and only necessary fact for Christian faith was a simple statement that "Jesus is the Christ." At this point Scott met Alexander Campbell for the first time and discovered they had been wrestling with similar questions. The two young men found themselves of a similar mind from the start. As Alexander Campbell began to make

20. Dwight E. Stevenson, *Walter Scott: Voice of the Golden Oracle* (St. Louis: Christian Board of Publication, 1946). This is the best biography of Walter Scott. An older but more comprehensive biography is that of William Baxter. William Baxter, *Life of Elder Walter Scott* (Cincinnati: Bosworth, Chase and Hall, 1874).

plans to publish *The Christian Baptist,* he and Scott discussed the project extensively. At Scott's suggestion the name "Baptist" was added to Campbell's proposal to call it "The Christian." Readers would thereby be gained among the Baptists. Scott contributed a series of four articles to the first volume.

The Campbells first had developed a plan of restoration of essential Christianity as a means to unite the church. Next they had become engaged in the distinction between the Old and the New Testament. In turn, this had led them to a more comprehensive study of baptism. None of this, however, gave an answer to the question: "How do people become Christians?" Scott sought to answer this and other questions in his series of articles on "A Divinely Authorized Plan of Preaching the Christian Religion." Individuals would be led to accept Christian faith step by step. From this time forward more emphasis would be put on the purpose of "restoring original Christianity," in the sense of committing individuals to Jesus Christ as Lord and Savior.

Alexander's opponents in the Redstone Baptist Association had become increasingly active and were furious over the publication of *The Christian Baptist.* He learned that the opposition determined to make a strong effort at the September 1823 meeting of the association to have him removed from the fellowship. He conceived of a plan whereby he could defeat them by leaving the association and uniting with the Mahoning Association of eastern Ohio. The Mahoning Baptist Association had been formed in August 1820, just two months before the Campbell-Walker debate, under the leadership of Adamson Bentley (1785-1864) of Warren, Ohio, and Sydney Rigdon (1793-1876), Bentley's brother-in-law. Bentley and Rigdon had visited Alexander at Bethany and had confidence in the Campbells and the correctness of their views.

The decision was made that Alexander should take membership with the congregation of Disciples which had been organized in Wellsburg on the river across from Ohio. This congregation took membership in the Mahoning Association. When the Redstone Association met, Alexander Campbell was no longer a member of it. In this way he out-maneuvered his opponents and remained free to preach among the Baptist churches. Since a number of members of Brush Run Church lived in the Wellsburg area, early in 1824 most of them took membership in Wellsburg. This brought to a close the Brush Run congregation and thus ended the Campbell's relationship with the Redstone Baptist Association.

Walter Scott moved to Steubenville, Ohio, early in 1826 and in August, in fellowship with Thomas and Alexander Campbell, attended the annual meeting of the Mahoning Association at Canfield, Ohio. He was well received and was asked to preach. The association next met at New Lisbon, Ohio, in August 1827 and, as the result of a request from one of its congregations, had decided to appoint an itinerant evangelist. Walter Scott was present at the meeting. He was offered the appointment; he accepted and began his work almost immediately. Earlier the evangelistic awakening under the leadership of Barton W. Stone and others had arisen among many of the churches of the area. From the first there were friendly relations between the Stone and Campbell followers. Preachers of both groups were active in the Mahoning Association.

The movement of the reformers on the Western Reserve, as northeastern Ohio was called, immediately began to receive new growth from Scott's energetic and novel preaching. His five-finger exercise of faith, repentance, baptism, remission of sins, and gift of the Holy Spirit was understood readily by unschooled pioneers. Scott was not a Baptist, except in his practice of immersion, but was a zealous student of the Bible and an inventor of revolutionary methods.

He persuaded schoolchildren to advertise his meetings. He called for immediate acceptance of Christ. He urged individuals in the phrases of the New Testament to be baptized for the remission of sins. Soon hundreds were being added to the congregations of the Reserve. It was only natural that some members of the Baptist churches were disturbed by the addition of so many new members who did not fully appreciate Baptist traditions. This tended further to increase the tensions developing between the reformers and the Baptists.

By March 1828 Alexander Campbell had become worried over reports of the growing success of Walter Scott on the Western Reserve. He wondered whether Scott had allowed his well-known impulsiveness to run away with him, or whether his evangelistic fervor had broken loose from the anchors of knowledge and Scripture. The Reserve was at this time the chief stronghold of Campbellian influence, and Alexander had no wish to lose it. Thomas Campbell, urged by Alexander, decided to visit the Reserve and examine for himself the results of Scott's endeavors. He saddled his favorite horse and visited such places as New Lisbon, Warren, Mantua, and Mentor where Scott had been preaching. The elder Campbell heard for himself some of Scott's sermons and witnessed his methods with both surprise and pleasure. He saw clearly that Scott had added to the movement for reform a new element which had been lacking in his own work and in that of his brilliant son.

The simple truth is that the Campbell movement to restore the unity of the church on the foundation of the New Testament did not take hold firmly until Walter Scott began preaching on the Western Reserve and Barton W. Stone's "Christian" movement spread to Ohio. Without the impetus given by those movements the Campbells' dream of Christian union on a biblical basis probably would have been passed over quickly on the rapidly changing frontier.

Considering the members added, the new congregations formed, and the large number of ministers attracted from the other denominations, the meeting of the Mahoning Association in Warren, August 1828 took on more than ordinary interest. Alexander Campbell delivered the opening sermon on the Christian religion and divided his subject into three sections: matters of knowledge, faith, and opinion. Over 1,000 additions for the year were reported. Walter Scott was thought to have recovered the "divinely appointed" and "effectual means" necessary to restore the purity of the church and ultimately the union of all Christians, if only they would listen and obey the simple commands of the Scriptures. In his report to the association for 1828, Scott recognized the help he had received from his fellow ministers: Bentley, Rigdon, and others. Such was the progress of evangelism in Ohio under Scott's leadership that, when the Mahoning Association met at Sharon, Pennsylvania, in the latter part of August 1829, the messengers learned that

another thousand converts had been added to the congregations.

The force and freshness of Scott's evangelistic appeal, the
exciting sense of rediscovery of a long-lost truth, the sense of
witnessing the beginning of a new period in Christian history,
all gave Scott's revival an extraordinary character. It was
different from other revivals. It was unlike the Great Western
Revival, which had stirred Kentucky and Tennessee thirty
years before and out of which had emerged the Stone movement. With Scott there was no frenzy of emotion, but a blend-
ing of rationality and authority, an appeal to common sense
and to Scripture suited to the temper of the frontier. Other
preachers in the association caught the new note and began to
sound it. Hundreds were converted. New congregations were
organized. The Campbell followers (and later the Stone and
Campbell movement combined) had no difficulty in accepting Scott's evangelistic method. It became the standard
emphasis for many years afterward.

Walter Scott later moved to Cincinati, Ohio, and still later
to nearby Carthage. Aside from the magazines edited by
Stone and Campbell, already mentioned, the most important
was Walter Scott's *The Evangelist,* which began publication
in 1832 and continued to 1844. The constant theme in all
these papers was the correct presentation of the gospel, the
restoration of the New Testament church, and Christian
union. News from the congregations and traveling evangelists
was of course included. Sometimes there was a discussion of
doctrine and of current questions such as abolition of slavery
and relations with slaveholders.

Scott's later career consisted of serving congregations in
the Cincinnati and Pittsburgh areas and editing several
papers after *The Evangelist.* The Disciples founded their first
institution of higher education, Bacon College, in 1836.
Walter Scott was made president, serving for a little over a
year. After an inaugural address on a carefully developed
philosophy of education, Scott, with the help of John T.
Johnson, spent the remainder of his tenure as president raising money and promoting the college.[20] He served on the committee on order of business at the first national convention of
Disciples held at Cincinnati in 1849. Scott, a widower, that

same year married a second time and moved to Mays Lick, near Maysville, Kentucky, where he served a congregation. Beginning in 1852 he operated the Covington Female Institute, Covington, Kentucky, but in 1855 he returned to Mays Lick. Shortly thereafter he married a third wife, a wealthy widow, with whom he made his home until his death in 1861.

By 1830 the Campbells and Walter Scott found themselves increasingly in dispute with the Baptists but they did not for a moment despair. They were convinced of the correctness of their views beyond any doubt and felt their cause would triumph. The inevitable dissolution of the Mahoning Baptist Association is discussed in Chapter 6. The situation on the American frontier was quite different from that which it had been when the Campbells found themselves separated from the Presbyterians in 1809, twenty years earlier. Different forces were at work in America. A new democracy had arisen, revealing its power in the election of Andrew Jackson to the presidency of the United States. Opportunity and optimism were the dominant themes of the new era. The vision of a church united on a scriptural basis was about to become manifest in a uniquely American religious movement.

6

THE STRUGGLE FOR IDENTITY

It has been said that one can believe just about anything and remain a Disciple. If that tongue-in-cheek remark assesses the mind and witness of the denomination with any degree of accuracy, present-day Disciples either ignore their heritage or regard it as excess baggage. Indeed, the Disciples fathers at their best championed wide diversity of opinion in matters "of which the Kingdom does not consist" and steadfastly refused to sanction a complete system of doctrine lest it undermine the authority of the Scriptures. Even so, the Campbells and their followers were not insipid thinkers lacking in theological decisiveness. Holding tenaciously to the fundamental convictions expressed in the *Declaration and Address,* they interpreted the New Testament with a view to uncovering the "ancient order of things" so as to unite the church and evangelize the world.

Their extraordinary sense of mission as a band of reformers bound them to each other but jeopardized their standing with the Baptists. Beginning with the Brush Run Church's acceptance into the Redstone Association in 1815, the formal relationship between Baptists and Disciples (or Reformers) ended in the early 1830s with a complex and lengthy process of separation. As a result, Disciples were free to unite with a sizable group of Christians in the West. The convergence of the two loosely organized movements, similar to each other in many respects, added yet another dimension to the already vast complex of Protestantism in the United States.

BAPTISTS AND REFORMERS

"I and the church with which I am connected are in 'full communion' with the Mahoning Baptist Association, Ohio; and, through them, with the whole Baptist society in the United States." Thus wrote Alexander Campbell in 1826. Notwithstanding his avowed intention to speak his mind and to censure views and practices at odds with the New Testament, he disclaimed the thought of "adding to the catalogue of new sects." The Baptists, he contended, "have as much liberality in their views, as much of the ancient simplicity of the christian religion, as much of the spirit of christianity amongst them, as are to be found amongst any other people." Turning his attention to the future, he predicted that at the turn of the twentieth century the historian of Baptists in the United States would be able to say: "We are the only people who would tolerate, or who ever did tolerate, any person to continue as a Reformer or a Restorer amongst us."[1]

Whether Campbell was stating his unvarnished opinion or merely engaging in a verbal game, he had changed his mind five years later. Mincing no words, he wrote in the December 1831 issue of *The Millennial Harbinger:*

Proscription and exclusion have done their utmost: and the Baptists, once thought to be the most tolerant, clement, and opposed to persecution, have gone farther than any sect in the New World in excluding persons for differences in opinion. No sect in this union has published more proscriptive, illiberal, and unjust decrees, than we can furnish from Baptist journals, associations, conventions, &c. against us.[2]

The Baptists already had shown their thoroughgoing disenchantment with Campbell. In 1830 the Franklin Association observed in a circular letter that Kentucky Baptists had enjoyed peace and harmony before Campbell made his first visit to the state. Taking into full account the strife and

---

1. *Christian Baptist,* February 1826, pp. 146-147.
2. *Millennial Harbinger,* December 1831, p. 567.

tumult brought about by Campbell, the letter advised the congregations in the association: "If you would protect yourselves as churches, make no compromise with error—mark them who cause divisions, and divest yourselves of the last vestige of *Campbellism*."[3]

The relationship between Baptists and Reformers deteriorated radically, to be sure, but it had been tenuous from the outset. When the Redstone Baptist Association admitted the Brush Run Church into its membership, Elder Pritchard and several others resisted the move. Campbell's "Sermon on the Law," delivered at a meeting of the association in 1816, confirmed Pritchard's judgment that the messenger from Brush Run was out of step with Baptist tradition. Strong opposition to Campbell surfaced in the meeting and swept through the association. Subsequently, Campbell wrote, "I itinerated less than before in my labors in the gospel, and confined my attention to three or four little communities constituted on the Bible—one in Ohio, one in Virginia, and two in Pennsylvania."[4] At the same meeting in 1816 Thomas Campbell, representing a congregation of immersionists in Pittsburgh, applied for admission to the association. The messengers refused to grant the request. One Reformer congregation was more of a problem than the Redstone Association had anticipated; receiving another one into fellowship would only compound the difficulties. Clearly the Baptists were having second thoughts about the wisdom of accepting Brush Run a year earlier.

Several factors contributed to the growing sense of estrangement between Baptists and Reformers. (1) Alexander Campbell never seemed content to be *only* a Baptist; he was a reformer first and a Baptist second. His association with Baptists provided him with a base of operations from which he could bring about change in the church. (2) During his years in the Baptist fellowship, Campbell was an iconoclast who urged the church to return from Babylon to Jerusalem. He understood his mission, in part at least, as that of excoriating the religious establishment. No denomination escaped his scathing denunciation. (3) Campbell was an editor and

---

3. Quoted in John A. Williams, *Life of Elder John Smith* (Cincinnati: R. W. Carroll and Company, 1871), p. 348.
4. *Millennial Harbinger,* September 1848, p. 522.

publisher, beginning in 1823. His journal gave wide publicity to his viewpoint and month after month agitated for reform. A prominent Baptist wrote in 1830: "I think I am warranted in the belief that the religious sentiments of Alexander Campbell are exerting a . . . deadly influence on the peace and prosperity of the Baptist churches—and are calculated . . . to injure the cause of vital godliness, wheresoever the *little* work, *called* the Christian Baptist, is read and *believed.*"[5] (4) Campbell married the only child of John Brown, a well-to-do farmer. In establishing his son-in-law on his fine farm on Buffalo Creek, Brown made Campbell financially secure. As a result, Campbell did not depend upon the Baptists for his livelihood. He could afford to be an iconoclast.

Even though the editor from Bethany and his band of Reformers felt obliged to specify and attack the grievous errors of sectarian Christianity, they shared some common ground with the Baptists. Most obviously, both groups recognized only consenting believers as proper subjects of baptism and immersion as the New Testament form of the ordinance. Both groups reflected the vital tradition of left-wing Protestantism. Both groups accepted the New Testament as the basis for the faith and life of the church in every age. It was necessary, of course, to interpret the New Testament as well as to acknowledge its authority. Here was the rub. Baptists and Reformers, like believers throughout Christian history, read the same Bible but reached different conclusions.

Among the differences in faith and practice were the following:

1- Baptists and Reformers shared with all other Christian bodies the aim to restore primitive Christianity, but there were no signs of solid and sustained interest among Baptists in the oneness of the church.

2- Baptists and Reformers agreed to the principle that creeds should not be used as tests of Christian fellowship. Many Baptist associations, however, accepted the Philadelphia Confession of Faith and made subscription to it a prerequisite for membership. The Philadelphia Confession, so named because of its adoption by the Philadelphia Association of Baptist Churches, was a slight modification of

---

5. *Millennial Harbinger,* January 1830, p. 25

the Westminster Confession against which Stone and the Christians rebelled. Reformers were unalterably opposed to the creedal basis of membership in Baptist associations.

3- According to Baptists and Reformers, no ecclesiastical body had the right to exercise authority over a local congregation. Nevertheless, Baptists organized their congregations into associations which functioned as advisory bodies. The Mahoning Baptist Association, to cite a typical example, acknowledged "the independence of every church" and disclaimed "all superiority, jurisdiction, coercive right and infallibility." This did not satisfy the Reformers. They refused to recognize associations as legitimate manifestations of the church and disbanded them at every opportunity.

4- Baptists saw no reason to question the appropriateness of their name. Reformers regarded it as sectarian and nonbiblical.

5- Baptists observed the Lord's Supper periodically, most frequently on a quarterly basis. Reformers spread the Table of the Lord every Sunday.

6- To be accepted into the membership of a Baptist congregation, a believer had to make a confession of faith, relate a personal experience which gave credibility to the confession, receive a favorable congregational vote, and submit to baptism. Reformers required only a confession of faith and baptism.

7- The act of baptism, reasoned Baptists, was a sign that remission of sins and regeneration already had transformed the believer. Reformers insisted that baptism was *for* the remission of sins; sometimes detractors referred to them as water regenerationists.

8- Baptists permitted only ordained ministers to administer baptism and the Lord's Supper. Reformers extended the privilege to all believers. In comparison with the Baptists, Reformers had a higher concept of the laity and a lower concept of the ordained ministry. To become an ordained Baptist minister, a person must have received a "special" call. Reformers neither expected nor required a "special" call to ministry.

9- Contrary to Baptist custom, Campbell made a radical distinction between the authority of the Old and New Testaments.

10- Experiential religion was far more characteristic of Baptists than Reformers. Campbell's emphasis on the reasonableness of revealed religion was ingrained in the mind of the Reformers.

Added to these differences were the petty misunderstandings and jealousies which arose from time to time and tended to lower the level of goodwill between Baptists and Reformers. All in all, their separation was not as surprising as had been their original decision to unite.

THE PROCESS OF SEPARATION

The process of separation extended over a period of several years. Adhering to the principle of local autonomy, each congregation and each association was forced to face the issues and choose sides. One could not act for another. Without a single exception, orthodox Baptists took the initiative in bringing about a division in the ranks. Although Reformers were the "separated" rather than separatists, it would be absurd to see them as innocent victims of Baptist intolerance and narrow-mindedness. As Reformers made headway in gaining a following, the apprehension of Baptists turned into alarm and then bitterness. The orthodox party, cherishing the character of their fellowship, had no alternative but to get rid of those who in searching thought they "had found a more excellent way." Right or wrong, the orthodox judged the very life of the Baptist Church, both present and future, to be at stake. The intensity of their feeling is understandable.

Of the converts to the cause of the Campbells and Walter Scott, several figured prominently in the Baptist-Reformer split. Among them was "Raccoon" John Smith (1784-1868). A Baptist farmer-preacher in Kentucky, Smith resolved to "preach the Ancient Gospel" after becoming acquainted with Alexander Campbell in 1824. Placed under censure by his association for reading Campbell's translation of the New Testament instead of the King James Version, Smith continued to press for reform as he preached within the circle of the Baptists. Resistance to him mounted; longtime associates in ministry became his staunch opponents. On one occasion, for instance, he met a friend and said: "Good morning, my brother." The man replied: "Don't call me brother, sir. I

would rather claim kinship with the devil himself."[6] Such
rebuffs reinforced Smith's will to advocate what he knew with
absolute certainty to be the *truth*.

A plain-spoken and colorful man, Smith was an unusually
effective evangelist. He immersed so many converts that
some people began to call him "the Dipper." After reviewing
the results of a few months' work in 1828, Smith commented
to his wife: "Nancy, I have *baptized* seven hundred sinners,
and *capsized* fifteen hundred Baptists."[7] "The Dipper's"
success did not lead to rejoicing among Baptists. They knew
that "baptized sinners" and "capsized Baptists" alike increased the size and strength of the Reformers.

In 1823, a year before Smith claimed the cause of the
Reformers as his own, Campbell and other members of the
Brush Run Church established a congregation at Wellsburg
which joined the Mahoning Association in 1824 to avoid
probable expulsion from the Redstone Association. For the
next decade Baptists and Reformers in scores of congregations went through the ordeal of dividing.

Many examples of divisions could be cited. The experience
of Philip S. Fall (1798-1890) at Louisville and Nashville is il-
lustrative. Fall, a young minister and immigrant from
England, had been the pastor of the Baptist church at
Louisville before moving to Nashville, Tennessee, in 1825.
Under his leadership some of the Louisville congregation had
accepted Campbell's program and formed a separate church.
Upon separation from the Baptists there was a friendly spirit
and a peaceable division of the church property. At
Nashville, Fall had a similar experience. After a visit from
Alexander Campbell in March 1827, the congregation (now
Vine Street Christian Church) withdrew from Concord Bap-
tist Association in August of the same year. After several
years in a succssful pastorate at Nashville, Fall returned to
Kentucky in 1831 where he became minister of the Disciples
congregation at Frankfort.

The experience of the May's Lick Church in Kentucky,
which split in 1830, followed a well-established pattern.
Orthodox Baptists, offended by the "unauthorized breaking

6. Quoted in Thomas W. Grafton, *Men of Yesterday: A Series of Character
Sketches of Prominent Men among the Disciples of Christ* (St. Louis: Christian
Publishing Company, 1899), p. 135.
7. Williams, *Life of Elder John Smith*, p. 385.

of the symbolic loaf" during Thomas and Alexander Campbell's visit, resolved to oust Reformers in the congregation. Charging that attempts "to produce a *reformation in society*" had thrown the congregation into "a state of painful confusion," they concluded that it was impossible to "live in some degree of peace" with the Reformers. Consequently they resolved:

That all of us whose names are hereunto subscribed, protesting . . . against the Reformation (falsely so called), are willing and determined to rally round the original constitution and covenant of the church, which has never been disannulled—

. . . .

And that no person shall be considered a member of this church who will refuse to acknowledge the above by subscribing their names, or causing them to be subscribed, or who will encourage the above-named Reformers [the Campbells, Smith, and others].[8]

As a result of the resolution, the congregation divided. Both parties claimed to be the original church and requested recognition from the Bracken Association. The minutes of the association's meeting described the problem and reported the decision of the messengers:

The church at May's Lick having divided, and each party presented a letter to the Association, claiming to be the original church—*Resolved,* That the majority be recognized as such; the minority having embraced a system of things called *Reformation,* thereby departing from the principles of the United Baptists in Kentucky and of the Association.

The principle of majority rule was not followed consistently. At the same meeting of the Bracken Association messengers dealt with the problem of the church at Bethel:

Two letters also having been received from the church at Bethel, both claiming to be the original church; and it appearing to the satisfaction of this Association that the majority of the church has departed from the original principles of the United Baptists—*Resolved, therefore,* That the minority be recognized as the church.[9]

Alexander Campbell published the minutes cited above in his journal to indicate the high-handed methods of the Bracken

---

8. Quoted in Williams, *Life of Elder John Smith,* p. 385.
9. Quoted in *Millennial Harbinger,* October 1830, p. 477.

Association. Then he observed: "It is true they have not gone so far as some others; for in one place in Tennessee, TWO persons were declared *'the church,'* against *one hundred and twenty-eight!!"* Doubtless, the ejected Reformers promptly formed a new congregation on the foundation of the ancient order of things.

Associations, of course, faced as many problems as their member churches. In 1826 ten orthodox churches in the Redstone Association excluded thirteen congregations which refused to subscribe to the Philadelphia Confession. Three years later the Beaver Association in Pennsylvania severed its relationship with the Campbell-Scott dominated Mahoning Association in Ohio. To justify its action, Beaver published a comprehensive list of Campbellite errors and circulated it widely. The Franklin Association in Kentucky adopted the so-called "Beaver Anthema" and "advised all the churches in her connection to discountenance the several errors and corruptions from which Mahoning has already suffered excision."[10] Before the close of 1830 practically all Baptist associations in Kentucky (including Boone's Creek, Bracken, Elkhorn, North District, and Tate's Creek) had taken a public stand against the Reformers and excluded them.

In the meantime, the Mahoning Association disbanded at Austintown, Ohio, in August 1830. The definite center of Reformer sentiment and activity, this association in northeastern Ohio already had ceased to be Baptist except in name primarily because of Walter Scott's remarkable success in evangelism. Although John Henry's fateful resolution to dissolve the Baptist body at the Austintown meeting caught Alexander Campbell and several others by surprise, it provoked little discussion and passed easily. The dissolution of the Mahoning Association was without a doubt the most decisive event in the entire process of separation between Reformers and Baptists. Subsequently, the churches which had constituted Mahoning met annually "for praise and worship, and to hear reports from laborers in the field." They gathered, however as one-time Baptists; now they were Disciples.

The division of the ranks spread from Ohio, Pennsylvania, and Kentucky to other states. The Appomattox Association

---

10. Williams, *Life of Elder John Smith,* p. 330.

in Virginia, for example, recommended in 1830 that its churches close their pulpits to ministers who persisted in believing the errors described in the "Beaver Anathema." Then the Dover Association in Virginia urged a complete break with Reformers. In response, Alexander Campbell admitted that "the Rubicon is passed" and counseled his followers to "suffer evil treatment with Christian dignity."[11]

The experience of division was painful for Reformers. Baptists endured a full measure of suffering, too, for they lost several thousand members and many churches. The Reverend Garner McConnico, described by Campbell as a "good, old, high-toned, Gillized Calvinist," must have summed up the sentiments of many Baptists when he wrote in mid-1830: "O Lord! hear the cries and see the tears of the Baptists, for Alexander hath done them much harm. The Lord reward him according to his works."[12]

THE MILLENNIAL HARBINGER

Campbell discontinued *The Christian Baptist* at the conclusion of volume seven in July 1830. "Hating sects and sectarian names," he explained, "I resolved to prevent the name of Christian Baptists from being fixed upon us, . . . "[13] As a replacement he had launched another monthly, *The Millennial Harbinger,* the preceding January.

The choice of a name for the new paper should not be taken to suggest that Campbell expected an imminent return of Christ from the clouds of heaven. Indeed he believed that ultimately Christ would reign on earth, but he doubted that any person was in a position to prophesy as to times or seasons. The millennium, in his judgment, would be realized gradually rather than by a cataclysmic event. Through his journal Campbell intended to work for reformation essential to the establishment of the kingdom. In this sense it was a harbinger of the millennium. To quote the words of the prospectus:

This work shall be devoted to the destruction of Sectarianism, Infidelity, and Antichristian doctrine and practice. It shall have for

---

11. *Millennial Harbinger,* November 1832, p. 574.
12. Quoted from the *Columbian Star and Christian Index* in *Millennial Harbinger,* December 1830, p. 542.
13. *Christian Baptist,* July 1830, p. 309.

its object the development, and introduction of that political and religious order of society called THE MILLENNIUM, which will be the consummation of that ultimate amelioration of society proposed in the Christian Scriptures.[14]

The church had to be purified and unified before Christ could exercise sovereign power on earth as in heaven. This goal claimed the mind and heart of the editor and publisher of *The Millennial Harbinger*.

On balance *The Millennial Harbinger* was more constructive and less iconoclastic than *The Christian Baptist*. The responsibility of leading a separate religious movement altered Campbell's point of view more than he was willing to admit. A more positive approach is evident in the second number of *The Millennial Harbinger*. Although Campbell suggested that he and his readers should continue to oppose the abuses of the age, he cautioned: "We must not run into the opposite extreme; or, in our haste to get out of Babylon, we must not run past Jerusalem."[15] The reformer had begun to be tamed.

Campbell edited and published *The Millennial Harbinger* for over thirty years. Advanced age and declining health moved him publicly to transfer the conduct of the paper to William K. Pendleton (1817-1899) in January 1864. Pendleton, assisted by several others, kept it going through 1870 by which time weeklies were beginning to command interest and support. Enormously influential among Disciples for a solid generation, *The Millennial Harbinger* increased Campbell's stature as religious leader of a growing people.

DISCIPLES AND CHRISTIANS

When Campbell made the decision to found *The Millennial Harbinger,* he was well acquainted with the Christians in Kentucky. He had visited the state for the first time in 1823 and had met Barton W. Stone the following year in Georgetown. The two men, quite different in many ways, never became close personal friends. Campbell was a

---

14. *Millennial Harbinger,* January 1830, p. 1. For a perceptive study of Alexander Campbell's millennial views, SEE R. Frederick West, *Alexander Campbell and Natural Religion* (New Haven: Yale University Press, 1948), pp. 163-217; also SEE Harrell, *Quest for a Christian America: The Disciples of Christ and American Society to 1866,* pp. 39-44.
15. *Millennial Harbinger,* February 1830, p. 91.

gentleman farmer of considerable wealth; the lack of adequate financial resources weighed heavily on Stone throughout his ministry. Campbell was an immigrant who studied at the University of Glasgow; a native American frontiersman, Stone had received a "log college" education. Of the two, Campbell was more articulate, more refined, more self-confident, more dominant in personality. Stone was gentler and warmer. Both men, however, deplored the "horrid divisions" in the Body of Christ and held to the conviction that the New Testament was the only solid and durable foundation for unity among Christians.

The rupture between Baptists and Reformers caught Stone's attention. Addressing Campbell in 1827, he wrote: "Not as unconcerned spectators have we looked on the mighty war between you and your opposers—a war in which many of us have been engaged for many years before you entered the field."[16]

The Baptist-Reformer split opened the way for Disciples and Christians to consider the possibility of uniting. Both groups had their greatest visibility and numerical strength in the same general area of the country—particularly in the Kentucky-Ohio region. Forced to withdraw from the Baptists, Disciples formed congregations in many communities that already had a congregation of Christians. (The Christians had been expanding as a separate communion since the dissolution of the Springfield Presbytery in 1804.) As the two groups became acquainted with each other, they came to see that they shared much in common. Both groups advocated Christian primitivism and affirmed the necessity of uniting the church in order to proclaim the Christian message with integrity and force. Both groups accepted the principle of unity in essentials, liberty in nonessentials, and charity in all things. Both rejected creeds as tests of Christian fellowship and the authority of church bodies which usurped the prerogatives of local congregations. Both recognized but two ordinances, the Lord's Supper and baptism, and practiced believers' baptism by immersion. Both opposed sectarian and unscriptural names. To their way of thinking, designations such as Baptist and Presbyterian promoted partyism and stood in sharp contrast to the biblical witness. In

---

16. *Christian Messenger*, July 1827, p. 204.

sum, the areas of agreement between Disciples and Christians were striking.

There were differences between the two groups, to be sure. Among the more significant were the following:

1- Disciples and Christians aspired to achieve Christian unity by restoring primitive Christianity. On balance, however, the Christians tended to emphasize unity at the expense of full-blown primitivism whereas Disciples were less willing to compromise their understanding of New Testament faith and practice for the sake of unity.

2- Disciples equated immersion and baptism; hence immersion was a prerequisite for membership in their congregations. Campbell even changed the name of John the Baptist to John the Immerser in his translation of the New Testament. His critics, intending to poke fun at his intransigence on the subject, wrote a pamphlet in verse (it could hardly be called poetry) and circulated it widely. One verse read:

> "Though your sins be black as jet,
> Never mind to mourn or fret—
> Come to me, no longer dream,
> I will plunge you in the stream,
> Up you'll come in garments white,
> Holy as a saint of light,
> Come to me each son and daughter,
> Here's the gospel in the water."[17]

The Christians were immersionists, too, but exercised patience and tolerance in their dealings with "the pious unimmersed." "I fear," wrote Stone, "forbearance, and such kindred virtues are overlooked in our great zeal for immersion, as that alone by which the blessings of the Kingdom can be enjoyed or obtained."[18]

3- Disciples observed the Lord's Supper weekly. Christians "spread the Table of the Lord" less frequently. In 1830 Stone became convinced that the apostolic church communed each week, but the Christians only gradually modified their practice of corporate worship accordingly.

4- The Christians had a higher conception of the office of the ministry and were less anticlerical than the Disciples.

---

17. Quoted in *Millennial Harbinger*, August 1831, p. 358.
18. *Christian Messenger*, February 1831, p. 38.

Campbell used the columns of *The Christian Baptist* to lambast the "kingdom of the clergy" repeatedly. His invective and sarcasm aimed at hirelings in ministry doubtless affected the attitude of Disciples. By 1830 the Christians had reached the point of developing a responsible ministry. Conference reports printed in the *Christian Messenger* frequently distinguished between elders (that is, ordained ministers) and unordained preachers. The experience of a quarter century as a separate religious group had taught Stone and his followers the importance of protecting congregations from unworthy ministers.

5- The two movements differed substantially in their respective programs of evangelism. The Christians in the West emerged from the fires of camp-meeting Christianity on the raw frontier. Although Stone condemned the excesses of emotional religion, he saw much of positive value in revivalism. Many of his brothers and sisters in the faith, moreover, used the mourner's bench. Disciples were more inclined to stress "reasons of the head" than "reasons of the heart" in winning converts. They viewed unbridled emotionalism with unmixed suspicion. Campbell shook his head in dismay at the spectacle of the typical camp meeting. Writing in 1843, he observed: "There are probably more wrangles by day and debauches by night within one mile of a camp of the usual size, than occurred in the whole nation of Israel at seven feasts of the tabernacles; . . . "[19]

6- The difference over the question of a name for the church has been treated at length in Chapter 1. Alexander Campbell expressed strong preference for "Disciples." Stone preferred "Christians." Both men claimed to have biblical precedent for their choice. Even when his father and Walter Scott sided with Stone, Campbell was unwilling to budge an inch on the matter. No wonder the Stone-Campbell movement wrestled with the problem of a name for well over a century before settling on the Christian Church (Disciples of Christ)!

Recognizing that their striking similarities outweighed their differences, substantive and trivial, Disciples and Christians felt their way toward a closer association with each other. As early as 1828 a Disciples congregation initiated cor-

---

19. *Millennial Harbinger*, October 1843, p. 463.

respondence with a Christian conference in Bourbon County, Kentucky. Members of the "Baptized Church" at Cooper's Run informed the conference that their "pulpits, meetinghouses and tables" were open to Christians in the area. The conference, meeting at Antioch on September 19, 1828, acknowledged the communication and expressed a willingness to "mingle" with Disciples at Cooper's Run "in social worship." Less than three years later, Christians and Disciples in Millersburg, Kentucky, united on April 24, 1831. According to the record book of the Millersburg Christian Church:

It was the practice of the brethren forming the two congregations to commune together at their several meetings, and finally finding themselves to be one so far as faith and practice were concerned they agreed to meet together without regard to differences of opinion, acknowledging no name but that of Christian, and no creed but the Bible. The result of these joint meetings was a union into one congregation in the year 1831, at which meeting they pledged themselves to each other not to indulge in speculations to the wounding of each other, but to regard the gospel as the power of God for salvation to all who believe and obey it.

There must have been some passage of time between event and account for the Millersburg recorder added: "This was the first union so far as we know or believe that had taken place between the 'Christians' and those called at that time 'Reformers.' "[20]

In the latter part of 1831 Campbell and Stone engaged in an extended and sometimes heated interchange on the subject of uniting Christians and Disciples. The *Christian Messenger* and *The Millennial Harbinger* gave full coverage to the discussion. Stone opened the correspondence by stating flatly that no reason existed to prevent union as far as the Christians were concerned. In essence the Reformed Baptists—as he called them—had accepted the doctrine taught by the Christians for a number of years. Stone's candor upset Campbell. Other antisectarian reformers were pioneers clearing forests and burning brush, Campbell replied, but only he and his followers had restored the ancient gospel. Stone was unwilling to concede the point. In his next letter he noted

---

20. Quoted in Alonzo W. Fortune, *The Disciples in Kentucky* (Published by the Convention of the Christian Churches in Kentucky, 1932), pp. 115-116.

Campbell's "plain denial" of the Christians' claim to priority and then observed: "I am aware of the deceptibility of the human mind, and of its strong propensity to make for ourselves *a great name.*" Campbell was infuriated. Writing in the last issue of *The Millennial Harbinger* for 1831, he observed that Stone "has a little of the *man* as well as of the *christian* about him." "I solicited a free, candid and *affectionate* correspondence on any points of difference," he continued. "But in asking for *bread* I did not expect a *stone.*"[21] If the union of Christians and Disciples had depended solely upon the goodwill between Campbell and Stone, it never would have been accomplished.

Meanwhile Stone had become acquainted with John T. Johnson (1788-1856). A one-time Baptist, Johnson was highly respected in and around Georgetown, Kentucky. So was his brother, Richard M. (1780-1850), who became a United States senator and in 1836 was elected Vice President of the nation in the Van Buren administration. For many years a member of the Kentucky legislature and thereafter a representative in the United States Congress, John T. Johnson abandoned his political career in 1831 to become a Disciples preacher. He examined Alexander Campbell's writings in the light of the Bible and was won over to the cause of reformation by restoration. "My eyes were opened, and I was made perfectly free by the truth," Johnson testified. "And the debt of gratitude I owe to that man of God, A. Campbell, no language can tell."[22]

Johnson quickly established a firm friendship with Barton Stone. Under their leadership two Georgetown congregations, one Disciples and the other Christian, agreed to worship together. The experience convinced them that they ought to be one people. Subsequently, a small group of Disciples and Christians met in Georgetown for a four-day conference, beginning on Christmas Day, 1831, at which Johnson and "Raccoon" John Smith played prominent roles. This meeting was followed by a larger one at the Hill Street Church in Lexington, Kentucky, on January 1, 1832. There the chief spokesmen were Stone and Smith. Smith urged the

---

21. SEE *Millennial Harbinger,* September 1831, pp. 385-392; *Christian Messenger,* November 1831, pp. 249-250; *Millennial Harbinger,* December 1831, p. 557.
22. John Rogers, *Biography of Elder J. T. Johnson* (Cincinnati: Published for the author, 1861), p. 21.

assembled no longer to be "Campbellites or Stoneites, New Lights or Old Lights, or any other kind of lights," but to come together on the basis of the Bible which would yield "all the light we need." In hearty agreement with the position stated by Smith, Stone extended his hand as a pledge of full fellowship. A handshake sealed the commitment to unite Christians and Disciples. According to Smith's biographer:

It was now proposed that all who felt willing to unite on these principles, should express that willingness by giving one another the hand of fellowship; and elders and teachers hastened forward, and joined their hands and hearts in joyful accord. A song arose, and brethren and sisters, with many tearful greetings, ratified and confirmed the union.[23]

An announcement of the union between Christians and Disciples—together with a spirited defense of the decision—appeared in the January issue of the *Christian Messenger*. Alexander Campbell was not present at the Lexington meeting. In view of his serious reservations about moving too quickly without giving due regard to all factors involved, it is not surprising that his response to the news was hardly enthusiastic. He nevertheless did express guarded hope for the success of the venture. Stone was elated; the union for him was the fulfillment of a dream. "This union," he reflected, "I view as the noblest act of my life."[24] Methodist circuit rider Peter Cartwright's description of the union is a model of distortion. He wrote in his *Autobiography:* "B. W. Stone stuck to his New Lightism . . . till he grew old and feeble, and the mighty Alexander Campbell, the great, arose and poured such floods of regenerating water about the old man's cranium, that he formed a union with this giant errorist, . . . "[25] Campbell supported the union, but Barton W. Stone clearly was the moving spirit behind it.

Neither Christians nor Disciples had any representative bodies with power to approve or disapprove the union. Authority was vested solely in local congregations. Members of both fellowships around the country, consequently, needed to be persuaded to join the new movement. The action taken in Lexington initiated the process of union. Implementation

---

23. Williams, *Life of Elder John Smith*, p. 455.
24. Rogers, *The Biography of Elder Barton Warren Stone*, p. 79.
25. *Autobiography of Peter Cartwright*, p. 35.

was achieved over a period of several years. To gain support for the union, the Lexington conclave selected John Smith of the Reformers and John Rogers (1800-1867) from the Christians "to ride together through all the churches, and to be equally supported by the united contributions of the churches of both descriptions; which contributions are to be deposited together with brother John T. Johnson, as treasurer and distributor."[26]

Architects of the union faced countless difficulties in building the road to full fellowship. Suspicions and misunderstandings developed. A number of Christians lamented that they had sacrificed some of their cherished beliefs to come together with Disciples. Just as many Disciples were certain that they had relinquished some of their views in order to embrace the Christians. Trivial concerns surfaced. The brethren in Alabama, for example, questioned the amount of income which Smith and Rogers received for their evangelistic labors. The *Christian Messenger* responded: "The brethren in Alabama are informed that the churches do not allow our Evangelists, Smith and Rogers, but $75 each, per quarter, and not $300 as they supposed."[27]

Key leaders in both parties were determined to keep the experiment in union from failing. In addition to defending the union with all the force they could command, they labored untiringly as evangelists. As a result of their uncommon success, many converts and proselytes came into the communion with no particular loyalty to either Christians or Disciples. In actuality, successful evangelism cemented the two groups together more than any other single factor.

The *Christian Messenger* and *The Millennial Harbinger* printed reports of the evangelistic work of Smith, Rogers, Johnson, and others. Typical of such accounts is the letter written by John Rogers from Carlisle, Kentucky, on May 16, 1832.

Dear Brethren—I have just returned from a two weeks tour through the counties of Harrison, Scott, Woodford, Jessamine, and Bourbon. Truth is on the march, conquering, and to conquer! I am happy to inform you that the following additions were made to the congregations at the following places: At Georgetown and its vicinity,

---

26. *Christian Messenger,* January 1832, p. 7.
27. *Christian Messenger,* September 1832, p. 286.

13 were added—At Clear Creek and Versailles, 11—at Nicholasville, 3; and at Cane-ridge 23—making in all 54 persons. At all the above named meetings, Brother Smith was present, and a prominent actor, except the last named.[28]

Rogers counted some of his additions twice, for the total amounts to 50 rather than 54. He was charged to be an evangelist, however, not a mathematician.

In view of the complications that could arise, it is not surprising that Christians and Disciples in some communities were slow to unite. In Lexington, of all places, the two groups did not get together until 1835. An "unfortunate blow up" occurred in 1832 over the doctrine of the ministry. Describing the situation, one of Campbell's followers commented: "It is the *Clergy*—the *hireling system*—the *called and sent*—the *rulers*—that keep us apart. No, we cannot unite under present *existing circumstances.*"[29] More precisely, Christians in Lexington insisted that one must be an ordained minister to administer the Lord's Supper. Disciples disagreed. The two groups finally overcame their differences three years later and united under the leadership of Thomas Miller Allen (1797-1871), one of Stone's closest associates. To cite another example, Stone moved from Georgetown, Kentucky, to Jacksonville, Illinois, in the fall of 1834. Upon arrival he found Disciples and Christians worshiping in separate places. In protest he refused to affiliate with either of them. When they united, he became a member of the new congregation.

Stone was unable to lead all of his followers into the merger. An undetermined number of Christians in the West remained aloof and in time established fellowship with Christians in other sections of the country. This group, known as the General Convention of the Christian Churches, united with Congregationalists in 1931 to form the Congregational Christian Churches. (Merging in 1957, Congregational Christian Churches and the Evangelical and Reformed Church formed the United Church of Christ.)

The merger of Christians and Disciples, nevertheless, was remarkably successful. Approximately 10,000 "Stoneites" and a larger number of "Campbellites"—perhaps 12,000—united in the early 1830s. By 1860 the Disciples of

---

28. *Christian Messenger,* July 1832, p. 218.
29. *Millennial Harbinger,* April 1832, p. 192.

Christ claimed a membership in excess of 190,000. The new denomination's rate of growth in the thirty years leading up to the Civil War was almost four times as great as that of the nation's population. As Disciples moved through this eventful period of rapid expansion, they asked over and over: "What does Mr. Campbell think?" It was a natural question, for the Sage of Bethany was by all odds their most prominent spokesman and influential leader.

THE CHRISTIAN SYSTEM

From their inception Disciples emphasized the disastrous effects of "speculation" and "human traditions" on the church through the centuries. A pronounced aversion to the word, *theology,* remained deeply embedded in the Disciples mind until the 1950s. "Not until 1952 do I recall hearing a group of our scholars publicly referred to as theologians," observed one of their most perceptive historians. "Not until 1958 did one of our institutions for the education of ministers name itself a theological seminary."[30] Despite their negative attitude toward theology the Disciples were not anti-intellectual or obscurantist in their approach to Christian faith. The reasonableness of the Christian religion was one of their cardinal principles.

Certainly Alexander Campbell was a theologian even though he never referred to himself as such and would have severely reprimanded anyone who so labeled him. An intellectual who aspired to be "the finest scholar in the Kingdom," he made known his understanding of Christianity through his journals and in his debates. Then in 1835 he published a synthesis of his thought entitled *A Connected View of the Principles by which the Living Oracles May Be Intelligibly and Certainly Interpreted.* Contrary to his usual practice, Campbell treated succinctly the subjects (including the universe, the Bible, man, God, salvation, the Christian hope, church, and ministry) covered in any systematic theology. Aptly retitled *The Christian System,* it provided a comprehensive statement on biblical doctrine which served as a textbook for generations of Disciples preachers.

---

30. Ronald E. Osborn, "Theology among the Disciples" in *The Christian Church (Disciples of Christ): An Interpretative Examination in the Cultural Context,* ed. by George G. Beazley, Jr., p. 82.

The Bible, Campbell maintained, was the matrix of his thought. Strange as it may seem, he firmly believed that he avoided the trap of "human opinion" in interpreting the biblical witness. In the preface to the second edition of *The Christian System,* published in 1839 and reprinted many times, he wrote: "While, then, we would, if we could . . . proclaim all that we believe, and all that we know, to the ends of the earth, *we take the Bible, the whole Bible, and nothing but the Bible, as the foundation of all Christian union and communion.* Those who do not like this, will please show us a more excellent way."

Critics of Campbell charged that in publishing *The Christian System* he had produced a creed for Disciples. He countered: "We speak for ourselves only; and while we are always willing to give a declaration of our faith and knowledge of the Christian system, we firmly protest against dogmatically propounding our own views, or those of any fallible mortal, as a condition or foundation of church union and co-operation."[31] Creeds were used invariably as tests of Christian fellowship and therefore had to be rejected, in Campbell's judgment. Although it was a representative statement of the Disciples position for several generations, *The Christian System* could be accepted or rejected without affecting one's status in the church. As a theological synthesis for Disciples, in any event, Campbell's volume had no competition until Robert Milligan's *Scheme of Redemption* appeared in 1869.

THE LUNENBURG LETTER

Of the particular subjects covered in *The Christian System,* Campbell had investigated none of them more thoroughly than the doctrine of baptism. Reaffirming his stand of many years, he argued in Chapter XVI that immersion was the proper form of baptism. Neither sprinkling nor pouring conformed to the New Testament practice. Yet in 1837 he acknowledged the presence of Christians in non-immersionist Protestant communions. A "conscientious sister" from Lunenburg, Virginia, expressed surprise that he recognized "the Protestant parties as Christian." She re-

---

31. Alexander Campbell, *The Christian System* (Bethany, Va.: Printed by A. Campbell and published by Forrester and Campbell, third edition, 1840), p. 12.

quested him to answer a series of questions. "Will you be so good as to let me know how any one becomes a Christian?" she asked. "Does the name of Christ or Christian belong to any but those who believe the *gospel,* repent, and are buried by baptism into the death of Christ?"

Campbell replied:

But who is a Christian? I answer, Every one that believes in his heart that Jesus of Nazareth is the Messiah, the Son of God; repents of his sins, and obeys him in all things according to his measure of knowledge of his will. *A perfect man in Christ,* or a perfect Christian is one thing; and "a babe in Christ," a stripling in the faith, or an imperfect Christian, is another. The New Testament recognizes both the perfect man and the imperfect man in Christ. The former, indeed, implies the latter. . . . Now there is perfection of will, of temper, and of behaviour. There is a perfect state and a perfect character. And hence it is possible for Christians to be imperfect in some respects without an absolute forfeiture of the Christian state and character.

. . . .

But every one is wont to condemn others in that in which he is more intelligent than they; while, on the other hand, he is condemned for his Pharisaism or his immodesty and rash judgment of others, by those that excel in the things in which he is deficient. I cannot, therefore, make any one duty the standard of Christian state or character, not even immersion into the name of the Father, of the Son, and of the Holy Spirit, and in my heart regard all that have been sprinkled in infancy without their own knowledge and consent, as aliens from Christ and the well-grounded hope of heaven.

He continued:

Should I find a Pedobaptist more intelligent in the Christian Scriptures, more spiritually-minded and more devoted to the Lord than a Baptist, or one immersed on a profession of the ancient faith, I could not hesitate a moment in giving the preference of my heart to him that loveth most. Did I act otherwise, I would be a pure sectarian, a Pharisee among Christians. Still I will be asked, How do I know that any one loves my Master but by his obedience to his commandments? I answer, *In no other way.* But mark, I do not substitute obedience to one commandment, for universal or even for general obedience. And should I see a sectarian Baptist or a Pedobaptist more spiritually-minded, more generally conformed to the requisitions of the Messiah, than one who precisely acquiesces with me in the theory or practice of immersion as I teach, doubtless the former rather than the latter, would have my cordial approbation and love as a Christian. So I judge, and so I feel. It is the image of Christ the Christian looks for and loves; and this does not consist in being exact in a few items, but in general devotion to the whole truth as far as known.

. . . .

There is no occasion, then, for making immersion, on a profession of the faith, absolutely essential to a Christian—though it may be greatly essential to his sanctification and comfort. My right hand and my right eye are greatly essential to my usefulness and happiness, but not to my life; and as I could not be a perfect man without them, so I cannot be a perfect Christian without a right understanding and a cordial reception of immersion in its true and scriptural meaning and design. But he that thence infers that none are Christians but the immersed, as greatly errs as he who affirms that none are alive but those of clear and full vision.

"All the Prophets and Apostles of both Testaments," Campbell concluded, sustained him in his reasoning.[32]

Some of Campbell's readers objected to his response, but he refused to modify his position. Although admitting "that the term *Christian* was given first to immersed believers and to none else," he added: "but we do not think that it was given to them because they were immersed, but because they had put on Christ."[33]

This correspondence reveals an important aspect of Campbell's thought that must be taken into account if the basic witness of the man is to be understood. A significant number of his followers, particularly one and two generations later, adopted his inflexible Christian primitivism but virtually ignored the Lunenburg Letter which he wrote at the height of his powers. Their distorted view of Campbell contributed to the rise of Disciples scholasticism and multiplied the problems of a developing denomination.

---

32. *Millennial Harbinger*, September 1837, pp. 411-414.
33. *Millennial Harbinger*, November 1837, p. 507.

7

CONSOLIDATION AND GROWTH

The thirty-year period from 1830 to 1860 was a time of consolidation and growth for the Disciples. From congregations mainly in Kentucky, southern and eastern Ohio, Indiana, western Pennsylvania and Virginia, the Disciples began to spread throughout the nation. Alexander Campbell was the acknowledged leader of the movement. After Barton W. Stone moved to Jacksonville, Illinois, in 1834 there was no doubt of that. The January 1832 meeting at Lexington, Kentucky, united the Reformer and Christian movements, and the combination began a period of development which ultimately changed its character. Growth in numbers of followers, congregations, and preachers made institutional development inevitable. Expansion took place in publishing, in education, and in district, state, and national organization. The Disciples proposal for a union of Christians on the basis of the New Testament came to be called "The Plea." Alliteratively, it was later said the Disciples grew on "Preaching, Publishing, Pedagogy (education) and the Plea."[1]

---

1. The four "P's" of the Disciples were suggested by Claude Spencer, leading Disciples historian, in a letter to the authors.

PREACHERS BECOME EDITORS

By 1830 the Disciples separation from the Baptists was generally acknowledged. A large number of religious journals made their appearance as a new self-awareness emerged. Many preachers watched with interest Campbell's successful venture in publishing and followed his example. Most of the publications lasted only a few years, but their combined influence contributed greatly to the growth of the movement. Considering the diversity of the population and the difficulties printers faced in securing helpers and supplies in frontier communities, the widespread circulation of their papers is remarkable.

Mention has been made of Alexander Campbell's pioneering in the publishing field. The change from *The Christian Baptist* to *The Millennial Harbinger* in 1830 was a symbol of his desire to move from a negative to a more positive position in regard to church organization and institutions. Under Campbell's financial genius and managerial ability his monthly magazine attained stability and stature. Agents and subscribers were to be found in hundreds of communities.

Campbell's publishing enterprise grew so rapidly he soon needed assistance. When he invited Dr. Robert Richardson (1806-1876) to come to Bethany in 1836 and help edit *The Millennial Harbinger,* Richardson was a physician at Carthage, Ohio. Originally an Episcopalian, son of a merchant in Pittsburgh, Robert had been a student in Thomas Campbell's school. Walter Scott was his good friend and teacher, and his regard for Scott probably led him to Carthage. When Richardson moved to Bethany, Campbell was freed to travel in the interests of the movement. Richardson became Campbell's biographer and one of the great leaders of the Disciples.[2]

Most of the magazines begun during this period had a short life. Not all the preachers who sought to emulate Campbell in the publishing field had his shrewdness or ability. Even Barton W. Stone's important journal, the *Christian Messenger,* lasted only from 1826 to 1837. Revived in 1839 it lasted another six years until 1845. Walter Scott's periodical, *The Evangelist,* appeared in 1832 and ceased publication in 1844.

---

2. Cloyd Goodnight and Dwight E. Stevenson, *Home to Bethphage* (St. Louis: Christian Board of Publication, 1949). This is the best biography of Richardson.

John Thomas began a paper known as *Apostolic Advocate.* Published at Office Tavern, Virginia, beginning in 1834, it lasted five years. Other publications of the period and their interesting titles included: *Gospel Advocate* (published at Georgetown, Kentucky, 1835-36 by J.T. Johnson and B.F. Hall); *Christian Preacher* (published at Cincinnati, 1836-40 by D.S. Burnet and J.T. Johnson); *Northern Reformer, Heretic Detector and Evangelical Review* (published at Middleburg, Ohio, 1837-42 by Arthur Crihfield); *Morning Watch* (published at Evergreen, South Carolina, 1837-40 by J.M. Barnes and C.F.R. Shehane); and *Gospel Proclamation* (published at St. Clairsville, Ohio, 1847, by Alexander Hall and merged with Benjamin Franklin's *Western Reformer* to become *Proclamation and Reformer,* Milton, Indiana, 1850).

In the December 1859 issue of *The Millennial Harbinger,* Alexander Campbell's son-in-law and assistant editor, W.K. Pendleton, indicated that three weeklies, twelve monthlies, and one quarterly were then being published. Two journals which were brought into being in the 1850s to represent the more conservative segment of the movement were the *Gospel Advocate* at Nashville in 1855 and *The American Christian Review* begun at Indianapolis in 1856. There can be no question but that the sheer number of new publications, the diverse viewpoints they expressed, and their news of progress and expansion did much to encourage and influence many people to support the movement and to become involved in its future.

THE BEGINNING OF HIGHER EDUCATION

The earliest leaders of the Disciples were men of considerable formal education. Barton W. Stone had been educated in David Caldwell's academy in North Carolina. Thomas Campbell was a graduate of Glasgow University and the Seceder seminary at Whitburn. Walter Scott was educated at the University of Edinburgh. Alexander Campbell had the winter of 1808-09 at Glasgow and was tutored by his father. The men who formed the Disciples recognized the importance of education and were soon zealous for the establishment of educational institutions.

The Disciples at first were active mainly in secondary education. Barton W. Stone conducted Rittenhouse

Academy for several years at Georgetown, Kentucky. Both Thomas and Alexander Campbell had experience as qualified teachers. Walter Scott conducted schools at Pittsburgh and at Covington, Kentucky. Many of their associates founded scores of academic institutes for young men and women as they pioneered in equal education. In Kentucky, for example, there were the Female Eclectic Institute (Poplar Hill Academy) near Frankfort, Greenville Institute at Harrodsburg, the Inductive Institute at Paris, Pinkerton's School for Young Ladies at Midway, and many others. In Tennessee there was The Female Seminary at Franklin (later Eclectic Institute for Young Ladies). In Indiana there were the Wayne County Seminary at Centerville, Cambridge Seminary, and Ladoga Academy. Similar institutions could be found in most of the states. All such schools were privately conducted and were supported by Disciples and others until public schools became widespread. This preoccupation of Disciples leaders with education meant an eventual interest in higher education. The education of a ministry, the development of culture, the retaining of young people as leaders, all seemed to demand that the churches become concerned with collegiate institutions.

Most higher education in the United States was church sponsored prior to 1860. There was an obvious need for colleges in the West. Almost as soon as the churches related to the Disciples became conscious of a separate existence there were proposals for the establishment of a college. Having tried in Ohio and Virginia and failed, John C. Bennett attempted to found a "Christian College" at New Albany, Indiana. The Indiana legislature granted a charter on January 24, 1833, to provide a place where "no religious doctrine or tenets peculiar to any sect of professing Christians shall ever be taught." The founder definitely did not want a sectarian college. Bennett was listed as president with the names of Barton W. Stone and Walter Scott as among the incorporators.[3] So far as is known the college never opened.

The first institution of higher learning of the Disciples to be established was Bacon College at Georgetown, Kentucky. Georgetown College, a Baptist institution, removed Thornton F. Johnson as professor of mathematics and civil engineering

---

3. *Millennial Harbinger,* 1833, p. 189.

because of his Campbellian views. The result was the forming
of a new college, organized November 10, 1836. Classes began
on November 14, and its charter was secured from the Kentucky legislature on February 23, 1837. First called "The
Collegiate Institute and School for Civil Engineers" as the
need for surveyors on the frontier was considerable, it was
eventually named for Francis Bacon, the scientist. It sought
to exemplify the spirit of empirical and rational inquiry
prominently expressed in Disciples thought. Students were
enrolled from twelve states and the District of Columbia the
first year. Walter Scott was elected president and professor of
Hebrew Literature. He was succeeded the following year by
David S. Burnet (1808-1867).[4] The institution was moved to
Harrodsburg, Kentucky, in 1839 and later united with Transylvania University in Lexington, Kentucky.

From Bethany, Alexander Campbell kept a watchful eye on
the developments in higher education in Kentucky. The
opening of Bacon College was duly announced in *The Millennial Harbinger* but Campbell was not altogether pleased. He
had given much thought to developing a college himself and
had lectured extensively on the subject of education. In a
series of articles on "A New Institution" he developed his
educational philosophy and in 1840 secured a charter for a
"Seminary of Learning" to be named Bethany College.[5]
Campbell donated the land on which the college's first
building was constructed.

From its opening in 1841 Bethany College rapidly rose to
become an important place for the education of Disciples
ministers and laity. Campbell served as president and
professor of moral sciences from the beginning of the college
until a few years before his death in 1866. The influence of
Bethany graduates in leadership of the Disciples and in establishing other colleges was considerable. Many families
hoped their sons might study with the renowned Alexander
Campbell. In turn he solicited money to finance the college in
his travels and through the pages of *The Millennial Harbinger*. The board of trustees at its second meeting received
word of the appointment of Robert Richardson and W.K.

4. Dwight E. Stevenson, *The Bacon College Story: 1836-1865*, The College of the
Bible Quarterly, Vol. XXIX, No. 4, October, 1962, p. 10ff.
5. *Millennial Harbinger*, 1840, p. 176.

Pendleton as faculty.[6] The selection of Andrew F. Ross and Charles Stewart as additional faculty was announced shortly thereafter. The school was purposely located away from city centers, as were most of the later Disciples colleges, so that "students could avoid worldly temptation."

The study of the Bible was central to Campbell's understanding of Christian higher education. He wrote:

Bethany College is the only College known to us in the civilized world, founded upon the Bible. . . .

It is founded upon the Bible in the following manner: The Bible is every day publicly read by one student in the hearing of all the other students. It is then lectured upon for nearly one hour, contemplated first historically; . . . the Christian apostles and evangelists, are, in order, exhibited, investigated and classified under appropriate heads.

. . . .

Those destined for the ministry of the Word, are thus furnished with all the grand materials of their future profession; and those assigned to other professions in life are prepared to enjoy themselves in the richest of all possessions.[7]

Campbell himself lectured when he was on campus, and many generations of students were inspired by his instruction. In his absence the daily lecture was given by W.K. Pendleton or another of the faculty.

With the successful establishment of Bethany College and the general approval given to higher education by Alexander Campbell, it was only a matter of time until there would be other colleges and institutions. The September 1845 issue of *The Millennial Harbinger* listed Bacon, Bethany, and Franklin as "our colleges." Preceded by several secondary schools, Franklin College was opened near Nashville, Tennessee, by Tolbert Fanning (1810-1874). Fanning later became a leader of the anti-organization churches in Tennessee and elsewhere. Franklin was closed in 1861, a casualty of the Civil War. Reopened briefly in 1865, it closed permanently when a fire destroyed its only building.

The Disciples quickly developed a number of colleges. Kentucky Female Orphan School (now Midway College) was organized at Midway in 1849 to serve girls who had lost

6. *Millennial Harbinger*, 1841, p. 270.
7. *Millennial Harbinger*, 1850, p. 291 ff.

one or both parents. Classes opened in 1850 at Western Reserve Eclectic Institute (now Hiram College) a new school established at Hiram, Ohio. Classes opened in 1850. James A. Garfield (1831-1881), the only preacher to become President of the United States, was its second president. The able Kentucky writer and educator, John Augustus Williams (1824-1903), was the first president of Christian College (now Columbia College) founded at Columbia, Missouri, in 1852. Fairview Academy, established in 1843, was the forerunner of Northwestern Christian University (now Butler University). Chartered in 1850 at Indianapolis, Indiana, classes began in 1855. Northwestern Christian University (named for the Northwest Territory) was brought into being by the Indiana convention of Disciples churches. This action by a corporate body was an exception to the usual pattern of colleges founded on the initiative of individuals.

The Illinois legislature in 1855 granted a charter to Eureka College. An outgrowth of Walnut Grove Academy, it was located at Eureka, Illinois. Sixty miles to the west, in the "military tract," Abingdon College was chartered in 1854. At first the more prosperous of the two colleges, Abingdon merged with Eureka in 1884 to form the present Eureka College. Christian University (now Culver-Stockton College) was chartered in 1853 and established in 1855 at Canton, Missouri. It was the first institution west of the Mississippi River to provide in its charter for coeducation; however, it did not register any women until 1867. Hesperian College in northern California (now Chapman College, Orange) was chartered in 1860 and began classes in March 1861. Oskaloosa College (now Drake University) was opened in Oskaloosa, Iowa, in 1861 and removed to Des Moines in 1881.

The above listing, with the exception of Franklin College, gives account only of those Disciples institutions founded before the Civil War which continue to exist until the present. Several other colleges were brought into being by dedicated Disciples leaders but soon withered away for lack of support. The Disciples did not always fully understand what was required to support an educational institution either academically or financially. Other colleges and universities, however, were to emerge later. Through the years the surviving colleges have provided a steady stream of leaders for both church and society.

THE BEGINNING OF ORGANIZATION

The Mahoning Association met at Austintown, Ohio, in 1830 and by this time was a Baptist association in name only. The large numbers of people in attendance gave the gathering the atmosphere of a convention. They spent the first day in evangelistic singing, preaching, and hearing reports. The next day the whole course of the movement was changed when, at the instigation of Walter Scott, a resolution was introduced proposing that the association be dissolved. With little thought of the future and almost without debate, the resolution was passed. Its implications were understood by Alexander Campbell and a few others, but they were not heard. Campbell took the floor immediately after the vote had been taken and asked: "Brethren, what are you going to do? Are you never going to meet again?" Without organization what was their future?[8] The same month the Stillwater Association of Ohio was dissolved in similar fashion.

Those persons who rejected any form of organization considered they were leaving "sectarian" ways. Campbell, however, was concerned that freedom from organization gained so impulsively might easily lead to anarchy. He felt that a tactical blunder had been made in this sudden move toward complete congregational independence. Campbell believed the brotherhood, as many now called the movement, could avoid many mistakes if it could keep somewhat within the framework of an association plan. His followers, however, were not ready to listen. They desired to break completely from previous forms of organization. The movement would struggle for many years over this question. Campbell and others sought to find a way to organize for the more efficient proclamation of its message. There were other leaders, however, who feared any form of organization beyond the congregation. Dissension, strife, and ultimately division were to result.

Because pioneer Disciples relied primarily on their own resources, they had to develop methods for propagating their views. It was difficult but necessary that they learn to cooperate. One of the early channels of cooperative work was the "Yearly Meeting" held in some regions usually in the fall. Suggested by Campbell as a means of keeping the movement

---

8. Henry Shaw, *Buckeye Disciples*, p. 58.

together, its purpose was preaching and fellowship. Time and again, in his new periodical and in speeches, Campbell began to stress the need for organization and cooperation among the churches. The first step toward cooperation came as congregations joined together to send out evangelists.

These evangelists were generally farmers, as were Stone and the Campbells, though some were schoolteachers, lawyers, doctors, or businessmen. At first they did not depend upon their preaching for a livelihood but freely offered their services to congregations and communities. Most of them were good, honest persons, though some took advantage of their position. With few exceptions, these early preachers and evangelists went where they pleased and generally were welcomed by the community. Frontier society enjoyed the diversion they provided from daily routine. In presenting the message of the Disciples they generally worked on a set pattern. They first expressed great tolerance of other denominations. Following this expression of open-mindedness they announced a sermon on Christian union at which time the evangelist would portray the evils of a divided church and human creeds. They would then propose a plan on which all reasonable people could unite: the restoration of New Testament teaching.

Though these evangelists were not always successful, there were usually a few individuals to accept their views. If half a dozen or so persons were interested, a congregation was formed. In the absence of ministerial leadership, laymen directed the services. The Lord's Supper, observed weekly, was the focal point of worship. Preaching became a means of bringing others to their viewpoint. Baptism of adult believers by immersion was practiced. Many of these churches died but some lived on to become substantial congregations.

The evangelists delighted in reporting their successes in *The Millennial Harbinger* and other journals. Campbell gave more space to church news in his new periodical than he had given such items in *The Christian Baptist*. These reports provide much valuable information on the growth and status of the movement. Features that stand out are: large numbers attending district meetings; reports on growing membership; lay-leadership developing within the movement; reliance on discussion in periodicals and books to define practice;

genuine fear on the part of some persons of organization beyond the local congregation; lack of financial support for preachers and evangelists; and attempts on the part of the more farsighted leaders to bring order out of chaos. As soon as Alexander Campbell became the responsible and representative leader of the movement, he had the insight and courage to abandon his earlier views and advocate cooperation.

While the Campbells were still associated with the Baptists, the Christians in Kentucky were already developing cooperation. The rise of conferences among the Christians in Kentucky has been discussed previously. A new phase of organizational development began in Clark County, Kentucky, when a general meeting in behalf of the "ancient order of things" was held at Mount Zion in October 1829. Another such meeting was convened at Mays Lick in April 1830. Lasting two or three days these meetings at first were for fellowship and for the discussion of common problems but later they were held for the purpose of planning cooperative work.[9]

For three years beginning in 1832 John Smith and John Rogers served the churches as evangelists. With John T. Johnson serving as treasurer, they urged the congregations of other sections of Kentucky to cooperate in sending out evangelists, for they said, "Cooperation is the life of any cause." The first cooperative effort consisted of all the churches supporting Smith and Rogers. As the churches grew stronger and learned to give for cooperative work, the support area grew smaller. In 1833 the congregations north of the Kentucky River cooperated to support these two evangelists. By 1835 four counties cooperating were doing a larger work than all the churches earlier.[10]

In May 1831 Campbell began a series of five essays on the subject of cooperation and organized work in *The Millennial Harbinger.* In the absence of Campbell the second and third articles were written by Walter Scott but do not materially change the viewpoint that was the logical forerunner of state and national organizations and societies. The essays

9. Alonzo W. Fortune, *The Disciples in Kentucky,* p. 111.
10. Fortune, *The Disciples in Kentucky,* pp. 198-200.

thoroughly explored the theme of cooperation culminating in the proposition that where the task is too great for a local congregation, many congregations should go together to perform it. Campbell wrote: "A church can do what an individual disciple cannot, and so can a district of churches do what a single congregation cannot."[11] Campbell soon urged the churches to take the steps necessary toward cooperation among themselves. When in 1832 a gentleman from Virginia wrote Campbell urging that an evangelist be employed on a yearly basis through general financial subscription, Campbell approved, saying: "The suggestion appears to us every way reasonable, just, and expedient."[12]

Within the next several years churches in districts of several states were cooperating in the employment of evangelists for their territory. The congregations of Brooke County, Virginia (in which Campbell lived), cooperated in employing an evangelist to work among them. Two counties in Indiana cooperated in sending out John O'Kane (1802-1881) in 1833. His work resulted in the founding of the first Christian church in Indianapolis. Great care was usually taken to explain that such "cooperation" raised up no authority over the congregations. Even so, some of the preachers were suspicious of the new arrangement.

It was only logical that sooner or later such county and district cooperation would lead to statewide organization. In 1834 several congregations were expelled from a "Christian Conference" in New York state and proceeded to organize a Pennsylvania Christian Conference. The Disciples in Pennsylvania date their annual state meetings from this event. About the same time a plan for statewide support of an evangelist was begun by several congregations cooperating in and around Springfield, Illinois. A notice in *The Millennial Harbinger* sent in by J. M. Mathes of Gosport, Indiana, announced a statewide meeting for Indiana for June 1839. The meeting, held in Indianapolis, June 7-11, was well attended. John O'Kane presided. Resolutions on education, on cooperation, and on supporting evangelists were made and discussed. Barton W. Stone was present and preached before a sizable audience. There were 139 congregations reported in the state

---

11. *Millennial Harbinger*, 1831, p. 237.
12. *Millennial Harbinger*, 1832, p. 598.

with nearly 8,000 members. Thus the churches of Indiana brought into being the first statewide assembly. Before adjourning, the next meeting was set for June 1840.[13]

Alexander Campbell, possibly thinking of the Indiana meeting, wrote in 1839 in *The Millennial Harbinger:*

An annual meeting in some central point in each state in the union, conducted on similar principles, exhibiting the statistics of the churches united in the primitive faith and manners, would in many ways greatly promote the prosperity of the cause. Co-operation and combination of effort is the great secret of success.[14]

Other states soon followed Indiana with organizations. The first Kentucky state meeting was held at Harrodsburg in May 1840 to explore "the Scriptural means of extending the Redeemer's Kingdom." A similar meeting was called for June 2 at Charlottesville, Virginia. Campbell promised to be there and also to attend meetings in Illinois and Missouri if at all possible.[15] The move toward organization and structure was in full swing.

TOWARD A NATIONAL ORGANIZATION

In the years prior to 1840 the trend was definitely toward cooperation; from 1840 on the question of formalizing this cooperation in organizations became ever more insistent. It was obvious that a means would have to be found to support the increasing number of employed evangelists, to nurture the growing number of congregations, to educate preachers, and to protect the congregations from unscrupulous and fanatical leaders. Some of the Disciples recognized the need for a means of cooperation on a national scale while other preachers and lay leaders were uneasy at the prospect. It is equally clear that they wished to do only that which was scriptural but were not quite certain what such a principle would or would not allow. All were agreed to proceed cautiously. To move quickly or indiscreetly would undoubtedly arouse controversy.

In 1842 Alexander Campbell began a series of essays on "Church Organization" in *The Millennial Harbinger* which

---

13. *Millennial Harbinger,* 1839, p. 284 and p. 352.
14. *Millennial Harbinger,* 1839, p. 353.
15. *Millennial Harbinger,* 1840, pp. 188-189.

ran for the next several years until 1848. The first essay is in a sense the most important as it represents a charter for organizational development beyond the local congregation. From this principle many organizational and structural developments were to emerge over the next century and a quarter. In this article he sets forth five arguments for organization, ending in a stated principle. Campbell wrote:

1. We can do comparatively nothing in distributing the Bible abroad without co-operation.
2. We can do comparatively but little in the great missionary field of the world either at home or abroad without co-operation.
3. We can do little or nothing to improve or elevate the Christian ministry without co-operation.
4. We can do but little to check, restrain, and remove the flood of imposture and fraud committed upon the benevolence of the brethren by irresponsible, plausible, and deceptive persons, without co-operation.
5. We cannot concentrate the action of the tens of thousands of Israel, in any great Christian effort, but by co-operation.

He then states a principle: "We can have no thorough co-operation without a more ample, extensive, and thorough church organization."[16]

Such concerns must have been in the mind of those "elders and teachers of the Christian Church" who "met according to previous arrangements from different parts of the United States and the Republic of Texas in the basement of the Church of Christ in Lexington, Ky. . . . on the 16th day of Nov. 1843." Sixty-seven persons are recorded as having been present; forty-five of that number came from Kentucky. Seven were from Ohio, six from Indiana, five from Illinois, and one each from New York, Pennsylvania, Tennessee, and Texas. Strangely, there were no representatives from Missouri. The gathering included D. S. Burnet, James Challen, Jacob Creath, Sr., Jesse B. Ferguson, John Allen Gano, John O'Kane, L. L. Pinkerton, James Shannon, and "Raccoon" John Smith. The meeting was held during the time of the Campbell-Rice debate. Although Campbell was in Lexington at the time, he must have chosen not to attend.[17]

---

16. *Millennial Harbinger*, 1842, p. 523. In the original article there is a second number five, probably a typographical error.
17. SEE the minutes of the meeting as recorded by D. Pat Henderson. Disciples of Christ Historical Society, Nashville, Tennessee.

John T. Johnson was selected to preside and D. Pat Henderson (1810-1897) was chosen clerk. The gathering agreed that the purpose of the meeting was to take up the question of church organization. A committee was appointed to draw up a presentation of the subject for discussion and only those brothers who "shall have had their names recorded. . . . shall be allowed to participate in this meeting." Apparently an attempt was made to form a missionary society, for Jacob Creath, Sr. (1777-1854) used his powers of persuasion to get the gathering to abandon the plan. Several important questions were raised by the holding of this meeting. Why was Campbell absent? Why was the meeting not reported in *The Millennial Harbinger* or the *Christian Messenger?* Henderson was working with Barton W. Stone on the paper at the time and was even publishing articles in favor of organization. Considering the ambivalent position of the Disciples on organization, it is only reasonable to assume that some of the leaders may have felt it would be wise to meet quietly and discuss the issues before proceeding further toward national organization.

In the fall of 1844 a meeting was requested by the churches of western Virginia and eastern Ohio to discuss church organization and cooperation. A preliminary conference, chaired by Alexander Campbell, was held at Steubenville, Ohio, in October. Proposals favoring organization were drafted to be discussed at a general meeting. Meetings were held at Wellsburg on December 26, 1844, and on April 1, 1845, at which time "propositions open to discussion but not demanded of anyone" were offered. They were not presenting "a system of resolutions or propositions to be adopted either as matters of expediency or moral obligation."[18] Campbell tried to make it plain that these meetings were only for the purpose of discussion. Other voices soon were raising organizational questions in several of the journals.

For some time D. S. Burnet had been giving leadership to numerous causes of the churches. He was an effective preacher and speaker, an editor and educator. It was as an organizer, however, that he made his most important contribution to the Disciples. Son of a prominent Cincinnati

---

18. *Millennial Harbinger*, 1845, p. 59 ff.

family, he was destined to be one of the outstanding Disciples leaders. When Burnet and other local supporters organized an "American Christian Bible Society" on January 27, 1845, at Cincinnati, the next step in a developing national organization was taken. Duly reported in *The Millennial Harbinger,* the announcement of such a society brought forth a variety of opinions. Aylett Raines (1788-1881) of Ohio suggested that if separate Bible society existence was justified at all for Disciples, it should be as an auxiliary to other Bible societies. As matters turned out, this was the position favored by Campbell. He argued in the pages of *The Millennial Harbinger* against "the propriety of any institution being got up under the patronage of any society . . . without a general understanding some way [being] obtained of the concurrence and support of the whole brotherhood in the scheme."[19] In this statement Campbell seemed to be putting into practice the principle of organization he had been arguing theoretically for several years.

D. S. Burnet was quick to respond to Campbell's opposition. Addressing a letter to *The Millennial Harbinger* he complained that Campbell had reported only negative reactions to the society. He asked if there had been a convention of the churches to establish Bethany College. To Campbell's objection that "our churches" cannot sustain more institutions than "our colleges," Burnet replied that it "has been shown we have *our* Bible Society as well as *our* Colleges and . . . the churches . . . have responded." To conclude the debate Campbell indicated that he would agree to support the new organization when his objections were answered.[20] This prolonged discussion brought the subject of organization into the open. The question was now taken up by editors far and wide: articles pro and con appeared in *Christian Review, Bible Advocate, Christian Record, Primitive Christian, Genius of Christianity,* and others. Later that year Campbell wrote:

Much has been written, a great deal said, and little done, on the whole subject of Christian organization. But there is a growing interest in the subject manifested, and there is a growing need felt for a more scriptural and efficient organization and co-operation.[21]

---

19. *Millennial Harbinger,* 1845, p. 372.
20. *Millennial Harbinger,* 1845, pp. 453-456.
21. *Millennial Harbinger,* 1845, p. 59.

The Bible Society never had much support and in 1856 the Ohio State Convention voted to terminate the society and turn its funds over to the American Bible Union.[22] Thus ended the first attempt at general organization.

The widespread discussion of the question of church organization and Campbell's essays on the subject between 1845 and 1848 produced a desire for some sort of general structure through which all the churches could cooperate to evangelize the world. By the spring of 1849 Campbell urged the "brethren" to forward to him their "objections, approval or emendations" and suggested that if his views were agreed upon, "we will despatch the matter with all speed and concur with them in the call of a general meeting in Cincinnati, Lexington, Louisville or Pittsburgh."[23] There was much in favor of holding the gathering in Cincinnati. The growing city was in the center of the largest number of Disciples congregations and was sufficiently near to the growing edge of the churches in Indiana, Illinois, and Missouri. Moreover, it was easily accessible by steamboat, the main method of travel in those days. October was the time agreed upon.

In the August 1849 issue of *The Millennial Harbinger* Campbell expressed his hopes and fears for the convention. He said:

> I am of the opinion that a Convention, or general meeting, of the churches of the Reformation is a very great desideratum. . . . I am also of opinion that Cincinnati is the proper place for holding such Convention . . . it should not be a Convention of Book-makers or of Editors, to concoct a great book concern; but a Convention of messengers of churches, selected and constituted such by the churches—one from every church, if possible, or if impossible, one from a district, or some definite number of churches. It is not to be composed of a few self-appointed . . . messengers from one, two, or three districts, or States, but a *general* Convention.[24]

In fact, the convention, planned for October 24-28, 1849, was set to coincide with the annual meeting of the Bible Society and a Sunday School and Tract Society organized in Cincinnati at approximately the same time as the society. The custom was for both agencies to meet in what were called

---

22. Earl I. West, *The Search for the Ancient Order* (Indianapolis: Religious Book Service, 1950). Vol. I, p. 165.
23. *Millennial Harbinger,* 1849, p. 273.
24. *Millennial Harbinger,* 1849, pp. 475-476.

"Anniversaries" on dates adjoining one another. The decision was made to broaden the purpose of these more-or-less localized meetings and announce a nationwide gathering. By word of mouth, private correspondence, and the various papers, the word was spread. The cooperative and organizational character of the movement was mandated in these actions of 1849. At the same time, the stage for future division was set.

On October 23, 1849, 156 delegates from nearly as many congregations and representing eleven states gathered in Cincinnati for the first national convention of the Disciples. The Christian Church at the corner of Fourth and Walnut Streets was host to the meeting. The session of October 23 concerned itself with the annual meeting of the American Christian Bible Society. D. S. Burnet gave an address and suggested adjournment at the earliest possible time so that the convention could get under way. L. L. Pinkerton was called forward to preside. The first order of business was the election of officers. Alexander Campbell, either because of poor health or for strategic reasons, was not present but was represented by W. K. Pendleton; nevertheless he was elected president. Four vice-presidents were chosen: D. S. Burnet, John O'Kane, John T. Johnson, and Walter Scott. A committee was appointed to plan the order of business for the next day.

The second session was held the next morning with D. S. Burnet presiding in the absence of Campbell. The first major issue to surface was the question of what constituted a delegate. Discussion followed as to who should be allowed to vote. The only state to send elected delegates was Indiana. Other individuals attending the convention had been officially designated by local congregations or by district meetings. The convention, however, was mostly composed of preachers and workers who had come on their own initiative out of interest and concern. With such a wide range of representation, and knowing the existence of an undercurrent of suspicion against "ecclesiastical authority," the convention voted to allow all present to participate fully and freely in the business of the meeting. The first national convention became a mass meeting in spite of Campbell's desire that it be a gathering of elected "messengers." Disciples conventions, though modified later, continued to be mass meetings until the constitution of the International Convention was amended in 1967, providing for voting representatives.

One of the first acts of the convention was to give approval of and encouragement to the American Christian Bible Society. The problem of obtaining an orderly ordination of ministers and a means of recommending qualified preachers to the churches was another early matter of business. The convention, for the most part, confined itself to practical aspects of Christian work. It resolved to seek organization of Sunday schools in every congregation and a strict observance of the Lord's Day. It urged the churches to form district and state meetings and to report the names and addresses of congregations and their leaders.

The basic concern of the convention, however, was the worldwide proclamation of the gospel. The lesser matters of officers, public morals, and agencies having been disposed of, the convention got down to the business of world evangelism. On the afternoon of October 24 John T. Johnson offered a resolution proposing the formation of a missionary society. The proposal was approved and a committee was appointed to draft a constitution for such an agency. The die was cast. There would be permanent organization.

The remaining business consisted of hearing the report of the constitutional committee and deciding such details as the name and function of a missionary organization. Should the purpose of the Bible society be expanded to include the missionary cause or should missions have a separate organization? Separate agencies were agreed upon. What name should be given the new agency? To be called the American Christian Missionary Society, its work was to include home as well as foreign missions. Annual meetings were to be held at Cincinnati the third week of October or at a time and place agreed upon at a previous annual meeting.

Before adjournment it was necessary to elect officers for the newly formed agency. Since Campbell previously had been elected president of the convention, it was decided he should be president of the missionary society. Twenty vice-presidents (distributed geographically) were chosen. They were: D. S. Burnet (Ohio), Dr. Irwin (Ohio), Walter Scott (Pennsylvania), T. M. Allen (Missouri), W. K. Pendleton (Virginia), John T. Jones (Illinois), John O'Kane (Indiana),

John T. Johnson (Kentucky), Tolbert Fanning (Tennessee), Dr. Daniel Hook (Georgia), Dr. E. Parmley (New York), Francis Dungan (Maryland), Richard Hawley (Michigan), Dr. James T. Barclay (Virginia), Francis Palmer (Missouri), J. J. Moss (Ohio), M. Mobley (Iowa), William Rowzee (Pennsylvania), Alexander Graham (Alabama), and William Clark (Mississippi). James Challen was elected corresponding secretary, George S. Jenkins, recording secretary, and Archibald Trowbridge, treasurer.[25]

The enthusiasm of the convention was contagious. Life memberships (at $20 each) and life directorships (at $100 each) were offered. Any church could appoint a delegate for a $10 annual contribution. The appeal was such that $2,140 was subscribed and enough pledges were taken to total over $5,000 before the convention closed on October 28.

Dr. James T. Barclay (1807-1874) of Virginia, elected vice-president of the ACMS at Cincinnati, was a graduate of the University of Virginia and of the medical department of the University of Pennsylvania. Barclay was later the first missionary of the society, serving in the Holy Land. He had been urging the missionary cause, had offered to accept service abroad, and had suggested that a New Testament approach to missionary effort should "begin at Jerusalem."

Scarcely had those individuals who were at Cincinnati got home before objections began to be raised against the actions they had taken.[26] Critics took exception 1) to the creation of any agency beyond the local congregation to do the work of the church and 2) to the agency's requirement of a cash payment (either in annual subscription, life membership, or directorship) to participate. Both these objections were a part of the complaint of the elders of the congregation at Connellsville, Pennsylvania, against the society.[27] One influential participant at the convention, Benjamin Franklin (1812-1878), agreed emphatically that such organizations were scriptural and acceptable. As a great admirer of Alexander Campbell, he at first followed Campbell's leadership in

---

25. *Millennial Harbinger*, 1849, p. 691.
26. Eva Jean Wrather, *Creative Freedom in Action—Alexander Campbell on the Structures of the Church* (St. Louis: The Bethany Press, 1968). Also, Ronald E. Osborn, "The Structures of Cooperation, Its Developments in the Historical Thought of Disciples of Christ," *Mid-Stream*, II, 1962, pp. 28-49.
27. *Millennial Harbinger*, 1850, pp. 282-284.

NINETEENTH CENTURY EDITOR BISHOPS

Isaac Errett   D. S. Burnet   Tolbert Fanning

J. H. Garrison   Benjamin Franklin   M. M. Goodwin

Moses E. Lard   David Lipscomb   J. W. McGarvey

An old cliche asserts, "Disciples do not have bishops; they have editors." Each of these editors exerted great influence over a group within the developing movement

organizational matters. Franklin had second thoughts, however, and soon held with equal positiveness that missionary societies were unscriptural.[28] Both Jacob Creath and Jacob Creath, Jr., wrote long letters to *The Millennial Harbinger* in opposition to the missionary society. These early complaints foreshadowed trouble to come.

On the whole, however, there was relatively little published discussion of the basic issues of organization. With the exception of the Creaths, Benjamin Franklin, and Tolbert Fanning most editors were favorable to the new directions. Interest in the first convention and the missionary society was expressed among many of the congregations. In time stronger opposition would arise. One indirect result of the national convention was the move toward further state organization. Anticipating the Cincinnati convention, formal organization of the Indiana Christian Missionary Society was accomplished October 6, 1849. Other states soon followed Indiana's lead. The first Kentucky state meeting was held at Harrodsburg in May 1840 with organization of the Kentucky Christian Missionary Society in 1850. The state convention of churches and Ohio Christian Missionary Society were formed in 1852. The pattern had been established for future state organizations.

One development resulting from the General Convention of 1849 was the launching of a brotherhood publishing enterprise. Even though it failed later, the American Christian Publication Society presaged the future. The convention had given recognition to a Cincinnati Tract Society. At the same time several men of the churches of the Western Reserve proposed to start a Sunday school library which would involve publishing study materials. The project, presented to the convention, was referred to a committee. Later a recommendation was made that the two ventures should be combined into one publication society. In 1851 they became the "American Christian Publication Society."

The American Christian Publication Society in May 1853 purchased a journal called the *Christian Age* published at Cincinnati. This magazine started in 1845 by T. J. Mellish had absorbed Walter Scott's *Protestant Unionist*. By 1850 D.

28. *Proclamation and Reformer*, 1849, p. 283; 1850, p. 88.

S. Burnet and Benjamin Franklin were the joint owners and editors of the magazine and using it to promote the national societies. The *Christian Age* in 1853 announced a plan for the formation of a new publishing concern to be called the "Bible Union." A $40,000 stock company was to be formed that would divide its profits among the interests of the movement and the stockholders. The company showed losses rather than profits, however, and the scheme was dropped. The publication society continued for a few years with the *Christian Age* as its journal.

Alexander Campbell and his associates at Bethany, who had a great deal to lose from such competition, opposed such a society. W. K. Pendleton, associate editor of *The Millennial Harbinger*, in a series of articles published in 1854 voiced strong opposition to the publication society.[29] This disapproval became a major factor in the defeat of the enterprise. When it is realized that Campbell's private press at Bethany was well established and with so many of the preachers eager to enter the publishing field, it is easily understood why the venture would fail. Many years later the plan for a "brotherhood publishing house" would be revived.

OPPOSITION TO THE "CAMPBELLITES"

The developments from 1830 to 1860 did not occur without opposition from other religious groups. As long as the Disciples were in fellowship with the Baptists, other denominations could loosely identify them as Reformers. After 1830 it became clear to the established denominations that a new religious group was among them. The strategy of the Disciples preachers and evangelists in entering a new community, preaching against creeds and confessions and advocating the "restoration of the ancient order of things," offended Baptists, Presbyterians, Methodists, Episcopalians, and other groups alike. Individually and cooperatively the various denominations used every means at their disposal to oppose the young movement.

The favored taunt was "Campbellite." A common form of attack was the attempt to place the Disciples with odd and already discredited sects. The term "Campbellite" was par-

---

29. *Millennial Harbinger*, 1854, pp. 338-347; pp. 451-453; pp. 531-533; and pp. 625-631.

ticularly offensive to Disciples as their opposition to "sectarian" names was well known (which is probably why it was
used). The Disciples willingness to contend earnestly for their
version of Christian faith in public debate did not make
friends for them. In general, all the debates, including those
of Campbell, were self-defeating to any long-range program
for Christian unity. The pages of *The Millennial Harbinger*
and other Disciples journals often carried items reflecting the
opposition encountered. By means of numerous books,
pamphlets, and articles published in religious journals, individual leaders of other denominations attacked
"Campbellism." Evidence of attacks on the Disciples in
general, and on Alexander Campbell in particular, abounds.

THE QUIET BEFORE THE STORM

After the dramatic events which led to the establishment of
the principle of national cooperation, the decade of the 1850s
settled into a period of quiet but steady growth. With an estimated 22,000 members in fewer than 1,000 congregations in
1832, the Disciples grew to almost nine times that number in
thirty years. "The Plea" entered hundreds of new communities throughout the several states and into Canada. The
Disciples first major strength was in the Ohio valley. Until
this time frontier conditions and habits characterized the
development of the movement. However, for the Midwest,
which was the stronghold of the movement, the frontier may
be said to have passed with the coming of the Civil War.[30]
The rapid growth of the Disciples can be accounted for partially by the following factors: 1) The widespread circulation
of *The Christian Baptist, The Millennial Harbinger,* the
Christian Messenger, and *The Evangelist.* These magazines
of the founding fathers, augmented by the circulation of a
score or more regional and local journals, gave wide dissemination to Disciples views. 2) Before 1830 many Baptist
congregations came over into the movement and large
numbers left other Baptist churches to form Disciples congregations. 3) There was a genuine enthusiasm for the view of
the Disciples which so nearly paralleled those attitudes

---

30. Garrison and DeGroot, *The Disciples of Christ: A History,* SEE Chapters XII,
XIII, XIV for a detailed story of state expansion.

toward individualism and freedom of the frontier American. 4) New communities and towns were being formed. The Disciples message that there was a basis for union in the gospel offered the hope that these communities need not be divided on sectarian lines. 5) Settlers migrated from the older parts of the country such as Ohio, Kentucky, or Tennessee to the newer settlements farther west. As families from Disciples background moved into new areas they took their religious convictions with them. 6) The fruits of cooperation began to be felt as area evangelists succeeded in establishing new congregations. 7) Visits by Alexander Campbell to a particular part of the country nearly always resulted in increased interest in Disciples views. Thomas Campbell also made visits in behalf of the movement. Barton W. Stone's presence in Illinois and visits in Missouri led to the establishment of congregations. These factors, and doubtless others, contributed to rapid growth before the Civil War.

The Disciples have never been numerous in the East and Northeast, but congregations and organizations going back to an early period are found in that area. Park Avenue Christian Church, the oldest existing congregation of Disciples in New York, goes back to 1810 and has a pre-Campbell origin. Work was established in Maryland as early as 1833 as the result of a meeting held by Alexander Campbell on a visit to Baltimore and the District of Columbia. A visit to Philadelphia shortly thereafter resulted in the organization of a congregation there. In Connecticut the Reformers were early represented by a church at Danbury. Organized in 1763, it was known as late as 1840 as the Reformed Baptist Society. A visit from Campbell resulted in its affiliation with the Disciples.

Campbell's fame in Virginia grew greatly after his services as a delegate to the 1829 constitutional convention at Richmond. Independent existence of the Reformers was thrust upon them by the action of the various Baptist churches in withdrawing fellowship from the advocates of "Campbellism." Separation took place in Richmond in 1832, following a visit there by Thomas Campbell, and out of it grew Sycamore Church (later Seventh Street Christian Church), mother of six congregations. As in Virginia, the Baptists of Georgia, North Carolina, and South Carolina were a fertile field for the Disciples proposals on Christian unity and a New Testament church. This was especially true after the visit of Thomas Campbell in 1833, when a district program of the Disciples was proclaimed and shortly thereafter a "Union Meeting" formed. North Carolina had early been the scene of religious experiments similar to those of Stone and the Campbells. A ready audience for Campbell's views was found when *The Christian Baptist* and later *The Millennial Harbinger* found their way into those regions. Many Disciples congregations in Georgia were organized by Nathan W. Smith (1813-1899) in more than sixty years of preaching.

Kentucky soon after 1832 led all the states in the number of congregations and members within the Disciples movement. The general lack of a paid ministry meant that many congregations had no pastoral oversight beyond that of the local eldership plus the occasional visits of traveling evangelists. They were enthusiastic, however, and the movement grew. Alexander Campbell attended the May 1850 convention which organized the Kentucky state missionary society.[31] The cause of the Disciples in Tennessee, as in Kentucky, rested on two foundations: the large number of Christian churches which entered the combined movement, and the many Baptist churches which adopted Campbellian principles after 1830. Between 1842 and 1860 it is estimated that thirty new congregations were organized. By 1860 Tennessee had a total of approximately 106 congregations.[32]

Churches in Alabama were the result of migrations from Georgia and Tennessee, bringing Disciples ideas into the region. The national convention of 1849, in which Alexander Graham was elected a vice-president, stimulated further growth in the state. Alexander Campbell made three tours through Alabama, Mississippi, and Louisiana (in 1839, 1857, and 1859) which resulted in the establishment of many Disciples congregations. Apparently upon requests received on his 1839 tour, Campbell sent an evangelist to do organizing work in Mississippi and Louisiana and appealed for support of his work through *The Millennial Harbinger*. There was also local interest in a simple New Testament Christianity which

---

31. Alonzo W. Fortune, *The Disciples in Kentucky,* p. 351.
32. Herman Norton, *Tennessee Christians,* Nashville: Reed and Company, 1971. p. 83.

soon received support from settlers migrating to the state already committed to similar ideals.

By 1853 Ohio counted approximately eighty congregations active in its state program but migrations of ministers and people to the West were causing concern.[33] The experience of Indiana Disciples was similar to that of Ohio. By 1845 the Indiana state convention was sending two evangelists into each of two districts, one north and one south of the National Road. The 1850 tour of Alexander Campbell through Indiana was a triumph for the Disciples in attracting attention to their movement. A second tour in 1860 with Mrs. Campbell and Isaac Errett in the party was equally successful.[34]

The Stone movement came first to several of the western states and was later joined by Disciples into one movement. Growth came rapidly as the land filled with those who were looking for a church professing the ideals of the Disciples. Periodicals were a strong asset to expansion in Indiana and Illinois as they were for growth elsewhere. Establishment of congregations in Michigan followed evangelism begun there about 1840. Isaac Errett moved to Michigan in 1856, and Benjamin Franklin held evangelistic services in the southern part of the state the same year.

A rush of migration from Kentucky, Tennessee, Virginia, and North Carolina made possible statehood for Missouri in 1821. This wave of settlers brought many followers of Stone and Campbell, making Missouri one of the strongest states of the Disciples. Disciples churches in Missouri, however, have kept the flavor of the "Christian" movement. Annual meetings for cooperation began in 1837, at Bear Creek church, Boone County. What was called the "state meeting" was first held in 1841 at Fayette. Alexander Campbell spoke for the 1845 gathering and received an offering of $400 for Bethany College; 196 congregations were reported with 13,057 members. Work was begun in Arkansas in much the same way it had been begun elsewhere. The first congregation at Little Rock was organized in 1832 as a result of the work of Benjamin F. Hall (1803-1873) of Kentucky. After listening to his preaching the members of a Baptist church, established

33. Henry Shaw, *Buckeye Disciples,* p. 176 and p. 187.
34. Henry Shaw *Hoosier Disciples* (St. Louis: Published by The Bethany Press for the Association of the Christian Churches in Indiana, 1966), pp. 100, 128, and 183.

in 1824, decided to join the Disciples. Again, westward migrations from the South, particularly Kentucky, led to "Christian" congregations being formed first in what is now the state of Texas. They were joined later by Disciples preachers and settlers to form a large number of congregations.

EARLY BLACK DISCIPLES

As the Disciples moved into the Deep South, it was inevitable that they should be drawn into the institution of slavery. By 1850 it is estimated that the Disciples had 310 congregations in the South. Urged to identify himself with the proslavery cause for the sake of further growth in the South, Alexander Campbell consistently refused. It was said that this attitude hurt the Disciples influence in the entire region.[35] There was some growth, however, and not all the growth was in white congregations.

For the most part in the period from 1830 to the Civil War, any Negro members of the Disciples were slaves enrolled by their masters as members of a particular congregation. However, a small number of black Disciples, preachers and people, were free. When slaves were members of their masters' congregations, they usually sat apart from the white members. The evidence is abundant to show that slave members generally were segregated either in a special section of the sanctuary or in a balcony if there was one. The balcony at Cane Ridge in Kentucky was used for this purpose. A balcony was set apart for slaves in the First Christian Church, Little Rock, Arkansas. The slave members of the Christian Church at Crittenden, Kentucky, sat in the last rows of pews at the rear of the church.

Slave members were commonly recorded under their owner's name. Apparently there was no difficulty anywhere in white preachers accepting the confession of black men and women and admitting them into the fellowship of the church. There is evidence Campbell himself baptized candidates of all races.[36] It is doubtful, however, if great numbers of slaves

---

35. *Millennial Harbinger*, 1857, pp. 502-507.
36. Robert L. Jordan, *Two Races in One Fellowship* (Detroit: United Christian Church, 1944). p. 24.

or freedmen at any time joined the Disciples. Not only were the Disciples a relatively new movement; they were growing most rapidly in areas outside the slave states.

Sometime before 1838 there is record of a congregation in Savannah, Georgia, led by Andrew Marshall, a mulatto, who was a convert from the Baptists to "Campbellism." He bought freedom for himself and his family, built a large congregation, and was an able and popular preacher. On a visit to the city Alexander Campbell preached to this congregation. Under white Baptist pressure Marshall later rejoined the Baptists.[37] Isolated instances of similar black congregations were to be found in other areas.

The separation of black Disciples, when they were sufficiently large in number, from white congregations began before the Civil War. A white congregation at Nashville, Tennessee, in 1849 reported it had two "colored Sunday Schools with 125 pupils." Ten years later, in 1859, one of these Sunday schools was organized into a congregation. Located in West Nashville and called Grapevine Church, it is considered the first black congregation of the Disciples in the South.[38] As the interracial congregation at Midway, Kentucky, grew, money was provided by the whites to erect a building for black members so that they might meet separately. The black congregation was led by a former slave, converted at Cane Ridge meetinghouse and freed to preach, who took the name of Alexander Campbell as his own. He obtained a job as a porter at Lexington, attended Transylvania University, led in the erection of the black congregation's building at Midway, and converted over 300 persons to Christ. After three years' work he was able to buy freedom for his wife, Rosa. Their two sons followed the father into the Christian ministry.[39]

Not all black members or congregations were in the South. Two early black churches are on record in Ohio during this period. An interracial congregation was formed with members at Stantontown and Marengo in Morrow County in

37. James Simms, *The First Colored Baptist Church in North America* (Philadelphia: J. B. Lippincott and Co., 1888), p. 93 ff. Also J. Edward Moseley, *The Disciples In Georgia* (St. Louis: Bethany Press, 1954), pp. 77-78.
38. *Christian Magazine,* 1849, Vol. II, p. 422. Also, Norton, *Tennessee Christians,* p. 129.
39. Robert L. Jordan, *Two Races in One Fellowship,* p. 29.

1842. The church existed until sometime after the Civil War. A black congregation was organized at Pickerelltown, Logan County, in 1838 and named the "Christian Disciple Church." Disbanded in 1856, this church was famous as an underground railroad station in pre-Civil War days.[40] A few additional congregations were to be found in other northern states.

Most of the membership of black Disciples prior to the Civil War was in predominantly white congregations. There were probably fewer than 1,000 members in separate black churches. The remaining black Disciples were members of white congregations. The slave-holding states of Kentucky, Tennessee, Virginia, and North Carolina had the largest number of black Disciples.[41]

WESTWARD TO THE PACIFIC

The Disciples organized their first congregation in Iowa, at Dubuque, on October 1, 1835. Settlers moving in from the East brought with them the ideas and practices of the Campbells. Cooperative meetings among the Iowa congregations began at Mount Pleasant in 1842 when organized congregations were reported as being at work in eight counties. The first state meeting was held at Marion in 1850. The state convention of 1859 received reports of ninety-one congregations with 4,859 members. The Disciples work in Minnesota began shortly before 1860. Nebraska came to statehood only in 1867, but by 1847 the Disciples were preaching to the white settlers of the territory and by 1854 had organized a congregation at Brownville, in Nemaha County. Pardee Butler (1816-1888) was chief among the pioneers who laid the foundations for the strength of the Disciples in Kansas, whose earliest congregations, meeting in sod houses of members or in schoolhouses, date from 1854-1855.

By 1850 the Disciples had gone overland to the Pacific coast. No sooner had the first scouts blazed a trail to Oregon than the Disciples followed them into the Willamette valley. Today the Disciples have many congregations in the state. In

---

40. Henry Shaw, *Buckeye Disciples,* pp. 143-144.
41. Hap Lyda, *A History of Black Christian Churches (Disciples of Christ) In the United States Through 1899* (Ann Arbor: University Microfilms, 1973), p. 37.

1843 a train of 1,000 persons arrived from Missouri with several Disciples in the group. The first congregations were formed in 1845 and 1846. By 1860 the Oregon Christian Missionary Society had been organized. The area now known as California, Nevada, Utah, Colorado, Arizona, and New Mexico was ceded by Mexico to the United States in 1848. With the discovery of gold by Sutter, the rush of Forty-Niners brought many Disciples to California. During the winter of 1850-51 the first Disciples congregation in California was organized at Stockton. Other congregations soon followed. Disciples were organizing congregations in Washington before it became a territory in 1853, but growth was slow.

Statistics for the Disciples before 1860 are to be found mainly in evangelists' reports to the journals. At best it is possible only to estimate their growth. Belcher's *Religious Denominations in the United States,* based on figures obtained from Alexander Campbell, shows 225,000 members, 2,700 congregations, and 2,225 ministers in 1857.[42] Other sources, however, indicate that by 1860 the Disciples most probably had a membership of no more than 195,000 persons (including 5,000 black members) located in 2,100 congregations, with 1,800 ministers scattered from the Atlantic seaboard to the shores of the Pacific Ocean, and from Upper Canada to the Deep South. It was the quiet before the storm. The nation would soon be at war and hopelessly divided.

---

42. Joseph Belcher, *Religious Denominations in the United States* (Philadelphia: John K. Potter, 1857), p. 811.

8

THE WRENCHING OF THE FELLOWSHIP

The entrenched institution of black slavery was a condemnation upon white America in the early period of the Disciples. Between 1808—the year before Alexander Campbell left Scotland to join his father in western Pennsylvania—and 1860, the slave population in the South increased from 1,160,000 to more than 3,500,000. Forced to respond to the volatile and overwhelming problem, Congress passed the Missouri Compromise, the Fugitive Slave Law, the Kansas-Nebraska Act, and other legislation. None of the decisions resolved the fundamental issue at stake, however, and the nation—half-slave and half-free—moved inexorably toward a date with disaster.

As fall turned to winter, in November 1860, Abraham Lincoln was elected President of the United States. Of the 1,866,000 popular votes cast for him, a mere 26,000 came from Dixie. Five days before Christmas South Carolina withdrew from the Union. A new government, the Confederate States of America, was formed in early February 1861. Speaking directly to the South in his First Inaugural, Lincoln said: "We are not enemies, but friends. We must not be enemies. Though passion may have strained, it must not break, our bonds of affection." Earlier in the address he had reminded the intransigents: "You have no oath registered in Heaven to destroy the government, while I shall have the most solemn one to 'preserve, protect, and defend' it." All hope of averting war was dashed on April 12 when Confederate forces opened fire on Fort Sumter in the harbor of Charleston.

For four solid years the Civil War spent its fury, leaving in its wake a pattern of death and destruction. Before Robert E. Lee surrendered to Ulysses S. Grant at Appomattox in 1865, North and South together suffered over 600,000 casualties—more than the total loss of American life in all the other wars in the nation's history from the Revolution through the war in Southeast Asia.

Writing for the January issue of *The Millennial Harbinger* in 1864, the aged and infirm Alexander Campbell gathered his wits and plaintively asked: "Shall we see our long labors go down in the storm of an hour, and give ourselves and our sacred charge, without an effort or struggle, up to the devouring elements?"[1] Alarmed and dismayed, the patriarch of Disciples had every reason to be concerned about the movement which had claimed his mind and heart for over half a century. Both Presbyterian bodies had divided north and south, and the slavery issue had split Methodists and Baptists in the mid-1840s. Clearly the situation of Disciples was precarious. In 1860 they had 829 congregations in the South and 1,241 in the North. Sparse in the deep South and sparser still in New England, they were strong in the strife-torn border states. Regardless of the threat to their unity and growing strength, Disciples could not avoid the trauma of war and the wrenching of their fellowship.

DISCIPLES AND SLAVERY

The founders of the Disciples were basically of one mind in their personal attitude toward slavery.[2] They opposed it unequivocally but did not accept abolition as an answer to the haunting question of what to do about it. There were shifts in the emphasis and variations in the intensity of their witness over the years, to be sure, but on balance their rejection of

---

1. *Millennial Harbinger*, January 1864, p. 4.
2. For an excellent treatment of Disciples and the slavery issue SEE David E. Harrell, *Quest for a Christian America: The Disciples of Christ and American Society to 1866*, pp. 91-138.

immediate emancipation was as pronounced as their opposition to slavery. An unyielding commitment to Christian unity as their cardinal principle figured prominently in their decision to stand against extremists on both sides of the issue. They were determined to keep Disciples from splitting over political disagreements. To justify their reasoning, they insisted that the New Testament did not explicitly condemn slavery. Having agreed to speak where the New Testament speaks and to remain silent where the New Testament is silent, they argued stoutly that one's position on slavery was a matter of "opinion" rather than "faith" and should not become a test of Christian fellowship. For this reason, they spoke out against the institution of slavery but maintained full communion with their brothers and sisters among the Disciples who were slaveholders.

Not a man of means, Stone nevertheless owned several slaves early in his ministry. Prior to the formation of the Springfield Presbytery, according to his own testimony, he emancipated them "from a sense of right, choosing poverty with a good conscience, in preference to all the treasures of the world."[3] Subsequently, he inherited a black child about six years old. When the slave reached the age of twenty-five, Stone freed him and cooperated with the Georgetown Colonization Society in sending him to Liberia. In 1830 a rumor circulated that Stone had changed his mind on slavery and was in fact a slaveowner. To set the record straight, he acknowledged that seven blacks—three adults and four children—were living with him and his family. Then he explained the circumstances: "They were bequeathed by my wife's mother, to her and her children, forever; . . . Over these you may see I have no control—nor have I any more right to emancipate them, than you or anyone else."[4]

In Stone's judgment, the practice of slavery was both immoral and unwise. "There is no intelligent man in our country," he wrote in 1833, "who does not confess that slavery is anti-Christian, . . . that it is ruining our country, and the morals of our children; and will ultimately, if persisted in, be the plague and destruction of the white population."[5] For a

3. *The Biography of Elder Barton Warren Stone*, p. 44.
4. *Christian Messenger*, December 1830, pp. 276-277.
5. *Christian Messenger*, September 1833, p. 274.

number of years Stone championed the work of the American
Colonization Society, founded in 1817 to send free blacks
back to Africa. The results of the society's work failed to
measure up to his expectations, however, and he spent the
declining years of his life in relative silence on the issue of
slavery.

As editor of the *Evangelist,* Walter Scott became embroiled in controversy over slavery in 1834. One reader asked
to have his subscription canceled because Scott refused to
open his "batteries upon this citadel of the devil." This request led to an extended and heated correspondence, all of
which appeared in the columns of the *Evangelist.*
Throughout the interchange Scott took issue with the argument that one must be proslavery if he rejects abolitionism.
Like Barton W. Stone, Scott deplored slavery but could not
see his way to work for the immediate emancipation of all
slaves.[6]

Both of the Campbells shared a personal aversion to the institution of slavery. Of the two, Thomas probably was more
forceful in his opposition. In 1819, for example, he spent an
afternoon reading the Bible and explaining it to a group of
slaves in Burlington, Kentucky. He had moved to this small
community over a year earlier to establish a school for youth
in the area. Upon learning that he had violated a state law
which prohibited any public address to blacks without white
witnesses, he promptly left Kentucky in protest and returned
to Pennsylvania.

A prosperous farmer in Virginia, Alexander Campbell had
a few slaves. His second wife, Selina (1802-1897), discussed
her husband's experience as a slaveholder in her published
reminiscences. Shortly before their marriage, she reported,
Campbell purchased two brothers, James and Charley Pool,
from a Methodist preacher. Honoring his promise, Campbell
freed them when they reached the age of twenty-eight.
Referring to another slave, Mrs. Campbell wrote: "There was
a young colored woman named Mary, who had such a bad
disposition and strong will of her own, that I was glad for Mr.
C. to make her a present to her father, who lived in Pennsylvania." She also mentioned "a boy named Ben" who

---

6. SEE Dwight E. Stevenson, *Walter Scott: Voice of the Golden Oracle,* pp. 150-
156.

"frequently sang for visitors and charmed them with the sweetness and pathos of his voice."[7] Although Mrs. Campbell did not say so, Ben lived to become a free person as did every other slave ever owned by her husband. Testified Campbell: "I have set free from slavery every human being that came in any way under my influence or was my property."[8]

Alexander Campbell's discussion of the slavery issue was subject to far more misunderstanding than his record as a slaveholder. Shifting his emphasis according to the mood of the nation and special circumstances in the church, he sometimes appeared to be antislavery, sometimes proslavery.[9] Proponents of both viewpoints could either quote him with full approval or marshal enough evidence to prove that he was one of their principal adversaries. All along Campbell made a distinction between his responsibilities as a citizen and his obligations as a Christian. As a citizen he was "constitutionally, religiously, and economically" antislavery even though he admitted: "Much as I may sympathize with a black man, I love the white man more." As a Christian he felt obliged to obey the law of the land (he urged compliance with the provisions of the Fugitive Slave Law in 1851, for example) and to accept the authoritative message of the New Testament. The law sanctioned slavery while the New Testament did not condemn it. Consequently, Campbell pressed for slavery to be humanized but not eradicated. Rejecting the inflammatory message of abolitionists in favor of a moderate approach, he was convinced that his mediating position if broadly accepted would enable Disciples of Christ to survive as *one* people.

Campbell's most extensive treatment of the slavery issue appeared in *The Millennial Harbinger* in 1845. A year earlier Methodists had divided "along Mason's and Dixon's line," and debate over the annexation of Texas had provoked a fresh wave of moral outrage among abolitionists. Both events prompted Campbell to write a series of eight articles entitled "Our Position to American Slavery."

---

7. Selina H. Campbell, *Home Life and Reminiscences of Alexander Campbell* (St. Louis: John Burns, Publisher, 1882), pp. 454-455.

8. *Millennial Harbinger*, June 1845, p. 259.

9. For an excellent discussion of Alexander Campbell's thought on slavery SEE Harold L. Lunger, *The Political Ethics of Alexander Campbell* (St. Louis: The Bethany Press, 1954), pp. 193-232.

Antislavery Disciples, not to mention abolitionists, found little in the series to bolster their sagging confidence in the moral leadership of *The Millennial Harbinger's* editor. Regardless of his intentions, his reasoning amounted to a defense of slavery in the light of the New Testament witness. He placed great emphasis on the Apostle Paul's insistence that every man should "abide in the same calling wherein he was called" (1 Corinthians 7:20). Instead of hedging, he stated flatly that "the simple relation of master and slave" is *not* "necessarily and essentially immoral and unchristian." Concluding the series, he summarized his position in three propositions: (1) The master-slave relation is not "in itself sinful and immoral." (2) Slavery, nevertheless, is "inexpedient." (3) No Christian community "governed by the Bible can constitutionally and rightfully" make slavery "a term of Christian fellowship or a subject of discipline."

Throughout the slavery controversy Campbell, a one-time iconoclast in the church, tried mightily to act as a moderate and judicious leader of a sizable religious movement. "To preserve unity of spirit among Christians of the South and of the North," he confessed, "is my grand object." He added:

Every man who loves the American Union, as well as every man who desires a constitutional end of American slavery, is bound to prevent, as far as possible, any breach of communion between Christians at the South and at the North. No sensible abolitionist, who either loves the Union or who desires the amelioration of the condition of the slave, can look upon the disruption of the Methodist community . . . but with the most profound regret. Any one pleased with such a result, as to its bearings upon slavery, is a fanatic rather than a philanthropist or a Christian.[10]

Without question, the welfare and unity of Disciples were more important to Campbell than either the amelioration or eradication of slavery.

A number of Disciples leaders in the South saw no reason to quarrel with Alexander Campbell's angle of vision. Whether they owned slaves or not, they accepted the pattern of life common to their section and remained content to ponder the mounting controversy over slavery without engaging in it. Southern Disciples by no means were unified in their

---

10. *Millennial Harbinger*, May 1845, pp. 195-196; in the same volume also SEE pp. 70, 145, 263-264.

outlook, however, as can be seen in the contrast between the approaches of Mrs. Emily H. Tubman (1794-1885) and James Shannon (1799-1859).

Emily Thomas, a native of Virginia, grew up in Kentucky and married the wealthy Richard C. Tubman of Maryland in 1818. The couple spent their summers in Kentucky and their winters in Augusta, Georgia, enjoying the benefits of aristocracy in both places. Although her husband was an Episcopalian, Mrs. Tubman became a Disciple. Baptized near Frankfort, Kentucky, in 1828, she affiliated with the Disciples in Augusta shortly after her husband's death in 1836. Having no children, Mrs. Tubman used her fortune to support church and other charitable causes. In addition to providing funds for many local church buildings, she contributed generously to several Disciples colleges and gave financial assistance to a number of young men in preparation for ministry. Among them were James S. Lamar (1829-1908) and William T. Moore (1832-1926), both highly respected preachers of the Disciples in the post-Civil War era.

In view of her wealth, it is not surprising that this Georgia woman was a large slaveholder. In the 1830s she gave her blacks the choice to accept freedom or to remain in slavery. Sixty-nine chose freedom and were sent to Liberia with their transportation underwritten by Mrs. Tubman. According to the historian of Georgia Disciples, two of the manumitted blacks were William Shadrach and Sylvia Ann Elizabeth Tubman. Their grandson, William Vaccanarat Shadrach Tubman, became the eighteenth President of the Republic of Liberia.[11] A moderate on the question of slavery and an uncommonly generous woman, Mrs. Emily H. Tubman earned the reputation as one of the great philanthropists among Disciples of Christ.

Unlike Mrs. Tubman, James Shannon was as much of a firebrand as any Disciple of his time. An intense Irishman, he emigrated to the United States after completing classical work at the University of Belfast. The study of Alexander Campbell's writings persuaded him to join the Disciples, and he became a forceful preacher as well as a brilliant educator. At one time a professor of ancient languages at the University

---

11. J. Edward Moseley, *Disciples of Christ in Georgia* (St. Louis: The Bethany Press, 1954), pp. 134-141, 183-184.

of Georgia, he later served as president of several colleges including Bacon College in Kentucky, the University of Missouri, and Christian University (now Culver-Stockton College) in Canton, Missouri.

Never one to temper his statements for any reason, Shannon was utterly militant in defending slavery. He opposed emancipation because slaves were inferior and could not be counted on to live wisely as free people. Socially expedient and in harmony with the natural order, slavery also was biblically sound in his judgment. Jesus and his Apostles must have approved the slave-master relationship, he argued; otherwise they would have condemned it. Recalling one of Shannon's proslavery speeches, W. C. Rogers (1828-?) wrote: "No man that I have ever been permitted to hear on this subject could array as many and as strong, plausible arguments from the Scriptures, in favor of this position, as could he."[12]

When Shannon was president of the University of Missouri, Congress in 1854 passed the Kansas-Nebraska Act, thereby intensifying the slavery debate in the border states. Instead of backing off from the wrangle on account of his politically sensitive position, Shannon made one inflammatory speech after another. Addressing a proslavery convention in 1855, he said:

And if, as we have seen, right of property in slaves is sanctioned by the light of Nature, the Constitution of the United States, and the clear teaching of the Bible, a deliberate and persistent violation of that right, even by government, is as villainous as highway robbery; and when peaceable modes of redress are exhausted, IS A JUST CAUSE OF WAR BETWEEN SEPARATE STATES, AND OF REVOLUTION IN THE SAME STATE.[13]

The unswerving radicalism of James Shannon must have caused Alexander Campbell and other moderate Disciples—Tolbert Fanning and Benjamin Franklin, for example—to cringe and to hope that at the very least he might lose his voice for a season.

In Campbell's judgment, however, outspoken abolitionists in the Disciples endangered the church's unity more than Southern fire-eaters. As early as 1834, Dr. Nathaniel Field

---

12. W. C. Rogers, *Recollections of Men of Faith* (St. Louis: Christian Publishing Company, 1889), p. 17.
13. Quoted in Harrell, *Quest for a Christian America*, p. 124.

(1805-1888) reported with obvious approval that the seventy-member congregation of Disciples at Jeffersonville, Indiana, had resolved "not to break the loaf with *slaveholders,* or in any way to countenance them as Christians."[14] Stirred by the awesome millennialism of William Miller (1805-1895), Dr. Field prepared for the second coming of Jesus in 1843 only to be disappointed. Then he set Oct. 22, 1844, as the correct date. Despite this diversion, he nonetheless remained a lifelong abolitionist.

John G. Fee (1816-1901), a Disciples minister in Kentucky, attained high visibility in the abolitionist movement. Founder of an interracial school in Berea, Kentucky, he wrote *An Anti-Slavery Manual* which was published in 1848 and circulated widely. After exploding the myth that the institution of slavery received divine sanction from the Old and New Testaments, he devoted separate chapters to the sinfulness of slavery and to the need for immediate emancipation. In concluding, he reminded his readers of the rapid increase in the number of slaves and pointed out that no people in the long stretch of history "remained perpetually in bondage." Appealing to the vested self-interest of whites, he thundered:

Three millions of slaves in our midst, are ready to rise at the tap of a drum. The day is fast approaching when forbearance will cease to be a virtue; and O! my brethren, what can we do in the day of calamity, when our iniquities are being visited on our own heads, and the vials of God's wrath are poured out upon us! We can, if we will, avert the impending ruin.[15]

Still another Disciples abolitionist, John Kirk of Ohio, refused to keep silent when Alexander Campbell urged all citizens to uphold the Fugitive Slave Law in 1851. Disenchanted and irate, Kirk wrote to Campbell: "I have come to the conclusion that I will neither patronize priest nor paper, that is not strictly anti-slavery. Your position to American Slavery I very much dislike." A smoldering Campbell replied tersely: "I wish you were emancipated from the tyranny of opinionism. Were I to form my opinion of you

---

14. Quoted in Dwight E. Stevenson, *Walter Scott: Voice of the Golden Oracle,* p. 150.

15. John G. Fee, *An Anti-Slavery Manual* (New York: Arno Press and The New York Times, 1969, reprint), p. 181.

from this communication, I would say that you are a very good miniature Pope. You are infallibly right, and every one that differs with you is infallibly wrong."[16] Although Campbell tried to destroy his adversary with sarcasm and invective, he must have been aware that Kirk's disaffection was typical of many Ohio Disciples at the time.

Pardee Butler was the James Shannon of abolitionism in the Disciples. The two men, one an antagonist and the other a champion of slavery, matched each other in the zeal and fervor with which they advanced their respective convictions. Outraged by the extension of slavery into the territories, Butler moved from Indiana to Kansas in 1855 to evangelize for the Disciples and to rout the proslavery forces. Settling on a 160-acre claim twelve miles from Atchison, he soon was instrumental in the gathering of seven congregations.

Southern sympathizers in the vicinity, annoyed and then infuriated by the fiery rhetoric of Butler, made his life miserable. Stripped to his waist on one occasion, he was tarred and feathered, put in his buggy, escorted to the outskirts of Atchison, and warned that he would be hanged if he returned. At another time a group of angry men painted the letter R (for Rogue) on his forehead and set him adrift on the Missouri River. To add to his problems, they placed on his crude craft a handmade flag with the inscription: "GREELEY TO THE RESCUE: I HAVE A NIGGER. THE REV. MR. BUTLER, AGENT FOR THE UNDERGROUND RAILROAD." "Gentlemen," he said as he swung away from the bank, "if I am drowned I forgive you; but I have this to say to you: If you are not ashamed of your part in this transaction, I am not ashamed of mine. Goodby."[17] Converting the forked flag staff into a paddle, Butler negotiated dangerous rapids and came ashore several miles downstream.

In 1858 Butler requested the American Christian Missionary Society to support his work. The only Disciples organization which even pretended to be national in scope, the society through its leadership faced a difficult decision. Isaac Errett, corresponding secretary of the society, expressed

---

16. *Millennial Harbinger*, January 1851, pp. 49-50.
17. Rosetta B. Hastings, *Personal Recollections of Pardee Butler* (Cincinnati: Standard Publishing Company, 1889), pp. 71-72.

interest in Butler's mission but cautioned: " 'It must . . . be distinctly understood that if we embark in a missionary enterprise in Kansas, this question of slavery and anti-slavery must be ignored." The prospect of being gagged did not set well with Butler. He fired back:

For myself, I will be no party, now or hereafter, to such an arrangement as that contemplated in your letter now before me. I would not make this "Reformation of the nineteenth century" a withered and blasted trunk, scattered by the lightnings of heaven, because it took part with the rich and powerful against the poor and oppressed, and because we have been recreant to those maxims of free discussion which we have so ostentatiously heralded to the world as our cherished principles.

Butler and Errett had reached an impasse, neither of them willing to compromise.

An antislavery man himself, Errett represented all Disciples in North and South and could not bring himself to commit funds to an evangelist-abolitionist. Although anxious to see the gospel preached in Kansas, Errett wrote to Butler: "If you still insist on the right to urge that question [abolition], and take part in the controversy raging in Kansas, *under the patronage of the A. C. M. S.,* I have only to say it is outside the objects contemplated in our constitution."[18]

Pardee Butler's request for funds as well as prayers touched a responsive chord among a group of Disciples in the Ohio-Indiana region. There, of course, antislavery views were vibrant and widespread. Ovid Butler (1801-1881), a strong abolitionist and an outstanding Disciples layman, was the principal supporter of North-Western Christian University (now Butler University) which was chartered in 1850 and established in Indianapolis. Alexander Campbell took a dim view of the Disciples school in Indiana because it competed with Bethany College for gifts and students. Besides, the institution was an antislavery stronghold; it even accepted several students who were expelled from Bethany for creating a disturbance by registering their protest against slavery.

John Boggs, a Disciples preacher in Ohio, edited and published the *North-Western Christian Magazine* in Cincinnati. The only abolitionist journal among the Disciples, it was

18. For a discussion of the Butler-Errett correspondence SEE Hastings, *op. cit.,* pp. 320-324; also SEE James S. Lamar, *Memoirs of Isaac Errett with Selections from His Writings* (Cincinnati: Standard Publishing Company, 1893), Vol. 1, pp. 214-218.

founded in 1854 and was superseded by the *Christian Luminary* in 1858. In the same year that Boggs mailed the first issue of his magazine, a few Disciples sponsored and attended an antislavery convention in Cleveland. Pardee Butler had like-minded friends in Ohio and Indiana. They did not disappoint him.

In protest against the American Christian Missionary Society, Ovid Butler and John Boggs along with several others (including two of Alexander Campbell's brothers-in-law) organized the Christian Missionary Society in 1859. Formed to give expression to antislavery sentiment and to back Pardee Butler, the rival society collected and sent him a modest amount of money before dissolving in 1863. It was not a thriving organization, but neither was the older American Christian Missionary Society.

Alexander Campbell and other moderate leaders strove with singleness of purpose to keep Disciples together as the nation erupted over slavery and moved toward war, but their efforts met heavy resistance.

DISCIPLES DURING THE CIVIL WAR

When the roar of cannons in Charleston Harbor signaled the onset of civil war, Disciples reacted like other mainstream Protestants in America. Able-bodied men, mustered into the army, made their way to the battlefields, certain that they bore arms for a just and a righteous cause. Women, elderly men, and children persevered, praying for the safe return of their loved ones or mourning their dead. Although there were notable exceptions, the rank and file of Disciples tended to reflect the sentiment of the section in which they lived.

As for the leaders of the movement, a significant number maintained neutrality throughout the conflict. Resisting the impassioned calls to patriotism, they chose to stand firmly for peace and just as firmly against war—particularly a war which jeopardized the health and unity of the church they loved and served. Others were either pro-Union or pro-Confederacy but struggled to express their loyalty in a manner befitting believers in Christ. Still others, vowing to thin the ranks of the enemy, read their New Testaments and loaded their rifles. In sum, Disciples leaders marched to the sound of different drummers during the Civil War; and many refused to march at all.

Living in the twilight of his career, Alexander Campbell was profoundly disturbed by the outbreak of hostilities. He wrote in June 1861:

Civilized America! civilized UNITED STATES! Boasting of a humane and Christian paternity and fraternity, unsheathing your swords, discharging your cannon, boasting of your heathen brutality, gluttonously satiating your furious appetites for fraternal blood, caps the climax of all human inconsistencies inscribed on the blurred and moth eaten pages of time in all its records.[19]

Campbell's biting comment did not catch his long-term readers by surprise. In the first issue of *The Christian Baptist* he had derided the chaplain at the elbow of the Christian general with his ten thousand soldiers "praying that the Lord would cause them to fight valiantly, and render their efforts successful in making as many widows and orphans as will afford sufficient opportunity for others to manifest the purity of their religion by taking care of them!!!" Responding to the Mexican War in 1846, Campbell observed that the Prince of Peace "had no beatitudes for heroes, no benedictions for conquerors." Two years later he delivered his memorable "Address on War," concluding that "there never was a *good* war, or a *bad* peace."

Campbell even refused to carry arms for self-defense. While traveling in Ohio on one occasion, he admitted to a stranger that his only weapon was a New Testament. " 'Sir,' " asked the stranger, " 'do you suppose that would defend you against robbers?' " " 'Certainly, much better than I could defend myself,' " replied Campbell. " 'The Author of this book has promised to preserve those that trust in him, and I know he is much more able to protect me.' "[20] No wonder the Sage of Bethany endorsed neither side in the Civil War. He was as consistent in his pacifism as any person of his time.

Jacob Creath, Jr. (1799-1886), Benjamin Franklin, and John W. McGarvey (1829-1911) joined Campbell in standing firmly on neutral ground. Creath's antiwar posture almost got

---

19. *Millennial Harbinger*, June 1861, p. 348.
20. SEE in order *Christian Baptist*, July 1823, pp. 17-18; *Millennial Harbinger*, November 1846, p. 641; *Millennial Harbinger*, July 1848, pp. 361-386; Robert Richardson, *Memoirs of Alexander Campbell*, Vol. II, p. 662.

him into serious trouble. During the middle of the war he held
a preaching mission in Paris, Missouri. When he stood up to
preach one evening, he found a letter lying on the Bible. It
read:

Reverend Sir: The loyal citizens of this town, and the United States
soldiers, would respectfully ask you to state publicly why you
neglect to pray for the President of the United States, and all in
authority. If you preach the doctrine of Christ and the apostles, you
should not forget the "powers that be" in your prayers. If you have
a satisfactory reason for this, it is but reasonable, in the present
troublous times, that we should know such reason. Should you
refuse, we shall take it for granted that you are disloyal, and shall
act in the premises accordingly. A Union Man[21]

After reading the letter aloud, Creath said that he was tend-
ing to his own legitimate business and did not intend to introduce politics into the pulpit. He lived to recount the incident.

Editor of the influential *American Christian Review,* Benjamin Franklin was a pacifist on pragmatic as well as
legalistic grounds. *"We will not take up arms against, fight
and kill the brethren we have labored for twenty years to
bring into the kingdom of God,"* he wrote in his journal.
McGarvey could have made the same statement. Convinced
that "the more prudent brethren" should "speak out plainly
for the benefit of the more rash," he stated flatly that he
"would rather, ten thousand times, be killed for refusing to
fight, than to fall in battle, or to come home victorious with
the blood of my brethren on my hands."[22]

McGarvey was one of fourteen Disciples to sign a "Circular from Preachers in Missouri" shortly after the outbreak
of war. The document is hardly a pacifist manifesto, for the
signers did not commit themselves as to the "propriety of
bearing arms in extreme emergencies." To preserve union
among the churches, however, they did argue against participation in the Civil War and urged all Disciples to join
them "in an utter refusal to do military service."[23]
Although they were sympathetic to the cause of the South,

---

21. Peter Donan, *Memoir of Jacob Creath, Jr.* (Cincinnati: R. W. Carroll and Company, 1872), p. 193.
22. Quoted from *American Christian Review* in Joseph Franklin and J. A.
Headington, *The Life and Times of Benjamin Franklin* (St. Louis: John Burns,
Publisher, 1879), p. 287.
23. The document is printed in *Millennial Harbinger,* October 1861, pp. 583-584.

a group of Disciples in middle Tennessee declared their neutrality in a communication prepared by Tolbert Fanning and addressed "To His Excellency The President of The Confederate States of America." They advised Jefferson Davis that the Bible was for them a higher authority than the "rules and regulations of any human government" and asked him to relieve them of "requirements repulsive to their religious faith."[24] The conviction that Christians should avoid entanglements in civil affairs helped to shape their thinking. One signer of the letter, David Lipscomb (1831-1917), decided as a matter of principle that he should not even vote in political elections much less maim or kill another person.

Notwithstanding the repeated appeals for moderation, most Disciples chose sides in the "fratricidal strife." The *Christian Record,* published by Elijah Goodwin (1807-1879) in Indianapolis, favored the Union and took issue with the neutral position of Franklin's *American Christian Review.* William T. Moore claimed partial credit for Kentucky's declaration of loyalty to the Union. A pastor in Frankfort, he preached a sermon on the "Duty of Christians in the Present Crisis" the Sunday before the badly split state legislature took final action. All but one of the five or six undecided legislators were Disciples and heard Moore's sermon. As a consequence, or so he was led to believe, they threw their support behind the Union and cast the decisive votes.[25]

James A. Garfield resigned as principal of Western Reserve Eclectic Institute (now Hiram College) to enter the Union army. He commanded the Forty-second Ohio Regiment and rose in rank from lieutenant colonel to major general. His military success, no doubt, contributed to his advance in politics which led to his election as President of the United States in 1880. Garfield's close personal friend, Isaac Errett, applied for a commission to form a regiment. Although his application was rejected, he prayed and worked for the Union.

James H. Garrison (1842-1931), coeditor and then editor of

---

24. For the full text of the letter SEE Earl I. West, *The Life and Times of David Lipscomb* (Henderson, Tenn.: Religious Book Service, 1954), pp. 87-89; SEE also Harrell, *Quest for a Christian America,* p. 151; Herman A. Norton, *Tennessee Christians,* pp. 103-104.

25. William T. Moore, "The Turbulent Period" in *The Reformation of the Nineteenth Century,* ed. by James H. Garrison (St. Louis: Christian Publishing Company, 1901), pp. 167-170.

The Christian-Evangelist in later years, enlisted in Company F of the Twenty-fourth Missouri Infantry and fought for the Union until he was wounded in battle at Pea Ridge, Arkansas. After recovering he spent the last three years of the war as a captain in command of Company G of the Eighth Missouri Cavalry Volunteers.

John B. Vawter (1838-1897), a respected Disciples preacher in Iowa after the war, was a soldier in the Fourth Kentucky Regiment of General Sherman's army. Captured by Confederate troops, he was imprisoned at Andersonville, Georgia. Vawter wrote *Prison Life in Dixie* under the pseudonym, "Sergeant Oats."

Dr. Lewis L. Pinkerton (1812-1875), a physician before he became a Disciples preacher in Kentucky, "was first, last, and always" in "the class of unconditional Union men," according to his biographer. Both surgeon and chaplain of the Eleventh Kentucky Cavalry, Pinkerton wrote:

I could . . . scatter flowers over the graves of the Confederate dead, and bedew them with tears; but I can not sell my principles. I must still say, if forced to it, even while scattering flowers over the Confederate graves, and weeping: These poor, brave young men fell in an unrighteous war against a beneficent government; they fell in a war in which enormous atrocities were committed by those who controlled them; they died in a cause which it behooves the rest of the human race to see overthrown. It were better that a million more should die than this continent should be belted by a great slave empire, whose existence would imperil liberty of every kind throughout the whole earth; . . .[26]

Many Disciples were as devoted to the Confederacy as Pinkerton was to the Union. Two sons of Disciples founders, Alexander Campbell, Jr. and Barton W. Stone, Jr., wore the gray of the Confederacy. Although Robert Richardson steadfastly opposed the "unhappy contest" and advised against engagement in it, his son David died in 1864 as a member of the "Morgan Raiders" commanded by General John H. Morgan. The judicious Dr. Winthrop H. Hopson (1823-1889) gave up his pastorate in Lexington, Kentucky, because of his well-known loyalty to the South. Arrested and then released, he was a chaplain under General Morgan. Of all Disciples ministers in the South, none were more extreme in their

---

26. *Life, Letters and Addresses of Dr. Lewis L. Pinkerton,* ed. by John Shackleford, Jr. (Cincinnati: Chase and Hall, Publishers, 1876), p. 77.

patriotism than Thomas W. Caskey (1816-1896) and Benjamin Franklin Hall (1803-1873).

Early in the war Caskey served as chaplain of the Eighteenth Mississippi Regiment of Volunteers. Against the wishes of his officers he went into the first battle of Manassas with a double-cylinder sixteen-shooter on his shoulder. When a fragment of a brigade broke ranks and fled, he cornered them in a narrow pass, "rallied them at the muzzle of a revolver," and led them back to the front line. "He faithfully discharged his duty to the sick and the wounded, attended to his prayer-meeting and preaching, but the trouble was to keep him out of the fights," wrote another chaplain.[27] Later on he assumed responsibility for administering a regimental hospital in addition to keeping his chaplain's duties. Still the desire for combat gripped him. "The old Adam would overcome the new," he confessed. "I would shoulder a gun, and go . . . into the fight. I do not think I killed any one or broke any arms, but I tried to break as many legs as I could." If an enemy soldier's leg is broken, Caskey explained, "it takes two men to pack him off, and they take care not to pack themselves back till the fight is ended."[28]

Dr. Hall, chaplain of the regiment commanded by Barton W. Stone, Jr., dared to wish that all people of the North could be hurled into eternity. If his word can be accepted at face value, he did not recognize a single moral restraint in the conduct of the war. To his mind, the Confederacy was engaged in a crusade rather than a just war and should act accordingly. A fanatic, Hall "rode a fine mule, carried a splendid rifle, and stipulated expressly that when there was any chance of killing Yankees he must be allowed the privilege of bagging as many as possible."[29] Few if any preachers in South or North presented and discharged arms with greater enthusiasm than this minister of the Disciples of Christ.

THE AMERICAN CHRISTIAN MISSIONARY SOCIETY

The intensity of feeling provoked by slavery and war was

---

27. *Caskey's Book*, ed. by G. G. Mullins (St. Louis: John Burns Publishing Co., 1884), p. 20.
28. *Caskey's Last Book*, ed. by B. F. Manire (Nashville: The Messenger Publishing Co., 1896), p. 34.
29. William Baxter, *Pea Ridge and Prairie Grove; or, Scenes and Incidents of the War in Arkansas* (Cincinnati: Poe and Hitchcock, 1866), pp. 114-116.

especially troublesome and threatening to the American Christian Missionary Society. Throughout the 1850s the society had attempted to maintain a neutral position so as to become a viable national organization of Disciples. Before turning down Pardee Butler's request for support in Kansas, the society had selected three missionaries for overseas service: a slaveholder, Dr. James T. Barclay; a former slave, Alexander Cross (1811?-1854); and an abolitionist, J. O. Beardslee (1814-1879). As North and South moved closer and closer to the brink of war, the society refused to yield to sectionalism.

After the Civil War began, however, it became even more difficult to avoid supporting one government or the other. The October 1861 national convention, for example, met in Cincinnati and was national in name only. Not one church leader from the South was present. During the meeting a one-time preacher and layman from Ohio, Dr. J. P. Robison (1811-?), proposed a resolution asking Disciples everywhere "to do all in their power to sustain the proper and constitutional authorities of the Union." Seconded by Lewis L. Pinkerton, it was declared in order by the presiding officer, Isaac Errett, after David S. Burnet questioned whether such a resolution was germane to the stated purpose of the society. "Raccoon" John Smith appealed the decision of the chair only to withdraw his appeal. A second appeal was sustained. Following a ten-minute recess the convention reassembled as a "mass meeting" with Burnet chairing the session. The same resolution was passed with one dissenting vote. In essence, the Society escaped from a precarious situation with its neutrality intact; the loyalty statement was approved only by a "mass meeting" without any official status whatsoever.

In 1863 the society met again in Cincinnati. This time a stronger resolution was introduced. Following the preamble, the text read:

Resolved, That we unqualifiedly declare our allegiance to said Government [the United States], and repudiate as false and slanderous any statements to the contrary.

Resolved, That we tender our sympathies to our brave and noble soldiers in the field who are defending us from the attempts of armed traitors to overthrow our government, and also to those bereaved and rendered desolate by the ravages of war.

Resolved, That we will earnestly and constantly pray to God to give to our legislators and rulers wisdom to enact and power to execute such laws as will speedily bring to us the enjoyment of a peace that God will deign to bless.[30]

When the convention approved the resolution by a wide margin, the American Christian Missionary Society had taken a firm stand against part of its constituency. Indeed, all in attendance were from the North and could not be expected to have voted otherwise; nevertheless, the society had abandoned its studied neutralism. The action was of more than passing significance.

SEEDS OF DIVISION

Shortly after the return of national peace Moses E. Lard (1818-1880) asserted that Disciples had passed through "the fierce ordeal of a terrible war" without dividing. "Not a rent in our ranks did the war produce," he boasted in 1866. "True, for the time being it cooled many an ardent feeling, and caused old friends to regard one another a little shyly. Still it effected no division." Turning his attention from past to future, he exclaimed: *"We can never divide."*[31]

The exuberant Lard either failed to sense or refused to acknowledge the full impact of the slavery controversy and Civil War on the Disciples, as have almost all historians of the movement since his time.[32] Technically, to be sure, Disciples avoided a formal division precisely because there was no ecclesiastical structure to split. Their loose connectionalism was a blessing in disguise, for no recognized church body above the congregational level had the power to render and enforce any decision. Yet the American Christian Missionary Society threw the weight of its influence, such as it was, behind the Union; and a substantial number of

---

30. Quoted from *Report of Proceedings of the Fifteenth Anniversary Meeting of the American Christian Missionary Society* (October 20-22, 1863) in Harrell, *Quest for a Christian America,* p. 163; also quoted in William T. Moore, *A Comprehensive History of the Disciples of Christ* (New York: Fleming H. Revell Company, 1909), p. 493.
31. SEE *Lard's Quarterly,* April 1866, pp. 330-336.
32. At least four historians have called attention to the tragic consequences of the Civil War on Disciples. SEE Frederick D. Kershner, "Stars," *Christian Standard,* May 25, 1940, pp. 497-498; Harrell, *Quest for a Christian America,* pp. 170-174; Earl I. West, *The Life and Times of David Lipscomb,* pp. 105-108; Henry K. Shaw, *Hoosier Disciples* (Published by The Bethany Press for The Association of the Christian Churches in Indiana, 1966), p. 155.

associations at the state level yielded to the pressures of sectionalism. Innumerable congregations, not to mention thousands of individual church members, followed the same pattern. Taking into account the total experience of Disciples in the Civil War, it is reasonable to conclude that they suffered an actual if not an official split.

Regardless of the complexity and ambiguity of the issue, the effect of the war on Disciples cannot be minimized. Seeds of discord, sown and cultivated, grew to full bloom with the separation of the Churches of Christ a generation later. The Civil War was nothing less than a watershed for the Christian Church (Disciples of Christ).

9

SECOND GENERATION LEADERSHIP

Their rapid growth interrupted and their confidence diminished if not shattered, Disciples sensed the pressing need to regain their momentum and to pursue their grand objective with renewed vitality after the Civil War. Over a half century had passed since the movement's founders had proposed a return to New Testament Christianity in response to the "bitter jarrings and janglings of a party spirit." Unswerving in his commitment to Christian unity as his "polar star," Barton W. Stone died in Hannibal, Missouri, on November 9, 1844. Following him in death were Thomas Campbell a decade later, John T. Johnson in 1857, and Walter Scott in 1861. Alexander Campbell, senile and lost in memories and fantasies, died at his Bethany home on March 4, 1866. David S. Burnet, the principal architect of organization for mission among the Disciples, died the following year and "Raccoon" John Smith in 1868. As Disciples of Christ moved into the uncertain years of Reconstruction, they remembered their fathers in the faith—particularly Alexander Campbell—but faced the necessity of accepting new leadership for understanding and direction.

ENTERING A NEW ERA

Less than a month after Alexander Campbell's death, his wife joined by four of her children requested Robert Richardson to write a biography of her late husband. A physician as well as professor of chemistry at Bethany, Dr. Richardson was a close personal friend of Campbell's and one of his most trusted associates. He reported his answer to Mrs. Selina Campbell in the April issue of *The Millennial Harbinger* for 1866. "In pursuance of a long-cherished purpose, and in accordance with the wishes of Brother Campbell's family as well as of many esteemed brethren and friends," he wrote, "I design to complete, the Lord willing, as soon as practicable, a memoir of this eminent servant of God."[1] Plagued with bad eyesight, he recruited his daughter, Emma, to take his dictation; other members of the family also came to his assistance. It was a labor of love for all of them. The first volume of the *Memoirs of Alexander Campbell,* published in 1868, was followed by the second volume two years later. A new edition, which bound the two volumes into one, was issued in 1871 and has been reprinted many times. Detailed and comprehensive as well as massive, Richardson's work of over 1,200 pages remains an extremely useful biography of Alexander Campbell.

While Richardson was compiling and sifting material for his manuscript, Robert Milligan (1814-1875) was hard at work on a systematic statement of theology for Disciples. His book, released in 1868, was entitled *An Exposition and Defense of the Scheme of Redemption as It Is Revealed and Taught in the Holy Scriptures.* Like Richardson's *Memoirs,* Milligan's *Scheme* became a classic in Disciples literature. Still in print, it served as a textbook for several generations of Disciples preachers. To quote one recent historian, *The Scheme of Redemption* "came as near to being a definitive theology of Disciples of Christ as any book that was ever written."[2]

A Presbyterian-turned-Disciple, Milligan was a native of Ireland and a graduate of Washington College in Penn-

---

1. *Millennial Harbinger,* April 1866, p. 185. Quoted in Goodnight and Stevenson, *Home to Bethphage: A Biography of Robert Richardson,* p. 218.
2. Dwight E. Stevenson, *Lexington Theological Seminary, 1865-1965* (St. Louis: The Bethany Press, 1964), p. 25.

sylvania. He taught at his alma mater for almost a decade
before accepting a professorship at the State University of Indiana in 1852. Then in 1854 he moved to Bethany College
where he taught mathematics for five years and assisted
Campbell, Richardson, and Pendleton in editing *The Millennial Harbinger.* In the course of his career as an educator
Milligan taught a full range of offerings in the arts and
sciences. Although he gained the reputation of being an excellent instructor in everything from mathematics and
chemistry to English literature and the Latin and Greek
classics, his great love came to be the study of religion. It is
striking that the most widely used systematic theology in the
full sweep of Disciples history was written by one who himself
had no formal theological preparation.

Scrupulously faithful to the tradition of Disciples, Milligan
did not understand his purpose as that of constructing
another theological system; there were too many of them
already. Rather he intended to provide a tool, so to speak,
which would help Disciples comprehend the "sublime and
gracious contents" of the Bible. "I have not attempted to *ex-
haust* any subject," he wrote, "but merely to give the reader
such hints, suggestions, illustrations, and explanations as
will enable and encourage him to study the Bible for
himself."[3] In terms of both approach and content Milligan's
volume bears a marked resemblance to Alexander
Campbell's *Christian System,* published over thirty years
earlier. As one recent interpreter observed, Milligan "says in
greater detail almost exactly what Campbell had said. . . .
The approach to the Scripture is no longer one of excited discovery. The truth had been discovered."[4]

Without a doubt the full length of Campbell's shadow fell
across Robert Milligan and Robert Richardson. Both men intended to make certain that the witness of the Sage of
Bethany would continue to inform Disciples in the years
ahead. Even so, the publication of Campbell's *Memoirs* and
The Scheme of Redemption tacitly acknowledged that the
era of the Disciples fathers had come to a close, that a change
in the ranks of leadership had occurred.

---

3. Robert Milligan, *An Exposition and Defense of the Scheme of Redemption as It Is
Revealed and Taught in the Holy Scriptures* (Cincinnati: R. W. Carroll, rev. ed.
1874), xiii-xiv.
4. George G. Beazley, Jr., "Who Are the Disciples?" in *The Christian Church
(Disciples of Christ): An Interpretative Examination in the Cultural Context,* p. 29.

THE POWER OF THE PRESS

To understand the development of Disciples from a small band of reformers in the early 1800s to a mainstream religious body a century later, it is imperative to recognize the unusually significant and sometimes decisive role of religious journalism in the life and thought of the movement. Loosely structured and disinclined to sanction authoritative bodies beyond the congregational level—representative or otherwise—Disciples turned to editors and to their journals for the formation of a common mind. The strongly emotional aversion to ecclesiasticism and all its trappings created a vacuum in leadership which resourceful editors, following the powerful example of Alexander Campbell, were pleased to fill. Whether the faithful gathered for worship in the backwoods or in a county seat or in a burgeoning city, their preacher more than likely could press an argument by quoting from the latest issue of a Disciples paper. As a result, it became a cliché to say that Disciples did not have bishops; they had editors!

Writing in 1909, William T. Moore insisted that "from the beginning of the movement to the present time, the chief authority in regard to all important questions has been the Disciple press."[5] James H. Garrison, himself an editor, agreed. "Did we ever have any trouble among us, on any question," he asked, "that wasn't worked up by our newspapers?"[6] Summarizing the importance of journalism for Disciples, Winfred E. Garrison (1874-1969) concluded: "The editor's chair has come nearer to being a throne of power than any other position among the Disciples."[7]

The assessment of Moore and the Garrisons, father and son, is entirely accurate if limited to the period prior to the establishment of a denominational publishing house in 1910 and the development of stronger national organization later in the same decade. Thereafter regional and national church executives, together with a number of widely respected pastors and heads of educational institutions, joined editors as the dominant figures in decision-making among Disciples.

5. William T. Moore, *Comprehensive History of the Disciples of Christ*, p. 699.
6. *Christian-Evangelist*, September 26, 1907, p. 1231.
7. Winfred E. Garrison, *Religion Follows the Frontier: A History of the Disciples of Christ* (New York, Harper and Brothers, 1931), p. 210.

Notwithstanding this expansion of the leadership base in the early twentieth century, the overall impact of religious journalism on Disciples has been enormous.

Of the founders, Alexander Campbell was the first to rely heavily on the printing press. Within a few years Stone and Scott joined him in the editorial fraternity as did many others. Prior to 1860 over one hundred papers had been established, including at least twenty in Ohio and a dozen or more in both Kentucky and Indiana. Many of them failed to attract a sufficient number of subscribers, and their editors—victims of competition if not apathy—were obliged to suspend publication. In spite of the high mortality rate, Disciples at any one time probably had as many editors per thousand members as any religious body in America. Before his death Stone lamented that aspiring journalists among Disciples failed to take into account the law of supply and demand. Campbell already had expressed his displeasure with the growing number of preachers who convinced themselves that they could land a telling blow for the Lord by issuing a prospectus for still another second-rate paper. Underscoring his point, he wrote in 1844: "Invidious though it may seem, duty, nevertheless, constrains this avowal, that we have entirely too many editors, or, what is the same thing, too many periodicals."[8]

Campbell's firm words failed to stem the tide; the rush into print continued, even accelerated. In time it became a demanding chore just to compile a reasonably accurate list of Disciples journals. One bibliographer estimated in 1957 that Disciples had "produced more than fifteen hundred periodicals above the local church level, and are producing more and more each year."[9]

It is hardly surprising that the most important leaders among Disciples after the Civil War enlarged their ministry and increased their visibility by editing and publishing a religious journal. They had learned from their predecessors to appreciate and utilize the power of the press. Besides, the publishing enterprise was growing rapidly throughout the church in America; the number of religious journals almost

---

8. *Millennial Harbinger*, April 1844, p. 171.
9. Roscoe Pierson, "The Literature of the Disciples of Christ and Closely Related Groups," *The College of the Bible Quarterly*, July 1957, p. 23.

doubled in the brief span of twenty years, increasing from 350 in 1865 to 650 in 1885. Disciples contributed more than their fair share of the total. The overwhelming majority of their journals were short-lived and inconsequential, to be sure, but several of them came to be solidly based and exercised wide-ranging influence out of all proportion to the size of their subscription list. In fact, the editorial witness of a few key papers provides a framework within which to comprehend the dynamics of the Disciples in the critical and turbulent post-Civil War era.[10]

EDITORS AND THEIR JOURNALS

Although *The Millennial Harbinger* had helped to shape the development of Disciples for three solid decades, its base of power eroded during the 1860s. Declining interest compelled the coeditors, William K. Pendleton and Charles L. Loos (1823-1912), to discontinue the paper at the close of 1870. In addition to the loss of Alexander Campbell's prestige and influence, the Civil War dealt a heavy blow to the journal. Faced with a problem which he saw no way to solve, the editor felt obliged to write shortly after the outbreak of war: "Owing to the discontinuance of the United States mail in certain States, we will not send the June No. . . . to our subscribers in those States, until we have further assurance of its reaching them."[11] Cut off by war from its southern constituency and accused of reflecting southern sentiment by some subscribers in the North, the paper's circulation dropped radically. Moreover, *The Millennial Harbinger,* a monthly, lost its hold on Disciples in part because of growing competition from papers which appeared each week.

The first important weekly in the movement was the *American Christian Review,* edited and published by Benjamin Franklin in Cincinnati. Founded as a monthly in 1856, it became a weekly two years later. In his introduction to the first volume, Franklin rejected the argument that circulating too many periodicals dissipated the resources of Disciples and

---

10. For a detailed study of periodicals among the Disciples from 1850 to 1910 SEE James Brooks Major, "The Role of Periodicals in the Development of the Disciples of Christ, 1850-1910" (unpublished Ph.D. thesis, Vanderbilt University, 1966).
11. *Millennial Harbinger,* June 1861, p. 357.

pulled them apart instead of together. "The more preachers and papers the better," he countered, "if they are the right kind."

A great-great-great-nephew of the American statesman with the same name, Franklin grew up in Ohio and moved to Indiana when he was twenty years old. By trade a cabinet maker, he abandoned his workbench for the Disciples pulpit and soon became an effective evangelist, baptizing over seven thousand people during his ministry. He engaged in a number of public debates and wrote two volumes of sermons, both entitled the *Gospel Preacher,* which appeared in over thirty editions. Franklin neither pretended to be a learned man nor apologized for his lack of education. Unusually popular among Disciples, he took great pride in being from and for the common people.

During the Civil War Franklin refused to take sides and could not avoid the difficulty of satisfying a constituency divided in its loyalty. The *American Christian Review* escaped the fate of *The Millennial Harbinger,* however. By 1869 Franklin had gained a considerable following for his paper. "The *Review,* in those days [the late 1860s], was regarded as *the* paper among us, by most brethren, and no doubt its patronage far exceeded all the rest."[12] So wrote another editor who had no reason to exaggerate the strength of the *Review.* A bastion of conservatism, the paper was called "The Old Reliable" by those who agreed with its editorial stand and feared that progressive ideas and "innovations" would spoil the Disciples and divert them from the course charted by Alexander Campbell.

The *American Christian Review* passed its heyday before Franklin's death. Thereafter the decline continued under the editorship of John F. Rowe (1827-1897). By the time Daniel Sommer (1850-1940) succeeded Rowe as editor in 1887 and changed the paper's name to the *Octographic Review,* it had moved from the center to the periphery of the Disciples. Neither Rowe nor Sommer had the vitality and personal appeal of Franklin, but they claimed to follow his lead in registering their protests from week to week. Apart from a small minority of conservatives, few appeared to notice, and still fewer cared.

12. *Christian,* December 26, 1878, p. 4.

In July 1855, six months before Franklin published the first issue of the *American Christian Review,* William Lipscomb and Tolbert Fanning founded the *Gospel Advocate* as a monthly periodical. Discontinued during the Civil War, it reappeared as a weekly in 1866 with David Lipscomb, brother of William, and Fanning as coeditors. The heavy demands of Fanning's farm and school, Franklin College, led him to turn the paper over to Lipscomb after only a few issues had been published. Lipscomb persuaded Elisha G. Sewell (1830-1924) to become coeditor in 1870, and the two like-minded men shared editorial responsibility for the *Gospel Advocate* until Lipscomb's death almost fifty years later.

A native of Tennessee, David Lipscomb belonged to a devout family. When he was only thirteen years old, he committed to memory all four Gospels and the Book of Acts. Baptized by Tolbert Fanning, he entered Franklin College and graduated in 1849. Having spent his childhood and youth on a farm, Lipscomb chose to earn his livelihood from the land. To the surprise of practically everyone, he began to preach and joined the large circle of Disciples farmer-preachers.

Although Lipscomb could not bring himself to bear arms for the Confederacy during the war, he was a man of the South. When the American Christian Missionary Society abandoned its neutrality in 1863 and passed a resolution supporting the Union, he joined other Disciples in Tennessee and throughout the South in expressing disappointment and resentment. Lipscomb's disenchantment with the power structure of Disciples in the North figured decisively in the rebirth of the *Gospel Advocate.* In typical candor he wrote: "The fact that we had not a single paper known to us that Southern people could read without having their feelings wounded by political insinuations and slurs, had more to do with calling the *Advocate* into existence than all other circumstances combined."[13]

The prospects for success were dim indeed at the outset of Lipscomb's venture in editing and publishing a religious paper. He acknowledged in 1866 that without new subscribers he would be forced to absorb a considerable loss. A year later he appealed to his readers for a thousand additional subscriptions. Apparently his urgent request prompted little

---

13. *Gospel Advocate,* May 1, 1866, p. 273.

response, for the journal ceased publication with the issue for November 7, 1867. Stubborn and determined, Lipscomb resumed publication at the beginning of the new year and by 1869 could boast that his journal had become self-sustaining. Published in Nashville, the *Gospel Advocate* gained a large following and exercised enormous influence among conservative Disciples in the South.

The *Gospel Advocate* stood with the *American Christian Review* in supporting a strict and legalistic Christian primitivism. Since the use of instrumental music in Christian worship and the cooperation of congregations through missionary societies had no apostolic precedent, the two journals waged a vigorous campaign to protect the faithful from these unauthorized and therefore dangerous innovations. Before the war Franklin had been a strong supporter of the American Christian Missionary Society and had filled the position of corresponding secretary for a brief period in 1856-57. Although Lipscomb questioned cooperative work beyond the congregational level, he was moderate in his criticism of the national organization. By the end of the war, however, both men were eager to oppose the Society with all the resources they could command. Clearly, the Society's loyalty resolution of 1863 inflicted deep wounds which failed to heal. At the very least, the political stance of the Society encouraged Franklin and Lipscomb to conclude that all missionary societies were human attempts to improve on the divine plan set forth in the New Testament.

The editorial witness of Benjamin Franklin after the Civil War alarmed many Disciples, including a number of respected leaders in the North. Convinced that his heavy barrage of criticism threatened to destroy the structure and distort the message of the Stone-Campbell movement, they moved promptly to challenge the "earth-born spirit" and "old-fogyism" of the *American Christian Review*. "The great truth for whose defense the Disciples are set," wrote James S. Lamar, "demanded a wiser, sweeter, better advocacy—an advocacy that should exhibit the apostolic *spirit* as well as the apostolic *letter*."[14] James A. Garfield, his political star on the rise, shared this conviction with Thomas Wharton

---

14. James S. Lamar, *Memoirs of Isaac Errett* (Cincinnati: The Standard Publishing Company, 1893), I, p. 301.

Phillips and his brothers, wealthy Disciples laymen from New Castle, Pennsylvania. They and others underwrote the Christian Publishing Association which issued the first number of the *Christian Standard* from Cleveland on April 7, 1866.

The journal's editor, Isaac Errett, needed no introduction to his readers. Born in New York City on January 2, 1820, he had been a member of the Disciples since 1832. After clerking in a bookstore, working as a printer's apprentice and teaching in a district school, he turned to the ministry at the age of twenty and became well acquainted with Walter Scott and the Campbells. In addition to serving as pastor of strong congregations in Ohio and Michigan, he had been coeditor of *The Millennial Harbinger* and corresponding secretary of the American Christian Missionary Society. It was a striking coincidence that Errett's first issue of the *Standard* reported the death of Alexander Campbell. A host of friends and admirers agreed that Errett was prepared to receive the mantle of leadership even though they recognized that no one could take the place of Campbell. "Among the preachers and writers of the nineteenth century who have plead for a return to primitive Christianity," William T. Moore wrote in 1868, Isaac Errett "stands pre-eminently among the most distinguished."[15]

Not even the obvious choice of Errett as editor assured the *Christian Standard* of success. The paper may well have "commanded respect from the very first," as his biographer insisted, but Errett found it difficult to convert respect into support. Disillusioned and unwilling to take further risks, the stockholders abandoned the enterprise as a financial failure in December 1867 and transferred the journal, debts included, to the editor. By purchasing the subscription list of Elijah Goodwin's *Christian Record,* Errett had been able to build a paid circulation of six thousand before it leveled off and began to drop. One friend of Errett aptly described the predicament of the paper: "In Ohio, the *Christian Standard,* first at Cleveland and then at Alliance, was trying its best to live, at immense sacrifices."[16] In spite of Errett's reputation

---

15. *The Living Pulpit of the Christian Church,* ed. by William T. Moore (Cincinnati: R. W. Carroll, 1868), p. 469.
16. *Christian,* December 26, 1878, p. 4.

and determined efforts, his journal was on the verge of folding.

The *Christian Standard* gained a new lease on life when R. W. Carroll and Company, leading book publishers in Cincinnati, agreed to publish the paper if Errett would continue as editor. He accepted the proposal and moved his journal to Cincinnati, where it rapidly received solid backing. In 1872, for example, the circulation reached fifteen thousand regular subscribers and was growing steadily. From the late 1870s until the turn of the century—twelve years after Errett's death—the *Standard* was doubtless the most powerful weekly among the Disciples. Established to manifest a progressive spirit and to withstand the tides of inflexible primitivism, the *Christian Standard* accomplished its purpose. "More than to any other journal and person," suggested Garrison and DeGroot, "it was to the *Christian Standard* and Isaac Errett that the Disciples were indebted for being saved from becoming a fissiparous sect of jangling legalists."[17]

In discussing the basic issues before Disciples, Errett found an ally in *The Christian-Evangelist*. The oldest continuously published journal among Disciples, *The Christian-Evangelist* was founded as the *Gospel Echo* by Elijah L. Craig at Carrollton, Illinois, in January 1863. Craig edited and published the *Gospel Echo* from 1863 to 1868 when John C. Reynolds (1825-1906) purchased the paper and moved it to Macomb, Illinois. In the final issue for 1868 Reynolds announced his selection of James H. Garrison as coeditor. A recent graduate of Abingdon College and associate to Reynolds at the Christian Church in Macomb, Garrison made his editorial bow in January 1869. "Little did I know what I was bowing myself into at the time," Garrison reflected many years later. "It is well that the Lord hides from our eyes the magnitude and difficult nature of the tasks to which he calls us."[18] For over sixty years—until his death in 1931—Garrison was associated with the paper, first as coeditor, then as editor, and finally as editor emeritus.[19]

---

17. Winfred E. Garrison and Alfred T. DeGroot, *The Disciples of Christ: A History*, p. 358.
18. James H. Garrison, *Memoirs and Experiences: A Brief Story of a Long Life* (St. Louis: Christian Board of Publication, 1926), p. 53.
19. Most of the material on editors and their journals, especially James H. Garrison and *The Christian-Evangelist*, can be found in William E. Tucker, *J. H. Garrison and Disciples of Christ* (St. Louis: The Bethany Press, 1964). SEE in particular pp. 38-60, 214-250. For a genealogical chart of *The Christian-Evangelist s* first seventy-five years, see *The Christian-Evangelist*, January 6, 1938, pp. 26-27.

Reynolds was content to remain in Macomb; the ambitious and aggressive Garrison grew restive. Meanwhile, another Disciples periodical, the *Christian,* failed. Garrison used the demise of this paper to his own advantage. Merging the *Christian* with the *Gospel Echo,* he converted a monthly into a weekly and moved to Quincy, Illinois. The initial issue of the *Gospel Echo and Christian* came off the press in March 1872. After the move to Quincy, Garrison assumed full financial responsibility for the paper. Reynolds faded into the background.

During his stay in Quincy, Garrison frequently caught himself day-dreaming about St. Louis as a logical center for a publishing house and Disciples journal. In the heart of the nation, St. Louis was central to the Disciples constituency; at the time no other periodical was being published for Disciples in the entire state of Missouri. The opportunity overshadowed the risk, and Garrison issued the first number of *The Christian* in 1874 from St. Louis.

About a year after he settled in St. Louis, Garrison's printing office burned. In desperate circumstances, he had prayed for help; hardly did he expect God to answer with fire. To make matters worse, the company's stockholders lost confidence in the publishing venture and refused further financial assistance. Alone, Garrison struggled on. One can understand why he wrote to his son two decades later: "I do not like to have my name associated with anything that fails. I had to pick up the C-E *[Christian-Evangelist]* once and carry it on my own shoulders about the time you made your advent into this mundane sphere [1874]."[20]

To accelerate the growth of *The Christian,* Garrison negotiated a merger with *The Evangelist* in 1882. Daniel Bates had started *The Evangelist,* originally named the *Western Evangelist,* at Mt. Pleasant, Iowa, in 1850. After several editorial shifts Barton W. Johnson (1833-1894) became associated with the journal in 1871 and transplanted it to Chicago eight years later. Edited by Garrison, Johnson, and Jerome H. Smart (1842-1913)—Mrs. Garrison's brother-in-law—the first issue of *The Christian-Evangelist* appeared on October 5, 1882. Three editors proving to be one too many,

20. Letter, James H. Garrison to Winfred E. Garrison, January 13, 1895. (The J. H. Garrison Papers, Disciples of Christ Historical Society, Nashville, Tennessee.)

Smart sold his interest in the company and moved to Kansas City. Garrison and Johnson worked together as coeditors until Johnson's death in May 1894. The two men were equal in rank but not in function. A former pastor, professor, college president, and corresponding secretary of the American Christian Missionary Society, Johnson supplied editorials on a regular basis and edited certain sections of the journal, but Garrison was clearly the dominant partner.

The Christian-Evangelist grew in circulation and influence. The subscription list increased from 16,000 in 1882 to 25,000 in 1884 and then fluctuated in that general range until Garrison's retirement in 1912. The journal's influence outdistanced its circulation, particularly in the period between Johnson's death and Garrison's retirement. Second only to the *Christian Standard* as a representative organ among Disciples at the turn of the century, *The Christian-Evangelist* surpassed its rival from Cincinnati during the Disciples controversy over church federation from 1902 to 1907. Decades later it circulated again as *The Christian* before merging with *World Call* to form a semimonthly, *The Disciple,* on January 1, 1974.

Many people contributed to the rise of *The Christian-Evangelist* from an inconsequential monthly to the most powerful weekly in the Disciples, but the achievement was largely the result of James Harvey Garrison's solid and sustained leadership. Unquestionably he set the tone of the paper and determined its week-to-week witness. Fundamental to his thinking was a concern for Christian unity. With unflagging zeal he urged Disciples to take the initiative in uniting a divided church by restoring New Testament Christianity. Where the Scriptures spoke, he spoke; and where the Scriptures were silent, he resorted to "sanctified common sense."

As long as Isaac Errett controlled the *Christian Standard,* his paper and *The Christian-Evangelist* took essentially the same position in responding to the majority of significant questions confronting Disciples.[21] Six weeks before his death

21. Garrison and Errett did differ over the most feasible method of opposing the liquor traffic. A prohibitionist, Garrison expressed grave concern when Errett came out in favor of "moral suasion." Heated disagreements between their two papers were caused by a marked increase in business rivalry after Errett relinquished control of the Standard Publishing Company in 1880. SEE William E. Tucker, *J. H. Garrison and Disciples of Christ,* pp. 214-220.

Errett wrote Garrison a letter which has been quoted frequently by historians of Disciples:

> We have been together from the beginning of this Foreign Missionary work. We have stood shoulder to shoulder in all the conflicts through which the society has passed and the two most effective instrumentalities in educating our people and bringing them into active co-operation in spreading the Gospel in all lands have been the *Christian Evangelist* and the *Christian Standard;* and indeed upon all points of doctrine and practice and expediency, as bearing on our great reformatory work, you and I have always worked on the same lines, in perfect harmony. I have always had unbounded confidence in you, and a sincere admiration of your spirit, your practical wisdom and your unostentatious consecration to the work of Christ.[22]

Just as important as the letter was Garrison's use of it. He cited it on a number of occasions to prove his close relationship with Errett. Garrison cherished Errett's favor, for Errett was his ideal and hero. Many historians have suggested that the editor of *The Christian-Evangelist* assumed the role of primary leadership among Disciples after Errett's death; none has recognized that Garrison self-consciously wore Errett's mantle.

In addition to the *Christian Standard* and *The Christian-Evangelist,* many other papers vied for the attention and backing of Disciples after the Civil War. The *Apostolic Times,* published in Lexington, Kentucky, attempted to develop a following among those who regarded the *American Christian Review's* position as counterproductive but refused to accept the progressive approach of Isaac Errett. Founded in 1869, the *Apostolic Times* faltered under the weight of its own inconsistencies and succeeded only in antagonizing just about everyone. It was merged with the *Old Path Guide* to create the *Apostolic Guide* in 1885.

During the war Marcia M. Bassett (?-1885), the only woman in the editorial circle of Disciples, edited and published the *Ladies' Christian Monitor* in Cincinnati. After marrying Elijah Goodwin in 1864 she moved to his home in Indianapolis. Continuing her paper, she also started *Mother's*

---

22. Letter, Isaac Errett to James H. Garrison, November 2, 1888. (The J. H. Garrison Papers.)

Monitor before combining the two into the *Christian Monitor* in 1866. A strong commitment to the missionary enterprise marked her career in religious journalism. Several months before her death she accepted the editorship of *Missionary Tidings,* the new monthly of the Christian Woman's Board of Missions. As if to condense her message of many years into a single sentence, she wrote in the first issue of *Missionary Tidings: "Failure* is a word which has never been written upon the banner of the sisters of the Church of Christ."[23]

For a brief period in the mid-1860s William W. Dowling (1834-1920) published the *Little Sower,* one of the first Sunday school magazines in the Disciples. In later years the author of many manuals and study guides, including *The Lesson Primer: A Book of Easy Lessons for Little Learners, on Bible Studies,* he also published the *Morning Watch* and the *Little Sower and Little Chief.*

In sharp contrast to the contents of Dowling's publications were *Lard's Quarterly* and the *Christian Quarterly,* both of which aimed to promote serious discussion and to sharpen the theological focus of Disciples. The conservative *Lard's Quarterly,* established by Moses E. Lard in 1863, attracted 1,700 subscribers in the first year. Claiming a need for a circulation of 3,000 but never reaching that level, he had no alternative but to discontinue his quarterly in 1868. The following year William T. Moore launched the *Christian Quarterly.* As scholarly and progressive as any periodical produced by Disciples in the nineteenth century, the *Christian Quarterly* even devoted considerable space to the review of theological literature in French and German. Far beyond the understanding of most preachers, not to mention the rank and file of laypersons, Moore's quarterly received favorable notice in Europe but appealed only to a tiny minority of Disciples. After sinking five thousand dollars of his own money into the venture, he wrote a "closing word" to his readers and suspended the paper in 1876.

As Moore and Lard could testify, religious journalism was a frustrating and costly business after the Civil War. Although the history of Disciples is cluttered with the remains of

---

23. *Missionary Tidings,* May 1883, p. 1. Quoted in Lorraine Lollis, *The Shape of Adam's Rib: A Lively History of Women's Work in the Christian Church* (St. Louis: The Bethany Press, 1970), pp. 65-66.

suspended papers, a few journals survived and thrived and gave their editors a solid base from which to assume and retain leadership in the second generation.

PROMINENT PREACHERS

The strong and pervasive influence of periodical literature on the Disciples by no means lessened the significance of the pulpit in the post-Civil War era. Whether or not most preachers in the movement understood themselves to be apostles of Alexander Campbell, with few exceptions they parroted his message to congregations large and small across the land. Regardless of their wrangling over theological nuances, they agreed that the Sage of Bethany had cornered the truth revealed in the Bible. What he discovered, so to say, they repeated almost by rote, recognizing little or no distinction between "Our Plea" and the New Testament witness. Deficient for the most part in education and in cultural awareness, they excelled in conviction and were effective if not sophisticated.

There was wide variety in the quality of Disciples preaching, to be sure. Some heralds of the Word consistently tested the patience of their hearers; many others proceeded from week to week in a workmanlike manner, all the while fired by the desire to convert and to nurture believers in the apostolic faith. Still others, endowed with rare gifts of mind and heart, rose to prominence in the pulpit and gained recognition far beyond the locale of their ministry.

To highlight what he judged to be "representative" Disciples preaching, William T. Moore edited *The Living Pulpit of the Christian Church* in 1868. A collection of twenty-eight sermons, the volume also contained the editor's introductory essay and a brief biography of each contributor. The preachers, selected by Moore, included David S. Burnet, Isaac Errett, Tolbert Fanning, Benjamin Franklin, Charles L. Loos, Robert Milligan, and William K. Pendleton. At the risk of showing a lack of modesty the editor added his own name to the impressive list. In the interest of propriety the sketch of his life was prepared by Dr. L. L. Pinkerton; a footnote assured readers that Pinkerton's laudatory comments were printed as received.

Knowles Shaw (1834-1878), the most successful revivalist in the Disciples from the early 1860s to his death, is not even mentioned in *The Living Pulpit*. His omission was hardly a glaring oversight, for Shaw achieved his reputation as a singing evangelist. Publisher of *The Morning Star* and four other religious songbooks, he composed a number of gospel hymns. His "Bringing in the Sheaves" was popular for many years, and countless congregations can yet sing the refrain without referring to a hymnal.

Shaw grew up in Rush County, Indiana, and was baptized in 1852. Beginning his evangelistic career six years later, he used his musical talents to advance his ministry. According to one of Shaw's admirers, "Many came to hear him sing, and remained to listen to his enthusiastic and convincing sermon." Although he devoted most of his time to strengthening Disciples in the Midwest, he led revivals in towns and cities from Michigan to Texas. Seldom at home with his wife and children, he observed a few months before his death that for the preceding thirteen years "he had not been out of a protracted meeting for two weeks in succession."[24] Shaw was killed in a train wreck near McKinney, Texas. Despite his death at the early age of forty-four, he received around 20,000 people into the membership of the Disciples.

Jacob V. Updike (1850-1907) succeeded Knowles Shaw as the best known professional revivalist among Disciples. Following the example of Dwight L. Moody and Ira D. Sankey, he and James E. Hawes (1862-1933) formed an evangelistic team. With Updike responsible for preaching and Hawes leading the singing, the two men met with great success before disbanding to take pastorates. Their "passion for souls" and their concern "to establish churches after the New Testament pattern" inspired other evangelistic teams to travel up and down the revival road in the name of the Lord and for the sake of the Disciples.

Dr. Lewis L. Pinkerton was utterly different from professional revivalists like Knowles Shaw and J. V. Updike in his understanding of Christian faith and in his approach to preaching. A provocative thinker and a serious student throughout his ministry, Pinkerton preached so as to stretch

---

24. William Baxter, *Life of Knowles Shaw: The Singing Evangelist* (Cincinnati: Central Book Concern, 1879), p. 40.

NINETEENTH CENTURY PEOPLE AND SCENES

John Rogers

"Raccoon" John Smith

John T. Johnson

Jacob Creath, Jr.

Robert Richardson

Thomas Munnell

Knowles Shaw

James A. Garfield

Sample church plans from
Board of Church Extension

St. Louis Christian Home

"Old Main" at Drake University

the minds of his hearers as well as to touch their hearts.

The personal influence of Alexander Campbell led Pinkerton to reject Presbyterianism and become a Disciple in 1830. After practicing medicine for a few years he gave up his profession in 1838 and began to preach. Of the several congregations which he served, he was most deeply attached to the one in Midway, Kentucky. During his ministry there he provided the key leadership in establishing Kentucky Female Orphan School (now Midway College).

Pinkerton did not hesitate to question accepted patterns of thought and practice among Disciples. As early as 1849 he abandoned the doctrine of biblical inerrancy. It was absurd, he reasoned, to suppose that all passages of Scripture were equally and fully inspired by God. He preferred the Presbyterian structure of church government; and he lashed out at fierce democrats among Disciples who attacked every effort at regional and national cooperation. "The greatest little tyrants I have known have been the greatest sticklers for what they call the independence of churches," he said. Pinkerton must have caused strict restorationists to wince when he wrote in 1873:

The New Testament is not a code of cast-iron laws for trembling slaves; but a rule of life for loving children—not a hole through a granite rock, through which fools and Pharisees are required to crawl on all-fours, but the "King's high-way," on which rational beings with free spirits, and with their heads turned toward the stars, are called to walk.[25]

---

25. For quotes from Pinkerton SEE *Life, Letters and Addresses of Dr. L. L. Pinkerton,* ed. by John Shackelford, Jr., pp. 108-111.

If candor is a cardinal virtue, Dr. L. L. Pinkerton achieved sainthood. Denounced as an eccentric and a heretic, he was the first real "liberal" among Disciples.

Moses E. Lard and Winthrop H. Hopson were at least the equals of Pinkerton in the pulpit. Many of the faithful judged that both men set a standard of excellence in preaching which the liberal from Midway never quite matched.

Lard grew up in poverty and received his early education in the school of adversity. Unable to write his name until he was seventeen years old, he entered Bethany College in 1845 and graduated at the top of his class. In time he became a gifted writer and an eloquent preacher. Although he was known to have disappointed congregations occasionally, at his best he was captivating. One of his ardent admirers was "Old Uncle Si Collins,"* a pioneer preacher in Kentucky. In the midst of one of Lard's masterful sermons, "Uncle Si" was so moved that he shouted to his friend, William Azbill: "Brother Bill, isn't he [Lard] a sugar stick!" The remark was quoted frequently to illustrate Lard's compelling power in the pulpit.

When asked if he or Lard were the greater preacher, Winthrop Hopson replied: "Up to thirty sermons Lard can beat anybody, after that, up to two hundred and fifty, I can beat him."[26] Hopson had the advantage of a good education; he was proficient in Latin before Lard could write his name. After completing a baccalaureate program and receiving a medical degree in Missouri, he chose to enter the Disciples ministry instead of pursuing a career in medicine. An evangelist and pastor, he served the important congregation in Lexington, Kentucky, from December 1859 to April 1862.

As a preacher Hopson was a craftsman. His most famous sermon was entitled "The Three-fold Aspects of Divine Truth." According to Jesse J. Haley (1851-1924), who heard the sermon twice, Hopson took two and one-half hours to deliver it each time. Despite its extreme length, dozens of Disciples preached the sermon as their own. Hopson prepared messages for more congregations than he knew. Presumably, the plagiarists improved on his time if not on his content.

Otis A. Burgess (1829-1882), able educator, skilled debater,

---

26. Quoted in Jesse J. Haley, *Makers and Molders of the Reformation Movement* (St. Louis: Christian Board of Publication, 1914), p. 98.

and pastor of Central Christian Church in Indianapolis from 1862 to 1869, and George W. Longan (1819-1891) of Missouri also received wide recognition for their pulpit ability. Their contemporary, Alexander Procter (1825-1900), deserves more than passing reference. Perhaps he was the preeminent preacher in the Disciples between the Civil War and the turn of the last century.

Alexander Campbell played a helpful role in Procter's preparation for ministry. Campbell provided a scholarship at Bethany College with income from the sale of his hymnbook in Missouri. The selection committee named Procter as recipient. He enrolled in Bethany in 1845 and graduated with distinction in 1848. Probably he was the first Disciples minister in Missouri to earn a college degree.

Procter spent his entire ministry in Missouri and for over forty years he served the congregation in Independence. A perceptive student of theology and philosophy with a genuine interest in all human life and thought, he read voraciously and kept at his fingertips the latest monographs from Europe. Some of his detractors called him a "Missouri rationalist" because he rejected the verbal infallibility of the Bible and accepted evolutionary theory without dismissing God from the universe. His spiritual and intellectual pilgrimage followed a trail far removed from the well-worn paths of narrow denominationalism. Wrote Jesse J. Haley: "Logic-chopping, hair-splitting, Shibboleth-pronouncing, prejudice-engendering sectarianism, under no guise of pretense or sanctification, had any attraction for him."[27] Members of his congregation admired and trusted him even when they could not comprehend the heights and depths he reached in the pulpit.

Procter was an unusual individual in many ways. He never answered letters and seldom wrote for publication, preferring instead to weed his garden or tend his roses or read and ponder. Yet he became known throughout and beyond the Disciples. When Burris Jenkins (1869-1945) entered Harvard University and mentioned that he had grown up in Kansas City, more than one professor responded: "Do you know Alexander Procter? Tell me about him."[28] If Procter aimed to

---

27. *Ibid.*, p. 154.
28. Burris Jenkins, *Where My Caravan Has Rested* (Chicago: Willett, Clark and Company, 1939), p. 75.

avoid public notice, he failed. It had no noticeable effect on him, however. He was content to preach in Independence and bear witness tó the fruits of an emancipated mind.

A one-time Disciples preacher, James A. Garfield substituted political platform for pulpit and advanced all the way to the White House. Unordained like most ministers of the Disciples in the late 1850s, he preached regularly on Sundays while engaged primarily as teacher and then as principal at Hiram College in Ohio. Following a brief period in the Ohio senate and notable service in the Union Army, he became a United States congressman in 1863 and won reelection to the House eight consecutive times. The Republican Party nominated him for President in 1880, and he defeated his Democratic opponent in the November election. A disappointed office seeker assassinated him less than four months after he assumed office; he died on September 19, 1881. Although James A. Garfield changed the focus of his career from religion to politics, he remained a devoted churchman and a respected leader among the Disciples until his death.

EDUCATION FOR MINISTRY

Second generation preachers and editors of the Disciples were alike in one respect: they moved into positions of power and influence without the benefit of theological education. Preparation for ministry, by and large, was informal and haphazard. Scores of preachers were recruited from the ranks of the laity and sometimes prepared for ministerial service by working with pulpit veterans. From time to time Alexander Campbell and Walter Scott gave special instruction to men aspiring to preach. So did others. Except for these scattered and short-term efforts, Disciples paid little attention to education for ministry.

To improve the situation, the Newburg (now Cleveland) yearly meeting authorized the establishment of a "School of the Preachers" in Ohio. Fifteen men attended the first session at New Lisbon in December 1835. They in actuality participated in a preaching seminar, for they delivered sermons and criticized each other. The first edition of Alexander Campbell's *Christian System* served with the Bible as their text. Continued annually until 1839, the program was absorbed by the regular session for preachers held during yearly meetings. When Campbell opened wide the doors of Bethany College the next year, he implemented a curriculum which required thorough study of the Bible as an essential of liberal education. To his mind, Bethany provided all the academic background a Disciples preacher needed.

A new era in ministerial education among Disciples began in 1865 with the founding of The College of the Bible (now Lexington Theological Seminary) in Lexington, Kentucky. Appropriately named, it was one of the colleges in the institution formed through a merger of Kentucky University and Transylvania University. Notwithstanding William K. Pendleton's and Isaac Errett's insistence that preachers like lawyers and physicians ought to have professional preparation beyond the college level, Benjamin Franklin and others vigorously opposed the concept of a "theological school." It is not surprising that the first venture of Disciples in theological education took the form of a "College of the *Bible*." Many decades passed before they felt free to describe this institution and others similar to it in name and function as theological seminaries or divinity schools.

The College of the Bible's first president, Robert Milligan, already was at work on *The Scheme of Redemption* when he walked into "Old Morrison" on the historic Transylvania campus to take up his administrative duties. John W. McGarvey, pastor of the Main Street Church in Lexington, and Milligan constituted the faculty for the first session in the fall of 1865. William T. Moore joined them the following semester. He commuted to Lexington from Cincinnati where he served as minister of Central Christian Church. From an initial enrollment of 37 the number of students increased steadily to 122 in 1870-1871 and then dropped sharply over the next six years. Although beset by numerous crises The College of the Bible not only survived but grew and developed into a graduate theological seminary.[29]

The impact of John W. McGarvey on The College of the Bible was nothing less than decisive. "For nearly half a century, from 1865 to 1911, the name of The College of the Bible was all but synonymous with that of John W. McGarvey," the historian of the Seminary has written. He added: "Although

---

29. For an account of the origin and early development of The College of the Bible SEE Dwight E. Stevenson, *Lexington Theological Seminary, 1865-1965*, pp. 11-36.

he did not become president of the institution until 1895, he emerged almost immediately in 1865 as its leading personality and its most influential teacher."[30]

"Brother McGarvey," as he was called by friend and adversary alike, graduated from Bethany College in 1850 and two years later was ordained by Thomas M. Allen and Alexander Procter. After serving the Christian Church in Dover, Missouri, for almost a decade, he moved to the Main Street Church of Lexington in 1862 and then on to The College of the Bible. In addition to his *Commentary on Acts,* completed and published while the Civil War raged, he wrote many other aids to biblical study including the popular and still useful *Lands of the Bible.* A "mentor of the brotherhood," McGarvey labored indefatigably to keep his students and Disciples everywhere from adopting the approach and findings of biblical critics. Praised as a stalwart defender of the true faith, he also was lambasted as a narrow-minded foe of liberal learning. However his contemporaries may have regarded his point of view, they did not minimize his influence.

John W. McGarvey claimed to be a faithful Disciple and to stand firmly in the Stone-Campbell tradition. So did David Lipscomb, Mrs. Marcia M. B. Goodwin, Isaac Errett, and Alexander Procter, to name but a handful of key leaders. They disagreed sharply, however, in their attempts to interpret a useful past so as to shape a viable future. Petty bickering led to heated controversy and engulfed the entire movement. The late nineteenth century was a period of dissension and division for the Christian Church (Disciples of Christ).

---

30. *Ibid.,* p. 11.

10

DISCORD LEADS TO DIVISION

Even the most farseeing and perceptive Disciple in 1865 could hardly have anticipated the bewildering complexity of the post-Civil War era in the United States. The North, prosperous and optimistic, channeled much of its vitality into commerce and industry. Northern entrepreneurs paved the way for Calvin Coolidge to remark many years later that "the business of America is business." Although Abraham Lincoln had insisted on "malice toward none" and "charity toward all" in his Second Inaugural, the South had no alternative but to endure the ordeal of Reconstruction. Embittered by the devastation of "the terrible swift sword" and stirred by haunting memories of a bygone age, southerners grimly set about rebuilding amid the dust and ashes of their shattered society. Cheap land coupled with discoveries of gold and silver lured a virtual flood of people into the vast area from the Mississippi to the Pacific. The conquering of the West became an American saga in record time. "As early as 1883," Henry Steele Commager observed, "Buffalo Bill found it profitable to turn his career into a show."[1] Seven years later the United States Census Bureau acknowledged the passing of the frontier.

---

1. Henry S. Commager, *The American Mind* (New Haven: Yale University Press, 1950), p. 44.

The population of the nation increased from 31,500,000 to 76,000,000 between 1865 and 1900. Accounting for much of the gain were the millions of European immigrants who joined native Americans in flocking to already burgeoning cities. In 1860 only one-sixth of the population lived in communities of 8,000 or more; forty years later townspeople numbered one in three. During the same period the population of Detroit quadrupled, while Chicago grew from a frontier outpost in 1833 to the fifth largest city of the world by the turn of the century. "In the generation following the Civil War," wrote Arthur M. Schlesinger, "the city took supreme command."[2]

Rapid industrial expansion created an enormous demand for bluecollar workers, prompting more and more families to crowd into urban areas and face the daily agony of tenement life. The nation's total wealth doubled and then more than doubled again in the thirty-year period following 1860. A rash of inventions—including the Pullman car in the 1860s and the incandescent lamp in the 1870s—added fuel to the "second industrial revolution." Striking advances in transportation linked the states and territories of the nation together. The Union Pacific and Central Pacific completed the first transcontinental railroad when the two companies joined their tracks with a golden spike west of Ogden, Utah, on May 10, 1869. By 1900 the nation could boast of more railroad mileage than all of Europe. In sum, the United States became an industrial giant during the life span of a single generation.

Intellectual ferment also marked the postwar era. Pioneers in science surprised the pious, arousing them from their dogmatic slumbers. Charles Darwin's theory of organic evolution, advanced in England, seemed to discredit the time-honored Genesis account of man's origin. An American edition of Darwin's book, *The Origin of Species,* appeared in 1860 but did not attract widespread interest until after the Civil War. A generation earlier Sir Charles Lyell and others had estimated the age of the earth in the millions of years, thereby suggesting that geology was at odds with the Book of Genesis. The testimony of the rocks, it appeared, substantiated neither a literal interpretation of the creation

---

2. Arthur M. Schlesinger, *Paths to the Present* (New York: The Macmillan Company, 1949), p. 223.

narratives in the Bible nor Archbishop Ussher's ingenious attempt to establish the marvelous "week of creation" in 4004 B.C. The new world of science and the old world of religion collided.

POSTWAR DISCIPLES

Disciples of Christ moved through the late 1860s and the 1870s preoccupied with the unfinished agenda of their prewar years. They reaffirmed their allegiance to the Stone-Campbell position without reaching consensus as to its fundamental meaning for their life together. A few outspoken thinkers—Lewis L. Pinkerton and Alexander Procter, to name but two—addressed themselves to fresh intellectual concerns, but they constituted a tiny minority. Many Disciples preachers and laypeople were content to travel on "the old paths" into a new era.

Although the center of power and influence in the United States shifted decisively from the country to the city, Disciples remained predominantly a rural and small-town communion. In 1890 only six and two-thirds percent of their membership resided in communities of 25,000 or more; and as late as 1917 over half of their members and eighty-two percent of their congregations were located in the country or in towns of 2,500 or less. Failing to develop an urban strategy, they stood little chance of attracting a significant following among the millions of immigrants other than English-speaking Protestants. Even so, Disciples grew at twice the rate of the nation's population in the post-Civil War era. Beginning with a membership of 192,000 in 1860, they increased to 400,000 in 1875 and then to 1,120,000 in 1900.

This extraordinary growth was an advance through storm. As Disciples developed into a major body in American Protestantism, they reflected what James H. Garrison aptly termed a "morbid fondness of controversy." From their inception, of course, they prized diversity and appeared to thrive on disagreement, clashing both with their religious neighbors and with each other. During and following the Civil War, however, dissension reached a new level of intensity and clouded the future of the movement.

Alexander Campbell's death in 1866 left Disciples un-prepared for an era of transit and tension. Notwithstanding their tendency to take issue with each other, they had sensed their oneness in his commanding presence. Their acknowledged leader, he symbolized both their strength and their potential. The news of his death neither shocked nor overwhelmed them, but they never recovered from the loss of his towering influence. "Even though they grew for a while," Ronald E. Osborn has suggested, "at Campbell's death they immediately began to fall apart. No one succeeded him, for his leadership was charismatic, not official, and the leaders who came after had diverse spirits."[3]

Animosity stemming directly from the Civil War posed a further threat to Campbell's followers. Long after the nation returned to peace and passed through the chaos of reconstruction, sectional bitterness continued to plague the movement. As a consequence, Disciples prayed for Christian unity but could not bring themselves to bury their differences.

The necessity of adjusting to a culture in the throes of social and economic change also contributed to discord among Disciples in the late nineteenth century. Those who attained some measure of financial success found it difficult to understand their brothers and sisters in the faith who reaped little benefit from the growing wealth of the nation. When Disciples moved into nicer and larger houses, they were not content to worship in simple and tasteless church buildings. Having purchased a melodeon for the pleasure of family and friends, they quite naturally mounted a campaign to get a musical instrument for the congregation. As they provided for their children to receive additional education in one of the many church-related colleges or newly founded state universities springing up across the country, they became increasingly uncomfortable in the presence of an un-sophisticated and self-taught preacher. Nontheological forces helped to shape the life and thought of Disciples of Christ as well as every other religious movement.

---

3. Ronald E. Osborn, "Dogmatically Absolute, Historically Relative" in *The Reformation of Tradition,* ed. by Ronald E. Osborn (St. Louis: The Bethany Press, 1963), p. 279.

The strife among postwar Disciples, however, was far more than a thinly disguised social and cultural clash. The doctrine of the church, long the central theological concern of the movement, became a problem of the first magnitude for them. As they pondered the nature and structure of the church in the light of the biblical record and their own self-understanding, they found themselves split into contentious parties. Pressed to determine the basic stance of their fellowship, they asked in essence: "What are the marks of the true church?" "Is the church primarily an inclusive or an exclusive community?" "Can the church respond to changing circumstances and remain receptive to the work of the Holy Spirit in every age without sacrificing either her catholicity or her apostolicity?" The more Disciples grappled with these and related questions, the less agreement they sensed among themselves.

Many years earlier Thomas Campbell unintentionally had laid the foundation for a full-scale debate. Aiming to reform a nineteenth-century church that in his judgment was neither catholic nor apostolic, he challenged Christians to close their ranks on the basis of New Testament Christianity. In the *Declaration and Address* Campbell proposed that followers of Christ accept the New Testament as the church's *constitution*. He added: "Nothing ought to be received into the faith or worship of the Church, or be made a term of communion among Christians, that is not as old as the New Testament." Rejecting all creedal affirmations in the interest of restoring "the ancient order," Campbell summarized his biblicism in the form of a motto: "Where the Scriptures speak, we speak; where the Scriptures are silent, we are silent."

In time this expression, accepted as a slogan by Disciples everywhere, created more problems than it solved. Strict constructionists or scholastics among the Disciples insisted that the church's organization and elements of worship must be derived from explicit scriptural commands and precedents. "That which the Bible does not specifically teach is prohibited," they maintained. The silence of Scripture was binding, to their way of thinking. Holding to this inflexible point of view, Benjamin Franklin wrote in 1875: "The brethren in Tennessee have not received the supplement to the last commission, to 'observe all things whatsoever I have not forbidden,' but are simply under the old commission, 'all things whatsoever I have commanded.' "[4]

Convinced that such legalistic primitivism utterly perverted Thomas Campbell's motto, moderate or progressive Disciples retorted that the silence of the New Testament was permissive rather than restrictive. Responding to the strict constructionists, they countered: "That which the Bible does not specifically prohibit is permitted." In 1869, for example, John A. Hoke asked the editors of the *Gospel Echo* to answer the question: "Is the Sunday School, as a *distinct* organization . . . authorized in the Christian scriptures?" The junior editor replied in the affirmative on the ground that "any means which is necessarily employed to carry out a command is authorized by the authority giving the command." He then applied his principle to uphold the establishment of Sunday schools:

The great fountain head of all authority for preaching or teaching the gospel . . . is the grand, world-wide commission given by our Savior to his Apostles . . . : "Go ye, therefore, into all the world and preach the gospel to every *creature*." Now, I think a little reflection will convince any one that the successful carrying out of this command, necessitates some such organization as the Sunday School.[5]

Where the Scriptures spoke, moderate Disciples spoke; but where the Scriptures were silent, they claimed the right—indeed the duty—to use "sanctified common sense" and to follow "enlightened judgment."

Unwilling to fossilize the living organism of the church, moderates sought to be adaptable without relinquishing or compromising the historic message of the Disciples. This approach alarmed strict constructionists. Accommodation, they argued, would lead inevitably to innovations; and innovations would result in the bankruptcy of "The Plea." Thus they decided to stand firm lest the grand design of New Testament faith and practice be swept away by a flood of change.

Among the staunchest opponents of change in the Disciples of Christ was Moses E. Lard. To shed light on the state of the movement in 1865, he wrote a widely quoted article entitled

---

4. *American Christian Review,* 1875, p. 220. Quoted in Earl I. West, *The Life and Times of David Lipscomb,* p. 136.
5. *Gospel Echo,* June 1869, pp. 224-225.

"The Work of the Past—Symptoms of the Future." No one needed to convince him of the unusual significance of the Stone-Campbell tradition. "Within the hands of this brotherhood, *and within their hands only,* is kept the cause which is the last hope of earth," he asserted. Lard was a deeply troubled man despite his certainty that the future belonged to Disciples. Having detected a growing tendency to push for innovations, he felt obliged to issue a stern warning with the hope of marshaling a solid flank of resistance:

He is a poor observer of men and things who does not see slowly growing up among us a class of men who can no longer be satisfied with the ancient gospel and the ancient order of things. These men must have changes; and silently they are preparing the mind of the brotherhood to receive changes. Be not deceived, brethren, the Devil is not sleeping. If you refuse to see the danger till ruin is upon you, then it will be too late. The wise seaman catches the first whiff of the distant storm, and adjusts his ship at once. Let us profit by his example.

Continuing, he thundered:

Let us agree to commune with the sprinkled sects around us, and soon we shall come to recognize them as Christians. Let us agree to recognize them as Christians, and immersion, with its deep significance, is buried in the grave of our folly. Then in not one whit will we be better than others. . . . Let us consent to introduce opinions in politics as tests of fellowship, and soon opinions in religion will become so. Then the door of heresy and schism will stand wide open, and the work of ruin will begin. Let us agree to admit organs, and soon the pious, the meek, the peace-loving, will abandon us, and our churches will become gay worldly things, literal Noah's arks, full of clean and unclean beasts. Too all this let us yet add, by way of dessert, and as a sort of spice to the dish, a few volumes of innerlight speculations, and a cargo or two of *reverend* dandies dubbed pastors, and we may congratulate ourselves on having completed the trip in a wonderfully short time. We can now take rooms in Rome, and chuckle over the fact that we are as orthodox as the rankest heretic in the land.[6]

Lard's assumptions may have been questionable and his conclusions unwarranted, but he understood the temper of Disciples in his time. An increasing number in the movement welcomed innovations as unmistakable signs of progress;

6. *Lard's Quarterly,* April 1865, Vol. II, p. 262. See also p. 251.

others saw them as harbingers of decline; still others waited for further developments before reaching any conclusions.

THE TABLE OF THE LORD

Before Lard's article appeared, Disciples already had adopted a more liberal approach to the observance of the Lord's Supper. In their early witness Alexander Campbell and the Reformers had yielded to the logic of an inflexible position and defended "close communion"—the practice of admitting only believers baptized by immersion to the service of Communion. Less rigid in their primitivism, Stone and the Christians refused to fence the Table of the Lord in order to keep out "defective believers." As Campbell moved into maturity, he modified his view and joined some of his followers in shifting from close to open communion. The impulse to reflect the oneness of God's people around the Lord's Table was stronger than the will to hold fast to an exclusivist interpretation of New Testament Christianity.

Basically Disciples had settled the communion question when Richard Hawley (1815?-1884) of Detroit wrote Isaac Errett in 1861, requesting him to comment on the practice of communing with unimmersed Christians. In reply Errett suggested that Disciples existed for the purpose of reuniting the scattered people of God and were under no mandate to "unchristianize" the pious unimmersed. Close communion could not be justified, Errett reasoned, precisely because many of the devout in other religious bodies were Christian despite their misunderstanding of baptism. He added: "For myself, while fully devoted to our plea, I have no wish to limit and fetter my sympathies and affections to our own people."[7]

Errett's letter, published in *The Millennial Harbinger,* brought about an extensive interchange in 1862. George W. Elley (1801-1884) wrote a series of articles supporting close communion. Each of them was printed and answered in *The Millennial Harbinger.* Elley stated his argument in capsule form. The church is composed only of those who are "born again"; only those who confess their faith, repent of their sins, and submit to immersion in water are "born again";

---

7. *Millennial Harbinger,* December 1861, p. 711.

they and only they "are citizens of Christ's kingdom" and "lawfully entitled to the ordinances of God's house." If Disciples could not or would not maintain the purity of the church, they were headed straight for Rome and not Jerusalem.[8]

Benjamin Franklin and Moses E. Lard agreed wholeheartedly. Lard went so far as to deny that Martin Luther, the great sixteenth-century Protestant reformer, was a Christian. To quote Lard's own words, "I mean to say distinctly and emphatically that Martin Luther, if not immersed, was not a Christian—this is what I mean to say." Assuming that he would be accused of Pharisaism and exclusivism, Lard wrote: "Be it so." "I stagger at nothing if true, at everything if false."[9]

William K. Pendleton and Robert Richardson sided with Isaac Errett. Denying that open communion would lead to the admission of the unimmersed into full church membership, Pendleton used the example of "Father [Thomas] Campbell" and the witness of the Apostle Paul to answer the strict primitivists. According to Pendleton, Paul got to the heart of the matter when he wrote to the church at Corinth: "Let a man examine himself, and so let him eat of this bread and drink of this cup." One's fitness to commune did not depend upon the judgment, however sound, of either priest or elders. "This is as it should be," wrote Pendleton.

The repast is, pre-eminently, a spiritual one; and as "no man can know what is in a man but the spirit of the man which is within him," it is most happy for us that the true fitness for participation in the Lord's Supper should be left to the discrimination of each man's own heart, under the searching scrutiny of the Holy Spirit, which penetrates into and reveals even the deep things of God.[10]

Pendleton nudged Disciples toward a wider fellowship by justifying their prevailing practice. In 1862, according to Isaac Errett, around two-thirds of Disciples congregations in the United States had lowered the barriers surrounding the Communion service. They spread the Table in the name of

---

8. *Millennial Harbinger,* January 1862, pp. 41-42.
9. *Lard's Quarterly,* September 1863, Vol. I, p. 44.
10. *Millennial Harbinger,* February 1862, p. 64.

the Lord and for his people, placing responsibility for sharing in the celebration of the Supper squarely on each communicant. Their slogan, "We neither invite nor debar," gave forceful expression to a firm position, at once legalistic and evasive. For many it was a mark of openness. Others retreated behind it, showing no cordiality or ecumenical tendency.

The controversy over the communion question ended as quickly as it began. Probably never since that time has so little clamor accompanied a major shift in practice among Disciples. Other innovations—particularly the replacement of peripatetic preachers with settled ministers, the use of instrumental music in worship, and the development of missionary societies—proved to be vastly more disruptive to the "Reformation Movement of the Nineteenth Century."

TOWARD A MORE EFFECTIVE MINISTRY

Surprising as it may seem, Disciples came into existence and expanded rapidly without the benefit of pastors or resident ministers. There were no full-time religious workers at the outset, for Disciples preachers had to farm or earn a living by some other means. Preachers served as part-time traveling evangelists. Congregations relied upon lay elders for week-to-week instruction and general oversight.

A practical necessity when congregations multiplied faster than the supply of preachers, this itinerant ministry also mirrored the strong anticlericalism of Alexander Campbell. At the time he launched *The Christian Baptist* he was as antagonistic toward the "professional minister" as any religious leader of his age. Practically everything that spoiled Christianity, in his judgment, could be traced directly to the "kingdom of the clergy." Ambitious and greedy, they lorded it over the churches and got paid for doing so. Reserving a full measure of his severest invective for men who fed their pride by using the titles of "reverend" and "doctor," he dedicated himself to cutting them down to size and closing the gap between long-suffering laypeople and the "hireling clergy." Campbell grew to appreciate the need for an educated and specially trained ministry, but the anticlericalism of his early witness made a deep mark on the Disciples of Christ.

In time several Disciples congregations became strong enough to support a resident minister. Probably the first two full-time pastors in the communion were David S. Burnet and Isaac Errett, both of whom served Ohio congregations in the 1840s. Within the next thirty years the settled pastorate gained gradual acceptance.

Strict primitivists found no precedent in the New Testament for what they termed the "one-man system." Rather than risk a concentration of power in one individual, each early Christian congregation vested authority in a "plurality of elders." So the argument went. Fearful of religious hierarchy in any form, Benjamin Franklin opposed "the building up of a new or older order of *clergy,* as a class, distinct from other members of the Church" and all "clerical conventions . . . or associations for their own government . . . or any other purpose not taught in Scripture, . . ."[11] No doubt economic privation merged with biblicism to shape the basis for opposition. Those who could not afford a resident minister were gratified to learn that there were none in the New Testament.

While conservative Disciples called attention to the potential for tyranny in the office of pastor, moderates were more concerned about the ineffective rule of uncommitted laymen. To their mind, the practice of choosing unqualified men for leadership merely to satisfy the requirement for a "plurality of elders" endangered the integrity and vitality of the church. James H. Garrison, for example, flatly rejected "the irrational idea that it is more scriptural to have a plurality of men *called* elders, who have not the capacity and do not discharge the *duties* of elders, than to have one real pastor or overseer who can feed and care for the flock."[12] Garrison welcomed the trend toward the parish ministry because he felt certain that generally the most qualified elder in a local congregation would be the resident minister. Disciples were growing up; moderates saw no reason to hinder a normal process.

Strict and moderate restorationists failed to reach agreement. Neither side was willing to compromise its understand-

---

11. Quoted from *American Christian Review* in *Biographical Sketch and Writings of Elder Benjamin Franklin,* ed. by John F. Rowe and G. W. Rice (Cincinnati: Published by G. W. Rice, 1881), Vol. I, pp. 53-54.
12. *Christian-Evangelist,* April 16, 1891, p. 242.

ing of the preacher's function and responsibility. From time to time small matters were blown up out of all proportion to their significance. Although Isaac Errett preferred to be called "brother" or "elder," a number of his friends in Detroit gave him a doorplate inscribed "Rev. Isaac Errett." The incident stirred up a tempest. Errett was soundly condemned for imitating "clergy-dominated denominations."

Errett's congregation in Detroit provoked still more controversy when it printed and circulated his statement entitled "A Synopsis of the Faith and Practice of the Church of Christ." "This declaration of our faith and aims is not to be taken as a creed," wrote Errett. "We assume no right to bind the conscience with any stereotyped formula." Regardless of his disclaimer, the "Synopsis" left many Disciples aghast. Exclaimed the volatile Moses Lard: "There is not a sound man in our ranks who has seen the . . . 'Synopsis' that has not felt scandalized by it."

When Aaron's calf came out had he called it a bird, still all Israel seeing it stand on four legs, with horns and parted hoofs, would have shouted a calf, a calf, a calf. The brethren meeting at the Corner of Jefferson Avenue and Beaubien Street, Detroit, may call their work in classic phrase a "Synopsis," or gently, a "declaration;" but we still cry a creed, a creed.[13]

A synopsis of faith! A doorplate inscribed with a clerical title! What next? Perturbed but resolute, inflexible restorationists struggled to lead Disciples back to the supposed purity of their golden age.

INSTRUMENTAL MUSIC IN WORSHIP

The debate on the implications of Christian primitivism reached fever pitch in the controversy over the use of instrumental music in the church's worship. The organ came to be a symbol of strife among Disciples. Conservatives argued that the New Testament prescribed the elements or acts of public worship; lacking explicit authorization in the New Testament, instrumental music was totally unwarranted in a body which claimed to restore apostolic Christianity. Moderates refused to grant the basic premise of the anti-

---

13. *Lard's Quarterly*, September 1863, Vol. I, pp. 100-101.

instrumental position. They defended the use of an organ on the ground that it tended to enhance instead of detracting from the worship experience of a congregation. As the contending parties advanced their respective viewpoints, citing the same arguments over and over, they turned a dispute into a brawl. All hope of reconciliation among the Stone-Campbell followers was lost in a welter of discord.

The question of instrumental music became a burning issue for Disciples around 1860 when congregations began to purchase organs and use them in worship. Probably the first congregation to do so was the one at Midway, Kentucky. "So far as known to me . . . I am the only 'preacher' in Kentucky, of our brotherhood . . . who has publicly advocated the propriety of employing instrumental music in *some* churches," admitted Dr. Pinkerton, the pastor at Midway. Benjamin Franklin denounced Pinkerton for offending good Disciples across the land. Pinkerton responded that he was willing to discuss the subject "with any man who can discriminate between railing in bad grammar and Christian argumentation; but I am as fully resolved as any man can be to have nothing to do with 'silly clap-trap.' "[14] Pinkerton and Franklin belonged to the same religious movement, but they approached both church and culture from different perspectives. The organ merely gave them an excuse to lash out at each other.

Interest in the "organ innovation" mounted while the Civil War raged. In March 1864, for example, a reader of *The Millennial Harbinger* asked the editor: "Will you inform me whether it is in accordance with the Scriptures to use in the churches organ or other instrumental music connected with the worship?" In his answer Coeditor William K. Pendleton confessed that he enjoyed all kinds of good music but counseled against forcing the instrument on anyone. Referring to the organ, he wrote: "I would rather never hear one again, than to have them interfering with the free, full, grateful, heartfelt singing of the whole congregation."[15]

That same month Moses E. Lard penned an article for his quarterly on "instrumental music in churches and dancing."

14. Quoted in Joseph Franklin and J. A. Headington, *The Life and Times of Benjamin Franklin,* pp. 410-411.
15. *Millennial Harbinger,* March 1864, p. 127.

"The day on which a church sets up an organ in its house," he warned, "is the day on which it reaches the first station on the road to apostasy." To deal decisively with congregations infatuated with the "infamous box," Lard proposed a threefold strategy: 1- Preachers should resolve never to "enter a meeting house belonging to our brethren in which an organ stands." 2- No layperson should transfer membership to a congregation using an organ. It would be better to "live out of a church than go into such a den." 3- If opponents of the organ fail to keep it out of their congregation, they should withdraw immediately "without even the formality of asking for a letter" and worship in good conscience elsewhere. Hostile as usual, Lard scorched "organ-grinding churches" and vowed to have "no fellowship with them"[16]

John W. McGarvey entered the fray later in 1864. Admitting that angels in heaven played musical instruments, he asked why a practice could be permissible in heaven and objectionable on earth. He answered: "Angels and saints in glory may be granted privileges which ought not to be granted to men in the flesh; for that may be harmless there which would be dangerous here, as children may be denied privileges which older persons may enjoy with impunity." The sheer dominance of an organ, in contrast to a tuning fork, reinforced McGarvey's conviction that the use of instrumental music in worship was inadvisable as well as unscriptural.[17]

Isaac Errett, preeminent spokesman for progressive Disciples, watched with interest and alarm as the controversy gathered momentum. Finally he broke his silence in 1870 and wrote several articles on instrumental music for his journal. Astute enough to recognize the social and cultural factors which led some congregations to prefer public worship with the aid of an organ, he observed: "A generation, educated to the use of instruments in school and parlor, will seek to use them in the churches; and mere denunciation of pride and worldliness will not cure the evil." In fact, he noted, instrumental music in worship among Disciples had increased in direct proportion to the bitterness with which the practice had been denounced. To Errett's mind, the organ was an ex-

---

16. *Lard's Quarterly*, March 1864, Vol. I, pp. 332-333.
17. *Millennial Harbinger*, November 1864, pp. 511, 513.

pedient in any case and for that reason ought not become a test of fellowship and a reason for division in the churches.[18]

The Christian-Evangelist joined the *Christian Standard* in attempting to persuade Disciples that the organ question was too insignificant to divide a great religious body. Barton W. Johnson, coeditor with Garrison, summarized the editorial stand of *The Christian-Evangelist:*

It *[The Christian-Evangelist]* holds that if the introduction of the organ into any congregation will mar its harmony that it would be sinful to introduce it; it holds that when a congregation is using one and is harmonious in its use no one outside has the right to interfere. It is not for or against the organ, but it is *for* peace and love and *against* discord and division all the time.[19]

The *Gospel Advocate* and the *American Christian Review* gave full and forceful expression to the antiorgan sentiment. Both papers insisted that those who refused to oppose instrumental music in worship were in effect pro-organ whether or not they admitted it.

No state or national assembly of Disciples ever resolved to back or resist instrumental music in worship, but local congregations could not avoid the issue. It was impossible for a congregation to live in harmony when some of the members favored the organ and others regarded its use as sinful. A news release, reprinted in *The Christian-Evangelist* from the *St. Louis Globe-Democrat,* illustrated the predicament in which Disciples found themselves at the local level.

Springfield, Mo., January 31 [1887] For several weeks a warm and at times acrimonious warfare has been waged in the Christian Church, of this City, between those who oppose the musical instruments in public worship and those who favored the organ. Yesterday affairs were brought to a crisis, and there were some sensational scenes. After the pastor, E. G. Laughlin, had read the opening hymn, the organist began playing and many joined in the singing, but at the same time the opponents of the organ started up another tune, and a pandemonium ensued. When the sacrament was announced, Brother Rogers arose and said he preferred not to partake with the organ people. After the sacrament, an anti-organ brother arose to smoothe matters over with a talk, but was in-

18. Quoted from *Christian Standard* in James S. Lamar, *Memoirs of Isaac Errett,* II. See pp. 34-40.
19. *Christian-Evangelist,* March 18, 1886, p. 168.

terrupted with a lively hymn volunteered by the organ crowd. At the close of the services, Mr. Bills, having consulted a lawyer, was advised to play the organ at all hazards, and he did so, and the meeting broke up in confusion.[20]

Unfortunately, the sound of organ music threw Disciples into chaos. Throughout the 1870s and 1880s congregations either split or lined up with one of the two contending parties. Clearly Disciples of Christ were moving toward division.

CHURCH STRUCTURE AND MISSIONS

The wrangle over missionary societies was yet another sign of the malaise of a movement in the process of shattering. With few but notable exceptions anti-instrumentalists opposed societies beyond the local congregation; and those who viewed the organ as an expedient defended societies as means by which all members of the communion could cooperate in responding to the missionary imperative of the church. (Of all the journals in the Disciples, only the *Apostolic Times* was prosociety and antiorgan.)

From their beginning, of course, Disciples had groped their way toward cooperative structures which would not infringe upon the rights of individual congregations. Every solid advance, however, led to apprehension if not outright resistance. The American Christian Missionary Society, founded in 1849, suffered from limited support and floundered particularly after abandoning its political neutrality during the Civil War. By 1866 the Society was in a state of virtual collapse. Growing opposition, compounded by resentment especially in the South, left in doubt the future of cooperation among Disciples. Vastly more was at stake than the survival of the American Christian Missionary Society.

When Benjamin Franklin, a one-time officer and champion of the Society, turned against it in 1866, progressive Disciples lost one of their strongest and most influential supporters. His paper, the *American Christian Review,* and the *Gospel Advocate* spearheaded the attack on the society principle. The two journals assailed the ecclesiastical machinery of national missionary societies and urged a return to New Testament simplicity. One outspoken Disciple voiced the viewpoint of

---

20. *Christian-Evangelist,* February 10, 1887, p. 83.

the *Review* and the *Advocate* when he wrote: "We want *more faith* and *less machinery, more work* and *less talk,* more faith and less planning. The Lord has given us the plan . . . ; but instead of going to work with the tools he has furnished, we spend all the day in making *new ones* which in our wisdom, we think will work better."[21]

According to strict restorationists, the only missionary organization in the New Testament was the local congregation. In addition to being man-made substitutes for the divine plan, societies tended to destroy congregational independence. Created to serve churches, missionary societies rejected the servant role and misused their power. A lifelong adversary of societies, Jacob Creath, Jr., expressed the wish to have the following epitaph inscribed on his tombstone: "Here lies Jacob Creath, who opposed all Societies to spread the Gospel except the individual churches of Jesus Christ, because he believed such Societies to be destructive of the liberty of the churches and of mankind."[22] Creath's testimony no doubt heartened all Disciples intent on resisting any deviation from "the ancient order revealed in the New Testament" and reproduced, so to say, in what they understood to be "loyal" congregations.

To counteract the arguments of the legalists and inspire support for the principle of cooperation, William K. Pendleton delivered a major address at the eighteenth anniversary meeting of the American Christian Missionary Society in 1866. He frankly admitted the precarious condition of the Society: "Advocates that once were eloquent, have withdrawn their plea; —friends that were liberal, have ceased to contribute; members that came up to counsel, have stayed away to chide; enthusiasm has been chilled . . . and wisdom made despondent of her hopes." Chiding antisociety Disciples for twisting the position of Alexander Campbell to their advantage, he pointed out that Campbell—his father-in-law and close associate—served as president of the American Christian Missionary Society and "from the first . . . threw his mighty influence in its favor."

After reminding his listeners that the Christian Association

---

21. *American Christian Review,* June 18, 1867, p. 194. Quoted in Earl I. West; *The Search for the Ancient Order,* Vol. II, pp. 60-61.
22. *Gospel Advocate,* January 12, 1871, p. 30.

of Washington was a missionary society which disavowed any intention of being a church, he spoke his mind on the critical issue before Disciples:

Let it not be said, then, that the disciples of Christ are to take the silence of Scripture on a given subject as a positive rule of prohibition against all freedom of action or obligation of duty. No rule could be more productive of mischief than this. That large freedom of thought and action, and that resistless spontaneity of benevolence, which makes a Christian a living power for good, wherever he goes, would be cramped and stifled by so narrow a principle, till Christianity would become a timid and cringing thing of forms, and afraid to expand itself in free and God-like charities, lest it might startle some slumbering knight of silence into crying, "Beware—beware—the thing is not spoken of in Scripture. There is no express precept or approved precedent for it in the word of God. Beware, for according to our canon, you may not do it."[23]

Pendleton's address, published in *The Millennial Harbinger,* served in a sense as a position paper for progressive Disciples in their defense of national missionary societies.

During the decades following the Civil War, Isaac Errett's *Christian Standard* and James H. Garrison's *The Christian* (later *The Christian-Evangelist)* were the most important advocates of the society principle. Both journals stood granitelike against strict restorationism and gave unwavering support to cooperative missionary work. Errett and Garrison shared the conviction that extreme individualism rather than tyrannical ecclesiasticism crippled Disciples and sapped their strength. Since the *Christian Standard* was more influential than *The Christian-Evangelist* before the turn of the century, it has been credited with saving "the principle of church cooperation through societies for the Disciples of Christ."[24]

The significance of *The Christian-Evangelist* and its predecessors should not be underestimated, however. Following the death of Errett in 1888, the *Christian Standard* became increasingly conservative, and Garrison's paper accepted primary responsibility for promoting missionary organizations. In the twilight of his career Garrison wrote his

23. *Millennial Harbinger,* November 1866. See pp. 495, 499, 502-503, 505.
24. Alfred T. DeGroot, *The Grounds of Divisions among the Disciples of Christ,* p. 117.

son, Winfred Ernest: "After Isaac Errett—great soul that he was—left us, I had almost to stand alone—so far as public agencies were concerned—against a strong legalistic and literalistic tendency in our brotherhood."[25]

All Disciples, conservatives and progressives alike, took seriously the missionary task of the church. They aimed to restore New Testament Christianity in order to unite the church for the purpose of winning the world to Jesus Christ. Committed as they were to the same ultimate goal, they could not agree on a common strategy. Neither segment of the movement could be persuaded to budge an inch. So the conservatives gravitated toward each other and gathered in independent congregations which worshiped without organs and responded to the Gospel without the assistance of societies. It is a striking coincidence that Disciples of Christ moved from dissension to division during the period of their most explosive growth.

A DIVISION IN THE RANKS

The disaffected congregations came to be known as Churches of Christ. Their estrangement from Disciples, rooted in political and cultural cleavage as well as in theological differences, intensified throughout the post-Civil War era and was recognized officially in 1906. In that year the United States religious census listed the Churches of Christ as an identifiable religious movement. A list of "loyal" preachers who had cut the ties binding them to the Disciples of Christ already was available. It had been compiled and made public by the *Gospel Advocate* in 1904 to validate the ministerial standing of men requesting clergy permits for reduced railroad fares.

David Lipscomb, editor of the *Gospel Advocate,* confirmed the schism on June 22, 1907. Answering an inquiry from the director of the United States Census Bureau, he wrote: "There is a distinct people taking the word of God as their only and sufficient rule of faith, calling their churches 'churches of Christ,' or 'churches of God,' distinct and

---

25. Letter, James H. Garrison to Winfred E. Garrison, December 2, 1924. (The J. H. Garrison Papers.)

separate in name, work, and rule of faith from all other bodies or peoples."[26]

According to the 1906 religious census, 159,658 members belonged to Churches of Christ.[27] Of this number, about 75,000 were in Tennessee and Texas. Almost two-thirds of the total membership lived in the eleven states which had comprised the Confederacy. The obvious sectional character of the division moved one historian to remark: "The sectional bifurcation of the Disciples of Christ—using the name to refer to the whole movement—is one of the most vivid American examples of the bending of the Christian ethos to fit the presuppositions of the community."[28]

The split in the Disciples, formally acknowledged in 1906, actually occurred before the turn of the century. It is impossible to establish the precise date of the division. Each congregation related to the Disciples had to confront the issues and decide whether to remain in or withdraw from the fellowship. No district or state or national manifestation of the church had the power to speak on behalf of a single local congregation. The process of separation consequently was complicated and lengthy, extending for at least twenty-five to thirty years.

By 1880 the two parties had taken shape; thereafter one incident after another gave definition to the schism and brought it into clearer focus. As early as 1883 Isaac Errett heard and reported the rumor "that there is already a combination of men" under the leadership of John F. Rowe "engaged in an organized effort to capture as many of our

---

26. See *Gospel Advocate*, July 18, 1907, p. 457. Quoted in Alfred T. DeGroot, *The Grounds of Divisions among the Disciples of Christ*, p. 130.

27. The Churches of Christ have grown rapidly since their separation from the Christian Church (Disciples of Christ). Although precise statistics are not available, the worldwide membership of the Churches of Christ probably exceeds 2,000,000 by a considerable margin. The two major journals in the movement are the *Gospel Advocate*, published in Nashville, Tennessee, and *Firm Foundation*, published in Austin, Texas. The best-known institutions of higher learning identified with Churches of Christ include David Lipscomb College and Freed-Hardeman College, both located in Tennessee, Abilene Christian College in Texas, Pepperdine University in California, and Harding College in Arkansas. In addition to their twenty or so colleges, Churches of Christ support over sixty benevolent institutions.

For a penetrating essay on the Churches of Christ, SEE Edwin S. Gaustad, "Churches of Christ in America" in *The Religious Situation: 1969*, ed. by Donald R. Cutler (Boston: Beacon Press, 1969), pp. 1013-1028.

28. David E. Harrell, Jr., "The Sectional Origins of the Churches of Christ," *Journal of Southern History*, August 1964, p. 264.

preachers and churches as possible, . . ."[29] Six years later officers of several antisociety congregations signed the "Sand Creek Address and Declaration," thereby repudiating the many innovations which had corrupted Disciples and pledging themselves to break fellowship with those who refused to turn away from "such abominations." A second declaration, written in 1892, urged strict primitivists to make certain that deeds to church property contain a statement prohibiting instrumental music and other equally defiling practices.

Thomas R. Burnett (1842-1916) minced no words in 1895 when he wrote in the *Gospel Advocate:*

> Brethren, proceed to re-establish the ancient order of things, just as if there was never a Church of Christ in your town. Gather all the brethren together who love Bible order better than modern fads and foolishness, and start the work and worship of the church in the old apostolic way. Do not go to law over church property. It is better to suffer wrong than to do wrong. Build a cheap and comfortable chapel, and improve it when you get able. It is better to have one dozen true disciples in a cheap house than a thousand apostate pretenders in a palace who love modern innovations better than Bible truths.[30]

Unlike his close associates David Lipscomb, the most respected leader among the disaffected, did not give up all hope for reconciliation until 1897. In August of that year he reprimanded Disciples for including in their yearbook "hundreds of churches and thousands of preachers and communicants that do not belong to [the Disciples movement] at all or have any more interest in it or sympathy for it than any other denomination." Citing this statement as decisive evidence, Arthur V. Murrell has concluded that the division of Disciples can be dated in August 1897 "even though Lipscomb would have to wait until the [federal religious census of 1906] to make it official."[31]

During the critical decade of the 1890s progressives also tacitly admitted that the Stone-Campbell communion had become two distinct groups. Although James H. Garrison dis-

---

29. *American Christian Review,* November 29, 1883, p. 380. Quoted in Earl I. West, *The Search for the Ancient Order,* Vol. II, p. 244.
30. *Gospel Advocate,* May 9, 1895, p. 291.
31. See Arthur V. Murrell, "The Effects of Exclusivism in the Separation of the Churches of Christ from the Christian Church" (unpublished Ph.D. thesis, Vanderbilt University, 1972), p. 222.

missed as "silly twaddle" the assertion of the *American Christian Review* in 1883 that the "dissolution of our people seems inevitable," he was not as unaware of the growing schism as he pretended to be. In 1895 he noted that the organ and society questions were dead issues among Disciples. "We have passed beyond them and are confronting vastly more important questions," he wrote.[32] Within the next three years he closed the columns of *The Christian-Evangelist* to further debate with the *Gospel Advocate*. When progressives and conservatives ceased to argue with each other, they no longer constituted one religious fellowship. Discord had turned into full-blown division.

In the hectic years of controversy Disciples founded a number of organizations and agencies at the national level. Each venture in cooperation rankled conservatives and gave them one more reason to resist the trend toward unbridled ecclesiasticism. Regardless of the opposition they were certain to encounter, progressives saw no other way to coordinate the work of congregations across the land and serve a rapidly growing membership.

---

32. James H. Garrison, "The Transient and the Permanent Elements in the Campbell Reformation," *New Christian Quarterly*, July 1895, p. 76.

11

RENEWED MISSION BRINGS
NEW LIFE

Americans were increasingly pragmatic and resourceful as well as incurably optimistic following the Civil War. To meet institutional needs, a committee could always be appointed or an organization formed. Experiencing the beginning of a new era and the end of an old one, the nation looked back upon its pioneer days and looked ahead seeking direction for the decades leading to the twentieth century. Disciples were part and parcel of these developments. Their preachers and organizing evangelists, utilizing the intricate system of connecting railroad lines, went to new areas and established congregations which were soon thriving in the general prosperity of the times.

The vast changes coming over America between 1870 and 1900 created tensions for the Disciples. While some Disciples looked to the past, longing for the old days, other Disciples, leaders and people, organized for more effective action in a new day. The period became an era of agencies and institutions as Disciples shared in the boundless drive of an expanding nation. Disciples seemed to have accomplished all they could through the old instrumentalities of crusading periodicals, debate, and with a few exceptions, poorly educated preachers. Future growth depended on a new evangelism, professional leadership in the ministry, settled pastors, better buildings, and improved cooperation among themselves and with other religious bodies. However, renewed criticism of such "innovations" soon began.

A PLAN THAT DIDN'T WORK

By the late 1860s enemies of the American Christian Missionary Society were jubilant as funds for the work dwindled. Tolbert Fanning considered the society as good as dead; David Lipscomb appeared to think it all a wasted effort. Their joy was considerably heightened when Benjamin Franklin and his paper, the *American Christian Review*, turned against organization. The ACMS, and state missionary societies as well, now faced the worst crisis of their history. A movement to unite the opposing forces of the brotherhood behind the ACMS was begun by Robert Milligan, president of The College of the Bible. He proposed to "place our Missionary Society on a true and scriptural basis" as a "golden mean" between extremes. His plan was to get rid of a constitution, by-laws, and other such objectionable features, and to organize the society into county, district, state, and national organizations.[1] In 1867 the ACMS did change its constitution, dropped the membership and directorship plan, and made other concessions, but the critics were not satisfied.[2]

So obvious had the disaffection with the ACMS become that something had to be done. At the convention of 1868 a committee of twenty leaders was appointed to consider the whole question, to devise a plan of work which would be free of the main objections, and to bring their report to the next convention scheduled to meet at Louisville, October 19-21, 1869. Among the twenty were William T. Moore, Isaac Errett, Moses E. Lard, Benjamin `Franklin, Alexander Procter, Charles L. Loos, William K. Pendleton, James S. Lamar, and Robert Graham (1822-1901). The committee met together for three days before the opening session and on Wednesday of the convention gave printed copies of its report to each person present so that it could be studied carefully.[3] William T.

---

1. *Gospel Advocate*, Vol. VIII, No. 45 (Nov. 6, 1866), pp. 709-711.
2. Earl West, *The Search for the Ancient Order*, Vol. 2, p. 93 ff.
3. *Apostolic Times*, Vol. I, No. 29 (Oct. 28, 1869), p. 227.

Moore, chairman of the committee, presented the proposed plan later adopted by the convention with only two dissenting votes, those of Lewis L. Pinkerton and John Shackleford (1834-1921).

The Louisville Plan, an attempt to give structure to loosely related congregations, proved to be highly impractical. Congregations were to send official "messengers" or delegates to district meetings, each district was to send delegates to the state meetings, and each state meeting was to be represented on the General Board of a General Christian Missionary Convention by its corresponding secretary, two delegates, and an additional delegate for each 5,000 members in the state. Special agents would not be necessary as local elders or pastors would request missionary offerings from the congregation. Missionary money raised by this means would be sent to the district organization. The district would keep one-half of the amount to employ local evangelists and send the other half to the state society. The state society would keep half the money it received and pass the other half to the General Convention.[4] The General Convention was to replace the annual meetings.

The Louisville Plan was received with apparent enthusiasm as a means whereby missionary control would be returned to the local congregation. Individuals would no longer support missionary work directly but the congregation acting as the church would be the responsible agent. The plan appeared ideal in principle but in reality it proved a disaster. Congregations at this time were not prepared to act responsibly in the raising of missionary funds. Adopted within a short time by eleven state meetings and thirty-six district organizations, the plan was ignored from the outset by most of these groups. Receipts for missionary work reached a new low. By the time the funds went through channels, each group holding out some of the money for local work, very little filtered through to the program of the General Convention. It now became clear that whatever was done to try to make the ACMS acceptable to its opponents, the conservatives were determined to accept no plan of organization beyond the local congregation.

---

4. *The Reformation of the Nineteenth Century*, ed. by James H. Garrison (St. Louis: Christian Publishing Company, 1901), pp. 296-305.

For the next several years the Louisville Plan was given considerable attention, but the records of the annual conventions during these years reveal that there was insufficient interest to make the plan work at any level. Barely enough money to pay the salary of the General Convention's corresponding secretary was received with nothing at all left to support missions. Theoretically, one-fourth of the amount given by a congregation to the district board was to be sent to the General Board for the work of the General Convention. John W. McGarvey, however, suggested that the congregations who gave the money be allowed to say where they wanted it spent. A strategy to avoid the criticism that the society was dictating to the churches, it proved a blow to the support of foreign missions as the congregations asked that their money be spent near home.

By 1870 only three missionaries had been sent out under the ACMS. Dr. J. T. Barclay reached Jerusalem on February 7, 1851 and continued until October 1861. Alexander Cross, a black man, reached Monrovia, Liberia, in January 1854, but died after two months of service. Julius O. Beardslee (1814-1879) began work in Jamaica in 1858 and continued until 1866 when the work had to be abandoned for lack of support. The society searched anxiously for some way to persuade the churches to support its work. Following the Franco-Prussian War (1869-1870) a mission to Germany was recommended but nothing came of it. Ten days before the convention was to meet at Cincinnati the great Chicago fire of October 1871 left thousands of persons homeless and several prominent Disciples bankrupt. Even a proposal for relief for Disciples caught in this disaster did little to bring support to the society.

With the adoption of the Louisville Plan the annual meetings became known as the General Christian Missionary Convention. The American Christian Missionary Society moved into the background as a corporate entity serving mainly as a collecting and disbursing agency for such funds as came to it. Those who had opposed the ACMS because they felt it was not scriptural were soon opposing the General Convention on much the same basis. For those leaders and persons willing to support the General Convention the question still remained: what could be done to sustain foreign missions? Failure of Disciples to obey the New Testament's "Great Commission" was a growing concern.

WOMEN LEAD THE WAY

During the last quarter of the nineteenth century women were active in American life as never before. Their new freedom found expression in greater opportunities for women to travel, to hold positions in business, to receive a college education, and eventually to work for the vote. This new stimulation to activity inevitably would find its way into the church and into the Disciples. Developing first in the well-established denominations, the desire of women to be active in the work of the church soon expressed itself. From 1869 to 1874 women's missionary societies came into existence in the Baptist, Congregational, Episcopal, Methodist, and Presbyterian churches. Nearly all these women's organizations had local, district, state, and national units for effective programing and for the raising of money. Disciples women soon would begin to organize and to participate in the mission and other work of their church.

No religious body was thought to hold more conservative views than the Disciples in regard to the participation of women in the work or services of the church. Without any written or spoken word on the subject there was a general understanding against it.[5] Among the leaders of the ACMS, however, there was a changing attitude. The men who were most active in the society were discouraged. They saw the Baptists, Methodists, and Presbyterians fully engaged in the great missionary movement of the time and desperately sought some means to awaken their fellow Disciples. Several of them began to consider the possibility of enlisting the support of the women.

A "Committee on the Cooperation of Women in the Missionary Work," chaired by James Challen, reported to the General Convention meeting at Indianapolis in 1870. Challen outlined what he believed church women could do, saying:

---

5. *Ibid.*, p. 45 f.

They may become missionaries at home and abroad like the Judsons and others. . . . They may organize and sustain chosen fields of labor, on which they can bestow their offerings and prayers. . . . The Woman's Boards of Missions in certain denominations around us have demonstrated this, and set a noble example to our sisters. . . . We feel assured that there is an element of power here, almost unknown to us, and unemployed, which needs to be called out into active labor.[6]

Thomas Munnell (1823-1898), corresponding secretary of the convention, added these words,

Recognizing that, as a people, we have never opened the way for the women of our churches to unite in any broad enterprise with us, we propose to invite their vast, though unemployed, abilities to "labor with us in the gospel," both as solicitors among ourselves and as missionaries in suitable fields.[7]

By this time missionary work, except locally, was at a standstill because of depressed economic conditions and the apparent breakdown of the Louisville Plan. The General Convention of 1872 recommended that the task of foreign missions be undertaken again as soon as practicable. Richard M. Bishop (1812-1893), prominent layman of Ohio, in his 1873 presidential address to the General Convention sketched the history of the ACMS. He recalled the Louisville Plan, adopted with such enthusiasm, and said, "But alas!, our fond expectations were not realized." A resolution was passed urging the General Board to make the next convention a time for reestablishing mission work. The men really did not seem to know what to do to change things. Women were about ready to "enter into the Gospel labors" and were awaiting a leader.

Mrs. Caroline Neville Pearre, wife of S. E. Pearre, minister at Iowa City, Iowa, became that leader. Mrs. Pearre subsequently recalled how frustrated she and others were because the Disciples had no missions, no missionaries, an organization on paper, and not much else. Why not a women's missionary organization? She later said,

Surely we could be led, if we had a leader. This matter pressed upon my heart and would not down. Finally, upon the 10th day of

---

6. Minutes of the ACMS, 1870, Indianapolis, UCMS microfilm.
7. West, *op. cit.*, Vol. 2, p. 98.

April, 1874, about ten o'clock in the morning, just after I had finished my private devotions the question came home to my heart almost like a voice "why can not *you* do it?"[8]

Knowing of Thomas Munnell's interest in such a project, she wrote to him about it. Munnell replied, "This is a flame of the Lord's kindling; and no man can extinguish it." She also engaged in a wide correspondence with leading women in Indiana, Illinois, Kentucky, Missouri, Ohio, and Pennsylvania, urging the organizing of local societies. James H. Garrison published a letter in *The Christian* about the formation of the Iowa City society in May and added an editorial encouraging other groups to organize. Soon local societies had been established in several of the states. In June, Isaac Errett visited Iowa City and while there wrote an enthusiastic editorial entitled "Help Those Women!" This editorial is credited with being the major encouragement in helping the women organize. He proposed that the women hold a convention the following October, at the same time as the General Convention at Cincinnati, to discuss a national organization. Mrs. Marcia M. B. Goodwin, editor of *The Christian Monitor,* a woman's magazine, also promoted the meeting.

Opening the 1874 General Convention at the Richmond Street Christian Church, President R. M. Bishop spoke cautiously and thoughtfully, reminding the convention that as a religious body they had reached a crisis. W. K. Pendleton of Bethany then reviewed the troubled twenty-five-year history of the ACMS. Other speeches of a discouraged nature were given. The most important event of that year's convention, however, was the organization of the Christian Woman's Board of Missions.

On Wednesday, October 21, 1874, women from nine states met in the basement of the church with Mrs. R. R. (Jane) Sloan (1815-1899), wife of an Ohio minister, presiding. A committee was appointed to draw up a constitution with Mrs. Pearre as chairman. Using the form of the women's missionary society of the Congregational church, the constitution for the CWBM proposed that the women engage in both home and foreign missions. They made certain that their new

---

8. *Missionary Tidings,* Vol. 17 (Aug., 1899), pp. 102-103.

262 JOURNEY IN FAITH

society would be under the complete control of women, a wise precaution considering the difficulty the men had experienced and a unique provision among church women's groups of the day. Their purpose was to "cultivate a missionary spirit; to encourage missionary effort in our churches, to disseminate missionary intelligence, and secure systematic contributions for missionary purposes."

The next day, after addresses before the full convention by Mrs. M. M. B. Goodwin and Mrs. Pearre, Issac Errett, newly elected president of the ACMS, offered a resolution asking recognition of the Christian Woman's Board of Missions. As a "board" it would report to the General Convention. The resolution was adopted unanimously by a standing vote. The first national officers were Mrs. Love (Maria) Jameson (?-1911), daughter of Ovid Butler, president; Mrs. William (Sarah) Wallace (Mrs. Jameson's daughter), recording secretary; Mrs. O. A. Burgess (1836-1902), treasurer; and Mrs. Caroline N. Pearre, corresponding secretary. Headquarters was established at Indianapolis as most of the officers lived there.[9] Before final adjournment at Cincinnati and after much discussion the women decided their first project would be to reopen the Jamaica mission. Nothing was to be done, however, until at least $1,000 was in the treasury.

Within a short time, by-laws were written and a sample constitution prepared for the use of local groups which the women hoped would be organized in every congregation across the country. Soon there were many local and state organizations. By 1876 the women had the money to send out their first missionaries, William H. Williams (?1842-1928?) and family of Platte City, Missouri, to reopen the mission in Jamaica. In 1880 the CWBM gave assistance to a program in France. In 1881 work among Negroes at Jackson, Mississippi, was begun. An important mission began in 1882 when four young women—Ada Boyd (?-1915), Mary Graybill (1846-1935), Mary Kingsbury (1857-1925), and Laura Kinsey—and two married couples (the S. L. Whartons and the Albert Nortons) landed in India. The CWBM was joined by the FCMS in this venture. Home missions were begun in Montana in 1882. At first the women published missionary material in

9. Lorraine Lollis, *The Shape of Adam's Rib*, pp. 32-33 and 41 ff.

the *Christian Standard, The Christian,* and other church journals. Later they decided to publish a monthly paper of their own entitled *Missionary Tidings.* The first issue came off the press in May 1883 at Indianapolis, with Mrs. Goodwin as editor. Beginning in 1884 missionary study materials, including monthly and quarterly materials for women's and children's groups, were published. CWBM had a significant influence upon the Disciples as an efficient organization and in the education of congregations and ministers regarding missions.

In the 1890s railroads began to offer reduced fares for ordained persons serving mission boards and the church. Disciples women were eager to use every opportunity to economize for the furtherance of their missionary program. Despite earlier conservatism regarding women in positions of leadership, at some time in this period the first woman Disciple was ordained. She was Clara Celestea Hale Babcock. Soon women were ordained in several regions, usually in order to take advantage of the railroad's generosity. Ordination of women as a theological issue was never discussed. By the first decade of the twentieth century a number of Disciples women had been ordained to Christian ministry and service.

AT LAST THE MEN ORGANIZE

At the same General Convention and in the same church basement that saw the formation of the Christian Woman's Board of Missions, William T. Moore called a group of men together to discuss what the Disciples as a whole could do to become active in foreign missions. After considerable discussion and prayer a committee was appointed to make definite plans to present to the next year's convention. On the committee with Moore were Isaac Errett, Joseph King (1831-1890), Alvin I. Hobbs (1834-1894), Thomas Munnell, and Benjamin B. Tyler (1840-1922). They met in Indianapolis the following summer during the sessions of the Indiana state meeting and drew up a tentative constitution for a proposed new society. The organization of a missionary society to work specifically in foreign missions was recommended. During the 1875 General Convention, meeting at Louisville, Isaac Errett

FOREIGN CHRISTIAN MISSIONARY SOCIETY

A. McLean

Royal J. Dye

W. T. Moore

The Foreign Christian Missionary Society was created October 22, 1875 to work exclusively in overseas mission. Its president, A. McLean, was probably the most influential Disciple mission spokesman of his time.

Among those who served under the Foreign Christian Missionary Society were W. T. Moore (in England), Royal J. Dye (in Africa), and A. L. Shelton (in Tibet).

A. L. Shelton

delivered a warm and touching address on the missionary imperative which deeply moved everyone present. Moore then presented the committee's proposals. With the adoption of these plans by the convention on October 22, 1875, the Foreign Christian Missionary Society came into being with Errett as president.[10]

The beginnings of new life among the Disciples came with the rise of an interest in foreign missions, and that arose largely through the unqualified support of the editors of brotherhood papers. The organization of the CWBM had been the first sign of a stirring of new life. Further enthusiasm was developed by the formation of the FCMS. Interest in foreign missions was expected to be a stimulus to home missions.

A charge was made that the convention was an organization gotten up by power-hungry persons wanting a means to control the congregations, but from this time forward little attention was given to opposition. The General Convention in the future was to be made up of interested individuals and not delegates of the congregations, thus abandoning yet another feature of the Louisville Plan. The next quarter of a century saw congregations, members, and preachers deciding for or against support of the missionary societies.

Instead of sending missionaries to non-Christian lands, as was at first planned, the FCMS for a time attempted to establish Disciples churches in some of the European countries. Henry S. Earl (1832-1919), who had formerly evangelized in England and then in Australia, was present at the 1875 convention and announced his intention to return to England. About the same time Timothy Coop (1817-1887), a wealthy layman of England, offered $10,000 on a matching basis if the American churches would send evangelists to his country. A proposal was made and accepted that Earl return to England under the FCMS and work among the people of Southampton. William T. Moore and several other Americans later went to various cities of England to establish congregations.

Encouraged by his pastor, Dr. A. O. Holck (1844-1907) of Central Church, Cincinnati, returned to his native Denmark

---

10. Archibald McLean, *History of the Foreign Christian Missionary Society,* (New York: Fleming H. Revell Co.), 1919, p. 35 ff.

in 1876 to establish congregations. This mission spread to Norway and Sweden where at one time twenty-two congregations were in existence. The FCMS sent Jules Delaunay (1813-1892) and his wife to Paris, in 1878. Delaunay, a former Roman Catholic seminarian, also came from Central Church, Cincinnati. This mission received some support from the CWBM in 1880. George N. Shishmanian (1837-1922), an Armenian, went to Turkey in 1879, where his mission headquarters was located at Constantinople. Other workers were added and later an Isaac Errett Memorial Chapel was erected in Smyrna. No lasting results were obtained from most of these projects.

In the midst of all this activity there was a concern that British and European projects were not foreign missions. Disciples longed to send missionaries to such fields as Asia and Africa. Growth of income was slow, however, and only after several more years would the FCMS have a secretary working full time. Until 1885 the only office of the FCMS was a storeroom of the Standard Publishing Company at Cincinnati. Even though the FCMS had few funds, it tried to do all it could with the little it had. The policy was conservative and program was not planned beyond available resources.

Three small children and James H. Garrison had an important part in leading Disciples to improved giving for foreign missions. In a missionary address in the General Convention at Louisville in 1880 Garrison told of an incident which had happened in his home on the evening before he left for the gathering. At family devotions he explained the purpose of his trip and discussed the speech on missions he was to give. At the end of prayers his two small sons (Arthur and Ernest) and a girl cousin left the room, put together the contents of their savings banks, a total of $1.13, and gave them to him, saying that they wanted "to send the gospel to children who have never heard of Jesus." The story of this touching sacrifice stirred the convention as Garrison reminded his audience that there was no fund into which he could put his children's offering. The convention recommended that the Sunday schools be asked to devote one offering each year to foreign missions on an occasion to be known as "Children's Day." From this time onward missionary receipts showed a general and rapid improvement.

The income of the FCMS for 1876 had been only $1,706.35, but by 1881 the income had risen to $13,178. Stimulated by the growing interest in Children's Day the offering nearly doubed in 1882, enabling the FCMS, joined by the CWBM, to send G. L. Wharton (1847-1906), Albert Norton (d. 1938), their families, and four young women to India. The year 1883 witnessed the opening of the mission to Japan under George T. Smith (1849-1920) and C. E. Garst (1853-1898) and their families. William E. Macklin (1860-1947), a Canadian physician, was appointed to Japan in 1886 but soon transferred his interest to China, where he served with distinction for many years. A return of the Disciples to Liberia was considered but in 1897 the Belgian Congo (now Zaire) was chosen for a mission. At its twenty-fifth anniversary celebration in 1900 the FCMS reported $180,000 received that year for support of its missionaries at work in nine countries. Isaac Errett served as president until 1888, followed by Charles L. Loos who served until 1900. The monthly paper of the FCMS was the *Missionary Intelligencer.*[11]

Much of the credit for the success of the program of the FCMS is due a remarkable man, Archibald McLean (1850-1920). Originally from Prince Edward Island, Canada, he attended Bethany College and for eleven years was pastor of the Christian Church at Mt. Healthy, a suburb of Cincinnati. When he entered upon his duties as secretary of the FCMS March 4, 1882, a new day had dawned for foreign missions and for the Disciples. For a short while (1889-1891) McLean served as president of Bethany College, while retaining his position as secretary of the FCMS. He returned full time to that position when he decided finally to devote the rest of his career to missions. The name "A. McLean" literally became a houschold word while his loadership in the development of a missionary consciousness among the Disciples and in the developing structure of the brotherhood was a contribution of great importance.

True to expectations, home missions benefited from the enthusiasm increasingly expressed by Disciples for foreign missions. Lacking in the glamor surrounding picturesque foreign fields, home missions developed more slowly. The

---

11. *Ibid.,* p. 51 ff.

ACMS revived as an agency for homeland missions as the foreign work was developed by the new societies. It shared in the planting of congregations in the West and in Canada and in the promotion of work in Sunday schools and among children and youth.

NEW AGENCIES FOR A NEW DAY

A special committee appointed by the General Christian Missionary Convention in 1878 to gather information about the Disciples for the United States Census of 1880 revealed the comparative strength of the Disciples in various parts of the country.[12] Claims were made that the statistics were inaccurate, but they were probably as nearly correct as could be obtained under the circumstances. They showed in general that the Disciples were a fast-growing body. Kansas and Texas were the most rapidly developing Disciples areas. A number of evangelists and itinerant preachers were working energetically in the home mission fields of the growing West. All this meant a new day for the Disciples.

It became obvious that congregations would need assistance if they were to have church buildings, as most banks were not interested in providing newly organized groups with building funds. Other Protestant bodies were establishing church extension funds and the Disciples, if they were to hold their own on the new frontiers, had to do likewise. Many thoughtful Disciples considered it poor stewardship to bring hundreds of people into new congregations without helping provide them with facilities. An agency to serve the needs of such churches emerged in the 1880s.

At the General Convention held in Cincinnati October 1883 Robert Moffett (1835-1908), corresponding secretary of the ACMS, recommended that a "Church Extension Fund" be created, "the principle to be loaned upon easy terms to such weak churches and mission stations as may stand in need of aid." A Committee on Church Extension was appointed. The first subscriptions were made by Joseph Smith, Jr., and W. S. Dickinson, Cincinnati; Timothy Coop, England; and Francis Marion Drake (1830-1903), Des Moines, Iowa. A year later

---

12. *The Evangelist,* November 4, 1880, p. 707.

the committee made its first report. Receipts totaled $12,105; three loans had been made. The convention of 1886, meeting for the first time "way out West," at Kansas City, received news that $14,711.83 had been collected with ten loans outstanding in eight states. Most of the loans were to Kansas congregations.

The Indianapolis convention of 1887 instructed Moffett to discover the number of Disciples congregations needing building assistance. The next year, at the convention held at Springfield, Illinois, he reported 1,628 homeless congregations ready to erect buildings provided they could be aided to the extent of one-third the cost of the building and land. This moved the 1888 convention to organize the Board of Church Extension within the corporation of the ACMS and reporting to the General Convention.[13] Members of the board and its offices were to be located at Kansas City, Missouri, since this was the center of the territory where most of the congregations needing assistance were located.

Francis M. Rains (1854-1919) of Topeka, Kansas, had been called to assist the committee in 1887. He became secretary of the newly formed board, serving until 1890. He was succeeded by George Waldo Muckley (1861-1926) who led the board most capably for many years. Over the next several years named loan funds were established and the first annuities were written. At first loans were for five years and were limited to $250 at six per cent interest. Staff members from the beginning were available to help congregations with their fund-raising campaigns. A special day for offerings to church extension was set up in 1890 and loans for more than $1,000 were granted for the first time in 1892. *Business in Christianity,* a magazine to supply information about the fund to older congregations and to help mission congregations, was begun in the fall of 1893. The board began to furnish architectural services in 1897.[14]

"Buggess' Ride" is one of the colorful events of Disciples history. The famous "Run" into the Cherokee Strip of Indian Territory (now Oklahoma) was held on October 16, 1893. Gathered on the border of Kansas to the north, and of Indian Territory on the east and south, approximately 150,000 per-

13. *Annual Report,* ACMS, 1888, p. 26.
14. G. W. Muckley, *Church Extension, a History,* n.p., 1909, pp. 1-14.

AMERICAN CHRISTIAN MISSIONARY SOCIETY

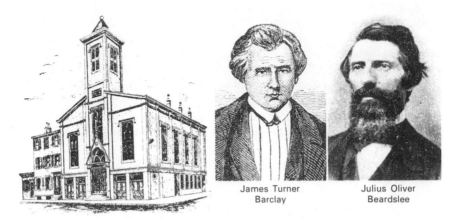

James Turner
Barclay

Julius Oliver
Beardslee

The American Christian Missionary Society was organized October 26, 1849 with Alexander Campbell as its first president. The national convention met in the church, pictured above, at the corner of Eighth and Walnut Streets, Cincinnati. In 1851 the Society sent out the first Disciple missionary, James Turner Barclay, who served two terms in Jerusalem. With the sending of Julius Oliver Beardslee to Jamaica in 1858 the society established the first continuing mission work of the Disciples of Christ.

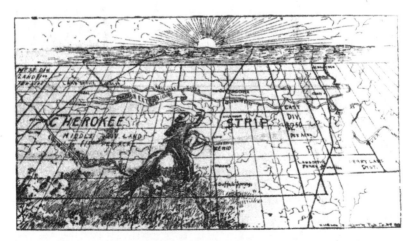

The American Christian Missionary Society has been called "the mother of cooperating organizations." This drawing from the January 1894 *Business in Christianity* depicts E. F. Boggess, pastor of the Guthrie, Oklahoma, church, as he ran in the opening of the Cherokee Strip in 1893 to secure lots for the Board of Church Extension.

sons awaited the time when they could make the run into the strip and claim land. Revivals were held among those waiting. One such revival with over 400 conversions was held near Caldwell, Kansas, by James M. Monroe (1843-1925), a well-known evangelist and state secretary of the Oklahoma missionary society from 1903 to 1911. George Muckley suggested to E. F. Boggess (1869-1931), pastor at Guthrie, Oklahoma, and a representative of the Board of Church Extension, that he train a fast horse and ride into the strip on behalf of the Disciples.

Immediately after the starting gun had been fired Boggess raced from Orlando, Oklahoma, northward and staked a claim for a church lot at Perry. It is not hard to imagine the boisterous group of settlers joining in the run. The original lot was lost in the general confusion of the time, but in a few days another site was bought. Boggess devoted his time over the next several weeks to getting building sites for the Disciples in railroad and county seat towns and in other places seemingly marked for rapid growth and development. He believed Disciples were at last getting into things the right way.[15]

By 1900 approximately 600 congregations in twenty-eight states had received aid and the total fund stood at $305,342. Almost 300 loans had been repaid in full with no losses to the board in the years since 1883. Hundreds of congregations owe their existence to the fact that the Board of Church Extension made funds available when they were most needed. The possibility of loans from a board of the church not only encouraged new congregations to build but also provided the means whereby established congregations were able to move forward with an expanded program. The board played its part in leading Disciples out of a frontier experience into a period in which the meeting house gave way to more worshipful and dignified buildings.

While the church was growing rapidly in the newer areas of Kansas, Oklahoma, and Texas, other Disciples were developing a concern for Christian benevolence. A decade after the formation of the CWBM not all church women were caught up in the excitement of foreign missions. Some concerned

15. *Christian-Evangelist*, August 24, 1899, p. 1071.

wives and mothers wished to help those persons in need closer to their homes. One particular group of women, including Mrs. James H. Garrison, Mrs. H. M. Meier, Mrs. Matilda Younkin (d. 1908), and Mrs. W. D. Harrison, gathered in a basement room in the First Christian Church of St. Louis on a bleak February day in 1886. The women discussed organizing an association for the purpose of aiding widows and orphans. No records were kept of these early meetings, but gradually their plans took definite shape and on March 10, 1887, the National Benevolent Association was incorporated under the laws of the State of Missouri. Its stated purpose was "to help the helpless, to give a home to the homeless, to provide care for the sick and comfort for the distressed."

Mrs. Matilda (Mattie) Hart Younkin, one of the leading spirits of the group, visited congregations in Missouri, Illinois, and Kansas in an effort to interest the women of the Ladies' Aid Societies in becoming auxiliaries to the NBA. Most of the Ladies' Aid Societies had resisted joining in the missionary organizations but might be interested in a program of benevolence. The membership fee for auxiliaries was $5.00, and the local society was to have the privilege of putting a child in the "Home" when it opened. Women in the church at Abilene, Kansas, were the first to take membership and pay the fee. Mrs. E. D. Hodgen was the first president of the association, with vice-presidents chosen from the four St. Louis congregations, and with Mrs. Younkin as the active agent and developer. When a widow appealed to Mrs. Younkin for help in the care of her three children, the time to open the "Home" seemed to have arrived. A fund had been started and amounted to $181.90. This money, together with $119.25 from the churches, constituted the total with which the first home of the NBA was opened in St. Louis in 1889.[16]

No recognition as yet had been made of the NBA as an agency of the Disciples. Unable to secure a hearing for its work in the General Convention, the women decided to have a convention of their own in 1892, and in September a well-attended two-day meeting was held at the First Christian Church in St. Louis. Petitions were presented to the General Conventions in 1895 and 1896 requesting recognition but objections were raised to such work and the petitions were "laid

16. *Fifty-Years' March of Mercy*, (St. Louis: NBA, 1937), pp. 9-12.

on the table." Not until 1899, twelve years after it was organized, was the work of the NBA recognized by the General Convention.[17] During the years of struggle the leaders of the work endured many hardships and met frequent rebuffs.

The women were given encouragement, however, by one or two local ministers and by the leaders of the Christian Publishing Company. The Christian Publishing Company at this time was managed by James H. Garrison but was a stock company. The women, wishing to provide a permanent building for the Christian Orphan's Home, held a conference in 1892 with Francis M. Call (1843-1915) and William W. Dowling (1834-1920), stockholders in the publishing company. The two men agreed to take the initiative in ráising funds for that purpose, resulting in the first building erected and owned by the NBA. In the spring of 1893 the board adopted Easter as the special day on which gifts would be solicited for Christian benevolence. Widespread criticism met this announcement as Easter was then still considered a Roman Catholic holiday and little recognition was given it by Disciples. The response of the churches was good, however; and another "special day" was added to the growing list. The first issue of *The Orphan's Cry* appeared in May 1894. Nine years later, aıter the NBA had entered the field of caring for the aged, the name of the paper was changed to *The Christian Philanthropist.*

The call became increasingly urgent to care for the needy aged. In order to emphasize the national character of the work a decision was made in 1899 to open a home for the aged in some state other than Missouri. The appeals for help became so persistent that the executive committee decided to furnish a six-room house adjoining the Christian Orphan's Home and take in the most needy of the applicants. Donations of furniture and other household necessities were solicited and in January 1900 the Home for the Aged was opened in St. Louis with three women residents. Meanwhile, the search for a permanent location finally led to Jacksonville, Illinois. A substantial gift by Mrs. Nancy Henderson (1828-1883) made possible the purchase of a residence there

17. *Proceedings of the General Christian Missionary Convention,* 1899, p. 100.

and on March 4, 1901, the Home for the Aged (now Barton W. Stone Home) opened.

Progress had been slow. By 1900 it appeared to the women that either they did not have the organizational ability of their sisters in the CWBM or local benevolence did not have the appeal of foreign work. The truth probably was that benevolence required such substantial sums of money that they needed a wider base of support than Ladies' Aid Societies. In any event, men became increasingly active in the program. In 1901 George L. Snively (1866-1955), pastor at Jacksonville, Illinois, became the first general secretary followed in 1906 by James H. Mohorter (1865-1929), pastor at Pueblo, Colorado. Miss Elizabeth Jameson (1879-1953), employed in 1903, became the first office worker. In this organization founded by women, women served in all the executive offices during its formative years, administering the work with the counsel of an advisory group of men. In 1906, however, James W. Perry was elected president of the association, serving from 1906 until 1910 when he was succeeded by W. Palmer Clarkson (1867-1941), a leading businessman of St. Louis. Frank M. Wright (1913-1950) was elected treasurer in 1901, succeeded in 1905 by Lee W. Grant (1863-1948) who had helped the women draw up their charter in 1887.

The development of the NBA was not the result of a centralized national movement but rather the expression of generosity of concerned Disciples in various localities. No broad general program characterized the growth of the NBA; its work grew from the desire of individuals and congregations for active participation in helping others. Within a few years homes were opened in Denver, Colorado; East Aurora, New York (later moved to Jacksonville, Florida); Cleveland, Ohio; Dallas, Texas; Atlanta, Georgia; and Beaverton, Oregon.

Disciples next turned their attention to a renewed and intensified interest in ministerial relief. The death of Ira J. Chase (1834-1895), preacher and former governor of Indiana, brought the matter to immediate attention. While holding an evangelistic meeting at Lubec, Maine, in 1895, Chase died. It became generally known that his widow and children at Wabash, Indiana, were in desperate need. A Union Army veteran, Chase was popular among Disciples, had served well as a pastor, and in 1888 was elected lieutenant governor of Indiana. Upon the death of Governor Alvin P. Hovey in 1891, Chase served out Hovey's term.[18] A close friend of Chase, Alonzo M. Atkinson (1833-1900) of Wabash was very much disturbed by the plight of the Chase family. Through brotherhood papers he proposed a "Chase Memorial Fund" to buy Mrs. Chase a home and to provide a yearly income. Notices in the journals brought a good response, and a Disciples conscience on behalf of their ministers and families began to stir. James V. Coombs (1849-1920), an Indiana evangelist, wrote,

> Bro. A. M. Atkinson of Wabash has proposed a Ministerial Relief Fund. He starts the fund with $1,000. No greater enterprise has been started since the organization of our Church Extension Society.[19]

There had been negative thinking among Disciples regarding ministerial support from the days before there were settled pastors. Church leaders recognized that the attitudes of the early leaders regarding salaries and the influence of others who had made a fetish of what they called "preaching without pay" would make it difficult to propose a general program of aid to indigent ministers and their families. Early concern for ministerial and dependent relief therefore expressed itself locally. Quite likely the first public appeal among Disciples for ministerial relief was that made by George Campbell (1807-1872) in the Indiana convention of 1859 on behalf of John Longley (1782-1867). The Ohio convention in 1869 had the first proposal for a ministerial relief "fund" though there is little record of its activities.[20] To Missouri, however, goes the honor of having the first organized system of ministerial relief. Gustavus A. Hoffman (1847-1937) appealed in 1881 for a statewide "old ministers pension fund" which was actually organized in 1883.[21]

The same year that the Missouri fund was organized the General Christian Missionary Convention, meeting at Cin-

---

18. *Indiana Christian,* May, 1895, p. 2.
19. *Indiana Christian,* November, 1895, p. 5.
20. Henry Shaw, *Buckeye Disciples,* p. 225.
21. *The Christian,* Aug. 25, 1881, p. 3.

cinnati, gave consideration to the problem of the brotherhood's aged and disabled ministers. As a result a Committee on Ministerial Relief came into existence and functioned off and on until 1895. The General Convention of that year, meeting for the first time in the Southwest, at Dallas, Texas, motivated by the appeals for the Chase Fund and urged by Atkinson, voted to organize a Board of Ministerial Relief. The new board was to report to the convention and had authority to raise funds for the aid of destitute ministers and their families. Three outstanding Indiana laymen were elected the first officers: Howard Cale (1846-1904), president; Alonzo M. Atkinson, corresponding secretary; and Amos Clifford (1838-?), treasurer. Headquarters was established at Indianapolis and at the first meeting of the board, November 6, 1895, help was given A. W. Fisher of San Antonio, Texas. The next applicant who received help was the sixty-eight-year-old widow of Knowles Shaw, well-known evangelist who had been killed in a train wreck in 1878.[22]

Such funds as existed in the states were turned over to the Board of Ministerial Relief after its organization, and, together with special gifts, the foundation of a permanent fund was laid by 1896. Formal organization of the board was delayed two years to work out relationships to the ACMS and the General Convention. The board became a legal corporation in Indiana in April 1897. At first all receipts were put into the permanent fund and invested principally in farm mortgages with only the interest used for relief. Atkinson, however, proposed that only three-quarters of all receipts be put into the permanent fund thus permitting a greater amount of money to be expended on relief. The board decided to adopt Christmas Sunday as its special day for an offering to be taken by the congregations for ministerial relief. By 1901 the board was aiding fifty-eight ministers and missionaries and showed receipts for the year of $9,676.95. The permanent fund showed a balance of $18,799.32. The Ministerial Relief plan provided little more than inadequate handouts from funds half-willingly given by the congregations. A more adequate relief and pension plan awaited a later day.[23]

---

22. *Indiana Christian*, December, 1895, p. 4.

The Disciples as a religious body could have withered away into an insignificant sect if they had not been challenged by the missionary emphasis introduced by the women, the renewed interest in foreign missions by the church as a whole, the growth and enthusiasm of the Sunday school movement, and the creation of service and benevolent organizations. The Christian Woman's Board of Missions, the Foreign Christian Missionary Society, the Board of Church Extension, the National Benevolent Association, and the Board of Ministerial Relief, together with the state and national Sunday school associations, were powerful stimulants that not only reawakened the movement but gave motivation for new endeavors by the churches. By the early 1900s the Disciples were an ongoing, forward-looking brotherhood.

Disciples were learning at last how to develop a conscience on Christian stewardship among themselves and in their congregations. In the earlier phases of their growing institutional structure, more than half of the money for most causes and agencies was obtained by emotional public appeals at the annual general and state conventions. The rest came from congregations on the "special days." It soon became evident that some better and more dependable way had to be found to support the various Disciples agencies. They were rapidly taking on the well-rounded character of a total church program.

Some church leaders urged that the informal pattern of giving among the Disciples must give way to more systematic and effective forms of stewardship. There needed to be a careful education of the ministry and the congregations on the support of all Disciples agencies and institutions.[24] The Disciples moved slowly, however, toward a program of local budgets, the every member canvas, and other forms of an educated stewardship. In the meanwhile, the appeals multiplied but somehow a considerable amount of money was raised and a significant amount of work was done by the assorted agencies and institutions of the developing Disciples communion.

---

23. William Martin Smith, *For the Support of the Ministry* (Indianapolis: Pension Fund of Disciples of Christ), 1956, pp. 49-63.
24. *Christian-Evangelist,* 1896, p. 338.

FELLOWSHIPING WITH OTHER CHRISTIANS

The nineteenth century was a time of rapid expansion of the church in America as each denomination sought to follow its constituency on the ever-receding frontier and to evangelize the great numbers of persons who were not related to Christianity in any manner. The Disciples were no exception to this pattern. The age of expansion passed and the early twentieth century saw the development of interdenominational and ecumenical relationships as Christians of various persuasions sought to understand one another and to work together.

Beginning with the Evangelical Alliance in 1867 through the last years of the nineteenth century, a number of interdenominational developments worked to bring Christians together. One of the first such developments was the Sunday school movement. During the 1870s it elicited from church people across the nation, including Disciples, a remarkable enthusiasm. The Sunday school became a center for experimentation in new ideas and methods and provided an outlet for the energetic leadership of dedicated lay people. Because it was not thought to be the church, it was freer than the church to adopt new ways of thinking. The Sunday school early transcended denominational barriers and led to various forms of cooperative effort.

Sunday school work furnished one of the first areas where Disciples began to look beyond themselves. The oldest Sunday school among Disciples dates from an organization in the congregation at Hanover, Shelby County, Indiana, in 1831. Other Sunday schools were reported at Georgetown, Kentucky, in 1834 and at Lexington, Kentucky, in 1837.

Both Stone and Campbell were at first suspicious of Sunday schools, partly on the ground that they were not derived from the New Testament church. However, their objections soon disappeared, and encouraged by the first national convention in 1849, Sunday schools soon were in favor across the brotherhood, though as yet by no means in every congregation. State Sunday school associations were formed, beginning with Indiana in 1861 and followed by Ohio in 1867. The need for some organization that would express and promote a sense of cooperation on a national scale became apparent.

This need found its expression in the organization of the General Christian Sunday School Association in 1882.

Disciples were throughly committed to Sunday school work by the time the 1869 convention of the International Sunday School Association, an interdenominational agency, took the actions which led to issuing the first Uniform Lessons in 1872. Christians working together on this plan for an orderly program of Bible study were brought closer together. The plan had serious faults, which were later corrected, but many persons were thrilled at the thought that pupils of every class in Sunday schools of every denomination were studying the same lessons every Sunday. Disciples were quick to adopt the International Uniform Lessons and soon had a representative on the Lesson Committee, Isaac Errett, who served from 1884 to 1888. He was succeeded by Benjamin B. Tyler, who was elected president of the International Sunday School Association in 1902.[25]

The Young People's Society of Christian Endeavor was founded in 1881 by a Congregational minister, Francis E. Clark. This program immediately caught the attention and won the favor of Disciples as well as the youth of most denominations. The Disciples entered heartily into Christian Endeavor, especially because of its interdenominational character. They enjoyed working with young people of other denominations, and many Disciples leaders had their first experience of interdenominational leadership in its ranks in state and national meetings. Later, when several denominations began to set up a separate young people's organization of their own, Disciples long continued to promote Christian Endeavor.

Another aspect of ecumenical cooperation was introduced when the Protestant Episcopal Church in the United States, followed by the Anglican Lambeth Conference of 1888, issued a four-point program for the reunion of the church, which came to be known as the Lambeth Quadrilateral. The suggested principles were: 1) the authority of the Scriptures, 2) acceptance of the Apostles' and Nicene creeds as statements of faith, 3) acceptance of baptism and the Lord's Supper as ordained by Christ, and 4) the apostolic succession

---

25. William C. Bower and Roy G. Ross, *The Disciples and Religious Education* (St. Louis: Christian Board of Publication, 1936), p. 100 ff.

of bishops. The main result of this statement was to stimulate among denominations frequently negative discussion of a long-neglected subject.

In 1891 the General Assembly of the Presbyterian Church in the U.S.A. offered a tentative proposal that the various denominations enter a federation for fellowship and cooperative action. Such federation would eliminate competitive effort and at the same time preserve the independence and special beliefs held by the several churches. A subsequent proposal of the Congregationalists in 1898 for a national convocation of denominations looking toward federation bore no fruit directly, but did encourage cooperation on a national scale which began with the creation of the National Federation of Churches and Church Workers in February 1901. Composed of interested individuals, some local congregations and one or two auxiliary church bodies, the organization did not represent the denominations officially. The weakness of such a body was obvious, and some of its spokesmen began at once to look forward to forming a federation of the denominations themselves.[26]

Federation as a principle had been discussed informally among Disciples for some years, but now the time had come for the first definite action. At the 1902 General Convention at Omaha, Edward L. Powell (1860-1933), minister at Louisville, gave an eloquent address on the subject of "Christian Union" followed by a brief presentation by Elias B. Sanford, secretary of the National Federation of Churches and Church Workers, on the proposed plan. James H. Garrison, editor of *The Christian-Evangelist,* immediately afterward introduced a resolution to the convention approving the federation principle. J. A. Lord (1849-1922), editor of the *Christian Standard,* objected to federation on the grounds that such action would "recognize the denominations." The resolution was adopted after much debate. From this time forward, however, the brotherhood's leading papers took opposite sides on the issue; and for the next several years federation was discussed intensely whenever Disciples gathered.[27]

---

26. Samuel McCrea Cavert, *The American Churches in the Ecumenical Movement, 1900-1968* (New York: Association Press, 1968), pp. 61-67.
27. Winfred E. Garrison, *Christian Unity and Disciples of Christ* (St. Louis: Bethany Press, 1955), pp. 123 ff. and 160 ff.

Disciples participated in the Inter-Church Conference on Federation held at New York City in November 1905 at which the plan for a Federal Council of the churches was put into final form and recommended for consideration by the various denominations. The thirty or more Disciples who attended were not "officially appointed," as there was no authority which had the power to do so, but were selected from among leaders who had been conspicuous advocates of federation. For some opponents of Disciples participation in the Federal Council the main question was that of having fellowship with the unimmersed. As the time for final decision came, however, a steadily increasing number of Disciples came to favor the federation proposal.

The Disciples, without a delegate assembly or other authoritative structure, were puzzled as to how they could enter into any sort of agreement with denominations having such bodies. The solution came as unofficial gatherings, having only the authority inherent in respected leadership, handled the plans for Disciples participation. At a widely publicized meeting, held at Cincinnati in March 1907, a committee was appointed with Frederick D. Power (1851-1911), long-time minister at Washington, D.C., as chairman, to prepare the Disciples response to the proposal for federation.

A public meeting, held outside the regular convention sessions, was called at Norfolk, Virginia, at the time of the next General Convention in October 1907. The Cincinnati committee reported, declaring support for the federation movement and approving the appointment of delegates to the Federal Council. The report was adopted with one dissenting vote. The Disciples, therefore, were members of the Federal Council of the Churches of Christ in America from its beginning in 1908. The name itself was the suggestion of James H. Garrison, at the time the Disciples leading advocate of federation. Disciples participation was made possible only after much searching and a long internal struggle, but the decision when it came received popular support. As local and state councils and federations of churches developed, Disciples were ready to take their place in them. Within two years the Foreign Missions Conference of North America and the Home Missions Conference had been formed. The

Disciples, along with other denominations, entered into membership at the time of formation.

Parallel with the discussion of federation and the beginning of the Federal Council's activities an almost continuous series of proposals and pronouncements on the whole subject of union were put forward. One brotherhood paper published a series of articles on the positions of several denominations, emphasizing points of agreement. James H. Garrison, deeply interested in the subject, published a book entitled *Christian Union Historically Considered.*

As president of the 1910 General Convention which met at Topeka, Peter Ainslie (1867-1934), stirred the Disciples with a dramatic call to return to their original commitment to the cause of Christian union and to take steps toward realizing that purpose. Minister of the Christian Temple, Baltimore, Ainslie became an ardent crusader for the ecumenical movement and the inspiration for subsequent generations of Disciples. More than any other leader he brought the Disciples appeal for Christian union to the attention of other religious bodies and, in turn, helped his own people become more involved ecumenically.

The time was propitious for Ainslie's concrete proposal to develop among Disciples a special agency to create a program of study and interest in Christian unity. The Federal Council of Churches was in its third year and the 1910 World Missionary Conference had just been held at Edinburgh, Scotland, attended by several leading Disciples. To avoid undue criticism, Ainslie called an open meeting, separate from the regular sessions at Topeka, to discuss the framework of such an organization. Approval was given his plans and a Council on Christian Union was incorporated in Maryland "to create and distribute literature bearing on Christian union, and to arrange conferences in important centers on the subject of Christian union." The name was changed in 1913 to Association for the Promotion of Christian Unity and still later to Council on Christian Unity. Among the first directors were such prominent Disciples as Thomas Carr Howe (1867-1934), Edward L. Powell, James H. Garrison, Finis Idleman (1875-1941), Ely V. Zollars (1849-1916), Allan B. (1856-1925) and James M. Philputt (1860-1932), Frederick W. Burnham (1871-1960), Z. T. Sweeney (1849-1926),

Charles S. Medbury (1865-1932), Frederick D. Kershner (1875-1953), R. A. Long (1850-1934), I. J. Spencer (1851-1922), B. A. Abbott (1866-1936), Jacob H. Goldner (1871-1949), and C. M. Chilton (1867-1962). Peter Ainslie became, and remained for many years, the organization's president.

With membership in the Federal Council of Churches and with the formation of the Council on Christian Union, the Disciples were well launched in the modern ecumenical movement. Undoubtedly the renewed emphasis on and interest in Christian unity helped Disciples escape introversion. Their participation in the mainstream of American Christianity and church life was now assured. The period from 1869 to 1910 had been a period of growth for agencies and institutions as well as of shattering controversy and not a little uneasiness as the leadership and the congregations moved out into wider circles of interest and influence.

12

BEGINNING THE SECOND CENTURY

At first mainly a rural people, the Disciples at the end of the nineteenth century were caught up in the social, industrial, and cultural turmoil of the cities. Their members, along with many Americans, migrated to the cities in great numbers. The years of the new century before World War I presented a special challenge to the churches. Separate congregations of Negro Disciples, brothers and sisters in Christ, were organized. Disciples churches in Canada came into closer fellowship with the American movement. Blessed during this period with a number of outstanding leaders, both laypersons and ministers, Disciples felt there was much to celebrate by the time of the centennial of the *Declaration and Address* in 1909.

GROWING INTEREST IN SOCIAL ISSUES

The unprecedented prosperity of the last part of the nineteenth century created so-called "Robber Barons" such as Jay Gould, Cornelius Vanderbilt, and John D. Rockefeller. Ostentatious displays of great wealth existed side by side with scenes of slum poverty defying description. Labor struggled to overcome injustice, and by 1881 the American

Federation of Labor had been organized. As unions sought to improve the condition of the working man, industrial strife broke out. The railroad strikes of 1877, the Haymarket riot at Chicago in 1886, the Carnegie steel strike at Homestead (Pittsburgh) in 1892 and the Pullman Company strike in 1894 all precipitated a deep bitterness between labor and management. These were only the highlights of a long series of labor disturbances the violence of which often shocked the nation. Other social issues of the last decades of the nineteenth century involved rights of private property, trusts, regulation of interstate commerce, child labor, and alcoholic beverages.

There began to develop a clearly discernible cleavage between labor and the church. The membership of Protestant churches was made up largely of employers, salaried persons, farmers, and those engaged in personal service for such persons, and as a result, naturally had the employer's viewpoint.[1] Even though Disciples sometimes criticized the greed of American corporations, they were not at all certain what should be done to control them. Editors of church papers expressed sympathy for the downtrodden in one issue and reacted with intolerant dogmatism in the next. The overall effect, however, was to stimulate interest in social questions.

Out of this conflict came the desire of American churches, including the Disciples, to apply the social teachings of Jesus. Here and there a few church leaders began to understand the social significance of the gospel and to speak out. Disciples leaders, however, were often perplexed by the discontent of the workers and puzzled as to what could be done to help. Isaac Errett in 1875 did recognize that social agitation was "a settlement of debts that had long accumulated," although he had no answers to propose.[2] James H. Garrison stated that the conversion of sinners was "the true mission of the gospel," but he also believed that the church must become informed concerning social issues.[3] Many Disciples, however, continued to think the only business of the church was that of changing the individual. As America's social disorders

---

1. William Warren Sweet, *The Story of Religion in America* (rev.), New York: Harper and Brothers, 1950. pp. 354 ff.
2. *Christian Standard*, June 19, 1875, p. 194.
3. *Christian-Evangelist*, May 28, 1891, p. 338.

mounted, some Disciples leaders became convinced that the basic illness was social and not personal.

Several factors led to this change in viewpoint. There was a new theology in addition to the rise of a new view of the role of economics. The most important factor, however, was the study of sociology. Developed toward the end of the nineteenth century, the purpose of sociology was to study human institutions and to draw attention to their effect on conditions resulting in human suffering. Christian reformers came to believe that the church had a responsibility to help change the social environment, especially if conditions tended to degrade individuals and families. Young Disciples ministers were encouraged to study sociology, and the subject was a favorite on convention programs well into the new century. Christian teaching combined with newly discovered sociological principles and applied to America's industrial and economic crises came to be known as the "social gospel."[4]

The central theme of the theology of the social gospel was the concept of the kingdom of God based on the brotherhood of man. Disciples leaders and their followers came to believe that the purpose of the church was to work for the redemption of society as well as the saving of the individual. By the first decade of the twentieth century this theology had permeated Disciples thinking. Many of the young ministers of the early 1900s preached with these assumptions clearly in mind. The social gospel movement among Disciples was not, however, primarily a theological understanding but a practical response to human need.

Few leaders of the social gospel movement in America greatly influenced the Disciples. Washington Gladden (1836-1918), Congregational minister at Columbus, Ohio, called for an application of Christian teaching to business. He was the hero of a rising generation of young ministers. Disciples journals published Gladden's speeches and recommended his books. Josiah Strong (1847-1916), minister of Central Congregational Church, Cincinnati, made an impression as an early ecumen-

---

4. David E. Harrell, Jr., *The Social Sources of Division in the Disciples of Christ* (Atlanta: Publishing Systems, Inc., 1973). pp. 85 ff. This is an excellent study of social issues as viewed by Disciples.

ical leader deeply interested in evangelizing the cities. The *Christian Standard* in the fall of 1885 helped promote an "Inter-Denominational Congress" organized by Strong. Held in Cincinnati to discuss urban problems, the meeting was supported by Isaac Errett, and he was one of the featured speakers. The General Convention by 1887 began distributing Strong's tracts on social issues. Walter Rauschenbusch (1861-1918), Baptist pastor and later seminary professor who gave theological expression to the movement, was little known among Disciples at this time. The social gospel spokesman most widely known among Disciples was George D. Herron (1862-1925) from Grinnell, Iowa. Herron was a popular speaker at a number of Disciples churches and meetings over the years. By 1900 he had become extremely controversial and his popularity waned.

Few Disciples became creative or prophetic leaders of the social gospel movement. Their ministers and leaders mainly responded to the challenge of the issues. By the 1890s James H. Garrison was writing, "It is high time the Church should come to the front as the champion of justice and equal rights among men."[5] Disciples preachers in general took the position that the Christian faith should be a balance between a desire to win the individual for Christ and a concern for correcting certain social ills, in that order. Editorials and leading articles in *The Christian-Evangelist* and the *Christian Standard* reflected this viewpoint. Both journals argued that churches should continue to evangelize individuals and at the same time give more attention to social justice. Reform-minded ministers preached challenging sermons on social questions. They organized forums to discuss social problems and invited representatives of labor to speak before study groups in the churches. Before the end of the century, liberal advocates of the social gospel arose among Disciples, particularly Frank G. Tyrrell (1865-1950), Errett Gates (b. 1870), and Alva W. Taylor (1871-1957).

One practical result of Disciples interest in social change was the development of institutional churches in several cities.[6] The idea of making a congregation the center of com-

---

5. *Christian-Evangelist*, June 21, 1894, p. 386.
6. Harrell, *op. cit.*, pp. 100 ff.

munity services came from the social gospel movement. Not every congregation so conceived its mission, but for a considerable number the idea was attractive. Disciples congregations with institutional church characteristics were to be found in Chicago, New York, St. Louis, Kansas City, Des Moines, Buffalo, Toledo, Pittsburgh, Baltimore, Dallas, and Louisville. Among the features emphasized by an institutional church were libraries, meals for those persons needing them, gymnasiums and other recreation facilities for youth. Some congregations sponsored a "labor exchange" to help find employment for the unemployed.

Probably the most widely publicized of the Disciples institutional churches was the Central Christian Church at Des Moines, Iowa, led by its pastor, Harvey O. Breeden (1862-1933). In 1894 the congregation began a "night school" to teach the illiterate and the immigrant such practical subjects as grammar, reading, shorthand, and bookkeeping. By the first decade of the twentieth century the congregation, in addition to its earlier programs, was providing reading rooms, a kindergarten, Bible studies, and a music program.

Somewhat similar to the institutional church was the social settlement house, an institution to aid slum victims. The *Christian Standard* in an editorial in 1891 suggested the idea for Disciples' consideration. Inspired by the example of Jane Addams and Hull House in Chicago, Hiram House was organized in 1896 at Cleveland. Located in a tenement district flooded with recent immigrants and led for fifty years by George Albert Bellamy (1876-1960), Hiram House became a model for Disciples social work. Supported at first by Disciples congregations of Cleveland, Hiram House was recognized increasingly as a community and interdenominational project. Flanner House at Indianapolis had similar beginnings in 1898 as a social service center in an area inhabited mainly by Negroes.

Two Disciples writers in the 1890s did much to clarify the major social issues. Barton W. Johnson of *The Christian-Evangelist* and Benjamin J. Radford (1838-1933) of the *Christian Standard* wrote articles and columns giving their observations on the economic problems of America. While most Disciples leaders and preachers gave only moderate support to organized labor, Johnson and Radford expressed definite prolabor views while abhorring any resort to violence. Their writings were eagerly read even though not all readers agreed with them. The foremost friend of the workingman among Disciples was William W. Hopkins (d. 1916), pastor of Second Christian Church in St. Louis. He became one of *The Christian-Evangelist's* most popular writers on labor-management issues during the 1890s. The number of pastors who openly supported labor increased as the twentieth century approached.

Government intervention in labor-capital conflicts received wide support by the last of the nineteenth century. Some Disciples leaders advocated compulsory arbitration and others profit sharing, but there was a consensus that legislation was needed. Nationalization of some major industries was discussed. Leaders were nearly unanimous in demanding antitrust legislation. Editors of Disciples journals supported the efforts of Congressman Thomas W. Phillips to establish study commissions to investigate the problems of capital and labor. Phillips, from Butler, Pennsylvania, was one of the most active and respected laymen in the church. A wealthy businessman, he had been one of the founders of the *Christian Standard.*

The late nineteenth century saw considerable discontent among farmers out of which grew the National Farmers Alliance and the Cooperative Union of America. These movements were carefully watched by Disciples leaders and received support from Johnson and Radford in their articles. A return to the farm was believed to be a possible solution to the nation's ills by some Disciples. Cheap land seemed a way to lure people from the crowded slums. A few Disciples became interested in colonization schemes which turned out to be a curious mixture of land reform and financial speculation. Some promoters simply advertised land in church papers. Others sought to establish new communities. Still others worked to form cooperatives. The most widely known colonization scheme among Disciples was that of Rufus A. Burriss (d. 1930) of Bowmanville, Ontario. Burriss began publishing appeals for settlers in 1897 for the Christian Colony on Rainy River in Canada. Early successes soon turned to failure in a period of bad crops.

Ultimately attention was drawn to the need for tax reforms as a solution to the nation's economic problems. Johnson and Radford in their articles called for a graduated income tax to secure equal taxation while others favored inheritance taxes. The most radical proposals were those arising from the followers of Henry George, a radical economic critic. George's plan seemed logical and simple as he proposed a single tax to be placed on all increments in land values due to "progress" and growth of the nation's economy. Although his plan had little long-term effect, he made some influential converts among Disciples.

One of them was Tom L. Johnson (1854-1911), a layman in the Cedar Avenue Christian Church of Cleveland. Johnson had made a fortune in street railways and from 1891 to 1895 served in the Congress. Elected mayor of Cleveland in 1901, he remained in that position until 1910, becoming known as one of the nation's outstanding reform politicians. When Johnson was elected mayor, Harris Reid Cooley (1857-1936), Johnson's pastor, was appointed director of the Board of Public Service and served in this office during the entire nine years of Johnson's administration. Cooley, also a promoter of the single tax, won fame for his enlightened reforms of Cleveland's charitable and correctional institutions. Cora, his talented wife, was a social worker and prominent lecturer on social issues.

In the last decade of the nineteenth century there was much unemployment and growing unrest. Disciples, however, had little respect or sympathy for "Coxey's Army" when in 1894 it marched on Washington to make demands on the government. Also widely publicized among Disciples was "Kelly's Army" which originiated in Oakland, California, with the encouragement of First Christian Church there. The "army," made up of about 1,500 men, arrived at Des Moines, Iowa, on its way to Washington and encamped. It was visited by several Disciples leaders, including Barton O. Aylesworth (1860-1933), president of Drake University. Encouraging his class in sociology to interview the marchers, Aylesworth himself made a statement to the press favoring the marchers' demands. His cordiality to the protesters offended many Iowa Disciples, including Francis M. Drake, chief patron of the university. The Board of Trustees issued a statement repudiating Aylesworth's actions. Kelly's army represented to many Disciples their worst fears of violence and anarchy.

The liquor industry, charged with political corruption and monopolistic tendencies, was regarded as one of the dangerous social evils of the day. Opposition to the manufacture and sale of intoxicants was a cause that liberal and conservative, revivalist and social gospel advocate alike, could support. Attracting great attention and commanding the dedicated zeal of thousands of persons, the temperance movement achieved nationwide prominence in the years before World War I. It was not long before the appeal for temperance became a demand for prohibition. The Prohibition Party was founded in 1869, the Women's Christian Temperance Union (WCTU) in 1874, and the Anti-Saloon League of America in 1895. By 1900 five of the forty-five states had adopted statewide prohibition. Some Christians worked for moderation; others for total abstinence. Some attacked the saloon and others thought political action best. Despite differing views temperance workers reached into every congregation. Protestantism in America had never before been so completely agreed upon a goal.

Disciples came to consider prohibition the most important question before the nation.[7] A majority of Disciples leaders connected the "liquor interests" with virtually every known social problem. Poverty, slums, labor agitation, and similar social evils were all directly related to the abuse of alcohol in the minds of Disciples. Mrs. Zeralda G. Wallace (1817-1904), an Indianapolis Disciple, was considered the originator of the temperance crusade in the early 1870s that led to the national organization of women. When the WCTU was formed in 1874, Disciples women, encouraged by their preachers, were soon drawn into its program. Although no Disciples women of the time gained national prominence in the organization, thousands of them were active leaders in state and local work. Disciples ministers by the hundreds joined with the women in supporting the cause.

Disciples journals took up the issue in the early days of the campaign. In July, August, and September, 1878, Isaac Errett and James H. Garrison engaged in a full-scale debate

7. Harrell, *op. cit.*, p. 210 ff.

on the prohibition question in the pages of the *Christian Standard* and *The Christian*. The main difference between the two men was the question of prohibition by law. Errett argued that such laws were useless unless supported by public opinion and practice. The question of the use of fermented wine in the observance of the Lord's Supper was debated in the papers a short time later. Many congregations began to use unfermented grape juice in this period. Prohibition remained the most discussed issue in church papers to the close of the century.

Disciples were in general agreement that Christians should use their political influence against the liquor industry, but they disagreed about the best political strategy. Usually Disciples leaders supported one of the established parties when it backed prohibition. When both major parties favored the liquor interests, they were moved to support the Prohibition party. In 1896 Disciples attending the national convention of the Prohibition party included Oliver W. Stewart (1867-1937), minister of the Christian Church at Mackinaw, Illinois, and permanent chairman of the convention. Josephus Hopwood (1843-1935), prohibition candidate for governor of Tennessee, was also at the convention which nominated Hale Johnson (1847-1902) of Newton, Illinois, widely known Disciples minister, for the vice-presidency.

Kansas in 1881 became the first state to enact legal prohibition since the Civil War. An active prohibition campaign among Disciples had been most effective. The heart of the Disciples prohibition leadership in Kansas was Pardee Butler, remembered from earlier days as an abolition crusader. Carry A. Nation (1846-1911) brought some attention to the Disciples as she became nationally famous as the "smasher" of saloons. The wife of David Nation, minister of the First Christian Church, Medicine Lodge, Kansas, she was active as a "jail evangelist." Working with the Barber County WCTU, she started her career in smashing saloons at Medicine Lodge in the late summer of 1899. After a raid at Kiowa and then a visit to Wichita early in 1900, her national fame was won.

Disciples in Iowa were led in their successful prohibition campaign by the most prominent preacher in the state, David Roberts Dungan (1837-1921). When Disciples layman Gen.

Francis M. Drake secured the governor's chair in 1896, Iowa prohibitionists were delighted. Assuming that he would resist efforts to change Iowa's prohibition stand, prohibitionists were profoundly shocked when Drake signed a bill passed by the legislature which allowed the licensing of distilleries in the state. In the coming months national Disciples journals and the Iowa papers were dominated by the debate over Drake's action. A resolution of censure against Drake was tabled at the next Iowa convention. He was reelected president of the convention but only after heated discussion. Refusing a second term as governor, Drake gradually worked his way back into favor with the church.

The General Convention in 1899 adopted the following resolution, "That we pledge our untiring hostility to the liquor business, and that we favor the prohibition of the manufacture and sale of intoxicating liquors as a beverage."[8] A majority of Disciples at the close of the century would have agreed with that resolution. Disciples concern for prohibition led the Norfolk convention in 1907 to set up a Board of Temperance with headquarters at Indianapolis under the direction of Dr. Homer J. Hall from Franklin, Indiana. In 1911 at the Portland convention the Disciples broadened the scope of the board's work to include social services. As a standing committee of the American Christian Missionary Society it was known as the Board of Temperance and Social Service. For the first ten years Alva W. Taylor, a leader in social reform among Disciples, served as the unsalaried secretary.

A younger generation of preachers and leaders, educated in sociological concerns, freely accepted the social gospel and its implications for the program of the church. In earlier days Disciples conventions, state and national, had been mainly concerned with missionary and organizational matters, but by the early twentieth century Disciples leaders and preachers began to express interest in social issues with prohibition becoming a major interest. Disciples were well on their way to taking their place with the rest of American Christianity in a consideration of social and ethical questions.

----

8. *Minutes of the General Convention,* 1899, pp. 99-100.

DEVELOPMENT OF BLACK DISCIPLES: 1865-1914

From the end of the Civil War to the beginning of World War I, Negro Disciples were primarily concerned with evangelism, education, and the organization of conventions. During this period Negroes knew what it was to have freedom but not equality. Blacks had difficulties making adjustments to emancipation in religion as well as in other aspects of life. They generally lacked the education, leadership experience, or money to be self-sustaining. White Disciples in this period became aware of, and in a limited way concerned for, their black brothers and sisters in Christ.

At the end of the Civil War the former slave states of Kentucky, Tennessee, Georgia, Virginia, and North Carolina had the largest number of Negro Disciples. There were few black congregations in northern states. Most Negro Disciples were members of predominantly white congregations, but within a few years of emancipation this pattern was broken. Where a sufficient number of black Disciples existed, they were encouraged to form their own congregations and were often aided financially by the whites to do so. When only a few Negroes were in a white congregation, the blacks withdrew from the church. The process was gradual, but by the end of Reconstruction the number of Negro Disciples congregations had multiplied considerably.[9]

After the Civil War concern for the evangelization of the southern Negro grew in both North and South. Some northern white Disciples considered carrying the gospel to the freedman a missionary cause. Disciples saw other denominations evangelizing blacks and felt that they should do as much. Southern white Disciples considered it their responsibility to care for the spiritual welfare of former slaves. Early efforts by the Disciples to evangelize the Negro were marked by the enthusiasm of a few leaders with little financial backing or organized effort. In the 1870s as much evangelistic work was carried on outside the ACMS as had been done through it.

The leading white preachers of Mississippi, including Thomas W. Caskey and Benjamin F. Manire (1828-1911), were quite active in preaching to former slaves. Manire made

9. Lyda, *A History of Black Christian Churches (Disciples of Christ) in the United States Through 1899*, pp. 38 ff.

frequent visits to northern Disciples congregations seeking support for Negro evangelism in Mississippi. Mrs. Emily H. Tubman of Augusta, Georgia, supported a Negro state evangelist. In the summer of 1867 there was a meeting of Disciples leaders, including Robert Milligan and Charles L. Loos, at Hiram College. Out of this gathering grew the Freedman's Missionary Society, an organization seeking to raise money to send an evangelist to the South. The organization passed out of existence by 1870 because of lack of support.

Disciples generally agreed during the 1870s that the best approach for Negro evangelization was to support black preachers who would preach to the black community. Negro Disciples preachers were agreeable to this idea as it gave them more responsibility for leadership. The plan produced only modest support, either North or South.[10] One exception was a revival in Mississippi in 1873-1874 led by George Owen (1813-1889), a white minister from Jacksonville, Illinois, aided by Mississippi Disciples. Among those converted was an influential Negro Baptist preacher named Levin Wood. With financial support from a number of Disciples, Owen and Wood were enabled to work among Mississippi Negroes with some success.

The 1879 General Convention was addressed by Preston Taylor (1849-1931), minister of the Colored Christian Church at Mt. Sterling, Kentucky. Destined to become the leading Negro leader for several generations, Taylor was appointed national evangelist by the General Convention in 1883 for work among black Disciples. The meager support given to Taylor was about all ACMS did for Negro work in the 1880s. Taylor traveled widely, holding evangelistic meetings, establishing new congregations, and giving Negro Disciples a sense of belonging. In 1886 Taylor settled at Nashville, Tennessee, as the minister of the Gay Street Christian Church. Two years later, in a dispute with some of the elders, he gave up the pulpit and established Taylor and Company, a funeral business in Nashville.

Probably the most successful black evangelist among the Disciples in the 1880s and 1890s was H. Jackson Brayboy of Alabama. Another prominent Negro evangelist of the time was S. W. Womack of Nashville. A number of southern white

10. Harrell, *The Social Sources of Division in the Disciples of Christ,* pp. 173 ff.

AMONG BLACK DISCIPLES

Mrs. Rosa Brown Bracy

Preston Taylor

During the twentieth century the Black Disciples church came of age and took control of its own destiny within the Christian Church (Disciples of Christ). What had begun as an American Christian Missionary Society home mission to Negroes in the South in the wake of the Civil War created institutions such as Southern Christian Institute, in Edwards, Mississippi. In 1917 the National Christian Missionary Convention was founded with its first annual meeting in Nashville. Leadership was provided by Black Disciples such as Preston Taylor. The National Convocation of the Christian Church was established in 1970 as successor to the National Christian Missionary Convention, but with its own administrative secretary, an assistant to the general minister and president of the Christian Church (Disciples of Christ). Its biennial assemblies continue to provide fellowship to Black Disciples.

Southern Christian Institute

Delegates to the first National Christian Missionary Convention, August 5-9, 1917 at Nashville

Delegates to the National Convocation, August 23-27, 1972 in Wilson, N. C.

A singing group at the National Convocation

School of Faith and Life and National Convocation, August 23-27, 1972

congregations went together to support Brayboy and
Womack as they organized new congregations. Their
successes only underscored the need for pastors trained in
evangelism and in ministering to newly organized congregations. Between 1865 and 1914 a number of promising
congregations of Negro Disciples were established in major
cities. In addition to the churches at Louisville and Nashville,
important congregations were established at Indianapolis,
Memphis, Dallas, Cincinnati, Kansas City, and St. Louis. A
congregation established in 1870 at Wheatland (Remus),
Mecosta County, Michigan, by Thomas W. Cross (1826-
1897), a Negro from Virginia, gathered blacks, whites, and Indians into a single congregation with considerable success.

Evangelists and preachers among Negro Disciples in every
region served at great personal sacrifice. They were mostly ill
paid and usually supported themselves with other labor.[11]
One outstanding Negro husband and wife team among black
Disciples was the Bosticks. Mancil M. Bostick (1864-1928)
attended the Negro congregation at Pea Ridge, Lonoke County, Arkansas. There he met Sarah Lue Young (1868-1948) and
after their marriage in 1892 they served the church for many
years. Bostick preached and reopened a number of congregations in Arkansas and neighboring states. By 1900 Mrs.
Bostick had become the organizer of women's missionary
work in Arkansas and a dozen other states.[12]

The basis for a more orderly development of Negro work
was laid when the General Convention in 1890 formed the
Board of Negro Education and Evangelization with headquarters at Louisville. The members of the original board
were E. L. Powell, H. I. Stone, Wm. J. Loos (1851-1930), J. T.
Hawkins, W. S. Giltner (1827-1921), J. I. Irwin (1824-1910),
and J. W. McGarvey.[13] A year earlier the convention had appointed John W. Jenkins (1857-1939), a former missionary to
Jamaica, "Superintendent of Missions and Schools Among
the Colored People." Jenkins urged the board to employ a
field secretary to give personal guidance to the Negro work.
He should be white since blacks had not come to trust any of

---

11. Lyda *A History of Black Christian Churches,* pp. 162 ff.
12. Bertha Mason Fuller, *The Life Story of Sarah Lou Bostick,* Little Rock, Arkansas, Private Printing, 1949. pp. 10-28.
13. Harrell, *The Social Sources of Division in the Disciples of Christ,* p. 177 ff.

their own leaders. After a lengthy search the board appointed Clayton C. Smith (1845-1919) secretary in January 1892. Smith brought considerable experience, a capacity for organization and a sense of dedication to his task. Within a few years the Disciples Negro program enjoyed a measure of success for the first time. The financial support of the Negro work improved steadily under his leadership. A special Sunday offering for Negro work was established in 1891. The Board of Negro Education and Evangelization was dissolved in 1900 when the Kansas City convention asked the Christian Woman's Board of Missions to assume responsibility for the work among black Disciples.

Disciples leaders early realized that an effective program of evangelization among Negroes would have to be combined with an educational program. Leaders and preachers among blacks were badly needed. There were several failures before a successful program was established. The most interesting of the early efforts among Negro Disciples was the proposal in 1868 of Peter Lowery, a Nashville Negro preacher, to establish Tennessee Manual Labor University. Lowery announced plans to buy a farm, build a mill, and provide students an opportunity to earn an education. His effort attracted a large number of young men, but the school came to a quick end in the midst of a financial scandal.[14]

Negro Disciples from the beginning were interested in district and state conventions and organizations.[15] The state missionary convention of the Colored Christian Church in Kentucky dated from 1872. District conventions were held as early as 1873 in middle Tennessee, becoming structured into the Annual Missionary Convention in 1880. The black Disciples of Missouri organized a missionary society and held their first convention in 1874. By 1880 black women decided to organize the Kentucky Christian Woman's Board of Missions Convention. Church school workers formed their own Sunday school convention shortly thereafter, giving Kentucky three separate conventions. Usually their meetings overlapped. This pattern of three separate conventions was

---

14. *The further story of educational institutions among black Disciples will be found in Chapter XIII.*
15. Lyda, *A History of Black Christian Churches*, p. 105 ff.

followed in several of the states. State meetings were being held in nearly every southern state by 1899.

As early as 1867 Negro Disciples tried to establish a national organization. At a meeting at Nashville several black preachers, led by Rufus Conrad, founded the American Christian Evangelizing and Educational Association. Receiving little support from either whites or blacks in the depressed post-Civil War economy, the effort failed. A more permanent organization was the National Convention of the Churches of Christ formed in 1878 by H. Malcolm Ayers and Preston Taylor of Kentucky. Ayers and Taylor spoke often before the General Convention asking for shared leadership with the white-controlled missionary societies for the work among Negroes but with little result. Taylor especially was concerned to work in cooperation with the General Convention. The National Convention held assemblies for many years but whether or not it met each year is uncertain. It is known to have met at Memphis in 1885, at Nashville in 1898, and at Kansas City in 1900. By the end of the century, congregations or individuals from at least a dozen states participated in its fellowship. It continued into the twentieth century, periodically issuing appeals to the white convention for support of Negro work.

Negro Disciples between 1865 and 1914 had few means of communication with one another. The *Christian Standard* tried to help by beginning a column in 1879 entitled "Our Colored Brethren." All the papers expressed willingness to report news of the Negro work, but it was irregularly done. This was not entirely satisfactory to Negro leaders, and they tried to start publications of their own. Two journals begun during the 1890s had only a brief existence: the *Assembly Standard,* published at Plymouth, North Carolina, and the *Christian Soldier* edited by D. R. Wilkins in Kentucky. The paper existing for the longest time among Negro Disciples was *The Gospel Plea,* edited by Joel Baer Lehman (1866-1942) at Southern Christian Institute. A weekly journal containing editorials, news, announcements, and occasional feature articles, it gave its largest amount of space to promotion of SCI. With the name changed in 1926 to *The Christian Plea*, the paper was published until 1965.

Negro Disciples in eastern North Carolina had a development all their own.[16] Between 1865 and 1873, with the help of the white Disciples, the black Disciples had organized themselves into a district and were busy evangelizing. After 1877 many congregations were formed in small towns and rural areas with the assistance of the white state organization. A number of Free Will Baptist congregations were brought into the fellowship. This has given a distinct character to the churches of the region.

A congregation, begun as a mission by an evangelist, was under the watchful eye of the district organization from its beginning. After a time the evangelist could apply to the district assembly for recognition of the mission as a congregation. If the assembly agreed that both the preacher and the church understood Disciples practice and belief, they were accepted as a congregation. If the preacher did not have standing as a "chief" (elder), he would have to meet certain additional requirements before being accepted. At the beginning of 1870 this region had perhaps six congregations of black Disciples. By 1914 it is estimated that there were at least 100 congregations in the area with approximately 8,500 members.

Discipline and organization gave strength to the program. Each local congregation held a Quarterly Conference at which the business of the church was considered, the footwashing ceremony was observed, and Holy Communion was held. On the weekend of every fifth Sunday the churches of one or more counties would gather for three days of fellowship and worship. Out of these gatherings grew the General Assembly of Eastern North Carolina governed by a council of seven elders or "chiefs." Since these assemblies were controlled by the men of the church, the women formed their own "Sisters Union" in a meeting at Plymouth, North Carolina, in 1892. Every congregation had an elected "church mother" who baked unleavened bread for the Lord's Supper and provided basins and towels for the footwashing ceremony. These organizations of black Disciples in eastern North Carolina pursued their own program and remained

16. William J. Barber, *Disciple Assemblies of Eastern North Carolina* (St. Louis: Printed for the author by The Bethany Press, 1966), pp. 3-78.

separate from the National Convention of the Churches of Christ for many years.

In general the Disciples Negro work between 1865 and 1914 met with numerous difficulties. White interest was not long sustained at any given time which led to a certain amount of Negro resentment. Although it did not often surface, a certain amount of racism persisted in Disciples thought and practice. There was little acceptance of social equality, as few Disciples abandoned the idea that blacks were inferior. Disciples did not grow as rapidly among Negroes as did Methodists and Baptists because Disciples in general were not as well known as the other two groups. The Disciples appeal to a rational religion based on New Testament study seemed to lack the warmth and emotional fervor found among the Methodists and Baptists.

By 1914 the question of self-determination arose among black Disciples leadership. White Disciples agencies did not include blacks in significant roles in the planning and executing of work among Negro Disciples. In many communities black Disciples congregations did carry out effective programs and activities. On the national level, however, they sought either to gain administrative authority or to structure themselves in order to achieve self-direction. By World War I black Disciples work and program seemed dormant. Much of the evangelical zeal and appeal of earlier days was missing. Leadership was not generally available when it was greatly needed. The best-known and ablest black Disciples leaders were growing older.

There were some gains nevertheless. The number of black congregations grew from only a few in 1865 to approximately 600 by 1914. Membership increased from a few thousand to approximately 48,250 persons by World War I. Black Disciples constituted between four and five per cent of the total membership of the Disciples in the United States. Negro Disciples found satisfaction in a movement which emphasized a united church based on a rational interpretation of the New Testament. The presence of black Disciples within the larger fellowship helped the movement to remain in contact with at least a portion of the American Negro Christian population. Black Disciples participation in the larger program of the Disciples, with all of its shortcomings, saved them from isolation.

DISCIPLES IN CANADA

Through the last decades of the nineteenth century Disciples in the United States became increasingly aware of fellow Disciples in the nation to the north. There had been adherents of the Stone-Campbell movement in Canada since the 1830s, but by the beginning of the twentieth century Disciples in Canada were still few in number. A variety of reasons accounted for the slow growth. The country was large and sparsely settled. Early communities in the Maritimes (Nova Scotia, New Brunswick, and Prince Edward Island) were rural and remained thinly populated. The province of Quebec was primarily Roman Catholic. By 1830 the immigration of the British into Ontario was in full swing, but there was loyalty to older institutions, including ancestral churches. It would be many years before the western provinces (Manitoba, Saskatchewan, Alberta, and British Columbia) would develop significantly.

Disciples congregations in the Maritimes were in the beginning Scotch Baptist (or Haldane). A Scotch Baptist congregation was formed at River John, Nova Scotia, in 1815 in the home of James Murray. Rigid and legalistic in their doctrines, such congregations grew slowly. Even before a congregation had been established at Halifax in 1832, Campbell's teachings had been brought northward by preachers who were agents for *The Christian Baptist*. The congregation at St. John, New Brunswick, was organized in 1834 by George Garraty (1811-1890). Later Maritime leaders included John McDonald (1806-1881) and Howard E. Cooke (b. 1856), a former sea captain.[17]

Prince Edward Island is the smallest province in Canada but has had great influence on Disciples through the years. Alexander Crawford (b. 1787), a Scotch Baptist minister, arrived in 1811. Educated at the school of the Haldanes in Scotland, he differed from the Baptists over creeds and soon

---

17. Reuben Butchart, *The Disciples of Christ in Canada Since 1830* (Toronto: Canadian Headquarters' Publication, 1949). This is the most complete history of Canadian Disciples. A more recent, shorter treatment is that of Shirley L. Muir, *Disciples in Canada* (Indianapolis: UCMS), 1966.

came to accept Campbell's beliefs. The congregation at New Glasgow dates from 1820. It was formed by silk weavers from Paisley, Scotland, and with John Stevenson as its leader, practiced immersion. Under the influence of John Knox (1817-1892), a graduate of the University of Edinburgh and a medical doctor, it joined the Campbell movement in the 1840s. Donald Crawford (1820-1911) was the minister of this congregation for over fifty years. A missionary society was formed by the three Maritime provinces in 1855 and by the 1870s nearly all of these Scotch Baptist congregations had become identified with the Disciples. This Scotch Baptist background has given a conservative cast to the Canadian movement and made it for a time less committed to church unity than Disciples in the United States.

Because of strong British immigration to Ontario in the 1830s, that province rose rapidly to become a major cultural and commercial center of Canada. The strength of the Canadian Disciples is to be found there. The migration brought James Black (1797-1886), a Scotch Baptist preacher, to Elgin County in 1820. Dugald Sinclair (1777-1870) came to Lobo in 1831. Both men were greatly influenced by reading *The Christian Baptist*. They traveled extensively over the province, evangelizing and organizing congregations which were transformed gradually from Scotch Baptist to Disciples beliefs and practices.

The first report of an Ontario "co-operation" was published in *The Millennial Harbinger* in 1843.[18] By 1846 there was a functioning provincial organization. Distinguished visitors to Ontario churches from the United States included Alexander Campbell and his wife in 1855, Isaac Errett in 1873, and Benjamin Franklin in 1875. In 1886 the Ontario Cooperation joined with the Wellington Cooperation to form the Cooperation of Disciples of Christ in Ontario, and Hugh Black (d. 1909) succeeded his father as its leader. Generally conservative in purpose, the cooperation majored in the support of an evangelist employed to organize new congregations. James Lediard (1847-1906) was an outstanding evangelist in Ontario throughout the 1880s. The first annual convention in Ontario was held at Guelph in 1887, the year that the Ontario Christian Woman's Board of Missions came

---

18. *Millennial Harbinger*, August, 1843, p. 376.

into being. Enthusiasm for foreign missions in the 1890s brought the Canadians together as never before. The Ontario Cooperation, meeting at Toronto in 1891, voted to send Mary Rioch Miller (1892-1916) from Hamilton to Japan as Canada's own missionary. Several of the provincial women's boards and the Foreign Christian Missionary Society supported her service from 1892 to 1916. Hillcrest Church of Christ (Disciples) at Toronto has long been the strongest Canadian Disciples congregation. It came into being in 1921 when Cecil St. Church, dating back to 1881, and Wychwood, a mission church of Cecil St. since 1899, united.

The first western province organized by Disciples was Manitoba. The promise of cheap, fertile land brought families with Disciples background from Ontario and northward from the United States. Andrew Scott (1857-1941), sent out by the Ontario women in 1881, organized the first Disciples congregation in Manitoba at Portage La Prairie. About 1901 a decision was made to gather all interested Disciples into the Western Canada Christian Missionary Association. In 1904 this organization became the Manitoba Christian Missionary Society. A congregation was organized at Winnipeg with the aid of John Abraham Lincoln Romig (1860-1938), evangelist of the ACMS. Over the next decade Romig organized many congregations throughout western Canada and was an important influence. By 1906 he reported to the ACMS seven congregations in the province with 600 members. George H. Stewart (1875-1958) of Winnipeg was an outstanding lay leader of the work in Manitoba.

From Manitoba the Disciples moved farther west to Saskatchewan which became a province in 1905. William G. Kitchen (1887?-1968) preached and evangelized in this territory in 1902. The E. C. Jones family arrived from Ontario about the same time and settled south of Regina. John A. L. Romig evangelized in the area and organized the first Disciples congregation about 1904. By 1909 a Saskatchewan Christian Missionary Society was formed after a successful evangelistic meeting held by S. S. Lappin (1870-1961). By 1920 a congregation had been formed at Regina with the help of the Board of Church Extension.

By 1905 Alberta had Canadian Disciples migrating from the Maritimes and Ontario, together with a number of

American families moving to virgin prairie farms, and establishing small congregations. The first annual convention in Alberta was held at Calgary in July 1909 at which time the Alberta Christian Missionary Society was formed. A colaborer with John Romig, H. Gordon Bennett (1870-1944), was appointed provincial evangelist and superintendent of missions. From 1911 to 1917 Matthias B. Ryan (1855-1955) labored successfully in evangelization. A lone congregation on the Pacific coast, Central Christian Church at Vancouver, British Columbia, was organized in 1905.

Several attempts were made to provide for education of Canadian Disciples who sought to enter the Christian ministry. At first Canadian young people came to the United States to study at Bethany College in West Virginia and later, at The College of the Bible at Lexington, Kentucky. The first effort on the home field was a school conducted by Donald Crawford (1820-1911) near New Glasgow, Prince Edward Island. He built his home to accommodate students and held classes there from 1845 to 1875. Realizing that their strength was unequal to the formation or support of an education institution, the congregations of Nova Scotia and New Brunswick established an Educational Loan Fund about 1887. From 1910 to 1915 there was a Maritime Bible College at West Gore, Nova Scotia, founded by O. H. Tallman and operated under a provincial charter. The Ontario churches became acutely aware of the need for an educational institution during the 1890s when the number of congregations in that province expanded rapidly and preachers were in short supply. With five students enrolled, arrangements were made in 1892 and 1893 for lectures to be given in the Cecil Street Christian Church, Toronto. Another educational attempt was made at St. Thomas in 1895. By 1897 St. Thomas had its own building, and by 1900 the school had nineteen students. In 1906 the name was changed to Sinclair College to honor Dugald Sinclair, the pioneer preacher. When the school closed its assets were made into a Sinclair endowment fund.

Though Canadian Disciples have been influenced greatly by the religious papers of the United States, they have had papers of their own. The oldest was the *Christian Gleaner* in 1832 at Halifax. The *Christian* was published at St. John,

New Brunswick, from 1839. Over the years at least eighteen various journals were begun and later abandoned. In 1892 the *Christian Messenger* was begun at Toronto and in 1923 combined with the *Christian* to create the *Canadian Disciple.*

Cooperation in evangelism and the organization of congregations between the Disciples in the United States and Canada dates from 1853. Beginning in 1858 with Wentworth Eaton (1811-1889), the ACMS for many years provided funds for evangelists in Nova Scotia and elsewhere in Canada. Through the years there was much cooperation through individual congregations and provincial societies. Between 1898 and World War I the ACMS gave $67,960 in financial assistance to help organize Canadian churches.

Few records from the early days survive. By the time of Canadian federation in 1867 the members of the Disciples in all Canada numbered an estimated 4,000. Ontario, the chief Disciples center in Canada, had approximately thirty congregations with an estimated membership of 1,600 persons. By World War I there were approximately 14,554 members throughout Canada. Canadians have given much to the development of Disciples missions, having contributed over thirty-six missionaries to various Disciples boards. Archibald McLean, William E. Macklin (1860-1947), Charles T. Paul (1869-1941), Susie Rijnhart (1868-1908), Mary Lediard Doan (1882-1959), Jessie Mae Trout (1895-), and Alice Porter (1926-) are among those who have come from Canadian congregations.

THE BLESSINGS OF LEADERSHIP

The period from the 1880s to World War I saw the rise of several important leaders. A new generation of Disciples, lay and ministerial, had arrived on the scene filled with a love for the gospel as understood by the Stone-Campbell movement and dedicated to its furtherance. The progress and development of this period were made possible by this remarkable group of writers, preachers, and lay leaders of great talent and ability. Many of them attained positions of leadership and influence at a relatively young age.

Two books were published during the 1880s that gave the Disciples a new pride in their leadership. John W. McGarvey published in 1881 a widely read story of the archeology and geography of Palestine entitled *Lands of the Bible*. In 1888 Z. T. Sweeney's *Under Ten Flags* gave stay-at-homes a view of the countries he had visited several years before with Isaac Errett. Benjamin B. Tyler's *History of the Disciples of Christ* in 1894 was the first attempt to tell the full story of the development of the Disciples. Thomas W. Phillips, Sr., was the author of *The Church of Christ* which was published anonymously ("By a Layman") in 1900. It met with instant success and thousands of copies were sold in fourteen or more editions. Among Disciples who became nationally known for their writings was James Lane Allen (1849-1925) whose *The Reign of Law*, published in 1900, put him among the best sellers. Equally popular as a novelist was Harold Bell Wright (1872-1944) with *The Printer of Udells* and *Shepherd of the Hills.* Vachel Lindsay (1879-1931) and Edwin Markham (1852-1940) were popular poets from Disciples families and were men proud of their religious heritage.

Well-known preachers of the period included George Hamilton Combs (1864-1951) and Burris A. Jenkins (1869-1945), Kansas City; George A. Campbell (1869-1943) and James M. Philputt, St. Louis; Charles S. Medbury, Des Moines; Z. T. Sweeney, Columbus, Indiana; Sylvester M. Martin (1857-1937), Seattle, Washington; Isaac N. McCash (1862-1953), Berkeley, California; Isaac J. Spencer (1851-1922), Lexington, Kentucky; and William E. Crabtree (1868-1930), San Diego.

Political figures and influential businessmen were prominent in the leadership of this period. Among them were, in addition to those mentioned earlier, Gov. Myers Y. Cooper (1873-1958), Cincinnati; Joseph I. Irwin (1824-1910) and Marshall T. Reeves (1852-1924), Columbus, Indiana; Robert A. Long, Kansas City; Mrs. Elizabeth "Mother" Ross (1852-1926), Eureka, Illinois; Charles C. Chapman (1853-1944), Los Angeles; Senator George T. Oliver (1848-1919), Pittsburgh; the Hon. Champ Clark (1850-1921), Missouri; Robert H. Stockton (1843-1923), St. Louis; George F. Rand (d. 1925), Buffalo; Albert R. Teachout (1852-1922), Ohio; and Hilton U. Brown (1859-1958), Indianapolis. These lay leaders were often seen among the churches in one role or another. All were committed to serving the gospel and the Disciples with their considerable talents.

Interest in further developing lay leadership was expressed at the New Orleans convention in 1908. A committee of seven men was appointed with power to organize a "Brotherhood of the Disciples of Christ" for the purpose of fellowship and to create interest among the younger men. With lumberman R. A. Long as president, national headquarters were established at Kansas City in Long's office building. The organization was complete with model constitutions for local and state "brotherhoods." It had a motto ("A Man's Work in a Man's Way") and a recognition button. Although it did not exist long, it was a forerunner of later laymen's groups.[19]

THE CENTENNIAL OF 1909

As the one hundredth anniversary of the *Declaration and Address* approached, Disciples leaders made plans for an appropriate celebration. They were anxious not only to celebrate the past but also to make a challenge for the future. As early as 1901 the General Convention appointed a committee, which reported at the Omaha convention in 1902, recommending a concerted effort to increase missionary, educational, and benevolent support for Disciples agencies. A Centennial Campaign Committee, with James H. Garrison, St. Louis, chairman, and William R. Warren (1868-1947), Pittsburgh, secretary, was selected in 1904. A Convention Committee, with W. R. Warren as chairman, was to work with the larger committee. The various agencies and institutions were encouraged to set long-range goals and projects; this was the first instance of cooperative planning among the Disciples. All plans were to lead to a Centennial Convention to be held in October 1909 at Pittsburgh.

One by one the agencies reported their goals. The ACMS planned to secure named memorial funds with a minimum of $5,000 each to underwrite its work in home missions. Twenty-one funds were received and invested with the income designated for the work. The CWBM earmarked $200,000 for buildings, one of which was the College of Missions at Indianapolis, the basic unit of the present Missions Building. The CWBM also planned to enter one new foreign field. The

---

19. *Program of the International Centennial* (Pittsburgh: ACMS, 1909), pp. 14-16; 46; 160.

FCMS desired increased support funds and $250,000 for buildings. The Board of Ministerial Relief sought to add to its endowment for the care and support of retired ministers and their families. The Board of Church Extension added to its funds for church loans. A new Christian Orphan's Home was erected at St. Louis by the NBA with additional funds given by Robert H. Stockton. Various educational institutions had goals such as the Garth student aid fund to assist ministerial students at Transylvania, The College of the Bible, and other colleges.

All goals were not for agencies and institutions. Members of congregations were challenged to participate in daily devotions and personal evangelism, to worship regularly, to read Christian papers, to tithe, to give an offering for church colleges, and to make every home "anti-saloon." Congregations were challenged to enlarge Sunday schools, to encourage prayer meetings, to pay all debts, to work with the state missionary society, and to form an active men's organization. There were even general goals: 1,000 recruits for the ministry; 10,000 adult Bible school classes organized; 200,000 trained Sunday school workers; and the promotion of Christian union by its practice.[20] Two histories of the Disciples were prepared and published for the centennial: William T. Moore wrote a ponderous *Comprehensive History of the Disciples* and James H. Garrison prepared a shorter volume, *The Story of a Century.*

A note of unpleasantness was injected when the *Christian Standard* opposed the selection of two of the more than forty main speakers for the centennial convention. The Centennial Campaign Committee invited Herbert L. Willett (1864-1944), biblical scholar of the University of Chicago, and Perry J. Rice (1867-1948), president of the Campbell Institute, to speak. There was immediate conservative reaction, but the committee refused to request their withdrawal. Another difficulty arose over the invitation to Samuel H. Church (1858-1943), a grandson of Walter Scott and avowed "open membership" advocate, to speak. These differences over convention speakers caused the *Christian Standard* to be critical of other plans for the convention. The controversy was regretted, but the program went forward as planned.

---

20. *Program of the International Centennial,* p. 69.

However, this tendency toward criticism on the part of the *Christian Standard* was to increase with the years.

As October 11-19, 1909, approached, Disciples everywhere were in a state of excitement. Disciples who did not attend had almost as much anticipation as those going. Most, if not all, of the goals previously set had been met. By October 11 over 50,000 Disciples had arrived at Pittsburgh, taxing the facilities of hotels and surrounding towns. Special trains arrived hourly from all over the United States and Canada. Parked on sidings, Pullman cars were used for housing. By a coincidence, the World Series of baseball was being played at Forbes Field where on Sunday morning the Lord's Supper was served to those attending the convention. Disciples chose as the convention theme their insight into Christian unity: "The union of all believers, on a basis of Holy Scripture, to the end that the world may be evangelized." There were simultaneous programs on various subjects at dozens of auditoriums, churches, and meeting places throughout the week. There was even a "Veterans' Camp Fire" where old songs of fifty years previous were sung and old-time preaching heard. Trips were arranged to Bethany where Decima Campbell Barclay (1840-1920), Alexander Campbell's daughter, received guests in Campbell's home. The highlight of the convention for many persons was the launching of the steamer, the *S. S. Oregon,* at a Pittsburgh shipyard. Dismantled after the convention, shipped to Africa and reassembled on the Congo River, the *S. S. Oregon* served missions and missionaries for over fifty years.

The Centennial Convention at Pittsburgh in 1909 was a "coming of age" for the Disciples. Their morale had never been higher as they achieved many of their goals. According to their own enthusiastic estimates they were celebrating 11,-647 congregations with 1,250,000 members and 8,904 Bible schools enrolling 931,000 persons. There were 6,877 ministers of the gospel urging the Disciples plea for Christian union. Disciples could claim thirty-three educational institutions of various standings and more than a thousand young people preparing for ministry. Future growth seemed certain. Divided on some issues but with overall good feeling, Disciples were well launched into the twentieth century. In their enthusiasm they could not foresee the social and cultural changes a new industrial and technological age was already shaping. The shock of World War I was less than a decade away.

13

THE FLOWERING OF A MISSIONARY SPIRIT

Although Disciples believed firmly that the future of the church on earth depended in large measure on the progress of their "Nineteenth-Century Reformation," they were slow to acknowledge the global dimensions of their responsibility as a religious communion. Clearly Alexander Campbell came to accept the missionary enterprise as the proper business of the church once he outgrew his squeamishness over Christian cooperation. "The church of right is, and ought to be, a great missionary society," said he at the height of his maturity. "Her parish is the whole earth, from sea to sea, and from the Euphrates to the last domicile of man." Walter Scott agreed wholeheartedly. Emphasizing the direct relationship between mobility and success in the proclamation of the Gospel, he paraphrased the missionary imperative at the heart of the New Testament message: "Go to those who water their steeds in the Rhine; to those who drink from the Seine, or who bathe in the Nile or the Niger, the sacred Ganges . . . and the Irawaddy."[1]

Notwithstanding the rhetoric of Campbell and Scott, Disciples for several decades failed to develop a solid base of

---

1. Quoted in Archibald McLean, *The History of the Foreign Christian Missionary Society,* pp. 29-30, 31.

support for missions. By and large they seemed more inclined to debate the merits of proposed programs than to implement them. Their first three ventures in overseas missions having ended in failure, they entered the 1870s without a single missionary on "foreign" soil. No wonder Joseph King, speaking at their national convention in 1874, reproved Disciples because they "were the only people who were not obeying the [Great] Commission *and not even trying to obey it.*" The self-respect of the movement, not to mention its integrity, was at stake. Archibald McLean described the predicament of Disciples: "When religious friends asked where our foreign missionaries were located, it was not easy to give a satisfactory answer. When they inquired what we did more than others since we claimed to have the truth and to be guided solely by it, we could make no effective reply."[2]

Following the formation of the Christian Woman's Board of Missions and the Foreign Christian Missionary Society in the mid-1870s, Disciples began to establish and sustain mission stations at home and around the world. Annual reports of financial support reveal a marked if gradual shift from indifference to concern in their witness. In 1876, for example, reported contributions earmarked for missions amounted to the modest sum of $9,517.59. Twenty years later the combined annual receipts of the movement's three missionary societies had increased to $217,075.07. Included in this total were designated gifts from 2,605 Sunday schools and regular dues from approximately 30,000 women who held membership in the CWBM. At last there was ample evidence to support the claim that Disciples were becoming a missionary-minded people.

As Disciples moved into the twentieth century, their enthusiasm for the cause of Christian missions continued to grow. The centennial celebration of 1909, commemorating the writing of the *Declaration and Address* a century earlier, highlighted the need for followers of Stone and the Campbells to honor their past by facing the future with a new level of commitment. In 1918, two years before the founding of the United Christian Missionary Society, giving to the CWBM and the FCMS exceeded $600,000 each. The American

2. Archibald McLean, "The Period of Foreign Missions" in *The Reformation of the Nineteenth Century*, ed. by James H. Garrison, pp. 380, 384.

Christian Missionary Society received $277,813.26 to undergird its homeland program in the same year. Over 100,000 women belonged to the CWBM. The FCMS supported 185 missionaries and pointed with pride to the work of 926 "native helpers." Disciples of Christ had joined mainstream Protestantism on the front lines of the missionary enterprise around the globe. Indeed the world—from the jungles of Africa to the mountains of Tibet—had become their parish.

In his massive history of the expansion of Christianity, Kenneth Scott Latourette labeled the years from 1800 to 1914 "the great century." Referring to this period of extraordinary activity in the life of the church, he concluded that "Christianity was now taken to more peoples than ever before and entered as a transforming agency into more cultures than in all the preceding centuries."[3] Apart from the tenacity and determination of a cadre of leaders, women and men alike, Disciples might have missed the most striking missionary crusade in the history of the church. When they did catch a worldwide vision, however, they seemed determined to make up for the time squandered in debate and lethargy.

A MISSIONARY PRESENCE: FAR AND NEAR

During the 1890s Disciples entered Mexico in addition to maintaining and expanding their witness in Jamaica, India, Japan, and China. As early as 1880 the FCMS had appointed Francisco de Capdevila to preach and teach without salary in Acapulco. His work, poorly planned and totally lacking in financial support, was short-lived and inconsequential. Fifteen years later a group of Texas women prevailed upon the CWBM to launch a program on the border of Mexico across the Rio Grande River from El Paso. Encouraged by an initial grant of $200, Merritt L. Hoblit quit his job with the Wells Fargo Express Company and moved to Juarez in December 1895. His ability to speak Spanish enabled him to establish a school and found a biweekly paper, *El Evangelista.* Recognizing the need for a more strategic location, Disciples transferred their work to Monterrey in 1897. Then in 1919

---

3. Kenneth S. Latourette, *The Great Century in Europe and the United States of America,* A. D. 1800-A. D. 1914 in *A History of the Expansion of Christianity,* Vol. IV (New York: Harper and Brothers, 1941), p. 7.

they entered into a comity agreement with other Protestant bodies and moved their base of operations from northern to central Mexico.

Samuel Guy Inman (1877-1965) became the best-known representative of the CWBM in Mexico. After marrying Bessie Winona Cox (1873-1968) and preaching for less than a year in Fort Worth, Texas, he began his missionary career on June 8, 1905. Several months later he wrote the corresponding secretary of the CWBM: "I attend and partially or wholly direct eight services each Lord's Day. And what a joy all of it is. . . .Great things are just ahead of us!"[4] Located first in Monterrey and then in Ciudad Porforio Diaz (now Piedras Negras), he founded the People's Institute and edited *La Revista Biblica,* a Sunday school weekly. After a decade in Mexico, he served as executive secretary of the Committee on Cooperation in Latin America from its inception in 1916 to 1939. An inveterate traveler and a highly respected student of Latin American affairs, Dr. Guy Inman gained high visibility as a frequent and sometimes controversial consultant to church and government for a solid generation.

The growing evidence of concern among Disciples for Latin America heartened the Inmans. The FCMS authorized and began a mission to Cuba in 1899, two years before its first missionaries to the Philippines, the William H. Hannas landed in Manila. In 1900 the CWBM opened the first Protestant orphanage in Puerto Rico; a decade later nine missionaries to the Philippines, the William H. Hannas, were at work on the island. Willis J. Burner (1870-1957) and his wife, both of Illinois, sailed for Argentina in 1905 and the next year established a mission in a suburb of Buenos Aires. Having completed a term of service in Argentina, the C. Manley Mortons became the first Disciples missionaries to Paraguay in 1918. Subsequently they accepted reassignment to Puerto Rico. There they taught in the Evangelical Seminary for two decades and led in the development of the McLean Conference Grounds.

Prior to the turn of the last century, the FCMS advanced into Africa. S. M. Jefferson (1849-1914), a Kentucky pastor, accepted an appointment to that "continent of the future" in

---

4. William J. Castleman, *Samuel Guy Inman, 1905-1916* (Indianapolis: Christian Communications Reporter, 1969), p. 65.

1885 but changed his mind and never reached the field. Twelve years passed before Ellsworth Faris (1874-1953) and Dr. Harry N. Biddle (1872-1898) arrived in Africa as Disciples missionaries. Dr. Biddle fell seriously ill and died before he and Faris had decided on a place for their mission. Shortly thereafter, in 1899, the American Baptists found themselves in a financial bind and sold their property at Bolenge in the Belgian Congo (now Zaire) to the Disciples for $2,500. The FCMS sent Dr. and Mrs. Royal J. Dye to replace Dr. Biddle in 1899. A physician, Dr. Dye (1874-1966) used the "white man's medicine" to counter the influence of a Congolese witch doctor named Bosekola. The Dyes and Ellsworth Faris made Bolenge a familiar name in congregations across the United States. To interpret the Disciples program in the Belgian Congo, Mrs. Dye (1877-1951) wrote a volume entitled *Bolenge* in 1909. Never one to restrain his enthusiasm, Archibald McLean observed in his Foreword: "In ten years one of the greatest churches in the world has been built up at that place out of the most unpromising materials."[5]

Meanwhile, the CWBM had begun to support Jacob Kenoly (1876-1911) in Liberia. One of thirteen children born to former black slaves, Kenoly grew up in Missouri and completed his education at Southern Christian Institute in 1902. His quiet but firm determination to serve the cause of Christ in Africa led him to Liberia in July 1905. He worked in the kitchen of the steamer on which he sailed and reached his destination without any possessions save for the clothes on his back. No financial aid was in sight. "I was landed in Africa, where I met the greatest trial of my life; insomuch I began to think it was a mistake to come, and God did not want me to do this work," wrote Kenoly to a friend in the United States.[6] Despite a siege of sickness and numerous other difficulties, he refused to concede defeat and opened a school for children in a log house which he himself built. When Clayton C. Smith, secretary of the Disciples Board of Negro Education and Evangelization, advised the CWBM of

---

5. Archibald McLean, "Foreword" in *Bolenge: A Story of Gospel Triumphs on the Congo* by Mrs. Eva N. Dye (Cincinnati: Foreign Christian Missionary Society, 1910), p. 3.
6. Clayton C. Smith, *The Life and Work of Jacob Kenoly* (Cincinnati: Privately printed, 1912), p. 43.

CHRISTIAN WOMEN'S BOARD OF MISSIONS

Mrs. Marie Jameson

Mrs. O. A. Burgess

Mrs. Caroline Neville Pearre

Jacob Kenoly

In 1874 women of the Christian Church took matters into their own hands and organized the Christian Women's Board of Missions. They were soon sending out missionaries such as Jacob Kenoly (to Africa 1905-11) and at home, the women launched the Bible chair movement at the University of Michigan in 1893 and established the College of Missions, the first school devoted exclusively to the training of missionaries.

Mrs. N. E. Atkinson

Mrs. Anna R. Atwater

Mrs. Helen E. Moses

College of Missions

Kenoly's plight, the women promptly adopted him as a missionary in 1907. Four years later the indomitable black drowned while fishing to provide a supply of food for the boys in his school.

Emory Ross (1887-1973) accepted the challenge to replace Kenoly in Liberia. The two men had been close friends at Southern Christian Institute where Emory's parents, the A. T. Rosses, taught. Recalled "Mother Ross": "There sprang up between the black man [Kenoly] and the ten-year-old white boy, Emory Ross, a love and a devotion that was like unto that of David and Jonathan. Their souls were knit together." Of an evening the two frequently sailed little handmade ships on the ponds of the plantation. "And they were always sailing, sailing off to some far country," added Emory's mother, "and it looked like boy's play, but in the light of what has since come to pass, it seems more like a prophecy, for the day came when the black man sailed the great waters and the day came when the white boy followed him."[7]

Ross agreed with the decision of the CWBM to discontinue its Liberia mission in 1916 and to cooperate with the FCMS in undergirding the well-established work in the Belgian Congo. A missionary with his wife in the Congo until 1933, he became one of Protestantism's most eminent authorities on Africa. He served for an extended period as secretary of the Africa Committee of the National Council of Church's Division of Foreign Missions. To name but two of the many other organizations which benefited from his insight and counsel, he gave leadership to the Congo Protestant Council and to American Leprosy Missions, Incorporated. Author of *Out of Africa* and *African Heritage,* he joined his wife, Myrta, in writing *Africa Disturbed* in 1959.

Fully as fascinating as the program of Disciples in the Congo was their ill-fated venture in Tibet. Dr. Susie Carson Rijnhart, a Canadian and member of the Ontario CWBM, got Disciples interested in that distant land sometimes called "the roof of the world." Before receiving an appointment from the FCMS, Dr. Susie already had spent four grueling years in Tibet. There she lost her husband,

---

7. Elizabeth W. Ross, *A Road of Remembrance* (Cincinnati: Powell and White, 1921), p. 41.

Petrus, and buried their only child. Alone and stricken with grief, she managed to survive, making her way to the China Inland Mission and then back to Canada. Refusing to retreat into the shadows of her own suffering, she insisted on resuming her work among the Tibetans. So in 1903 the FCMS commissioned Dr. Albert L. Shelton (1875-1922) and his wife, Flora Beal, to go with her. In the course of their journey the three missionaries spent some time in Tachin Lu, China, where Dr. Susie married her second husband, James Moyes. The James C. Ogdens soon joined the two couples to pioneer in Tibet. Failing health prompted Dr. Susie and her husband to resign in 1906, but their associates remained on the field.

Dr. Shelton made few converts but gained the confidence and admiration of hundreds through his practice of medicine in and around the village of Batang. Dr. Zenas S. Loftis (1881-1909) volunteered to take charge of the Batang clinic but developed typhus fever and died six weeks after reaching Tibet. About a year later another physician, Dr. William Hardy (1883-1961), and his wife assumed responsibility for the mission so that Dr. Shelton could begin a furlough.

While traveling over treacherous mountain paths leading to the Chinese border, the Sheltons were attacked by robbers. Mrs. Shelton and their two daughters escaped, but Dr. Shelton was captured and had to endure life with the marauding band for over two months. During this period he kept a diary on the blank pages and margins of a book in his possession. On one occasion he scribbled:

It was difficult to sleep last night. If I were turned loose I couldn't do anything. I couldn't walk a mile. If I could only eat I might get a little strength. . . .It looks as if the end of my work [is] at hand. I hoped to accomplish so much, only to wind up in a hole like this. Thy ways, O God, are past all finding out, but help me to say, "Not my will but Thine be done."[8]

Weakened to the point of exhaustion and desperately sick, he was abandoned only to be found by chance and taken to China. In time he met his family and sailed for home.

---

8. Quoted in Flora B. Shelton, *Shelton of Tibet* (New York: George H. Doran Company, 1923), pp. 241-242.

After regaining his health, Dr. Skelton grew restless and sought permission to go back to Tibet. The FCMS hesitated but gave its consent. Shelton said goodbye to friends and well-wishers not knowing he would never see them again. Upon returning to Batang, he began to plan for the establishment of a mission station further into the interior of Tibet. Before completing final preparations for the move, he was shot and killed by bandits. He was buried beside the grave of Dr. Loftis in a land which claimed both their hearts and their lives. Disciples had to terminate Tibetan work a few years later, but the saga of Shelton in Tibet gave them a very special reason to commit themselves anew to the overseas mission of the church everywhere.

Among the thousands stunned by the news of Dr. Shelton's death were the fifty-four students at the College of Missions in Indianapolis, Indiana. This institution, like so many others, began as a project of Disciples women. In 1909 the CWBM oversubscribed a goal of $100,000 to found a missionary training school. Indiana women set the pace in the campaign. Mrs. Maud D. Ferris made the largest individual contribution, an annuity gift of $25,000, in memory of her mother, Mrs. Sarah Davis Deterding (1853-1890).

The College of Missions opened in 1910 with Charles T. Paul as principal. A Canadian and a former missionary in China, he was recognized as an extraordinary linguist. Under his leadership the college designed a highly specialized graduate program of missionary education based on recommendations stemming from the 1910 World Missionary Conference at Edinburgh, Scotland. The regular curriculum included courses ranging from "Medicine and Hygiene" to "Colonial Government and International Law." Enrollment climbed to forty-seven in 1919 and peaked at fifty-five two years later. Within the first decade of the college's history, over one hundred of its students accepted overseas appointments; several others chose to serve in the church's homeland mission program. Responding to changing needs and circumstances, the College of Missions transferred its teaching operation in 1927-28 to the Kennedy School of Missions of Hartford Seminary Foundation in Connecticut. The affiliation of the two schools continued for a number of years.

The pronounced interest of Disciples in overseas missions did not detract from their homeland missionary endeavors. Archibald McLean of the FCMS, for instance, traveled over 40,000 miles in 1895-1896 to visit Disciples and observe their work around the globe. In the book which he wrote to report on his world trip, he devoted a full chapter to "A Plea for Missions in America." "The Gospel must be carried into every city and hamlet of this broad land. Wherever the beer keg can go the Bible must go," McLean said. "Wherever men go to mine gold or silver or copper, or to raise corn or wheat or fruit, or to engage in any form of work, there the ministers of the Gospel must go and preach the unsearchable riches of Christ."[9]

Writing in 1920, Mrs. Ida W. Harrison (1851-1927) reviewed the forty-five-year history of CWBM and praised the board for its response to needs at home as well as abroad. "One of the glories of the Christian Woman's Board of Missions," she contended, "is that it is built on such broad lines that it knows no distinction between home and foreign missions."[10] An abundance of evidence gave credibility to her claim.

In addition to joining the ACMS in supporting evangelistic and pastoral work throughout the nation, especially in western states and territories, the CWBM established and maintained a number of educational and social service centers. To cite but a few examples, Disciples women assumed responsibility for Hazel Green Academy in 1886. A mountain school in Kentucky, it had been opened six years earlier to provide both elementary and high school education for young people in the area. Livingston Academy, located in Tennessee, was founded in 1909. Other "highland schools" were sustained for several years at Morehead, Kentucky, and Beckley, West Virginia.

In 1891 the CWBM began a mission for Chinese immigrants in Portland, Oregon. Fifteen years later the Chinese Christian Institute was established in San Francisco. A similar program for Japanese in Los Angeles, started in 1908, later flowered into All Peoples Christian Center which still

9. Archibald McLean, *A Circuit of the Globe* (St. Louis: Christian Publishing Company, 1897), p. 15.
10. Ida W. Harrison, *History of the Christian Woman's Board of Missions* (1920), p. 110.

continues. Mexican Christian Institute (now Inman Christian Center) began in 1913 to serve the Mexican-American community in San Antonio, Texas. The center provided a free medical clinic, a day nursery, a kindergarten, and a variety of course offerings. Organized work among American Indians was slower to develop. Yakima Indian Christian Mission near White Swan, Washington, did not open until 1921.

Viewed in terms of measurable results, efforts to evangelize among Negroes met with little success, so Disciples placed their emphasis upon the improvement of educational opportunities for black Americans. Winthrop H. Hopson, a respected minister in Kentucky, was responsible in large measure for opening the doors of Louisville Christian Bible School in 1873. One of the school's students, H. Jackson Brayboy, graduated in 1875 and became probably the best-known black evangelist among Disciples of his time. Financial difficulties forced the school to close in 1876. A new Louisville Bible School, started in 1892, aimed to educate Negro preachers. Disciples established several other schools for Negroes in the South. Among these were the Lum Grade School in Alabama, the Martinsville, Virginia Christian Institute (subsequently known as Piedmont Christian Institute), and Warner Institute in Jonesboro, Tennessee.

Excepting only Jarvis Christian College in Texas, Southern Christian Institute was by all odds the most substantial and influential Negro school related to and supported by Disciples of Christ. Founded in 1874 on a plantation near Edwards, Mississippi, Southern Christian Institute educated hundreds of Negroes at the elementary and secondary levels. Over the years its college enrollment was small. In 1954, when a more adequate system of public education had become available to blacks in Mississippi, the school was merged into Tugaloo College. Flanner House, a "settlement house" in Indianapolis, gained strong support across denominational lines and in time initiated an imaginative inner-city program under the dynamic leadership of Dr. Cleo Walter Blackburn (1909-). However inadequate their response to massive needs, Disciples did attempt to reflect the mind of Christ through a network of homeland missions.

The growing expression of a missionary conscience among Disciples was undoubtedly a tribute to the forceful leadership of their society executives. Archibald McLean, of course, was the moving spirit behind the Foreign Society for almost four decades. He more than any other individual among the Disciples earned the right to be called an apostle of overseas missions. Robert Moffett, Benjamin L. Smith (1859-1933), and Grant K. Lewis (1868-1937) accepted the challenge of stirring Disciples to expand their program of homeland missions. Each of the three labored for a considerable period as corresponding secretary of the ACMS.

Of the many women whose witness gave vitality and strength to the CWBM, Mrs. Helen E. Moses (1853-1908) and Mrs. Anna R. Atwater (1859-1941) deserve special mention. Taking into account the full sweep of Disciples history to 1941, Dr. George Walker Buckner, Jr. suggested that these two women "stand out distinct and lustrous for the quality of their leadership and the measure of confidence accorded them by their associates."[11] Although Mrs. Moses was "frail as a sea shell" and was plagued by poor health, she served as corresponding secretary and then as president of the CWBM from 1899 to 1908. Mrs. Atwater, affectionately called both "Queen Ann" and "Aunt Anna," succeeded Mrs. Moses and remained with the CWBM until 1920. Later she became the first woman to be named vice-president of the United Christian Missionary Society. Mrs. Atwater and Mrs. Moses, together with Archibald McLean and others, played a decisive role in giving shape and substance to the missionary presence of the Christian Church (Disciples of Christ).

EVANGELISM AND EVANGELISTS

In the early twentieth century the evangelistic record of Disciples hardly matched the growth of their programs in homeland and overseas missions. Claiming a membership of 1,120,000 in 1900, they suffered a sizable loss in the withdrawal of Churches of Christ and twenty years later could count only 1,178,079 members in the United States and Canada. While their numerical growth rate doubled that of the United States between 1860 and 1900, they failed to keep pace with the continuing surge of population in the nation

11. Quoted in Lollis, *The Shape of Adam's Rib: A Lively History of Women's Work in the Christian Church*, p. 107.

after the turn of the century. Regardless of the expectations of their nineteenth-century forebears, Disciples no longer could talk themselves into supposing that they would sweep the country in time. Indeed there were some who wondered whether the Stone-Campbell movement could avoid a steady if not precipitous decline.

To accelerate their growth, Disciples placed great emphasis on evangelism between 1900 and 1910. For several years, beginning in 1904, a Board of Evangelism functioned within the framework of the ACMS. Thereafter a coterie of professional evangelists organized the National Evangelistic Association. Structurally unrelated to any other Disciples organization but meeting at the time of the general convention, this association promoted and encouraged a spirit of evangelism among preachers across the land. Its leaders took some of the credit for persuading the United Christian Missionary Society to appoint a superintendent of evangelism in 1920.

Meanwhile, these professional evangelists traveled from one place to another holding revival campaigns so as to revitalize congregations and "win souls for Christ." None of them gained the visibility of Billy Sunday who enjoyed his greatest success from 1908 to 1918. They nevertheless attracted widespread attention and numbered their converts in the hundreds and thousands. James H. O. Smith (1857-1935), one-time state evangelist of Indiana, later served the congregation in Valparaiso. During the first five years of his ministry there, the congregation's membership increased from 80 to 1200. James V. Coombs (1849-1920) and George F. Hall (1864-?) also held pastorates before entering the general evangelistic field. By far the best-known and most successful Disciple in professional evangelism at the time was Charles Reign Scoville (1869-1937). Jesse M. Bader (1886-1963) rose to prominence after World War I and earned national and ecumenical recognition for his leadership in evangelism.

Scoville held "protracted meetings" in cities throughout the United States and in 1912 led his evangelistic team on a mission around the world. One of his six assistants on this tour, Charles R. L. Vawter (1879-1935), subsequently formed his own campaign company. Scoville moved like a general into a community and demanded unconditional surrender.

Large numbers of people responded to the man and to his message. He received over 1,500 converts during his extended meeting at Anderson, Indiana, in 1906. His seven-week Little Rock, Arkansas, campaign in 1923-1924 resulted in 1,302 conversions; more than 400 agreed to become tithers, and fifty-one committed themselves to enter the Christian ministry. Following the pattern of Dwight L. Moody and Billy Sunday, Scoville developed a large and effective campaign organization. Local committees carried out precise instructions in planning and handling a myriad of details. Nothing, except possibly the weather, was left to chance. Although Scoville preached for the purpose of getting results, he did not turn his crusades into emotional binges. Said he: "When a person at a revival meeting sits and wrings his hands and rolls his eyes and groans and sighs like a dying calf, that's not religion, that's foolishness."[12]

Jesse Bader adopted the slogan, "Each one win one," and relied heavily upon a program of visitation evangelism during his years as a pastor in Atchison, Kansas, and in Kansas City, Missouri. The first superintendent of evangelism in the United Christian Missionary Society, he resigned in 1932 to head the Department of Evangelism in the Federal Council of Churches. Retiring in 1953, Bader then accepted a full-time assignment with the World Convention of Churches of Christ which he had founded in 1930. He became the first general secretary of the organization and served in that capacity until his death. Jesse Bader never tired of prodding ministers and lay people into taking the task of evangelism seriously. "What our Lord made primary," he said repeatedly, "we have no right to make secondary."[13]

PAPERS AND PUBLISHERS

Plagued for decades with more papers than they could support or even cared to read, Disciples entered the twentieth century lacking a publishing house and a weekly magazine they could call their own. Dozens of journals had floundered and collapsed, leaving their publishers in financial straits.

---

12. Quoted in Harry H. Peters, *Charles Reign Scoville: The Man and His Message* (St. Louis: The Bethany Press, 1924), pp. 171-172.
13. Quoted in Samuel McCrea Cavert, "Jesse Moren Bader: Evangelist and Ecumenical Churchman" in *Herald of the Evangel*, ed. by Edwin T. Dahlberg (St. Louis: The Bethany Press, 1965), p. 17.

Others—the *Gospel Advocate,* for example—shifted their loyalty and attention to the Churches of Christ. *The Christian-Evangelist* in St. Louis and the *Christian Standard* in Cincinnati, both of them privately owned, remained enormously influential among Disciples. The *Christian Oracle* appealed to a circle of liberal-minded Disciples but faced an uncertain future in its struggle to gain a national constituency.

The *Christian Oracle,* founded in 1884, barely managed to survive. Moved from Des Moines to Chicago in 1888 and renamed the *Christian Century* in 1900, it was offered for sale eight years later. Charles Clayton Morrison (1874-1966), pastor of the Monroe Street Christian Church in Chicago, paid the purchase price of $1,500 and launched his career in religious journalism. Under his vigorous leadership the *Christian Century* gradually cut its denominational ties and in 1918 became "an undenominational journal of religion." Thereafter it developed into the most scintillating and widely read interdenominational weekly in the United States.

The Christian-Evangelist and the *Christian Standard,* once so close in editorial stance, began to represent different positions after the death of Isaac Errett in 1888. While *The Christian-Evangelist* continued to support the organized work of Disciples and encouraged full participation in the emerging ecumenical movement, the *Christian Standard* came to be the most outspoken "critic of the brotherhood." Suspicion replaced mutual trust and widened the gap between the two papers. Their interchanges grew more and more caustic; their clashes, increasing in frequency and intensity, spelled serious trouble. Thoughtful leaders recognized the gravity of the situation and pondered the consequences of mounting controversy.

Attempting to deal directly with the problem, Disciples in their 1907 convention appointed a "Committee of Twenty-five" to consider the formation of a national publication society. Sensing the unmistakable signs of growing estrangement within their ranks, they felt obliged to protect their "holy cause" from further "paroxysms of newspaper controversy." In effect, the convention—meeting in Norfolk, Virginia—charged the committee to explore the possibility of effecting a merger between the Christian and Standard Publishing Companies.

James H. Garrison, the Christian Publishing Company's principal stockholder, reacted favorably and assured the committee of his full cooperation. In fact, he made no effort to conceal his outright enthusiasm. Heavily in debt and nearing retirement, Garrison had spent almost forty years editing or coediting *The Christian-Evangelist*. Writing to his younger son, Winfred E., in the spring of 1908, he said: "It cannot be long before I must either lay down my pen, or cut off a large part of the burden of responsibility I am now carrying."[14] Later in the year he confessed: "I owe altogether too much, and my purpose is to sell a controlling interest in the company to somebody who would like to be my succesor if possible, but at least enough of my stock to meet my indebtedness."[15]

The thought of merging with Garrison's concern did not appeal at all to those who owned and ran the Standard Publishing Company. They accused *The Christian-Evangelist* editor of conniving with the "Committee of Twenty-Five" to advance his own interests. Further, they insisted that the whole scheme was concocted by ambitious men who aspired to positions of power. The committee therefore had no alternative but to report its lack of progress to the Centennial Convention at Pittsburgh in 1909.

In the meantime, Robert A. Long, a wealthy Kansas City businessman and an ardent Disciple, learned of Garrison's need to sell out. Early in 1909 he expressed a willingness to buy some of the stock owned or controlled by Garrison provided others could be found to do likewise. The two men entered into correspondence, and Long quickly suggested that he would be "rather surprised if we do not work something out of it." Before the end of the year they reached a firm agreement.

An editorial leader entitled "Change of Ownership" appeared in *The Christian-Evangelist* on December 9, 1909. It was announced that Long had purchased the Christian

---

14. Letter, James H. Garrison to Winfred E. Garrison, April 26, 1908. (The J. H. Garrison Papers.)
15. Letter, James H. Garrison to Winfred E. Garrison, November 1, 1908. (The J. H. Garrison Papers.)

Publishing Company for the purpose of turning it into a "brotherhood publishing house." A self-perpetuating board would direct the business of the nonprofit enterprise. The Christian Publishing Company changed hands in 1910, and the Christian Board of Publication received its charter in April of the following year. According to a provision in the charter, all surplus income not needed for improved services and plant expansion "shall be . . . paid into the treasury of some one or more of the missionary, benevolent, church extension, educational societies or other agencies of the Christian Churches (Disciples of Christ), as the Board of Directors may select."[16]

Thus, eighty-seven years after Alexander Campbell issued the first number of *The Christian Baptist,* the Disciples gained their own publishing house. For the first time a national journal belonged to the Disciples rather than to a private publisher (or his creditors). The move, advantageous as it was for *The Christian-Evangelist,* almost inevitably pushed the *Christian Standard* into a role of continuous opposition.

Long was named president of the board and held the office for the remainder of his life. Garrison stayed with *The Christian-Evangelist* as editor and then as editor emeritus. In retirement he continued to write his popular column, "The Easy Chair." Among the long-term directors at a later time were W. Palmer Clarkson (1867-1941) and Oreon E. Scott (1871-1956).

HIGHER EDUCATION

If the history of Disciples is littered with the remains of discontinued journals, it also is filled with the wrecks of abandoned schools and colleges. Scores of well-intentioned individuals, aiming to assure the growth of the small communities in which they lived, founded institutions in order to transmit the Stone-Campbell message to coming generations. In many instances the experience was an exercise in futility; vacant buildings and dismissed faculties testified to the folly of attempting to build a school on the foundation of un-

---

16. *The Story of the Beginning* (St. Louis: Christian Board of Publication, n.d.), p. 31.

restrained optimism mixed with unsecured pledges. "Doubtless some mistakes have been made with respect to the matter of education among the Disciples," William T. Moore admitted. "The supreme independency which controlled in the organisation of churches controlled also in the organisation of colleges."[17]

By 1964 Claude E. Spencer, Disciples archivist and bibliophile, could compile the names of 485 educational institutions which had been "founded by individual members, congregations or conventions of the Christian Church (Disciples of Christ)." Spencer's list is mind-boggling even after making allowances for the numerous cases in which an institution operated under several names over the years. The overwhelming majority of the schools closed within a brief period after they opened, the victims of incredibly bad planning and woefully inadequate financial resources. A small number of them survived and became fully accredited centers of church-related higher education in the twentieth century.

Disciples started sixteen educational institutions—far more than they needed or could possibly support—prior to the Civil War. Speaking his mind on the state of the movement and its prospects for the future, Moses E. Lard wrote in 1865: "Our great centres of learning must be sustained. Their decline could be looked upon as nothing short of a calamity. Only we are committing this great folly—we are building ten where we should have but one." He elaborated:

Up to this writing not a semblance of a necessity has existed among us for more than one college. Had we only one, and had that one all the money which from first to last we have spent on colleges, and the control of all the young men we are now sending to eight or ten unbuilt, half-built, and imperfectly endowed institutions, the results, we have no hesitation in saying, would be both far more and far better than we are now realizing. With us a cherished principle is—but few institutions of learning, and these of the highest order.[18]

Although the ultraconservative and volatile Lard called attention to a problem which Disciples needed to solve, they preferred to safeguard local autonomy even to the point of

---

17. William T. Moore, *A Comprehensive History of the Disciples of Christ*, p. 682.
18. *Lard's Quarterly*, April 1865, vol. II pp. 252-253.

risking anarchy. Any congregation, indeed any member or group within a congregation, was free to organize a school and encourage others, near and far, to save it from impending disaster. So the proliferation of institutions continued at an alarming rate.

Most Disciples-related colleges organized between the Civil War and World War I were actually junior colleges which also offered preparatory work at the high school level. They were able to drop their secondary programs without severely curtailing enrollment only after states accepted responsibility for funding a system of public education and enacted compulsory school attendance laws.

Two brothers, Addison (1842-1911) and Randolph Clark (1844-1935), founded AddRan College at Thorp Spring on the cattle frontier of Texas in 1873. Moved to Waco and then to Fort Worth, the school was renamed Texas Christian University in 1902. Transylvania University, originating in a Virginia land grant of 1780, and Kentucky University, erected upon the ashes of Bacon College at Harrodsburg in 1858, consolidated in 1865 on the Lexington campus of Transylvania with the name of the Harrodsburg institution—Kentucky University. In 1878 the University's agricultural and mechanical college withdrew to become a separate institution and evolved into the present University of Kentucky. That same year another school in the University, The College of the Bible, obtained its own charter but did not move to a new campus until 1950. The liberal arts college of Kentucky University maintained its connection with Disciples and readopted the Transylvania name in 1908.

Cotner College, started in 1888, closed in 1934 and reopened in 1946 as a center for the teaching of religion in Lincoln, Nebraska. William Woods College, originally named the Female Orphan School of the Christian Church in Missouri, was established by Missouri Disciples in 1890. Ashley S. Johnson founded The School of the Evangelists (now Johnson Bible College) in 1893 at Kimberlin Heights, Tennessee. Located adjacent to the University of Oregon in Eugene, Northwest Christian College began in 1895 as Eugene Divinity School under the leadership of Eugene C. Sanderson (1859-1940). A year later the Bible College of Missouri (now the Missouri School of Religion) opened next to the University of Missouri in Columbia with William T. Moore as dean and teacher. The North Carolina Christian Missionary Convention, meeting in 1901, agreed to purchase Kinsey Seminary in Wilson and converted it into Atlantic Christian College the following year. Established as Virginia Christian College in 1903 by Dr. Josephus Hopwood (1843-1935), Lynchburg College received its present name in 1919. Phillips University had its beginning at Enid, Oklahoma, in 1907—only fourteen years after the United States government opened the Cherokee Strip to homesteaders. In 1909 Disciples organized and assumed responsibility for The Drury School of the Bible (renamed the Drury School of Religion) which served as a department of religion at Drury College, a Congregational institution in Springfield, Missouri.

A gift of 418 acres of land by Major (1884-1937) and Mrs. J. J. Jarvis paved the way for Jarvis Christian College to open in 1913 at Hawkins, Texas. Like Southern Christian Institute, Jarvis was founded for the primary purpose of increasing educational opportunities for Negroes in America. Without a single exception, these colleges overcame countless obstacles and passed through distressing times in their quest for stability and prominence.

While most church-related colleges struggled to avoid bankruptcy in the late nineteenth century, state universities entered a period of rapid growth and expansion. Recognizing the need to provide religious instruction for students at tax-supported institutions, Disciples pioneered in the establishment of Bible chairs and thereby made a unique contribution to American higher education.[19] Leonard W. Bacon, a Congregational minister in New England, proposed in 1882 that churches begin to sponsor and undergird the teaching of religion in state university settings. He further suggested the University of Michigan as a possible site for such a venture. It remained for Disciples to implement his plan in the early 1890s.

Charles A. Young (1881-1927), Disciples pastor at Ann Arbor, Michigan, no doubt persuaded the CWBM's national of-

---

19. For the only detailed and comprehensive historical study of the Bible chair movement, see Ronald B. Flowers, "The Bible Chair Movement in the Disciples of Christ Tradition: Attempts to Teach Religion in State Universities" (unpublished Ph.D. thesis, University of Iowa, 1967).

ficers to back him in launching an experimental program. In the course of her presidential address at the 1892 CWBM assembly, Mrs. Otis A. Burgess (1836-1902) said:

The way is open, if we have the courage to undertake it, for the establishment of an English Bible Chair at the seat of the University of Michigan, where the courtesies of that great institution are offered to us. The demand there for Bible Study can be met by endowing a Chair, and putting a competent teacher in charge.[20]

The women, responding with enthusiasm, agreed to take on the project.

As a result, the first Bible chair program in the United States was inaugurated at the University of Michigan in October 1893. Herbert L. Willett and Clinton Lockhart (1858-1951) constituted the first faculty. Classes were taught in the Disciples church building. Later the CWBM raised an endowment of almost $40,000 and purchased a residence for the use of the Bible chair.

The success of the Michigan experiment encouraged Disciples to move to other state university campuses. The Virginia Christian Missionary Society began a short-term lecture series at the University of Virginia in 1896. There the work eventually received solid support when gifts totaling $50,000 endowed the John B. Cary (1819-1898) Memorial Chair of Biblical History and Literature. Around the turn of the century comparable programs also were started at the University of Georgia and the University of Kansas. The generosity of Mrs. M. M. Blanks enabled Frank L. Jewett (1874-1969) to found a Bible chair at the University of Texas in 1905. These and other chairs gave students in state universities the chance to study Judeo-Christian history and thought under some of the ablest teachers in the Disciples of Christ.

As institutions multiplied from decade to decade and competed with each other for students and financial resources, Disciples became painfully aware of the need for some measure of cooperation and coordination in the enterprise of church-related education. In response the ACMS formed a nine-member Board of Education in 1894. The board received

---

20. Quoted in Ida W. Harrison, *History of the Christian Woman's Board of Missions*, p. 123.

no funds for its work and accomplished little other than preparing occasional articles for church journals and reminding Disciples that a viable religious movement required an educated ministry. Sixteen years later an Association of Colleges of the Disciples of Christ was established to bring schools into a closer relationship. Then in 1914 thirty-seven institutions (including a dozen or more which later closed) agreed to affiliate with a new Board of Education of Disciples of Christ which subsequently led to the incorporation of the present Board of Higher Education. Richard H. Crossfield (1868-1951) of Transylvania served as first president of the board and was succeeded in turn by Charles E. Underwood (1875-1917), Carl S. Van Winkle (1875?-1935), and Harry O. Pritchard (1876-1936). Finally an instrumentality had been devised with the potential to represent the overall cause of Disciples-related higher education.[21]

MEN AND MILLIONS MOVEMENT

The newly formed Board of Education and almost all of its member institutions participated fully in the Men and Millions Movement, a comprehensive stewardship project launched by Disciples in 1913. The program began to develop a year earlier when the FCMS decided to raise one million dollars for expansion of overseas missionary work. Both the ACMS and the CWBM—together with the Board of Ministerial Relief, the National Benevolent Association, and the Board of Church Extension—joined the FCMS in the venture, and the suggested goal was more than doubled. Shortly thereafter Robert A. Long argued with telling effect that church-related colleges and universities should be included in any massive fund-raising effort. He offered to give a million dollars provided others would match his gift with an additional $5,300,000. Disciples accepted the challenge in 1913, and the campaign was under way.

Using the motto, "We seek not yours but you," the Men and Millions Movement publicized a threefold aim: to enlist

---

21. For a study of organizational developments leading to the formation of the Board of Higher Education, see Griffith A. Hamlin, "The Origin and Development of the Board of Higher Education of the Christian Church (Disciples of Christ), 1894-1968" (unpublished M.S.E. thesis, Southern Illinois University, 1968). See especially pp. 23-42.

1,000 young people for full-time ministry at home and abroad; to raise $6,300,000 for missions, education, and benevolence; and to encourage each congregation to conduct an "every member canvass." Abram E. Cory (1873-1952) and Raphael H. Miller (1874-1963) gave executive leadership to the enterprise while Archibald McLean headed the executive committee. Countless individuals represented the cause in districts and states across the nation. The involvement of the United States in World War I and the disruptions brought about by a wartime economy put church institutions in a serious financial bind, so Disciples held a War Emergency Drive in conjunction with the final phase of their Men and Millions campaign.

By 1919 over 8,000 young men and women had signed pledge cards declaring their intention to attend college and to consider entering some form of Christian ministry. Financial commitments totaled $7,105,342.63 of which $6,010,750.67 was collected over the next decade. Up to that time no other religious body in America had accomplished as much in a broad-gauged stewardship program. The Men and Millions Movement was a striking example of solid cooperation among Disciples at every level of church life.

DISCIPLES AND WORLD WAR I

A large majority of Disciples let their national loyalty color their religious convictions after the United States entered World War I in April 1917. Although they faced the grim prospect of war with genuine apprehension, they backed President Woodrow Wilson in his determined bid "to make the world safe for democracy." In the minds of many faithful churchgoers, the global conflict took on the character of a holy war with the United States upholding the cause of righteousness in the crusade.

Probably James H. Garrison came as close as anyone to stating the mind of rank and file Disciples at the time. Taking a cue from Allied propaganda, he described the war as a struggle between democracy and tyranny and argued that civilization hung in the balance. "We know what we are fighting for," Garrison wrote in his "Easy Chair" column. "President Wilson has clearly defined our aims. The man who is unwilling to lay down his life, if need be, for these principles, lacks the heroism of Jesus and . . . the army of martyrs."[22] It seemed clear to Garrison that countries should be chastened with the restraining power of force if they persisted in defying the basic principles of justice and mercy. He therefore urged Americans to march forth and end the villainy of Germany. Ahead of them, he felt certain, was a warrior Christ.

Not all Disciples agreed with Garrison, to be sure. Peter Ainslie, pastor of Christian Temple in Baltimore, consistently spoke out against the war and insisted that "the sin of Europe is the sin of the whole world." Reflecting on the proceedings of a peace conference which he attended in 1914, he wrote:

Instead of blaming the Kaiser, which is the easy thing to do, let us remember that war is barbarism, and no nation can lay claim to civilization that practices war any more than an individual can lay claim to culture who pommels with his fist on the street those who get in his way, and shoots down in cold blood those who protest against his encroachments.[23]

Frederick D. Kershner (1875-1953), editor of *The Christian-Evangelist* from the winter of 1915 to mid-1917, also expressed strong pacifist leanings and took exception repeatedly to the view that only the Allies had sufficient reason to ask for and receive God's favor. Kershner and Ainslie, however, aroused a storm of protest and found few to agree with them.

To coordinate their response to the needs of the nation's military establishment, Disciples formed a War Emergency Committee. This organization, which was related to the General Wartime Commission established by the Federal Council of Churches, supervised a variety of programs. Dozens of churches near Army cantonments got financial assistance. A congregation in Illinois, for example, received a grant of $25.00 per month, while the minister was sent an additional monthly appropriation of $20.00 to help pay for his travel expenses to and from Camp Grant. Edgar DeWitt Jones (1876-1956), then pastor at Bloomington, Illinois, was

22. *Christian-Evangelist*, March 28, 1918, p. 325.
23. *Christian-Evangelist*, September 3, 1914, pp. 1138-1139.

one of many to serve as short-term ministers at military camps. Like other large religious bodies in the United States, Disciples greatly expanded their chaplaincy force. In 1915 they had but two chaplains, one each in the Army and the Navy. Four years later the number had increased to seventy-seven. Despite a shortage of funds, the War Emergency Committee arranged to provide each chaplain with essential equipment including a portable typewriter and two communion sets.[24]

In sum, Disciples thought and acted about like the rest of mainstream Protestants in America during World War I. They on balance gave enthusiastic and unabashed support to the Allied cause and greeted the signing of the armistice with jubilation and prayers of thanksgiving.

---

24. For a survey of the War Emergency Committee's work, see *War-Time Agencies of the Churches: Directory and Handbook,* ed. by Margaret Renton (New York: General Wartime Commission of the Churches, 1919), pp. 35-40.

14

DEVELOPMENT AND UNIFICATION

After World War I Disciples of Christ began to lose their complacent and naive view of church life. So much that had appeared transparently clear and simple at the beginning of the century was becoming obscure and complex. Great changes were taking place in the patterns of American life. Sharing in these changes, Disciples lost some of their self-assurance. The idea that the whole religious world would eventually turn to them and accept their ideas of reformation was on its way out. Disciples developed a wholesome desire for self-improvement and created new conventions, agencies, and institutions to serve new needs. It was a new era with new problems. The church's concern for world peace increased. Wartime optimism among Christian leaders led to the launching of campaigns of advance, but postwar disillusionment led to isolationism, declining idealism, and growing nationalism. Interest in the church and its agencies declined throughout the 1920s.

The years 1917-1920 saw the culmination of the long struggle shared by Disciples to bring about the adoption of an amendment to the Constitution of the United States prohibiting the manufacture and sale of intoxicating beverages. Adopted by Congress in 1917, the year the United

States entered World War I, the prohibition amendment went into effect on January 6, 1920.

These years found the Disciples struggling with the establishment of an adequate general convention, the unification of its various boards and societies, and the creation of a more responsible retirement fund for their ministers and missionaries. The rate of growth for Disciples had slowed considerably and this caused general concern. Out of the reorganization which followed came the International Convention of the Disciples of Christ, the National Christian Missionary Convention, the United Christian Missionary Society, the 1919 Pension System, and the All-Canada Movement.

THE INTERNATIONAL CONVENTION OF DISCIPLES OF CHRIST

For many decades the need for a general convention of the brotherhood had been recognized. The 1909 Centennial Convention had set a precedent for a convention which had more authority than to receive the reports of missionary societies. Thereafter the practice was followed of having "joint" or "general" sessions to consider all interests of the churches. Not until 1912 at Louisville was a constitution for "The General Convention of Churches of Christ" approved, and then only after considerable discussion and debate. Its provision for election of delegates from each of the congregations, however, met with considerable disfavor from the beginning, and the plan never gained general support. Fear of "ecclesiasticism" and loss of congregational autonomy still prevailed.[1]

There were other problems. Theoretically the convention consisted of annual meetings of the various boards and societies, but actually its programs were filled with sermons and addresses of an inspirational nature with little time left for the necessary reports. When a sermon or other presentation was cut short or eliminated because of overtime business sessions, both speakers and listeners were frustrated. Furthermore, it was difficult to get a clear-cut decision on any matter without a great deal of discussion and argument.

---

1. Grant K. Lewis, *The American Christian Missionary Society* (St. Louis: Christian Board of Publication, 1937), pp. 154 ff.

Tensions and disagreements were growing within the brotherhood between the more progressive leaders of agencies and societies and the *Christian Standard,* whose editors and owners were more and more reluctant to accept the changes and the newer ideas being proposed.

Throughout the history of the convention ambiguity about its structure and purpose had persisted. The Louisville Plan of 1869 had long since been rejected. The first experience of a delegate body under the new constitution at Toronto in 1913 was less than satisfactory. At a mass meeting called to register protest, Z. T. Sweeney of Columbus, Indiana, said, "The delegate convention is dead: I say, it's as dead as last year's bird nest." Many nondelegates attended the 1914 convention at Atlanta and the 1915 convention at Los Angeles. Only a few hundred elected delegates came to either convention. Obviously something else would have to be done, and Sweeney decided to do it.

At the 1916 convention, held at Des Moines, Iowa, he offered a motion since known as "the Sweeney Resolution," asking for a committee of five persons to meet with the officers of the convention, representatives of the societies, and editors and owners of church papers, to modify the 1912 constitution in such a way as to provide for a more orderly business procedure. The convention approved the resolution, and the committee was appointed. Sweeney and Frederick D. Kershner, then editor of *The Christian-Evangelist,* were good friends and had doubtless discussed the difficulties of the convention many times. Shortly after the Des Moines convention a brief editorial appeared in the November 2, 1916, issue of *The Christian-Evangelist* in which Kershner proposed twin conventions. He suggested that a democratic convention copy in large measure the bicameral form of civil government, combining the delegate feature in one house and the mass meeting in another. The *Christian Standard* replied with strong support for a mass meeting only.[2]

The Committee on Revision of the Constitution was ready to report at the next general convention held at Kansas City in October 1917. The revised constitution was mainly the work of Judge Frederick A. Henry (1867-1949) of Cleveland,

---

2. Lester G. McAllister, *Z. T. Sweeney: Preacher and Peacemaker* (St. Louis: Christian Board of Publication, 1968), pp. 86 ff.

Ohio, but it was based on ideas of Sweeney and Kershner. It proposed abandoning the idea of a delegate convention (thus giving all members of the congregations attending the convention the privilege of voting on all matters). Instead it provided for a Committee on Recommendations, representative of states, provinces, and areas on a proportional basis to meet before the mass convention of registered individuals. Reports and resolutions were referred first to the Committee on Recommendations and then to the floor of the convention. Inasmuch as congregations of both the United States and Canada were represented, the name was to be the International Convention of the Disciples of Christ.

Every attempt had been made to meet the *Christian Standard's* objections. It was thought a time of peace and understanding had come when the revised constitution was presented by Sweeney from the platform at Kansas City and was approved with great enthusiasm. Within a few years, however, the *Christian Standard* became even more disenchanted with the reorganized convention and attacked it repeatedly. There was disagreement especially over the powers and duties of the Committee on Recommendations. Robert Graham Frank (1873-1954) who had served as the efficient part-time general secretary of the convention since 1913 continued in this office until 1946, carrying the heavy burden of planning and managing each convention while serving a demanding pastorate in Dallas. Amiable and good-natured, Graham Frank injected his infectious humor into the business sessions, making endurable many a dull moment and lightening the tension when controversy arose.

THE NATIONAL CONVENTION OF THE CHURCHES OF CHRIST

By 1917 black Disciples were ready to consider reorganizing the convention of their congregations. A National Convention made up of individuals had met for fellowship off and on for many years. Since early in the twentieth century a Workers' Conference had been held at Southern Christian Institute in which many of the state leaders and evangelists had opportunity for fellowship and received training, but it was still not a convention of the churches. Negro Disciples leaders believed a convention of black congregations would give needed leadership experience to ministers and laity. A convention of Negro congregations would relieve their frustration with white Disciples leaders who refused to share leadership with them. Early in 1917 two calls went out proposing to organize such a gathering. Preston Taylor sent out a call for a meeting at Nashville, Tennessee, to be held in August. William Alphin (1865-1937) suggested a meeting of black Disciples to be held at the time of the general convention set for October at Kansas City.

Representatives of Negro leadership from fourteen states and a large number of black congregations met at the Lea Avenue Christian Church in Nashville on August 5-9, 1917. Led by Preston Taylor and others, the National Convention of Churches of Christ (later changed to National Christian Missionary Convention) was more formally organized, with Taylor as the first president. White leaders present included Robert M. Hopkins (1878-1955) of the American Christian Missionary Society, Mrs. Anna R. Atwater of the Christian Woman's Board of Missions, Stephen J. Corey (1873-1962) of the Foreign Christian Missionary Society, and Joel B. Lehman (1866-1942), superintendent of Negro work for the CWBM. They were in agreement that the Negro constituency was too hasty in organizing and suggested that there be only one convention, an International Convention, where the Negro would be as welcome as any white person. The blacks were determined to have their own convention and so a compromise was reached to make the National Convention an auxiliary of the proposed International Convention. An Advisory Board was established, composed of black members to be elected by the National Convention and white members representing the boards responsible for Negro work.[3] The purpose of the National Convention was to create a means of self-expression and cooperative endeavor for development of Negro congregations.

WORLD CALL MAGAZINE

As early as 1913 the unification of the various papers published by the boards and societies had been urged. The

---

3. Robert L. Jordan, *Two Races in One Fellowship* (Detroit: United Christian Church, 1944), pp. 55 ff.; pp. 62 ff.

idea had merit for joint promotion was increasingly practiced. Most of the magazines had inadequate subscription
lists and had to be subsidized. The editorial board of the
CWBM's *Missionary Tidings,* the strongest of the journals, opposed the merger for a time, but a joint magazine was finally
agreed upon in 1918. It was named *World Call.* Prospects for
the uniting of most of the boards interested in the magazine
appeared so good that it was thought best to proceed at once
with the new publication. The first issue came off the press in
January 1919 under the sponsorship of the Men and Millions
Movement. *World Call* combined the material formerly contained in five journals: the *American Home Missionary*
(ACMS), *Missionary Tidings* (CWBM), the *Missionary
Intelligencer* (FCMS), *Business in Christianity* (the Board
of Church Extension), and the *Christian Philanthropist*
(NBA). In August 1921 the new magazine became a publication
of the United Christian Missionary Society and related agencies. The first editors of *World Call* were W. R. Warren (1868-
1947) and Effie Cunningham (1858-1945) who served from
1919 to 1929 and were followed by Bess White Cochran
(1908-), 1929 to 1932 and Harold E. Fey (1898-), 1932 to 1934.

THE UNITED CHRISTIAN MISSIONARY SOCIETY

For some time the numerous agencies, state and national,
which had come into being to administer the various
programs of missions, education, and benevolence, had found
themselves competing for support. Each organization
depended heavily on one or more special days in the church
calendar for an offering to its cause. Ministers and congregations were weary from repeated appeals. Early in the
twentieth century the societies and boards began to cooperate
in budget-making and in promoting their causes jointly to
reduce competition. This development, linked with the increasing use of annual budgets by congregations, led to a demand for unification of the various boards. The "every-
member canvass," combining requests for both local expenses and missionary and benevolent causes, gave added
impetus to the development. The demand for unification and
simplification of organization grew with each succeeding
year.

A calendar committee had been appointed at the Buffalo Convention in 1906. Its mandate was to reduce the number of special days. The committee went beyond its assignment and proposed that the various boards and societies should be united into one organization with one board of administration. While a decade or more was to pass before the proposal could be implemented, it was a harbinger of the future. The experiences of the next several years combined to forward unification. The unforgettable 1909 Centennial Celebration had been instructive as a unified program of goals and projects was planned and carried out. The cooperative Men and Millions Movement was launched in 1913 and succeeded in its objectives. The establishment of the International Convention further convinced the leadership of the need for new directions.

After the Kansas City convention in 1917 a committee made up of representatives of the several boards and societies began a series of meetings looking toward the formation of a united organization. No convention was held in 1918 because of World War I, but after two years of careful and painstaking preparation the International Convention, meeting at Cincinnati in 1919, heard a report from the committee on unification. It recommended the formation of a new cooperative venture to be called The United Christian Missionary Society.[4]

Six former boards and societies were to be united in one organization: 1) the American Christian Missionary Society, Cincinnati; 2) the Christian Woman's Board of Missions, Indianapolis; 3) the Foreign Christian Missionary Society, Cincinnati; 4) the Board of Church Extension, Kansas City; 5) the National Benevolent Association, St. Louis; and 6) the Board of Ministerial Relief, Indianapolis. Frederick W. Burnham, president of the ACMS, was to be president of the new society; A. McLean and Anna R. Atwater were to be vice-presidents. Burnham's services were requested from the ACMS so that he could give as much time and thought as possible to launching the new organization. Annual meetings of the UCMS (open, with voting privileges, to all Disciples) were to be held in conjunction with the International Convention. General oversight of the organization was to be given to a Board of Managers representing states,

---

4. Grant K. Lewis, *American Christian Missionary Society,* pp. 172 ff.

provinces, and areas. Its membership consisted one-half of men and one-half of women. A smaller Board of Trustees of twenty-two members, again composed equally of men and women and meeting bimonthly, set policies between meetings of the Board of Managers.

The provision that one-half of the Board of Managers and one-half of the Board of Trustees of the UCMS should be

Portion of crowd at communion service climaxing the 1909

composed of women was unique. It was a concession forced by
the women of the CWBM whose organization was bringing
the greatest assets into the new society. As a result of the
arrangement, the editor of the *Christian Standard* charged
that the UCMS would be dominated by women and this
would lead to further weakening of the Disciples position on
scriptural reform. The *Christian Standard* used as convincing

centennial convention held in Forbes Field in Pittsburgh.

argument a recent decision of the CWBM to enter into a comity arrangement with other mission boards on the development of missions in Mexico.[5]

On June 22, 1920, the United Christian Missionary Society came into being. By August the various boards, together with their staffs and families, were in process of moving to the new headquarters at St. Louis, chosen because of its central location. For legal and financial reasons several of the agencies kept their own charters. The UCMS, however, became the coordinating agent of all the participating boards. Not everyone was pleased with the changes taking place. Conservatives often expressed the fear that such a massive organization would wield too much power. The fears were often repeated. In 1928 the UCMS moved to the College of Missions building at Indianapolis. The College of Missions had transferred its operation to Hartford, Connecticut, and a study revealed that Missions Building, owned by the former CWBM, was suitable for offices. By terms of the bequest under which construction funds had been given, the building must be used for missionary purposes or revert to the estate of the donor. Thus Indianapolis became the chief center of organizational life for the Disciples, and 222 South Downey Avenue became the best-known address among the churches.

The same Cincinnati convention that authorized the formation of the new society directed the old boards and the Board of Education to participate in the Interchurch World Movement. The day after the armistice was signed, November 12, 1918, the proposal had been made that the various Protestant communions in America cooperate in a great forward movement in foreign missions. Expansion of home missions was included later. Difficulties plagued the movement. A war-weary nation was disillusioned from the beginning, and ultimately the movement failed. The UCMS was burdened in its first year of operation with the responsibility for paying off the Disciples portion of the debts incurred by the unsuccessful Interchurch World Movement. Under the leadership of the new society Disciples congregations accepted quotas and the debt of over $600,000 was soon paid.[6]

---

5. Editorial, *Christian Standard*, April 19, 1919, p. 701.
6. *Year Book, Church of Christ* (Disciples), Cincinnati: ACMS, 1920, p. 19.

The United Christian Missionary Society organized itself into four divisions: 1) an Administrative Division with Departments of Foreign Missions, Home Missions, Church Erection, the Ministry (including recruitment, relief, and pensions), and Benevolence; 2) an Educational Division with Departments of Religious Education and Missionary Education; 3) a Promotional Division; and 4) a Service Division, including the treasury and office management.[7]

The Department of Foreign Missions took over the work formerly carried by the FCMS and CWBM in fields abroad. The Department of Home Missions undertook to administer the varied types of work formerly carried by the ACMS and CWBM. Included in its portfolio were evangelism, church maintenance, Negro work, mountain schools, work with ethnic minorities (Spanish-speaking Americans, Orientals, Indians), community houses for immigrants, evangelism among coke-workers in Pennsylvania and the French-speaking in Louisana. In addition several interdenominational projects sponsored by the Home Missions Council of North America were to be continued. The Department of Religious Education had been under the capable and energetic leadership of Robert M. Hopkins since it had become a part of the work of the ACMS in 1910. By 1914 the department had a national staff of five workers including Hazel A. Lewis (1886-) in children's work and Cynthia Pearl Maus (1880-1970), pioneer leader in youth work. The Department of Missionary Education and Organizations continued the activities in this area conducted by the CWBM. Soon a field staff was developed with workers in every state or area, and gradually the national program was coordinated with state and provincial programs. The Department of Church Erection continued the work of the Board of Church Extension, the Department of the Ministry carried forward the program of the Board of Ministerial Relief, and the Department of Benevolence worked in the area of the National Benevolent Association. By 1924 the UCMS was known as "A Board of Missions and Education." In an early reorganization the Department of Religious Education became the Division of Christian Education as the Board of

7. *Year Book and Annual Reports,* St. Louis: UCMS, 1921. p. 6.

TWENTIETH CENTURY PANORAMA

Herbert L. Willett

Peter Ainslie

Thomas W. Phillips

F. F. Burnham

R. A. Long

Alva W. Taylor

F. E. Smith

Z. T. Sweeney

Jesse M. Bader

Temperance and Social Welfare and the Board of Education were included in an enlarged society. In 1928 Hopkins resigned to become executive secretary of the World Sunday School Association and was succeeded by Roy G. Ross (1898-).

To celebrate the fiftieth anniversary of the organization of the Christian Woman's Board of Missions, a "Golden Jubilee" was planned for 1923-1924. Proposals were advanced to organize 500 new women's groups, to secure 50,000 new *World Call* subscriptions, and to raise a jubilee fund of $1,000,000 for fifty new buildings for home and foreign fields. This campaign was successful and the funds were presented in a colorful ceremony at the International Convention held at Cleveland in 1924.

In connection with the projected Golden Jubilee a plan was developed to make a thorough survey of all the cooperative tasks of the Disciples administered through the International Convention. State and provincial missionary societies and institutions of higher education were included in the scope of the survey. Each particular agency, society, or institution surveyed was to present an accurate report on present work and an evaluation of how well the organization was performing its tasks. It was five years before the survey was completed, although the original time table proposed only two years. The survey was authorized by the International Convention at Winona Lake in 1922. The result was published by the Christian Board of Publication in 1928 under the title *Survey of Service*. The overall purpose of the survey, to throw light upon the process of unification among Disciples, was realized.[8]

THE 1919 PENSION SYSTEM

By the end of World War I leaders in all denominations believed that ministerial "relief" was neither dignified nor the best answer to the church's responsibility for support of ministers in retirement. A move was started to develop sound contractual pensions in which both the minister and the congregation might participate. Among the Disciples the two

---

8. *Survey of Service*, ed. by William R. Warren (St. Louis: Christian Board of Publication, 1928), pp. 11-18.

men who took leadership in developing such a plan were William R. Warren and Francis E. Smith (1877-1960). As early as 1916 an actuary was employed by the Board of Ministerial Relief "to prepare deferred annuity rates for ministers." Outlined in general terms in 1916 and detailed in the board's annual report in 1917, a plan was put forward proposing the establishment of a pension system. The plan called for the regular payment of dues from ministers and asked for a regular additional contribution from congregations. Anticipating funds from the Men and Millions Movement, the board was encouraged to think that the system could be made into a funded pension plan.

What was known as the "1919 Pension System" was adopted by the general convention at Kansas City in 1917 at the time of the organization of the International Convention. The cancellation of the 1918 convention because of the war gave an extra year to improve the plan, allowing actuaries to change the dues for younger members and to broaden the disability benefits. Inaugurated on January 1, 1919, the plan provided a pension of $500 per year at age sixty-five after thirty years' service, if both church and member had paid their share. The church's share was an amount equal to six per cent of the salary. The widow would be allowed $300 per year where full payment had been made. All ministers and missionaries between the ages of twenty-one and sixty were eligible for membership. With 229 persons on relief rolls in 1919, the new plan was welcomed as a means of better serving ministerial needs. In 1971 the remaining beneficiaries and benefits of the "1919 Pension System" were moved into the present Pension Plan by increasing each member's pension twenty percent and fully funding the remaining obligation.

On September 1, 1918, Francis E. Smith came to the Board of Ministerial Relief as secretary from a successful pastorate at Muncie, Indiana. By September 1919 only 405 ministers and missionaries had enrolled in the plan. Pastors' salaries were small, and there was difficulty in getting either the ministers or the congregations to recognize the need. Smith promoted both the continuing work of ministerial relief and the new Pension System. When membership in the plan closed on June 30, 1928, over 800 persons were enrolled. Two difficulties with the plan were apparent from the first: the relatively small number of persons participating and the lack of consistency on the part of the churches in payment of their share of the pension reserve.

Although it was one of the smaller agencies, the Board of Ministerial Relief joined wholeheartedly in the movement to unite the several boards and societies. When plans were in their final stages for the creation of the UCMS, however, it became apparent that the board would face difficulties. The problem was that of an agency involved with reserve funded pensions attempting to operate with other organizations primarily receiving gift money. Arrangements were made for the Board of Ministerial Relief to participate but also to retain its charter of incorporation. Under direction of the Indiana regulatory agencies, dues for the 1919 Pension System were required to go directly to the Board of Ministerial Relief. Ministerial relief money was to be sent through the UCMS.

General dissatisfaction with the limitations of the 1919 Pension System and the handling of ministerial relief grants led the International Convention in 1928 to approve the development of a completely new pension plan unrelated to the old system. The new board was incorporated as The Pension Fund of Disciples of Christ, but was to operate under the original Indiana charter of the Board of Ministerial Relief. It was continued as a separate organization from the UCMS and was authorized to take full responsibility for ministerial relief grants as well as pensions.

THE ALL-CANADA MOVEMENT

Many of the difficulties of the Canadian Disciples were related to the vast geographical size of their nation. Except for the province of Ontario many of the Canadian Disciples congregations were isolated and had difficulty in relating to a larger movement. The provincial organizations experienced a degree of cooperation with the general agencies at work in Canada, but after the organization of the International Convention and the United Christian Missionary Society, in which Canadian Disciples participated, the arrangements were felt to be inadequate. Forward-looking Canadian leaders recognized something more was needed.

---

9. Smith, *For the Support of the Ministry,* pp. 77-94.

In 1921 representatives from both eastern and western provinces attended the annual meeting of the Ontario cooperation. Led by George H. Stewart (1875?-1958) of Winnipeg, a movement was begun to unite all Disciples in Canada in fellowship and program-building. An All-Canada team was organized to tour the country and sound out the congregations. Out of the visits made in the fall of 1921 came six identifiable needs: 1) the desire for closer cooperation with fellow Canadians, 2) the appointment of an All-Canada secretary, 3) a headquarters at Toronto, 4) Sunday school literature directed to Canadian needs, 5) a program for children, and 6) a stewardship program.

An All-Canada convention was held in Ontario in 1922 to approve and to launch a new program to be known as the All-Canada Movement. The UCMS loaned John Stuart Mill (1878-1965) to be the first All-Canada secretary and Mrs. M. V. Romig (1866-1947) to be women's worker. Marian V. Royce (1901-) of Toronto was employed as educational worker and children's specialist in May 1924. Upon the resignation of Mill shortly thereafter, she served as acting secretary. In September 1926, Hugh B. Kilgour (1892-) began his many years of service as All-Canada secretary. An All-Canada Committee administered the affairs of the Canadian program. This committee created an Extension Fund for Canadian congregations and established a College of the Churches of Christ in Canada at Emmanuel College, Toronto, for the education of Canadian young people interested in the ministry.[10] *The Canadian Disciple* in 1924 became the publication of the All-Canada Committee.

DEVELOPMENTS IN HIGHER EDUCATION

Throughout the 1920s Disciples of Christ expanded their existing colleges and universities and added one or two new institutions. In spite of the rapid growth of state colleges and universities, church colleges in general considered it necessary to add to their own physical plants, to build dormitories, and to increase endowment just to keep competitive. Never adequately financed by the churches sponsoring them, denominational colleges found themselves seek-

---

10. Butchart, *Disciples of Christ in Canada Since 1830*, pp. 175 ff.

ing support from the localities in which they served and from the business community. A growing secularization of both curriculum and student life raised questions in the minds of many Disciples as to how closely related to the church their institutions of higher learning really were.

Two new endeavors in higher education were launched in the 1920s. California Christian College, continuing the tradition of Hesperian College, was organized in 1920 at Los Angeles. Within a few years the name was changed to Chapman College, honoring Charles C. Chapman (1853-1944) of Fullerton, a leading contributor to the institution. In 1924 under the leadership of Will G. Irwin, Z. T. Sweeney and his wife, Butler University at Indianapolis was persuaded to establish a College of Religion (later School of Religion and now Christian Theological Seminary). Frederick D. Kershner was chosen dean and the first classes were held in September 1925.

THE NATIONAL CITY CHRISTIAN CHURCH CORPORATION

For many years a small congregation of Disciples met in the nation's capital, Washington, D.C. At first gathering in homes and rented halls, the congregation by 1871 was housed in a small frame building on Vermont Avenue. This was the building in which James A. Garfield worshiped with some embarrassment to his coachman who thought it undignified for the President of the United States to stop before such an undistinguished edifice. It was said that during the services the driver waited with his carriage before a more imposing church near by. Frederick D. Power (1851-1911), minister of the congregation from 1875 to 1911, proposed a new building to the general convention in 1880 and with brotherhood support erected a new structure which was dedicated in 1884.

A worthy "national" building and congregation continued to be the dream of a number of Disciples. Beginning in 1926, a concrete proposal was advanced for the building of a monumental structure on a choice lot on Thomas Circle, at the heart of the nation's capital, in which to house the Vermont Avenue congregation. Kansas City lumberman, R. A. Long, agreed to assist in financing such a building, contingent on a nationwide campaign for funds. The National City Christian Church Corporation, representative of all regions of the nation, was formed. Offices were established at St. Louis and plans were laid for raising the funds. A stately and beautifully appointed building was dedicated at the time of the International and World Conventions in October 1930. Not all Disciples were enthusiastic about the project. It was finished just at the time of the Great Depression, and many of the pledges of support were never paid. After prolonged effort and many years the debt was eventually paid. The building is owned by the Christian Church (Disciples of Christ) but is maintained by the congregation.

THE DISCIPLES AND THE KU KLUX KLAN

An organization formed early in the twentieth century brought to the surface deep spiritual problems among Disciples and in American Christianity in general. On Thanksgiving night, 1915, William J. Simmons, a Methodist minister of Stone Mountain (Atlanta), Georgia, founded the Ku Klux Klan and became its first Imperial Wizard. Patterned after the organization of the same name which had been organized in the South during reconstruction years, it had little influence until 1920 when it began to spread throughout the nation. Then two promotional experts, Edward Y. Clarke and Mrs. Elizabeth Tyler, organized an intensive campaign for members in exchange for a large percentage of the $10 initiation fee. Playing upon well-established prejudices such as anti-Catholicism, anti-Semitism, and white supremacy, they attracted a large following among theological conservatives and those who felt threatened by the new biblical interpretation. There were night marches with torches, white hoods and robes, and flaming crosses on lawns. Churches with congregational government under lay control were especially vulnerable to the Klan's campaign.

Perhaps the greatest drawing power of the Ku Klux Klan to some persons was its portrayal of a 'possible takeover of America by the Roman Catholic Church. In the presidential campaigns of 1924 and 1928 the Klan became politically important and was partially responsible for the defeat of Alfred E. Smith, a Roman Catholic, as he sought the presidency.

During the period from 1920 to 1926 the Klan maintained substantial political power in Indiana, Illinois, Kansas, Nebraska, Colorado, Oregon, Texas, Arkansas, Oklahoma, and Louisiana. After several years of success the Klan began to decline in numbers from several millions of members in 1924 to less than 350,000 in 1926.

The growth of the Ku Klux Klan in the 1920s was phenomenal, but even more astonishing was the large number of ministers and laymen who became active in its program. Those preachers who opposed its activities did so at their peril. In some instances entire congregations were dominated by the Klan. The program of the Ku Klux Klan was modeled after a religious order with profession of faith in Christ as a qualification for membership and with the use of the cross as a religious symbol in ceremonies. Conditions in the 1920s contributed to the flourishing of such an organization. Amidst the rapid changes after World War I many desired to hold on to old values and old ways. The liberal-fundamentalist controversy was raging. Large numbers of Roman Catholics had recently arrived in America. The immigration of American Negroes from the rural areas to the cities had just begun. The Klan thrived on the fears, prejudices, and controversies of the time. Its main support came from blue-collar workers of limited education.[11]

Disciples in numerous places gave strong support to the Klan. Many members of Disciples congregations were from rural areas. They were hard-working, poorly educated, and often theologically conservative. The constituency of the Disciples, their loose congregational structure, and their tensions between "liberals" and "conservatives" during the 1920s all made it possible for the Klan to capture key laymen in a number of congregations and occasionally the minister as well. The Klan had three major ways of getting the minister to come to its side: 1) by getting elders and leading members of the congregation to apply pressure, 2) by buying off the minister with money or giving it to the church he served, and 3) by forcing the minister to cooperate by means of physical or psychological threats. Many ministers gave in and were ex-

---

11. Arnold Forster and Benjamin R. Epstein, *Report on the Ku Klux Klan* (New York: Anti-Defamation League of B'nai B'rith, 1965), pp. 15ff.

ploited by the Klan. Others who kept silent or openly opposed the Klan were threatened and driven from their pulpits. By these methods, the Klan gained control of many congregations. The Klan used the minister to encourage recruitment of members and to secure prestige for the movement. It preferred to meet in church buildings as this gave the members a feeling of respectability.

Representative of the Klan's tactics was the treatment of Frank E. Davison (1887-1960), a minister in Indianapolis at the height of the Klan's activity. When Davison took a stand against his congregation's using its property to house Klan meetings, he was waited on by three of the elders. Promised lucrative speaking engagements if he would withdraw his opposition, he refused. When his resignation was demanded and he was fired, the matter made the headlines of the local papers.[12]

The Klan also appeared in Williamson County, Illinois, but with a different result. On the evening of May 20, 1923, Charles Reign Scoville, the evangelist, was conducting a service at the First Christian Church at Marion. As he started to take up the offering, seventeen men in masks and long white robes marched down the center aisle, handed the minister a letter, and departed. The letter contained a statement of appreciation for the evangelist and his efforts in the community along with three ten-dollar bills.[13] Across the nation congregation after congregation had similar experiences with the Ku Klux Klan. After 1925 the influence of the Klan declined. Wherever it had been, however, congregations were divided and ministerial reputations tarnished.

INTO THE JAZZ AGE

The mid-1920s found the Disciples apparently at the peak of their strength and influence. By 1925, however, a downward trend in giving, attendance, and Sunday school enrollment was evident to the more observant. It is clear in retrospect that the many years of growth and advance for the Disciples were at an end. For two decades Disciples, along

12. Frank E. Davison, *Thru the Rear View Mirror* (St. Louis: Bethany Press, 1955), pp. 75 ff.
13. Paul M. Angle, *Bloody Williamson* (New York: Alfred Knopf, 1974), pp. 134-135.

with other Protestant groups, had with enthusiasm and energy sought to build and expand at home and abroad. Innumerable crusades had been fought ranging from prohibition to missionary expansion. The prosperous 1920s produced a period of overexpansion for the church as well as for business. Missions boards, church colleges, and other agencies of the church were overstaffed and overbuilt. Congregations all over the country entered into a period of building costly structures, often with borrowed money. A day of economic reckoning was not far distant.

Considerable disillusionment came over the church after the intense idealism of the war years. That postwar generation also suffered from a breakdown in public and private morality. As the movement from the farms to the cities accelerated, it became a time of so-called liberation, a time to relax and enjoy life. A new era known as the "jazz age" came into being. Advanced by "flaming youth" and "flappers," the revolution in morals of the 1920s led to "speak-easies" and bootleggers. The change went deeper than this, however. It was an era that tore people loose from old certainties. Automobiles were increasingly available and their use changed patterns of life for all. Millions of persons who did not know the names of John Dewey or Sigmund Freud were influenced by their theories. Intensive advertising campaigns influenced multitudes to buy products unheard of a few years before. The coming of the radio with its instant communication and entertainment affected the church. As if all these external changes were not sufficient to slow the advance of the church, internal conflicts broke out in the 1920s, dividing Protestantism into "modernists" and "fundamentalists" and Disciples into "liberals" and "conservatives." Many ministers and congregations sought without success to take a middle way. One by one ministers and congregations were led into two hostile and often embittered groups.[14]

---

14. Oliver Read Whitley, *Trumpet Call of Reformation* (St. Louis: Bethany Press, 1959). This book gives a good sociological understanding of this period in Disciples history.

15

IN THE THROES OF CONTROVERSY

Thomas Campbell, writing in 1809, called attention to the "heinous nature and pernicious tendency of religious controversy among Christians." "Tired and sick of the bitter jarrings and janglings of a party spirit," he expressed a desire to be "at rest" and to "adopt and recommend such measures as would give rest to our brethren throughout all the churches."[1] It is ironic that Disciples honored the elder Campbell as a father of their movement yet manifested the same contentious spirit which he so thoroughly deplored and repudiated.

However much Disciples yearned for harmony and concord, they found themselves in the awkward position of acting out their faith in the midst of strife. Freedom of expression, regardless of the consequences, was a way of life as well as a cherished principle among them. Holding tenaciously to the notion that each believer had the high responsibility to think and speak for himself in the light of the biblical witness, they seldom hesitated to take issue with each other; and on occasion they pursued an argument as if the kingdom of God hung in the balance. Embroiled in controversy from

---

1. Thomas Campbell, *Declaration and Address.* Reprinted together with the *Last Will and Testament of the Springfield Presbytery* and an introduction by Frederick D. Kershner (St. Louis: The Bethany Press, 1955), p. 24.

generation to generation, they struggled in vain to keep dissension from polarizing them into contending factions and leading them to the disaster of division. "When the free and independent tradition of the Disciples is considered," Howard E. Short has observed, "it is somewhat remarkable that more divisions have not occurred."[2]

The first large-scale rupture in the movement, resulting in the formation of the Churches of Christ, has been discussed at length in Chapter 10. This turn of events failed to leave the denomination in a state either of tranquility or of consensus. Thousands of legalistic restorationists, inflexible and conservative, maintained their connection with the Disciples but grew increasingly restive in the fellowship. They reacted negatively to what they termed a bureaucratic and heresy-inclined octopus at the national level and became convinced that the communion was in the process of losing its peculiarity if not its identity. As a result, Disciples of Christ moved through the early- and mid-twentieth century on a collision course. Personality clashes and thwarted ambitions plus other social and cultural factors provided a rich mixture of fuel for the flames of controversy. In addition, the storm of protest—which eventually gave birth to another restorationist body known as "Christian Churches and Churches of Christ"—cannot be understood without taking into full account the impact of American liberal theology around the turn of the century and thereafter.[3]

AMERICAN RELIGIOUS LIBERALISM

There is no doubt but that fresh stirrings in the American intellectual climate after the Civil War baffled traditional Christian thinkers and flabbergasted the church. As if Charles Darwin had not created enough of a tempest with his theory of organic evolution, a growing number of scholars began to subject the Bible to rigorous historical and literary analysis. In the view of many churchgoers the world of scholarship seemed bent on destroying some of the Christian

2. Howard E. Short, *Doctrine and Thought of the Disciples of Christ* (St. Louis: Christian Board of Publication, 1951), p. 81.
3. Most of the material on Disciples in controversy is condensed from William E. Tucker, *J. H. Garrison and Disciples of Christ.* For an account of the controversy from 1900 to 1950, see Stephen J. Corey, *Fifty Years of Attack and Controversy* (St. Louis: The Committee on Publication of the Corey Manuscript, 1953).

community's cherished beliefs. This undeniable challenge to religious faith prompted the rise of liberal theology as a diverse but distinctive movement within American Christianity. Strengthening the movement from the outset were the theological students in post-Civil War America who flocked to German universities, studied under Albrecht Ritschl and Julius Wellhausen, and returned home to spread the liberal insights which they had gained on the continent.

The genius of liberal theology was its openness to all truth and its insistence on genuine dialogue between church and world. Fearing nothing more than an outmoded faith, liberals reconstructed Christian theology in order to harmonize it with prevailing currents in philosophy and science. Their emphasis on historical optimism, the immanence of God, the dignity of man, and the humanity of Christ stood in vivid contrast to traditional Christianity. Exponents of liberalism resolved the apparent conflict between Moses and Darwin by insisting that evolution could have been "God's way of doing things." They defended the principles of biblical criticism on the ground that the Bible was not only the record of divine revelation but also an intensely human collection of documents.

To a large segment of the church in America, this new theology was a wrong-headed attempt to improve the Gospel handed down by the apostles and expounded in the creeds. Countering the preaching of Henry Ward Beecher and Lyman Abbott from the famous pulpit of Plymouth Church in Brooklyn, conservatives charged Charles Darwin with rank atheism and argued that nothing could be gained by succumbing to his wild propaganda. They urged the devout to defend the true faith rather than accommodate it to the changing circumstances of time. Liberals accused conservatives of obscurantism, and conservatives upbraided liberals for making a mockery of the Gospel.

The highly charged controversy raged out of control in the late nineteenth century and opened gaping wounds in several denominations. Heresy trials marred the peace of Presbyterianism. Charles A. Briggs, professor of biblical theology at Union Theological Seminary in New York City, was censured for departing from the Westminster Confession of Faith and suspended from the Presbyterian ministry. The crisis at Andover Seminary in Massachusetts disrupted Congregationalism. Northern (now American) Baptists established rival institutions to offset the liberalizing influence of Crozer Seminary in Pennsylvania and the University of Chicago. To a striking degree, the battle over beliefs was concentrated in urban centers of the Northeast. Although Disciples were primarily a rural-small town and midwestern people, they, too, were plagued with theological dissension around the turn of the last century.

As early as 1869 a few Disciples began to consider the strange new world of Darwin. In August of that year, for example, one participant in an Illinois "preachers' institute" gave an account of Darwinism and defined the word *protoplasm*. By 1874 Barton W. Johnson felt obliged to criticize Darwin for passing on guesses to the public as proven facts. The theory of evolution was even ridiculed from the relatively progressive platform of the Missouri Christian Lectureship in the late 1880s. George Plattenburg (1828-1904), blistered the evolutionists: "They cast an 'obscure glance,' find an "apparently,' rise to a 'probably' and 'must have been,' and—presto! out of a tadpole comes a man." He suggested a religious creed for Darwinians in the same address: "Hail, all-sufficient atom! By thee worlds were made. Hail, infinitesimal molecule! we worship thee—we praise thee, oh! ineffable particle! for out of thee, and through thee, and into thee, are all things!"[4] Several Disciples refused to equate evolution and infidelity, to be sure, but they constituted a tiny minority and in the main kept their thoughts to themselves.

The revolt against the traditional formulation of the Christian faith did not inflame Disciples until the winter of 1889-1890. At that time Robert C. Cave (1843-1923), outspoken minister of Central Christian Church in St. Louis, preached a series of sermons which shocked his congregation. Forced to resign, he retreated to the safe confines of a "nonsectarian church." The Cave incident received an airing in the public press and left a host of Disciples around the country shaking their heads in utter dismay.

---

4. George Plattenburg, "Materialistic Evolution" in *The Missouri Christian Lectures, selected from the courses of 1886, 1887, and 1888* (Cincinnati: Standard Publishing Company, 1888), pp. 162, 166-167.

Cave's conversion to liberal theology was thoroughgoing. From the pulpit of Central Christian Church he argued that God did not command Abraham to slay his son or require Jephthah to offer his daughter in sacrifice. In interpreting the New Testament message, he advocated the "open membership error," denied both the virgin birth and the bodily resurrection of Jesus, and asserted that Christians might believe Christ to be a myth so long as they accepted the "Christ idea."[5] Following his withdrawal from the Disciples, he continued to speak his mind through regular contributions to a religious journal, the *Non-Sectarian.* Repeatedly he derided the principle of Christian primitivism, defined sin in terms of ignorance, affirmed the divinity within all people, and labeled the atonement of mankind by the substitution of Christ as a moral outrage. No wonder Cave touched sensitive nerves and aroused righteous indignation. Although he lost his pulpit because of his "modernistic" preaching, he dealt openly and candidly with issues which were to keep Disciples in turmoil for decades to come.

THE BATTLE OVER THE BOOK

Robert C. Cave was certainly not the first Disciple to question the dominant attitude toward the Bible which nineteenth-century believers had inherited from their forebears. Alexander Campbell himself utilized the principles of historical criticism in his study of the Scriptures. When a prominent biblical scholar at Andover Seminary reasoned that "the best standard of orthodoxy is the application of the principles and rules of interpretation to the Bible, which are applied to all other writings of the age in which they appeared," Campbell "thanked God and took courage." To clarify his position, Campbell listed seven principles of interpretation, of which the first is the most important: "On opening any book in the Sacred scriptures, *consider first the historical circumstances of the book. These are the order, the title, the date, the place, and the occasion of it.*"[6] At times he

---

5. *Christian-Evangelist,* January 9, 1890, p. 23. See also an article reprinted from the *St. Louis Republic* in *Christian-Evangelist,* December 26, 1889, p. 825.

6. Alexander Campbell, *A Connected View of the Principles and Rules by Which the Living Oracles May Be Intelligibly and Certainly Interpreted, . . . Containing the Principal Extras of The Millennial Harbinger, Revised and Corrected* (Bethany, Va.: M'Vay and Ewing, 1835), pp. 95-96.

took issue with those who claimed that each jot and tittle of the Bible was verbally inspired, but he was reluctant to concede the possibility of error in the Scriptures. Obviously, Campbell's understanding of the inspiration of the Bible was not sharply defined. Both liberals and conservatives were able to quote him to bolster their respective arguments.

One of Campbell's converts, Lewis L. Pinkerton, flatly rejected the doctrine of biblical inerrancy. Within a few years of Pinkerton's death in 1875, George W. Longan and Isaac Errett also groped their way to a more liberal view of the Bible. A member of *The Christian's* editorial staff in 1881, Longan wrote an article in which he insisted that the theory of verbal infallibility not only led to "most mischievous consequences" but also furnished "men like [Robert] Ingersoll with their sharpest weapon of attack."[7] Errett, the most influential Disciple of his time, delivered the 1883 Missouri Christian Lectures on the general theme of biblical inspiration. After distinguishing between inspiration and infallibility, Errett concluded:

Admitting the fact of inspiration, have we in the inspired Scriptures an *infallible* guide? Are they absolutely free from error? That all truth is infallible needs no proof. But, is the *communication* of truth, in the inspired Scriptures, absolutely free from error? I do not see how we can answer this question affirmatively, unless we can prove that human language furnishes an absolutely certain method of communication between mind and mind. Nor do I see how this can be proved.[8]

Errett and Longan raised the anxiety level of conservatives. John W. McGarvey, who later directed the attack within Disciples against "higher critics," was especially troubled. Admitting that he "was pained to hear from Bro. Errett the concession that the Scriptures are not infallible," he reproved Longan for taking a "long stride in the direction of infidelity."[9] McGarvey's rebuttal was to be but an opening skirmish in the lengthy battle over the book among Disciples of Christ.

---

7. *Christian*, May 12, 1881, p. 4.
8. Isaac Errett, "Inspiration" in *The Missouri Christian Lectureship* (St. Louis: John Burns, Publisher, 1883), p. 167.
9. *Ibid.*, p. 183; *Christian*, June 16, 1881, p. 1.

Beginning in 1893 the major phase of the controversy continued until 1917.[10] For a quarter of a century, laypeople as
well as preachers and seminary professors argued vehemently
over the authorship of the Pentateuch. Few questions seemed
to be more pressing than the date of the Book of Daniel.
Disciples originally had rallied around the Scriptures, but by
1900 irreconcilable approaches to the Bible had polarized
them into contending factions. The principle adversaries in
this denominational struggle were *The Christian-Evangelist*
and the *Christian Standard.*

By and large *The Christian-Evangelist* was receptive to the
basic viewpoint of biblical critics, although its witness was
ambiguous until after the death of James H. Garrison's
coeditor, Barton W. Johnson, in 1894. Johnson made no
apology for his conservatism, for he thought that the critics
posed a greater threat to Christianity than avowed atheists.
To his mind, biblical criticism if unchecked would destroy
both the integrity of the Scriptures and the vitality of the
church. In response to Johnson's death, McGarvey wrote: "I
especially feel his loss at the present time, because he was so
strong a writer on Biblical criticism, and wrote so perfectly in
harmony with my own views on this important theme."[11]
McGarvey had reason to grieve. The stilling of Johnson's pen
left no one to counteract the editorials of Garrison in *The
Christian-Evangelist.*

Garrison's response to biblical criticism was neither that of
indiscriminate hostility nor wholesale acceptance. He certainly did not accept and endorse many of the critics' conclusions. It appeared to him that they frequently advanced
theories on the basis of flimsy evidence, and he told them so.
Still he championed the right of Christian scholars to pursue
honest investigation and to report their findings. His genuine
openness to any new light which could be thrown on the
history and literary character of the Scriptures strained his
relationship with McGarvey.

The conflict between the two men sharpened in 1899 when
Garrison engaged Herbert L. Willett to write the weekly arti-

---

10. In 1893 John W. McGarvey began a department of "Biblical Criticism" in the
Christian Standard. Although it is artificial to date the battle over the Book,
McGarvey's feature did more than any other single force to precipitate and sustain
the major phase of the controversy. In 1917 liberals won a decisive victory over conservatives at The College of the Bible.
11. *Christian-Evangelist,* June 14, 1894, p. 375.

cle on the Sunday school lesson in *The Christian-Evangelist.* The best-known biblical critic among the Disciples, Willett had been introduced to the historical criticism of the Scriptures by William Rainey Harper at Yale. When Harper became the first president of the University of Chicago, Willett transferred to that institution and received the Ph.D. degree in 1896. He was dean of Disciples Divinity House in Chicago at the time Garrison named him as a regular contributor to *The Christian-Evangelist.*

In ensuing years Willett wrote numerous scholarly articles and books, including *The Bible Through the Centuries* and *The Jew Through the Centuries,* and taught scores of Disciples seminarians. His most significant contribution to the life of Disciples, however, was not in the seminary classroom. Throughout his career he tried to bridge the chasm between biblical critics and laypeople. In addition to preparing a wealth of materials for church schools and Christian Endeavor societies, he lectured throughout the United States. Willett's success as a popularizer of liberal biblical scholarship prompted Lyman Abbott to remark that "no man in America had done so much to open to popular understanding the new Bible that historical criticism had illumined."[12] While writing the weekly commentary on the Sunday school lesson for Garrison, Willett raised the eyebrows of conservatives more than once. Although Garrison could not support every position taken by his associate, he refused to stifle biblical scholarship and censure Willett. Conservatives therefore accused *The Christian-Evangelist* of sheltering a heretic.

Conservatives channeled their response to biblical criticism through the columns of the *Christian Standard.* One issue of the *Standard* in 1909 contained a full-page cartoon which summarized the paper's editorial policy during the battle over the book. The drawing, a striking example of religious satire, pictured a blind clergyman using the "scissors of unbelief" to cut the last page of the Book of Revelation out of the Bible; the rest of the Scriptures lay scattered on the floor. The caption read: "The Spirit of

---

12. Quoted in Herbert L. Willett, Jr., "A Living Benediction" in *My Dad: Preacher, Pastor, Person,* ed. by George A. Campbell and J. Edward Moseley (St. Louis: Christian Board of Publication, 1938), p. 190.

Higher Criticism: 'And what remains of the Bible, beloved, is divinely inspired.' "[13]

John W. McGarvey served as field general for the Cincinnati paper in its war on the critics. His conception of the Bible was typical of the conservative mind. Since the Bible is the word of God, it has to be verbally inspired and absolutely inerrant. According to the infallible Scriptures, Moses wrote the Pentateuch and David the Psalms; Jonah spent three days in the belly of a whale, and God literally created woman from Adam's rib. Describing McGarvey's point of view, one commentator wrote: "Isaiah was Isaiah, Daniel was Daniel, Job was Job, Jonah in particular was Jonah, the great fish and all, and Baalam's ass spake as good Hebrew as his master, and what else?"[14] To say less, in McGarvey's opinion, impugned the veracity of the Scriptures. He consequently did everything in his power to protect the Bible from the plunder of "destructive criticism."

From 1893 to 1911 McGarvey wrote a regular feature on biblical criticism in the *Christian Standard.* Week after week he stung the critics through sarcasm and ridicule. Objects of his abuse included Herbert L. Willett, Charles A. Briggs, and William R. Harper. His readers must have chuckled when, for example, he borrowed the principles of "higher criticism" to prove beyond reasonable doubt that Harper was not, in fact, the author of a series of lectures published under his name. Citing numerous grammatical errors and misquotations of Scripture, he concluded that the lectures could not possibly have been written by the learned president of a university. Many of McGarvey's contributions were less witty and more caustic. By nature a gentle and hospitable man, he sometimes dipped his pen in gall so as to expose the fallacies of what he judged to be misguided scholarship. The critics, particularly Willett, grew to expect regular verbal lashings from McGarvey. They rarely were disappointed.

A fresh wave of discord engulfed Disciples as they prepared to celebrate their centennial at Pittsburgh in 1909. Upon learning that Willett and Perry J. Rice had been invited to address the centennial convention, conservatives thundered their oppostion. Tainted with liberalism, Rice was bad enough;

13. *Christian Standard,* August 7, 1909, p. 1377.
14. *Christian-Evangelist,* May 14, 1914, p. 624.

Willett was worse. The *Christian Standard* ran a clever series of articles contrasting Willett's teaching with the Bible and the Disciples fathers. The paper also published pages of letters protesting his inclusion on the program. In spite of all the ranting and extensive negotiations, Willett remained on the program and spoke to an overflow audience.

The Standard Publishing Company, having agreed to publish a *Centennial Convention Report*, inserted a special statement in the front of the volume. This "publisher's note" disavowed any responsibility for the appearance of Willett's and Rice's names in the report and concluded: "We regard this statement as due, not only to ourselves under the circumstances, but to the integrity of this report. On no other condition would we have permitted the use of our imprint."[15] The battle continued, much to the chagrin of many thoughtful Disciples.

The controversy over biblical criticism culminated in 1917 at The College of the Bible. Rumblings within the school at that time turned into an earthquake, to use Dwight Stevenson's word.[16] Six years earlier President McGarvey had died and was succeeded by Richard H. Crossfield (1868-1951). Although McGarvey had groomed Hall L. Calhoun (1863-1935) for the presidency, he became dean instead. During the same period William Clayton Bower (1878-), Alonzo W. Fortune (1873-1950), George W. Hemry (1874-1924), and Elmer E. Snoddy (1863-1936) were chosen to fill vacancies in the seminary faculty.

All four of the new professors were theological liberals; their dean was an ultraconservative. Calhoun received his Ph.D. degree from Harvard University, graduating with his orthodoxy unscathed. Dean Calhoun labored to preserve The College of the Bible as a stronghold of conservatism but met solid resistance from his liberal colleagues. The Seminary took on the character of a powder keg.

In 1917 the *Christian Standard* set fire to the fuse by publishing a letter previously sent to approximately three hundred Disciples ministers. Written by Ben F. Battenfield,

---

15. Russell Errett, "Publisher's Note" in *Centennial Convention Report* (Cincinnati: Standard Publishing Company, 1909).
16. For a detailed account of the controversy at The College of the Bible in 1917, see Dwight E. Stevenson, *Lexington Theological Seminary, 1865-1965*, pp. 165-207.

a student at The College of the Bible, the letter blistered the liberal contingent on the faculty and asserted that a majority of the student body had been deluded into discarding the true faith. The *Standard,* shocked by the radical departure of McGarvey's school from his spirit and teaching, called for an impartial investigation and printed many expressions of alarm. One reader wrote: "I cannot see why anyone wants to teach such stuff as comes from Chicago." Another asked: "Can you name a college where I can send my two boys and know that they are not subjected to the influence of destructive criticism, cards, dancing, etc.?" There were seven pages of such comments in the April 14 issue of the *Christian Standard.* Through their journal conservatives attempted to instigate a heresy trial at The College of the Bible.

The Lexington seminary's Board of Trustees convened in May to consider the charges against a majority of the faculty. Having investigated the situation to their satisfaction, the trustees exonerated the accused professors. As reported in the public press, they concluded in part:

> The Board has found no teaching in this College by any member of the faculty that is out of harmony with the fundamental conceptions and convictions of our brotherhood which relate to the inspiration of the Bible as the divine word of God, divinely given, and of divine authority, or to the divinity of Jesus Christ or to the plea of our people.
>
> The Board has found no student whose faith in any of these things has been shaken, but has had evidence that the faith of many students has been strengthened.[17]

Shaken and defeated, Dean Calhoun resigned and presented his case to Disciples everywhere through a series of articles featured in the *Christian Standard.* His cause was lost, however, and he knew it. Several years later he admitted as much when he transferred his church membership to the Churches of Christ.

The outcome of the struggle for control of The College of the Bible had far-ranging consequences among the Disciples of Christ. To lodge their protest more effectively, conservatives in time established the fundamentalist McGarvey Bi-

---

17. *Ibid.,* p. 183; quoted from *Lexington Herald,* May 10, 1917.

ble College in Louisville. Instead of restricting freedom of inquiry and encouraging heresy hunts, progressives in the movement confirmed their commitment to intellectual openness. They were gripped by the conviction that their uncompromising stance had saved the Stone-Campbell tradition from disaster. James H. Garrison, retired but still enormously influential, no doubt spoke for a large majority of Disciples: "Our whole educational future, as a religious people who have emphasized intellectual freedom along with simplicity and soundness of faith, has a brighter outlook because of this [The College of the Bible] incident."[18]

EXPANDING HORIZONS IN MINISTERIAL EDUCATION

Advances in ministerial education among Disciples played a major role in shaping the battle over the Bible. Prior to the 1890s educated Disciples preachers with few exceptions had prepared for ministry in little denominational colleges which awarded no degree beyond a Bachelor of Arts. Thereafter divinity students in increasing numbers found their way to the nation's great theological centers. These were the men who later plagued McGarvey and his partisans. It is clear that American liberal theology seeped into the Disciples of Christ by way of Yale, Union in New York and the University of Chicago.

Levi Marshall, the first Disciple to seek admission to Yale Divinity School, submitted his application about 1875. Having heard that Disciples were troublemakers, the faculty requested a full statement on his religious beliefs before processing his application. Marshall and a handful of others must have made a favorable impression over the next decade or so, for in 1890 Yale began to advertise for students in *The Christian-Evangelist*. The immediate results were less than impressive. Only five Disciples were enrolled in 1892, but the number increased to eleven by 1901. During one period in the twentieth century Disciples had more students at Yale Divinity School than any other denomination.

The University of Chicago was far more influential than Yale in raising the level of Disciples ministerial education. Incorporated in 1890 and opened in 1892, the University en-

---

18. *Christian-Evangelist*, June 21, 1917, p. 711.

TWENTIETH CENTURY PANORAMA

Edward Scribner Ames

F. D. Kershner

P. H. Welshimer

W. E. Garrison

Edgar DeWitt Jones

Disciples Divinity House,

University of Chicago

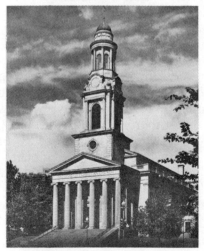

National City Christian Church

couraged various denominations to take advantage of its faculty and facilities by establishing affiliated "houses" for their divinity students. At the 1893 national convention, convened in Chicago, President Harper urged Disciples to undertake such an enterprise. The following May it was announced that the Disciples Divinity House of the University of Chicago had been constituted and that Herbert L. Willett had been elected dean of the institution.[19]

James H. Garrison and *The Christian-Evangelist* gave unqualified support to the new venture, but conservatives immediately sounded an alarm. Benjamin C. Deweese, noting that the University was a Baptist school, feared the corrupting influence of Baptists on Disciples students. Besides, he argued, the curriculum at Chicago would add nothing to the program of ministerial education already in effect among Disciples. Why, therefore, sink money in an institution which could not keep from competing with poverty-stricken Disciples colleges for funds and students? McGarvey joined in the attack. Pointing out that "it is not easy to handle lampblack without smutting your fingers," he advised Chris-

---

19. For the story of the first seventy-five years of the Disciples Divinity House of the University of Chicago, see William Barnett Blakemore, *Quest for Intelligence in Ministry* (Chicago: The Disciples Divinity House of the University of Chicago, 1970).

Scene from recent Quadrennial of the International Christian Women's Fellowship

tian parents against sending their children to a school staffed by infidels and biblical critics. Conservatives fired all their heavy artillery in the direction of Chicago. W. Barnett Blakemore, a perceptive and respected interpreter of the Disciples mind, succeeded Ames as dean of Disciples Divinity House in 1945 and held the position until his death three decades later.

Despite heavy opposition, Disciples Divinity House opened in the fall of 1894 and survived to become for several decades a dominant factor in Disciples life and thought. The signal success of the enterprise was due in large measure to the leadership of three individuals who served successively as dean of the House: Herbert L. Willett, Winfred E. Garrison, and Edward Scribner Ames (1870-1958). Joined by Charles Clayton Morrison, long-term editor of the *Christian Century* in Chicago, these men literally constituted the intellectual center of the Disciples for many years. Brilliant and determined, they led the Stone-Campbell movement into and through the heyday of American liberal theology. "Through their teaching and writing, and that of their students," wrote Ronald E. Osborn, "they brought home to Disciples, too long isolated from the currents of contemporary thinking, the full impact of liberalism."[20]

THE CAMPBELL INSTITUTE

Willett, Garrison, and Ames were instrumental in forming the Campbell Institute during the 1896 national convention of Disciples at Springfield, Illinois. The organization restricted its membership to college graduates and adopted a threefold purpose: to encourage a scholarly spirit, to inspire contributions to the literature and thought of Disciples, and to promote spiritual maturity. Mrs. Albertina Allen Forrest, the only woman to be a charter member, was the first secretary of the Institute. Beginning with fourteen members in 1896, it claimed a membership of 101 in 1906 and 177 a decade later. Frederick D. Kershner remarked with a note of mild sarcasm that at one time (the mid-1930s) the "journal of

---

20. Ronald E. Osborn, "Theology Among the Disciples" in *The Christian Church (Disciples of Christ): An Interpretative Examination in the Cultural Context,* ed. by George G. Beazley, Jr., p. 104.

the Institute . . . attained the colossal circulation of almost four hundred copies."[21] As a liberalizing force in the life of Disciples, however, the organization's influence was out of proportion to its size.

Although the Campbell Institute aimed to be a group of thinkers rather than a school of thought, conservatives regarded all of its members as shameless modernists. Caricaturing the conservative temper in 1924, James H. Garrison wrote: "Already we have some good brethren who would refuse to accept the Ten Commandments if they should be issued in a circular from the Campbell Institute."[22] There was truth as well as humor in Ames's observation: "The Campbell Institute is unique in one respect: it is evidently less loved by its members and more feared by its enemies than any other organization in the world."[23]

In addition to publishing the *Bulletin of the Campbell Institute,* renamed the *Scroll* in 1906, the Institute held annual meetings usually in Chicago to hear and discuss papers. For many years it has sponsored evening "after-sessions" during the International Conventions and later the General Assemblies of Disciples. These lively sessions sometimes attracted large crowds and provided a rare opportunity for frank interchange on controversial issues.

THE CONGRESSES OF DISCIPLES

Prior to the origin of the Campbell Institute, James H. Garrison began to promote the idea of a forum for open and uninhibited discussion among Disciples. As early as 1890 he called attention to a cluster of "living questions" which Disciples as a group could evade only at peril to themselves. "What are the modifications, if any, which Time and Experience have made Necessary, in the Doctrinal Aspects of our Movement?" he asked. "What, if any, are the new obligations imposed upon us by recent Developments in the Religious world, in relation to the great question of Christian Unity?" To discuss these and related questions, he suggested that a congress be held "next December" (1890) in St. Louis.[24] Almost a decade passed before his proposal was adopted.

---

21. *Christian Standard,* August 10, 1940, p. 772.
22. *Scroll,* July 1924, p. 285.
23. *Scroll,* April 1926, p. 252.
24. *Christian-Evangelist,* May 1, 1890, p. 274.

In 1898 a group of Disciples ministers, vacationing at Macatawa Park—a small resort on the eastern shore of Lake Michigan—made plans for the first congress which convened in St. Louis on April 25, 1899. Garrison served as general chairman. The program covered a wide variety of topics including the history of doctrine, biblical study, city evangelization, Christian worship, and church organization. Among the speakers were Edward Scribner Ames, Jesse J. Haley, Ida W. Harrison, James A. Lord, William T. Moore and Allan B. Philputt. The success of the event exceeded the expectations of even its most ardent backers.

Excepting only 1920, Disciples continued to hold congresses on an annual basis through 1926. Conservatives participated in the sessions for the first five years or so. Subsequently, they stayed at home, leaving the congresses mainly to those who approved of and supported the Campbell Institute. Their absence was but another sign of growing polarization within the Disciples.

THE ONE CHURCH AND THE PIOUS
UNIMMERSED

Progressives, including moderates and liberals alike, made full use of the congresses to highlight and promote the cause of Christian unity. The Cincinnati Congress in 1907, for instance, devised the strategy which enabled Disciples to cooperate with other communions through the newly formed Federal Council of Churches. For five years conservatives had fought the federation proposal only to see Disciples endorse it at a mass meeting held "in connection with" but officially unrelated to their 1907 national convention in Norfolk, Virginia. John B. Briney, editor of *Briney's Monthly,* alone cast a dissenting vote. He represented a host of conservatives who preferred to live in "splendid isolation" rather than get entangled with the "denominations."

Born to heal the brokenness of the church, Disciples from their beginnings intended to restore New Testament Christianity so as to unite the church in order to proclaim the Gospel more effectively. As generation followed generation into the twentieth century, many Stone-Campbell followers either lost sight of or chose to ignore the parameters of their plea. Conservatives defended a simplistic understanding of the restoration of primitive Christianity and forgot the goal of Christian unity. Liberals, on the other hand, worked diligently to reflect the essential oneness of Christ's church and refused to be straightjacketed by the strictures of a rigid restorationism.

The clash between the two points of view came to center on the issue of open membership—that is, the practice of accepting persons into the full membership of Disciples congregations even though they had not received baptism as consenting believers and by the method of immersion. Forced to choose between closed and open membership, thoughtful Disciples found themselves in an exceedingly difficult position. If they refused to accept nonimmersed Christians into their congregations, they were in effect reinforcing the tragic divisions in the Body of Christ. If they accepted nonimmersed believers into their congregations, they were tacitly sanctioning a form of baptism other than that practiced in the New Testament church. The long-term controversy over the pious unimmersed opened deeper and more painful wounds and generated more heat than any other problem among Disciples in the twentieth century. It shook the very foundations of the movement.

Although some of Barton W. Stone's followers held that the form of baptism was a matter of opinion rather than an essential of Christian faith and practice, almost all Disciples in the 1840s and 1850s agreed that their congregations should consist *only* of immersed believers. This closed membership policy was virtually unchallenged by the time of the Civil War.

Lewis L. Pinkerton, as was his custom, raised a voice of concern in 1869. An avowed advocate of open membership, he argued that Disciples of Christ questioned the Christian character of a pious unimmersed Protestant when they denied him or her the right to enter their communion. Pinkerton refused to administer baptism except by immersion, but he did not think that the form of the ordinance should constitute an insuperable barrier to Christian fellowship.

Less than a decade later William T. Moore became pastor of a Disciples congregation in London, England, where he put Pinkerton's idea into practice. Around the turn of the century a few congregations on this side of the Atlantic also waived the requirement of immersion at the instigation of their ministers. Probably the first to do so was the Cedar Avenue Church of Cleveland, Ohio, in 1895. The South Side Christian Church in Indianapolis opened its membership the next year. Despite a vigorous and unrelenting conservative protest, these congregations and several others—the Monroe Street Church in Chicago, for example—braced themselves for battle and took definite stands favoring some form of inclusive fellowship. Ames, Willett, Morrison, and Peter Ainslie followed the lead of Thomas Munnell, one-time secretary of the ACMS, urging Disciples to lift the barrier of immersion and strike a telling blow for Christian unity. Their forceful witness drew a bead on committed restorationists.

In 1929 Alfred T. DeGroot completed the first comprehensive investigation of open membership in the Disciples and found only nineteen of the denomination's 8,399 congregations in the United States and Canada to be openly receiving the unimmersed into their fellowship. He later discovered that the practice was more widespread than he realized at the time. As he wrote:

> Conversation with large numbers of ministers since that time [1929] has revealed that many of them, probably some hundreds, employ the practice with or without official approving action by their churches, and at least scores of churches have adopted open membership, but for the sake of allaying controversy they give no general publicity to this policy.[25]

By 1940, in any event, Carl S. Ledbetter could substantiate his claim that at least 106 Disciples congregations in addition to fourteen federated churches had ceased to insist on immersion as a test of Christian fellowship. More recently, Professors Garrison and DeGroot estimated that in 1958 "nearly 1000 churches practice open membership openly or quietly."[26]

This major shift in the direction of inclusive fellowship raised the temperature of conservatives to the boiling point. They flailed away at the "radicals," insisting that open membership was a misguided scheme designed to undo the "brotherhood" and frustrate its providential mission. Their

---

25. Alfred T. DeGroot, *The Grounds of Divisions Among the Disciples of Christ*, p. 189.
26. Winfred E. Garrison and Alfred T. DeGroot, *The Disciples of Christ: A History*, p. 440.

arguments and emotional outbursts, however, failed to sway a growing number of Disciples of Christ.

SOCIETIES UNDER FIRE

In the early twentieth century Disciples quarreled at every level of church life. No organization found a way to insulate itself from the tumult and the shouting. No agency managed to miss the cross fire of charges and counter charges, attacks and reprisals. Missionary societies, in particular, felt the full force of the conservative onslaught.

While in the process of losing the struggle to save Disciples from the Federal Council of Churches, the *Christian Standard* opened fire on another front. In 1907 it assailed Archibald McLean and the FCMS for accepting three gifts amounting to $25,000 from John D. Rockefeller, Sr. To James A. Lord, editor of the *Standard*, Rockefeller was an unscrupulous individual who made his fortune by fleecing the American people. No good could come from using "tainted money" to spread the Gospel. Thomas W. Phillips, Sr., a leading Disciple and wealthy oil man, added a loud *amen* and threw the weight of his influence behind the protest. He had tried in vain to compete with the gigantic Standard Oil Company and knew from firsthand experience of Rockefeller's "immorality." It added insult to injury for the FCMS to accept money which Rockefeller had "stolen" from Phillips. Observed Frederick D. Kershner: "To take money secured in that way for missionary purposes was, to him [Phillips], like accepting the loot of a highwayman who has robbed the elders of the church while on the way home from the communion table."[27]

Many stood shoulder to shoulder with McLean, president of the FCMS. William J. Lhamon pointed out that Jesus did not ask the rich young ruler how he acquired his money. "The simple fact was that he had it, and Jesus told him to give it," wrote Lhamon. "Possibly giving is the only thing that can save Mr. Rockefeller and others greatly in danger. Why should we not help him give by receiving?"[28] The editor of *The Christian-Evangelist* entered the fray. Commending

27. *Christian Standard*, August 24, 1940, p. 829.
28. *Christian-Evangelist*, January 31, 1907, p. 158.

Rockefeller for using his resources to assist worthy causes, James H. Garrison distinguished between the accumulation and distribution of wealth: "The one may be very wrong; the other . . . altogether right."[29] Only God can judge whether a contribution has been earned honestly, he maintained. The church's responsibility was limited to the proper use of funds which it received. Garrison's position made good sense to members of the FCMS's Board of Managers. They retained Rockefeller's gifts but agreed in the interest of harmony never to solicit him again. This compromise did not appease the *Christian Standard.* The breach between it and missionary agencies widened.

Dissension increased when Disciples merged six boards and societies to form the United Christian Missionary Society in 1920. For years a comprehensive organization had been needed to unify and simplify the communion's expanding missionary and benevolent work. Competition for funds, not to mention other matters, had become a nagging and pervasive problem. Congregations were plagued with "special days" at which time a particular agency presented its appeal and received an offering. Before one "special day" could be observed, publicity on the next one was in the mails. The continuous round of promotion exhausted nearly everyone. Weary congregations and preachers asked: "Will there be no night of rest?" The UCMS was organized partly in response to that often repeated question.

While *The Christian-Evangelist* backed unification without reservations, the *Christian Standard* encouraged resistance to the merger. It promoted a "Restoration Congress" held just before the 1919 International Convention which ratified the constitution of the UCMS. At this rally, attended by those who were "resolved to maintain the Restoration plea intact," conservatives plotted their strategy for opposing the unification plan. Then they moved in a body to the floor of the convention and leveled a stinging attack on the recognized agencies.

An editorial in *The Christian-Evangelist* gave an account of their sweeping accusations:

The abuses charged against the societies—often in almost cruel

---

29. *Christian-Evangelist,* August 8, 1907, p. 1005.

personalities—ranged from personal grievances and old strifes
. . . to such allegations as "open membership," "infant dedication"
on the foreign field, unjustifiable meddling with the local churches
and pastors by the secretaries, the ignoring of the deity of Christ,
and the willingness to see our own church work supplanted by
others.[30]

Fearful of an ecclesiastical machine gaining in power as it
expanded, conservatives obviously saw what they took to be
solid evidence that "modernism" had infiltrated the national
bureaucracy to an alarming degree.

The primary source of discord in the 1920s was the issue of
open membership. The "*Standard* crowd" believed that the
United Society condoned the practice of open membership on
the mission field. The UCMS Board of Managers unequivocally denied supporting any missionary who received
unimmersed believers into Christian fellowship. Further, the
board agreed to a policy statement which was approved by
the 1922 International Convention at Winona Lake, Indiana:

> In harmony with the teachings of the New Testament as un-
> derstood by this Board of Managers, the United Christian
> Missionary Society is conducting its work everywhere on the princi-
> ple of receiving into the membership of the churches at home and
> abroad, by any of its missionaries, only those who are immersed,
> penitent believers in Christ.
> Furthermore, it is believed by this Board of Managers, that all of
> the missionaries and ministers appointed and supported by this
> Board, are in sincere accord with this policy, and certainly it will
> not appoint and indeed it will not continue in its service any one
> known by it to be not in such accord. It disclaims any right and
> disowns any desire to do otherwise.[31]

This statement antagonized liberals without satisfying
conservatives. To the former it smacked of creedalism,
and to the latter it bore no resemblance to what they believed were the facts.

Shortly after the Winona Lake International Convention,
the *Christian Standard* published John T. Brown's inflammatory report on his investigation of Disciples mission
stations around the world. In identifying places where he
thought missionaries were accepting the unimmersed into full

---

30. *Christian-Evangelist*, October 23, 1919, p. 1108.
31. *Christian-Evangelist*, September 7, 1922, p. 1144.

church membership, Brown confirmed the suspicion of conservatives that the UCMS could not be trusted. Subsequently, the *Standard* ran a series of articles entitled "The
United Society Has Broken Faith" and edited by Robert E.
Elmore.

To dispel misunderstanding and bring order out of chaos,
the Cleveland International Convention in 1924 took action
which led to the appointment of a "Peace Conference Committee" consisting of representatives from the contending
factions. Reporting at the next convention, held in Oklahoma
City, the committee recommended:

That no person be employed by the United Christian Missionary
Society as its representative who has committed himself or herself
to belief in, or practice of, the reception of unimmersed persons into
the membership of churches of Christ.

That if any person is now in the employment of the United Christian Missionary Society as representative who has committed
himself or herself to belief in, or practice of, the reception of unimmersed persons into the membership of churches of Christ, the
relationship of that person to the United Christian Missionary
Society be severed as employee. And that this be done as soon as
possible, with full consideration given to the interests of the person
involved without jeopardy to the work of the Society.[32]

Following intense and extensive debate, the recommendation
carried.

As a result, the UCMS named and dispatched Cleveland
Kleihauer, John R. Golden, and Robert N. Simpson to study
conditions at missions of Disciples in the Orient. The three
men uncovered no instances of open membership and
returned to the United States confident of their findings.
When the Memphis International Convention in 1926
received and endorsed their report, conservatives gave up on
the UCMS and resolved to pursue missionary activity independently. It was a fateful decision. Already slim, the
prospects for reconciling a polarized people vanished.

THE EMERGENCE OF A NEW FELLOWSHIP

For some time conservative Disciples had been organizing
for action. Their preconvention rally in 1919 has been mentioned. The next year "permanent officers" were elected at a

---

32. *Christian-Evangelist*, October 15, 1925, p. 1336.

Restoration Congress in St. Louis. They formed a New Testament Tract Society in 1921 and passed a resolution "urging all churches to discontinue fellowship with the United Christian Missionary Society and the General Convention until present abuses are rectified."[33] Continuing discontent spawned the Christian Restoration Association in 1925.

To give wider publicity to their protest, conservatives founded two journals. *The Touchstone,* originally named *The Spotlight,* was short-lived. Issued for the first time in 1925, it folded in 1927. *The Restoration Herald,* organ of the Christian Restoration Association, proved to be more permanent. In addition to these two papers, the *Christian Standard* welcomed articles written for the purpose of exposing and embarrassing the UCMS. The *United Society News,* launched in 1925, entered the melee as a UCMS publication.

Despite these ominous developments, Disciples did not appear to be in immediate danger of splitting until the International Convention in Memphis. Up to that time, friends and enemies of the UCMS wrangled but remained in the same international assembly. At least they were within shouting distance of each other. Before leaving Memphis, however, the dissidents decided not to be outvoted again and agreed to establish a convention of their own. The first North American Christian Convention, as they styled their meeting, convened in Indianapolis in October 1927. Conservatives continued to designate themselves as members of the Disciples of Christ, but in reality they constituted an identifiable group moving inexorably toward a separate fellowship.

Meanwhile, some of these disenchanted Disciples had taken initial steps to provide a "sound ministry" for "faithful" congregations. Unwilling to condone much less to support the so-called "modernism" of Disciples-related colleges and universities, they proceeded to found both McGarvey Bible College and Cincinnati Bible Institute in 1923. The two united and became Cincinnati Bible Seminary a year later. James D. Murch (1892-1973) served as acting head of the school until Ralph Records was named president in 1926. Milligan College, Johnson Bible College, Minnesota Bible College, and Kentucky Christian College already were in operation and provided an approach to ministerial edu-

---

33. *Christian Standard,* December 17, 1921, p. 2997.

cation which conservatives found acceptable. Although each of these institutions struggled for survival, not knowing from one year to the next whether its doors could remain open, over thirty more Bible colleges came into existence within the next three decades. To list but a few of them together with their dates of beginning, they included: Manhattan Bible College in Kansas, 1927; Atlanta Christian College in Georgia, 1928; Ozark Bible College in Missouri, 1942; Lincoln Bible College in Illinois, 1944; Intermountain Bible College in Colorado, 1946; Roanoke Bible College in North Carolina, 1948; and Dallas Christian College in Texas, 1950. Of all these schools, only Milligan College received strong financial backing and gained standard accreditation for its degree programs.

Contrary to the traditional witness of Disciples and to sound academic practice, a surprising number of the Bible colleges required their professors to subscribe to a doctrinal statement. According to the constitution of Great Lakes Bible College in Michigan:

> . . . every trustee and teacher or other worker in any capacity must be a member of the church of Christ (undenominational) and must believe, without reservation, in the full and final inspiration of the bible to the extent that it is to him the infallible Word of God, and therefore the all sufficient rule of faith and life; in the deity and supreme authority of Christ; obedience to the Gospel; the edification of the church; and the restoration of its unity on the New Testament basis.[34]

Some of the other schools specified essentially the same requirements for their teachers and trustees. The unwavering opposition of Stone and the Campbells to creeds as tests of fellowship was lost in the strenuous effort to guarantee theological orthodoxy. It is obvious that the dissidents distorted the Disciples tradition when it served their purpose to do so.

Committed to Bible colleges which protected students from a clash of ideas in the academic marketplace, conservative restorationists disclaimed any relationship to the UCMS and therefore engaged in direct-support missionary

---

34. Quoted in Alfred T. DeGroot, *New Possibilities for Disciples and Independents* (St. Louis: The Bethany Press, 1963) pp. 65-66.

and benevolent work. Instead of using an agency of the church to develop and implement a global strategy for witness and mission, each congregation was free to channel contributions directly to particular individuals and stations. This procedure provided little or no opportunity for the careful screening of missionary candidates and for the coordination of their varied programs in an increasingly complex world.

Among the best-known directly supported missionaries in the 1920s and the 1930s were the Leslie Wolfes in the Philippines, the W. D. Cunninghams and M. B. Madden in Japan, Dr. and Mrs. S. G. Rothermel and the Harry Schaefers in India, the J. Russell Morses in Tibet, C. B. Titus and Simon B. Sibenya in South Africa, G. Vincent Hall in Jamaica, and Enrique T. Westrup in Mexico.

By 1949 the *Christian Standard* could count fifty-two direct-support missionaries at work abroad plus another seventy-one either on furlough or making plans for overseas service. The total number increased rapidly and reached 280 ten years later. To maintain the flow of gifts to their stations, these missionaries gave priority to heavy promotional activity among interested congregations. Lacking any alternative, they found it necessary to convert their furloughs into stateside fund-raising tours. In reporting on the nature and scope of their work for Christ, they seldom missed the chance to underscore their opposition to the practice of open membership.

Although the disaffected preachers and congregations—many of them—established their own instrumentalities for missions and benevolences, they referred to themselves as Disciples and continued to be listed in the yearbook of the denomination. This ambiguity marked the organized life of Disciples for many years. Generally distinct lines of separation had been drawn between the polarized factions, to be sure, but there was some overlapping. A few spokesmen on both sides still held out the hope that division could be averted. They were hard pressed to cite even the slightest evidence of reconciliation, however.

Sensing the need to bring the situation into clearer focus, Vernon M. Newland took it upon himself to issue a *Directory of the Ministry of the undenominational fellowship of Chris-*

tian Churches and Churches of Christ in 1955. Since Newland published the names of "loyal" preachers and the congregations they served (without, it should be noted, bothering to confirm the accuracy of his list), one prominent historian concluded that "1955 may be termed the birthday" of a new restorationist body in the United States.[35] If his judgment was premature, he anticipated a fresh outbreak of agitation and rancor in the 1960s.

Following a lengthy period of study and discussion, Disciples began the complex process of reorganizing into the Christian Church (Disciples of Christ). As a consequence, over 3,000 congregations with an estimated membership exceeding 750,000 took legal action to withdraw from the fellowship. Then in 1971 the *Yearbook of American Churches* was asked to list the "Christian Churches and Churches of Christ" as a separate religious communion in addition to the Christian Church (Disciples of Christ) and the Churches of Christ. The formal acknowledgment of division came as no surprise to anyone familiar with the tumultuous course of Disciples history in the twentieth century.

A loosely knit and splintered body of self-governing congregations, "Christian Churches and Churches of Christ" resist any threat—real or imagined—to their complete autonomy. Like the Churches of Christ, they champion the restoration of New Testament Christianity but cannot agree among themselves as to the precise details of "the ancient order of things." It is impossible to determine their numerical strength with any degree of confidence because no procedures have been devised and approved for the orderly gathering of reliable statistics. Their North American Christian Convention, held annually, maintains a full-time staff and attracts an attendance that sometimes reaches 10,000.

The "Christian Churches and Churches of Christ" claim to stand squarely in the great tradition of Stone and the Campbells. So do Disciples and Churches of Christ. Yet the existence of three distinct communions, sharing a common past, provides vivid testimony that the Stone-Campbell movement itself failed to overcome the forces of divisiveness let alone lead a fragmented church into a new day of unity.

---

35. Alfred T. DeGroot, *Church of Christ Number Two* (Privately published, 1956), p. 4.

16

THE GREAT DEPRESSION AND
RECOVERY

The energy, endless expansion, and easy optimism of the 1920s were dissipated by the faltering, contracting, and gloomy economic depression of the 1930s. Its effect was felt in all areas of the church's life. Congregations which had gone into debt, assuming that prosperity would make payment easy, floundered. Many could not pay their ministers. Regional and national agencies retrenched, cutting back programs. Not until World War II were some services restored. The Depression forced a deeper level of understanding onto the churches. Concern for social justice and for a means to overcome economic inequities led to a revival of the social gospel. By the mid-1930s Disciples reflected an interest in pacifism, and in the slogan, "Keep America Out of War," which was expressed by other American churches at the time. National institutions and agencies experienced considerable change and development throughout the 1930s. In the days preceding December 7, 1941, and Pearl Harbor, the Disciples gave evidence of a new maturity in their outlook. By the end of the war in 1945, Disciples were once more ready to move forward.

THE GREAT DEPRESSION

Few individuals were prepared for the intensity of the
social displacements of the Great Depression which began
with the stock market crash of October 1929. Americans
could not believe that the expansion and growth of the 1920s
were over. Many Disciples did not immediately recognize
what had happened, but by 1930 the impact of the Depression
was being felt throughout the churches. In near despair, the
editor of *The Christian-Evangelist* early in 1931 said, "We
should never have thought that anything like this would or
could come to America."[1]

By the summer of 1932 the Depression was having a
noticeable effect upon Disciples congregations. The classic
principle of church giving, "the first to be cut and the last to
be increased," was in operation. Attendance and offerings
were down, forcing a reduction in local expenses and missionary budgets. A few congregations had begun to employ
Christian education workers who were often the first to be
dropped from the staff. As congregations suffered reduced income, they ran deeply into debt. Mortgages went unpaid and
were sometimes foreclosed. Some congregations discontinued
a preaching ministry entirely or sought only weekend services
of a minister. On every hand congregations were behind in
salary payments to their ministers. Many ministers worked
at reduced salaries. No statistics reveal the total number of
ministers unemployed, but it must have been considerable.
Disciples ministerial salaries had not been high before 1929
and were lower than ever during the Depression.

The Depression continued into the mid-1930s without
much sign of economic recovery. All Disciples agencies and
institutions were affected, but the Depression was particularly hard on the United Christian Missionary Society.
During this period the vast majority of Disciples missions and
benevolence work was conducted through this agency. Actually the UCMS was somewhat in financial trouble before
the crash of October 1929. Loss of income was due to the
economic problems of the nation, but in some quarters the
"liberalism" of UCMS leaders was blamed. For whatever
reason, income was down and a slight budget cut was made

---

1. Editorial, *Christian-Evangelist*, February 5, 1931, p. 184.

beginning in July 1929. The leadership of the UCMS advised against panic as the deficit increased during the missionary year 1929-1930, and every effort was made to economize without curtailing program.

A total deficit of $712,133.95 had been accumulated by 1930. This reflected financial difficulties going back to the creation of the UCMS in 1920. Expansion had been entered into in many areas of work at home and abroad with the anticipation of increased giving which never materialized.[2] At the end of the summer of 1931 Stephen J. Corey (1873-1962), president of the UCMS, reported reduced staff and office personnel. Every possible economy in travel and promotional expense had been made. For some time the closing of the mission to Tibet had been contemplated. It was now begun. Missionaries were withdrawn from Jamaica and almost all the missionaries from the Philippines. Some missionaries were brought home from Japan, and the mission in Mexico continued with limited staff. Such reductions in missionary activity were made with the greatest reluctance.

In spite of all economies, the deficit of the UCMS by June 20, 1932, was $829,000 and reached its peak of $1,126,952.34 by December of that year. A decision was made by the administration of the UCMS that 1) the indebtedness would not be increased further and 2) salaries would be reduced at once, with most severe adjustments at the headquarters at Indianapolis. Beginning in 1932-1933 a greatly reduced budget, based on the previous year's receipts, was instituted. The UCMS followed this approach to budget-making for many years. Among the economies, headquarters staff was asked to work for two months each year without pay. Staff vacancies were not filled. Field staff and home missionary projects were greatly reduced.

Basically, the UCMS was financially sound. A difficult period of adjustment had been entered which was faced with courage and discipline. The UCMS went from an income of $2,918,056.76 in 1929 to its lowest income of $1,394,465.15 in 1935. It was 1936 before the income of the UCMS showed a gain over the previous year. Every effort was made to alert the churches to their responsibility, but congregations were in

---

2. William O. Paulsell, "The Disciples of Christ and the Great Depression" (unpublished Ph.D. thesis, Vanderbilt University, 1965), pp. 441 ff; 143 ff; 292 ff.

trouble themselves and could do little additional to help. In terms of money spent and total program at home and abroad, the UCMS by 1933 was back to 1912. Changes were made gradually and by June 1934 the worst was apparently over. Morale began to rise among staff and workers. Another sign of encouragement came when *World Call* magazine reported that it had overcome its own deficit and was in the black.

One result of the Depression was an increased concern for the relationship of the church to social reform. A renewal of interest in the social gospel was apparent, and the concept of governmental involvement in social change found general approval. At the International Conventions held annually throughout the Depression, a number of resolutions were introduced and passed regarding the state of the nation. In 1933 the convention approved a "Message on Social Justice" to the churches. This resolution sought to lead the churches to a deeper concern for social reform. In 1934 the International Convention at Des Moines passed a resolution on "Economic Justice" asking for guarantees against unemployment, a shorter work day, and old-age security.

The Depression profoundly affected the institutional life of the Disciples. It damaged all the institutions and agencies of the church. Two educational institutions were closed: Piedmont Christian Institute, Martinsville, Virginia, and Cotner College, Lincoln, Nebraska. Cotner reopened in 1946 as a foundation to provide religious studies for students attending the University of Nebraska. Nearly all Disciples colleges emerged from the Depression with heavy burdens of debt. Further effects of the Depression were felt in a major reorganization of the UCMS and the creation of new agencies to serve the churches.

NEW DEVELOPMENTS AND INSTITUTIONAL CHANGES

One new development was a renewed fellowship with Disciples in Great Britain and other English-speaking nations. American Disciples had known of churches in England with views similar to theirs ever since William Jones, minister of an independent congregation on Windmill Street, Finsbury Square, London, heard of the work in America in 1833. In 1835 he began publication of a British

Millennial Harbinger to disseminate the views of Alexander Campbell. The British Churches of Christ (Disciples) have had an annual conference since 1842 and missionary work overseas since 1893. Campbell himself visited the British churches in 1847. David Lloyd George, Prime Minister of Great Britain, was a Disciple. After the period in the 1880s when American Disciples ministers and evangelists had organized congregations in England, little contact had been maintained.

Disciples churches were brought to New Zealand from England in 1843, and have been there ever since. They cooperate through an annual conference and have had mission work in Africa. R. Garfield Todd, a New Zealand missionary, became Prime Minister of Southern Rhodesia. Disciples congregations in Australia date from Thomas Magarey's arrival from New Zealand in 1845. Working through annual conferences, the Australian Disciples have had mission work in India and other lands. Disciples missions began in South Africa in the last years of the nineteenth century. In more recent years Basil Holt (1902-) from the United States helped develop a number of congregations now joined with a united church.

Disciples from the various English-speaking nations became more aware of one another after the 1910 World Missionary Conference at Edinburgh and the ecumenical gatherings of the 1920s. In 1925 Jesse M. Bader became the first fraternal delegate from the International Convention to the annual conference of the British Churches of Christ (Disciples). Knowing of Disciples in at least thirty nations around the world, including those with mission work, he proposed to the British a world convention of Disciples. Encouraged by the British leaders, Bader visited New Zealand and Australian Disciples in 1926 to solicit their support for such a world gathering.[3]

Since 1930 was to be celebrated by Christians everywhere as the 1900th anniversary of Pentecost, this was the year chosen for the first World Convention of Churches of Christ. Disciples ignored the depression as plans were made for a combined International and World Convention to meet in

---

3. *Christian-Evangelist*, August 30, 1930, p. 1125.

October 1930 in Washington, D.C. Over 8,000 delegates attended the convention and enjoyed a well-planned program. From this first convention have come successive World Conventions in England, the United States, Australia, Canada, Scotland, Puerto Rico, and Mexico. Conventions, normally held at five-year intervals, are for the purpose of fellowship and inspiration. The undenominational fellowship of Christian Churches and the Churches of Christ cooperates with the Christian Church (Disciples of Christ) in planning, supporting, and enjoying the World Convention. In recent years special effort has been made to receive delegates from mission churches as well as English-speaking lands. Through a Study Committee topics of general interest are studied in preparation for the conventions and for study at breakfast groups. Governed by elected officers and an executive committee, there is a headquarters office and a general secretary under whose leadership conventions are arranged. Jesse M. Bader became the first secretary of the convention, serving full time after 1954.

One of the surprises of the 1930 convention was the appearance of a group of "Gospel Christians" from Russia announcing themselves as a part of the Disciples movement. They were descendants of a movement in Russia begun in the 1860s. Not since the General Convention at Louisville in 1912 had representatives of the All-Russian Union of Evangelical Christians visited American Disciples. The Russians represented congregations having similarities of origin, belief, and practice to the Disciples in the United States. During the Russian Revolution this group of "Gospel Christians" had been persecuted, but as the Russian situation began to stabilize, the Soviet government permitted a limited number of church organizations to resume operation. Shortly after the Russian delegation was received at Washington in 1930, most Protestants in Russia were put into one grouping to be known as "Union of Evangelical Christians and Baptists." There the remnants of the "Gospel Christians" remain.[4]

Changes came in this period to the Pension Fund of Disciples of Christ. A pension plan was sought that would meet the needs of a growing ministry adequately. A report by J. H. Mohorter made at the Cleveland International Conven-

---

4. McAllister, *Z. T. Sweeney: Preacher and Peacemaker,* pp. 80 ff.

tion in 1924 led to the passing of a resolution calling for a campaign to raise an "endowment Pension Fund." The resulting Commission on the Ministry, composed of 210 representative Disciples and chaired by Thomas C. Howe (1867-1934) of Indianapolis, met regularly over the next several years to outline what was needed in a pension plan. It was agreed that ministerial relief as well as pensions should be adequately funded. The new plan, in addition to a retirement pension, was to provide lump sum cash death benefits to the widow (or estate), widow pensions, minor-child pensions, and disability pensions. A campaign for $8,000,000 to underwrite such a plan was proposed, but the first task of the new Pension Fund was the enrollment of 2,500 ministers and congregations. Approved by the International Convention in April 1928 at Columbus, Ohio, the new plan was to be set in operation on January 1, 1931.

While the financial campaign failed because of the effects of the Depression, the churches and ministers became aware of the need. During the period 1930-1935, less than $3,500,000 was pledged and less than $1,000,000 in cash collected; nevertheless, the plan went into effect on schedule. Congregations particularly were slow to accept the idea of lifetime ministerial support. The plan was hampered by the lack of full funding, and these difficulties were compounded by the state of the economy. Recovery came only in the 1940s. Abram E. Cory, Bert Wilson (1877-1943), Paul G. Preston (1884-1966) and Francis E. Smith of the staff labored long and hard at the task of keeping pension reserves up to the level necessary to cover liabilities. The determination and persistence, especially of F. E. Smith, made it possible to maintain the Pension Fund.[5]

The original plan of a unified organization of all the agencies and boards of the Disciples was disrupted first by the legal requirement of the separation out of the Pension Fund in 1928. For some of the remaining boards it proved more difficult than anticipated to merge with the diversity of interests, programs, and funds represented in the UCMS. The well-intended merger of Disciples boards and agencies had brought into the UCMS functions which could be carried better by separate boards. After the removal of the Pension

5. William Martin Smith, *For the Support of the Ministry*, pp. 116-156.

Fund, two additional boards petitioned the International Convention to be released from the UCMS.

Leadership clashes, misunderstandings, and general dissatisfaction led the National Benevolent Association to withdraw in 1933 and to resume its status as a free agency reporting directly to the International Convention. The lack of sufficient income led the NBA to adopt the policy of making the support of its various institutions the responsibility of the congregations of the regions the institutions served. The International Convention also authorized the creation of the Board of Church Extension of Disciples of Christ as a separate agency in 1934. Its new charter, for the first time, made it possible to help congregations acquire parsonages. By 1946 the board was able to offer interest-free loans to congregations needing them.

For a brief time, from 1934 to 1938, the Board of Higher Education became a part of the UCMS. The board came into the UCMS as the Department of Higher Education in the Division of Christian Education. At the same time a separate and independent College Association of Disciples of Christ was created to become an academic consultation service to educational institutions. Dr. Harmon O. Pritchard served as secretary for both the department and the association. Experience proved that higher education did not really belong in a missionary society, and approval was given by the Denver International Convention in 1938 for its separation. The College Association was dissolved and the Board of Education of Disciples of Christ (now Board of Higher Education) was created. Dr. Harlie Smith (1900-1970) began service as secretary in April 1939 and served until 1941. He was succeeded by Dr. John L. Davis (1904-) who served during 1942-1946, and Dr. Henry Noble Sherwood (1882-1956) who served from 1946 to 1950. Following a reorganization in 1950, Dr. Harlie Smith returned and served until his retirement in 1969.

The removal of the work of the National Benevolent Association, the Board of Church Extension and the Board of Education necessitated a reorganization of the UCMS. In 1941 the work of the Department of Social Education and Social Action was divided into two parts. The Division of Home Missions, led by Willard M. Wickizer (1899-1974), accepted responsibility for social action by creating a Department of Social Welfare headed by James A. Crain (1886-1971) who served until 1954. The Department of Religious Education assumed responsibility for social education. The Department of Church Development and Evangelism had responsibility for evangelism, church maintenance, aid to small congregations moving toward self-support, the organization of new congregations, and a program for rural churches. The Division of Foreign Missions and the Division of Administration stayed much the same.

During this period the Division of Christian Education continued to develop a significant program under the leadership of Roy G. Ross. He was followed by Tilford T. Swearingen (1902-) in 1936. The age-group program begun by the American Christian Missionary Society was continued under the UCMS. The children's program expanded rapidly until the depression. State, provincial, and area committees developed programs when field workers and national staff were not available. Cynthia Pearl Maus continued in youth work after the creation of the UCMS. The highly successful young people's summer conference movement was begun in 1919 under her leadership. For a number of years, beginning at Memphis in 1926, a series of youth conventions was held in connection with the International Convention. Christian Endeavor continued to be the Disciples youth program until a new inclusive program known as Christian Youth Fellowship was proposed and adopted at the International Convention in 1938.

CYF was a program designed under the leadership of Myron T. Hopper (1903-1960) and the youth committee to develop young people in churchmanship. From the beginning it was extremely popular. At Lakeside, Ohio, in 1944 an International CYF Commission was organized with youth and adult leaders representative of the convention areas of the United States and Canada in attendance. For a number of years this racially inclusive commission met annually to plan the major themes and emphases of the Disciples youth program. By 1960 thirty-five states, provinces, and areas had organized regional commissions of CYF. Disciples young people participated in the ecumenical movement through the United Christian Youth Movement and its interdenominational camps, conferences, and committees.

The summer conference movement continued to grow. Based upon the concept of leadership education, it helped prepare young people for service in the church. A significant number of young people was recruited for Christian ministry through the conference movement. In 1939 a camping program for junior high young people was begun. Some areas began weekend gatherings for youth during the school year. These programs developed in 1941 into missionary study sessions known as World Fellowship Youth Meets. Work with college and university students was not neglected. Lura Aspinwall Hunt (1893-1955) became the first full-time national director of student work in 1934. She served until the withdrawal of higher education from the UCMS in 1938. Responsibility for student work was left with the Department of Religious Education, but because of financial difficulties only part-time staff leadership was available until 1945. At first a part of Christian Youth Fellowship, the Disciples Student Fellowship was formed in 1946 as an organization ministering to Disciples students on numerous campuses throughout the United States and Canada.

With the creation of the Department of Religious Education of the UCMS in 1920, the former Lesson Committee of the Disciples became known as the Curriculum Committee. Responsibility for missionary education was added in 1924. In a major reorganization of the Curriculum Committee in 1929, sections on children's work, youth work, student work, and adult work were created. Planning sections were provided also for leadership education, evangelism, stewardship education, and social education. The editors of the Local Church Curriculum Division of the Christian Board of Publication joined with the staff of the UCMS in the work of this committee. In 1953 a Curriculum and Program Council and a Christian Education Assembly were set up by the UCMS and the Christian Board of Publication to develop a total program of Christian education.

By the 1930s church leaders, including many Disciples ministers and missionaries, were taking a definite stand against war. This was undoubtedly a reaction to the uncritical support of the war effort given by the American churches during World War I. There was a firm determination to oppose participation in any future war, and to keep the churches from being used for war purposes. Pledge cards were circulated asking individuals to promote peace, to oppose war, and to prevent the cause of war by striving for a just social order. This position was encouraged by the Department of Social Education and Social Action of the UCMS and through editorials and articles in *The Christian-Evangelist* and *World Call.*

Interested individuals in several state and area peace organizations began to talk of a national organization. A forceful presentation at the Indiana Disciples convention in 1935 by persons interested in the peace movement led to the organization of the Disciples Peace Fellowship that same year during the International Convention at San Antonio. Interested individuals adopted a constitution, signed a covenant to work for world peace, and elected Joseph B. Hunter (b. 1886) of Little Rock, Arkansas, as first chairman.[6] Since that time the DPF has sought to educate youth and other persons in the issues involved in world peace. Cooperating with the Department of Social Education and Social Action and successor departments, DPF has advised on draft registration options, worked with conscientious objectors, and, in general, has served as a conscience for Disciples on world peace.

One immediate result of the organization of the DPF was the promotion of a Disciples Peace Poll. In 1936 the International Convention authorized such a poll to be directed by the Department of Social Education and Social Action. Over 16,304 ballots were received and tabulated. They came mostly from urban and metropolitan individuals and congregations. The polling revealed a strong pacifist opinion among those responding on questions of armament reduction, American neutrality, and personal attitudes toward participation in future wars. Kirby Page and other Disciples leaders wrote and campaigned for world peace.

The organization of the UCMS in 1920, intended to help reduce the multiplicity of appeals to the congregations for financial assistance, did little to relieve promotional pressures. The creation of a Commission on Budgets and Promotional Relationships by the International Convention

---

6. *Christian-Evangelist,* October 31, 1935, p. 1432. See also, Editorial, *Christian-Evangelist,* April 16, 1936, p. 499 and *Christian-Evangelist,* April 15, 1937, p. 493.

at Colorado Springs in 1923 was another attempt to solve the problem. The Commission, composed of ministers and laymen, sought to advise on good business practice, to monitor the budgets of the various agencies, and to encourage cooperation in promotional efforts. All organizations cooperating in and through the International Convention were asked to submit their proposed budgets for review by the Commission. The printed program of the International Convention each year carried annual audited reports of the agencies for the information of the churches.

Cooperation in budget-making and promotion proved advantageous. By the time of the 1931 International Convention held at Wichita, Kansas, further unification seemed possible. A study commission was appointed which drafted a set of cooperative promotional principles and reported to the International Convention meeting at Indianapolis in 1932. These principles were endorsed by the Pittsburgh convention in 1933. By the time of the Des Moines convention in 1934, the proposed plan had been approved by seven national boards, twenty-three state missionary societies, and five colleges. Unified Promotion came into being as a cooperative promotional and distribution agency on July 1, 1935. Clarence O. Hawley (1890-1963) was called as the first director of Unified Promotion. After that date the major portion of the money obtained by the agencies reporting to the International Convention was raised through Unified Promotion. Unified Promotion achieved what the creation of the UCMS had failed to accomplish: the joint promotion of Disciples causes.

Not all cooperative agencies reporting to the International Convention joined in Unified Promotion. Some institutions, boards, and state societies preferred to continue on their own, necessitating the continuation of the Commission on Budgets and Promotional Relationships, which continued to review askings and receipts. Later a Board of Review, separate from the Commission on Budgets and Promotional Relationships, was formed to review the programs and promotional plans of participating agencies.

Funds at first were distributed to member agencies of Unified Promotion on the basis of a five-year history of giving established prior to the creation of Unified Promotion. After

1950 distribution of funds was based upon annual allocations made by the Commission on Brotherhood Finance. This commission was created by Unified Promotion to review the askings of member agencies and to make allocations on the basis of need and anticipated receipts. Unified Promotion continued until 1974 when the Church Finance Council was organized. Unified Promotion was an effective means by which most of the national and state boards, societies, and many of the colleges cooperated in their appeals to the churches. Its leadership was respected and accepted by the churches. Each agency joined in the total promotion of all the causes, sharing staff time and promotional expense.

For years it had been recognized that the program of the Division of Home Missions of the UCMS and the programs of the various state and provincial missionary societies had many interests in common. This common concern was recognized in 1938 with the creation of the Home and State Missions Planning Council of the Disciples of Christ under the forward-looking leadership of Willard M. Wickizer. An interagency organization made up of representative national and area workers, ministers, and other interested individuals, the Council met annually. The work of the Council was divided among nine standing committees: Local Church Life, Evangelism, Effective Ministry, Town and Country Church, Christian Service, Missionary Policy and Strategy, World Outreach, Urban Work, and Stewardship. The Home and State Missions Planning Council served effectively until 1972, giving innovative leadership in local church program and in home missions program for the Disciples. Out of the work of this Council grew a new understanding of church mission.

In the late 1800s suggestions had been made for some form of preservation of historical materials of the Disciples. The organization of a historical society to promote interest in the Disciples heritage was proposed by Errett Gates as early as 1901.[7] Nearly forty years were to pass, however, before concrete action was taken at the International Convention meeting in Richmond, Virginia, in 1939 when a committee was appointed to discuss the formation of a society. As a

---

7. Errett Gates, *Christian-Evangelist*, September 12, 1901, p. 1170. SEE also *Discipliana*, Jan. 1943, p. 36 for Gates' account of this attempted organization.

result of the committee report the St. Louis convention in 1941 approved the constitution for the Disciples of Christ Historical Society with J. Edward Moseley (1910-1973) as president. Its purpose was to stimulate interest in the collection, preservation, and use of various materials relating to the Stone-Campbell movement.[8] Its temporary headquarters were located at Culver-Stockton College, Canton, Mo. Claude E. Spencer (1898-), the librarian of the college, was elected curator of the society. From the start materials began to pour into the new organization. By 1946 the society had taken over the administration of the Henry Barton Robison collection of the college. As the materials of the society and its work grew, it became apparent a new home would have to be found. Disciples leaders at Nashville, Tennessee, in 1951 secured the use of space in the Joint University Libraries (sponsored by Peabody College, Scarrit College, and Vanderbilt University) to house the collection and raised $50,000 to assist DCHS in relocating there in April 1952. The Robison collection remained at Culver-Stockton College. However, a few years later DCHS received many volumes and other material from the collection on a permanent loan. Through the generosity of the Phillips family of Western Pennsylvania a building program was begun in 1955 and in 1958 the Thomas W. Phillips Memorial building was dedicated near the university center section in Nashville.

One of the speakers at the World Convention in 1930 was Dr. Ludwig Von Gerdtel of Germany. By means of his own study he had come to views similar to those of the Disciples. After the convention he remained in America and taught at Butler University, during which time he formed the German Evangelistic Society. In 1932 he attempted to return to Germany, but because of the Nazis he was unable to stay and once again lectured briefly at Butler. The work was reorganized as the European Evangelistic Society in 1943. The purpose of the organization was to have conversation in a university setting with German scholars in applying the New Testament to present-day European culture. Earl Stuckenbruck and his wife opened a work at Tübingen in 1946 where ground for a seminary was purchased and a hostel and office

---

8. *Christian-Evangelist,* May 15, 1941, p. 591. See also, *Christian-Evangelist,* April 3, 1946, p. 346 and *Christian-Evangelist,* December 12, 1951, p. 1200.

Thomas W. Phillips
Memorial

were maintained. Annual reports of the European Evangelistic Society have indicated a continuing interest in the services of the society.

As a result of the many organizational changes which came about after the Depression, and the realization of changing Disciples practices, the urgent need for a careful reexamination of the Disciples position with reference to their earlier principles became apparent. The International Convention meeting at Des Moines in 1934 authorized a standing Commission on Restudy of the Disciples of Christ. Commission personnel included leading ministers and laypersons and represented almost every shade of opinion. The Commission submitted to the International Convention in 1946 a report outlining the principle areas of tension. Diverse views were presented and possibilities for the future were suggested. The work of the Commission was considered closed after its 1949 report to the convention as Disciples became involved in other postwar developments.

MINISTERIAL STATUS AND OUTSTANDING LEADERS

During the 1930s and 1940s the quality of academic preparation of Disciples ministers improved steadily. The attendance at interdenominational and graduate centers of learning by students for the ministry came to have a positive bearing on the outlook of the Disciples and their institutions. For over three decades several hundreds of Disciples ministers, educators, and leaders had received their education at such institutions as Yale Divinity School, Union Theological Seminary, the Divinity School of the University of Chicago, and Hartford Theological Seminary. Disciples colleges and seminaries, in the meanwhile, had been lifting their standards. By 1940 it was assumed that a ministerial candidate would have an undergraduate degree and three years of graduate seminary education before ordination. At that time it was estimated that over half of the ordained ministry of the Disciples had attended seminary.

Outstanding ministers and leaders of this period included Raphael H. Miller, Washington, D. C.; Lin D. Cartwright (1886-), St. Louis; Daisy June Trout (1882-1956), Indianapolis; Clarence E. Lemmon (1888-1963), Columbia, Missouri; Pearl H. Welshimer (1873-1957), Canton, Ohio; Edgar DeWitt Jones, Detroit; Harry B. McCormick (1884-1974), Cleveland; Alonzo W. Fortune, Lexington, Kentucky; Hampton Adams (1897-1965), St. Louis; Edward Scribner Ames, Chicago; Winfred E. Garrison, Chicago; L. Nathaniel D. Wells, (1876-1963), Dallas; Leroy D. Anderson (1876-1961), Fort Worth; Isaac J. Cahill (1868-1945), Cleveland; Homer W. Carpenter (1880-1964), Louisville; Daniel W. Morehouse (1876-1941), Des Moines; and Roger T. Nooe (1881-1969), Nashville.

Laymen and laywomen who made significant contributions in the 1930s and 1940s included Thomas C. Howe (1867-1934), Indianapolis; Edward S. Jouett (b. 1863), Louisville; Oreon E. Scott (1871-1956), St. Louis; Charles M. Rodefer (1881-1965), Bellaire, Ohio; Mrs. Myrtle S. Morehouse, Des Moines; Mrs. Leila Rothenburger (1881-1942), Indianapolis; Frank Buttram (1886-1966), Oklahoma City; James R. McWane (1869-1933), Birmingham, Alabama; Wilber V. Crew (1868-1949), Dayton, Ohio; G. Carlton Hill (1901-), Cincinnati; William H. Book, Jr. (1898-1965), Indianapolis; and Harry Hines (1886-1954), Dallas, Texas.

During this period dedicated leaders were serving the National Christian Missionary Convention. P. H. Moss (1880-1935), long-time national director of religious education among black Disciples, served until his death in 1935. That same year R. H. Peoples became general secretary of the National Convention. From 1915 to 1938 Mrs. Rosa Brown

Bracy served as the first national secretary of Negro Disciples women's organizations. These leaders, along with other black Disciples, worked hard to give encouragement to the programs, conventions, and congregations of the Negro Disciples. Social and economic conditions were such during this period that only those with deep commitment were able to challenge the people.

In every state, province, and area where Disciples congregations were serving, thousands of similarly dedicated men and women ministers and laity, black and white gave unstintingly of their time and substance to serve Christ and the church.

NATIONAL RECOVERY AND THEOLOGICAL RENEWAL

World Call, along with other Disciples publications, approved of church involvement in social reform during the years of the Depression. At first *The Christian-Evangelist* supported the policies of President Herbert Hoover, but after he left office the tendency was to criticize his administration.[9] The editorial policy of *The Christian-Evangelist* and *World Call* changed in favor of the program of President Franklin D. Roosevelt after he assumed office. While deploring Roosevelt's attitude toward prohibition (he wanted it repealed), they praised him for restoring confidence and optimism to a depressed nation. Frederick D. Kershner, then a columnist for *The Christian-Evangelist,* frequently supported the New Deal in his writings.

By the time of the Depression, the Disciples had been discussing social issues for several generations. It was only natural that their publications would appraise and evaluate the social issues of the Depression and the New Deal in relation to Christian faith. As the nation slowly recovered from the worst economic effects of the Depression, Disciples leaders found themselves advocating and supporting a variety of programs to aid the economically depressed. The Civilian Conservation Corps, a program to provide employment to young men in reforestation, conservation, national park and flood control projects, was approved with the reservation that it not be made a part of universal military training. Disciples

---

9. Paulsell, pp. 154 ff; 162 ff; and 236-255.

favored aid to farmers. They praised the Tennessee Valley Authority, a program involved in building dams and selling electric power to rural areas as well as economic and social planning for communities in the valley of the Tennessee River. Disciples spoke out in general on the economic and social problems related to the Depression. Their great fear was not the threat of a move toward socialism, but the possibility that a fascist order would arise. They insisted on the right of all sides of an issue to be heard.

Even as the nation was recovering from the effects of the Depression, important developments were taking place in theology. The thought of a German theologian, Karl Barth, was introduced into America in 1929 at the beginning of the Depression. Within a few years his concepts of a transcendent God and man's total depravity were being discussed widely in academic circles. Barth emphasized the sinful nature of man and man's inability to do anything to save himself. His system of thought came to be known as "neo-orthodoxy," a return to orthodox Reformation theology, but with the addition of social concern. Barth's theology and teachings, while influencing many denominations, never really excited the Disciples. Due to the stimulus of the Depression, however, there was a revival in the 1930s of the social gospel.

More appealing to some Disciples was the theology of Reinhold Niebuhr. A pastor in Detroit during the labor controversies of the 1920s, Niebuhr in 1928 became a professor of Applied Christianity in New York's Union Theological Seminary. Niebuhr in his personal experience shifted from an easy-going, naive idealism to a stern, complex realism. For Niebuhr it was important that man face the facts of life, including the fact of sin and evil. The promises of God should mean more to man than the delusion of self-sufficiency. One of his first books, *Moral Man and Immoral Society,* published in 1932, called for man to make an honest appraisal of his condition. A later book, *The Irony of American History,* pointed toward man's present posture. Niebuhr called for a reevaluation of history's forces and man's true tendencies. There are certain unavoidable facts of history: war, greed, exploitation, prejudice, poverty, cruelty, injustice, and lust. Rarely is the choice before us a clear one between good and evil, but rather it is an ambiguous one between lesser evils, between degrees of violence and toward an ethic of proximate justice. The Christian view of man is that of both angel and beast. Because he is a child of nature, man tempers his optimism; because he is a child of God, he escapes from cynicism.

The theological renewal which began in the seminaries during the 1930s had barely begun to penetrate the ministry and the churches when World War II broke upon America. The task of theological reconstruction was delayed until after the war. The thought of Niebuhr did inform a sufficient number of American and Disciples ministers and churches so that the mistakes of World War I were avoided. American Christianity in general, and Disciples in particular, gave full support to the war effort, and looked upon the war not as a crusade of godly forces but as the lesser of two evils.

War began in Europe in September 1939. The question in the mind of many Disciples ministers was what the future would bring. Opinion was divided; some ministers and leaders advocated neutrality; others were for early intervention; still others were not certain. The International Convention of 1939, influenced by a general interest in neutrality among church people, established procedures whereby conscientious objectors among Disciples could enroll with their home congregations. Draft boards could then certify them to Civilian Public Service camps for alternate service. That they were to be supported by church funds caused some tension.[10] A series of twelve convocations was held across the United States in 1941. National leaders addressed these meetings and led discussions on the question of what the churches could do to meet the religious needs of people in a time of national defense.

DISCIPLES AND WORLD WAR II

After the Japanese attack on Pearl Harbor in 1941 the United States became directly involved in World War II. Disciples reacted along with all Americans to support the nation in its need. America, under President Franklin Roosevelt's leadership, earlier had entered into a period of

10. *World Call*, April, 1940, p. 42. See also, *Disciples of Christ Year Book, 1941*, Indianapolis: Year Book Publication Committee, p. 8.

military preparation. Several millions of young Americans were drafted into the armed forces. The churches in various areas of the country felt the effects of these dislocations of people as military camps and war industries were built. The new theological perspective so recently introduced by Reinhold Niebuhr and other theologians alerted churchmen to Christian responsibility. There was a new attitude toward the church's participation in war which emphasized not only national need but also human values.

Among the first Disciples to suffer upon America's entry into the war were the missionaries and their families in foreign lands. At one time there were sixteen men and women and three children interned in various countries. The first to arrive home were the members of the W. H. Edwards family in 1941, having survived the sinking of the *S. S. Athenia* on which they were first traveling. Lois Anna Ely (1888-1972) arrived from China and detention camp on the *S. S. Gripsholm* in 1943. The Allen Hubers, the Harry Fongers (and son Burton), and the Joseph Smiths (and son Freddie) were interned in the Philippines for the duration of the war. Burton Fonger died in prisoner of war camp in 1944. Oswald J. Goulter (1890-), interned in China by the Japanese, was one of the last to be released in 1945. Many accounts of Christian perseverance and heroism have been told as a result of these experiences. Ultimately all Disciples missionaries trapped by the war were released or repatriated.[11]

The Chaplaincy Endorsement Commission of the International Convention of Disciples of Christ was the clearing house for Disciples ministers seeking to serve as chaplains in World War II. Nearly 400 Disciples chaplains served in the Army (which at that time provided chaplains for the Air Force), and approximately 60 chaplains served in the Navy as Disciples sought to fill their quotas. The Chaplaincy Commission served on a voluntary basis with Carrol C. Roberts (1896-1973) as chairman. The congregation of the Ninth Street Christian Church at Washington, D.C., provided office facilities for the commission.

In January 1941, as the nation prepared for war, Disciples formed a Committee on War Services to serve the needs of

---

11. *Disciples of Christ Year Book, 1945,* Indianapolis: Year Book Publication Committee, pp. 8; 19; 38 ff. and 87.

the church during the emergency. This committee directed the appropriation of funds to sixty-six congregations in areas where military camps were located to help develop programs for men and women in the armed forces. Financial aid was granted to fifty-one congregations in war industrial areas to assist persons displaced by the war. A secretary was provided for the Chaplaincy Endorsement Commission. Assistance was rendered Disciples chaplains in publishing a chaplains' news bulletin, in helping with correspondence and reading materials, and in making field communion sets available.

The Committee on War Services also gave assistance to Japanese-American Disciples who were interned by the United States government in camps located in Arkansas, Arizona, California, Colorado, Utah, and Wyoming. The committee cooperated with the War Relocation Authority in finding new homes for these uprooted people. The committee also provided the means to keep these Disciples in touch with each other through a newsletter, as well as providing a number of scholarships to Disciples young people of Japanese descent. The Committee on War Services was renamed the Committee on Military and Veterans Services in 1946 and functioned in its new task for several years.

Two committees were formed to aid Disciples who refused to participate in the war because of religious convictions. A Committee on Conscientious Objectors worked with the more than fifty Disciples young men assigned to Civilian Public Service projects as conscientious objectors. A Committee on Ministerial Exemption worked with young men seeking exemption from military service as ministerial students.

In 1941 the Disciples were in the fourth year of a Five Year Program of Advance, a program of stewardship emphasis. The fifth year of the program was revised to become an Emergency Million drive to raise an extra million dollars to provide special services for wartime needs. The idea was presented to the International Convention at St. Louis in May 1941 before America's entry into the war. The fund, as proposed and approved, was to be used to clear all Disciples agencies of debt, to undergird a forward-looking program, and to assist congregations affected by the war. The Emergency Million for Life and Work project was under the direction of

Unified Promotion with C. O. Hawley as director. Originally to be completed between July 1, 1941, and June 30, 1942, it was not until June 30, 1943, that it could be announced that the fund was "over the top" at $1,052,525.[12] The money raised was applied to its agreed upon purposes immediately.

In 1943 Disciples accepted a financial goal of $250,000 to meet the needs of the Committee on War Services and a newly organized interdenominational Church Committee on Relief and Reconstruction. The Church Committee on Relief and Reconstruction had been formed by American Protestant denominations to give assistance to refugees and orphans of the war, war prisoners, relief for China, and orphaned missions. The week of February 20-27, 1944, was proposed as the time when Disciples everywhere would observe a Week of Compassion during which the funds for these causes would be raised. The proposal was enthusiastically received and the goal successfully underwritten.[13] Thereafter, the Week of Compassion became a permanent part of the program of the Disciples.

As America moved into the third year of war, Disciples and other Christian groups began to consider the shape of the postwar world. Questions were formulated as to how the world could be reconstructed so as to prevent future wars. Much discussion and interest were expressed in a possible organization of the nations of the world to aid and protect weaker nations and to help keep the peace. In the fall of 1943 it was announced that Drake University would join with a minister's study group known as the Midwestern Seminar-Lecture Committee in sponsoring a lectureship and conference. Set for the first week of February 1944, the theme of the conference was to be "The Church and the New World Mind."[14] Limited to no more than 300 delegates because of scarce hotel accommodations and wartime travel restrictions, the conference drew its full quota of delegates. It was composed of ministers, laypersons, educators, young people, and seminarians.

Lecturers of national reputation addressed the conference, held on the campus of Drake University and in University

12. *Christian-Evangelist,* July 3, 1941, p. 785 and August 4, 1943, p. 753.
13. *Christian-Evangelist,* November 24, 1943, p. 1132 and March 9, 1944, p. 142.
14. *Christian-Evangelist,* October 27, 1943, p. 999. See also, *Christian-Evangelist,* November 10, 1943, p. 1093.

Christian Church. Among the speakers were Rufus Jones, Haverford College; William Ernest Hocking, Harvard University; Cleo W. Blackburn, Flanner House, Indianapolis; Georgia Harkness, Garrett Theological Seminary; M. Searle Bates, Union Theological Seminary, New York; and Walter W. Van Kirk, Federal Council of Churches. William F. Rothenburger (1874-1959), minister of the Third Christian Church in Indianapolis, served as director of the conference and assisted in the publication of the lectures. John L. Davis prepared a study guide to accompany the book for study classes and nationwide convocations planned as a follow-up of the conference. The spirit of much of the Disciples leadership was captured in an editorial in *The Christian-Evangelist* prior to the conference. The editor said,

It is believed that unless the church people are set to the task of informing themselves on the opportunities and responsibilities of the church toward a world of brotherhood, the postwar world is sure to lapse into the same pagan system of competition and selfishness which has already precipitated two world wars.[15]

In 1944, the last full year of the war, a Christian Literature Commission was formed for the purpose of helping to prepare citizens and Christians for a new kind of world, for postwar rehabilitation and enduring peace.[16] It was believed Christians could help in fashioning and directing the new world coming into being. There was a reaching out for God, for the fulfillment of life, and for assurance of the things of the Spirit. Considered a part of the church's postwar planning, a Christian Literature Week was promoted to be observed by the congregations. A packet of materials was sent out by the commission suggesting that a study of the Bible be revived in home, church, church school, women's societies, and youth groups. The theme, "You Are What You Read," recurred for years. In later Christian Literature Weeks the establishment of church libraries was encouraged and the purchase of books relating to Christian faith and experience was promoted. A Week of Observance was begun in 1950 and a permanent commission was formed in 1959 which served until 1973. It

15. Editorial, *Christian-Evangelist*, November 24, 1943, p. 1143.
16. *Christian-Evangelist*, September 13, 1944, p. 880.

was transferred to the Church Libraries and Christian Readers' Department of the Christian Board of Publication.

With the end of the war in August 1945 Disciples had recovered from the "Great Depression" of the 1930s and had begun to look forward toward a new world order. Disciples played their part in supporting the formation of the United Nations later that year. Economic recovery made possible the projection of plans for institutional and program development thought impossible of attainment a few years previously. The International Convention and the other agencies of the church were stronger than they had been in many years. Delayed building programs of congregations and institutions could now proceed. Some concern was expressed for the adjustment of returning servicemen to civilian life, but in general the transition went smoothly from a wartime society to peace. It was to be mainly in the area of denominational structure, however, that the Disciples were to develop in the coming decades.

17

POSTWAR PROSPERITY OF CHURCH
AND NATION

The period immediately following World War II was a time of prosperity for the church. Idealism was somehow rekindled in the process of bringing the war to a conclusion. Most Americans felt as though a new opportunity was being given to create a better world. This spirit was reflected in the plans and developments within the church. Disciples began to make operative long-postponed plans in building and program. The ecumenical movement flowered in a wave of international goodwill. Minorities demanded and received recognition. Theological discussion was resumed among the churches. Disciples especially were to wrestle with theological renewal. There was a resurgence of interest in and support for Christian higher education.

A CRUSADE FOR A CHRISTIAN WORLD

As World War II ended, Disciples leaders considered a challenge to the churches that would take them forward in many program areas. Remembering the successful Men and Millions Movement thirty years previously, leaders desired to bring Disciples to a new appreciation of their origins and their mission. The various Disciples agencies named a "Committee of Twenty-five" (later expanded to thirty-three persons) to plan a cooperative program to encompass the total life of the churches. A new commitment to the faith, life, and work of the church universal caught the imagination of those who met at Indianapolis in May 1946.[1] Approval for such a program was given by the International Convention meeting in August at Columbus, Ohio.

The name given the program was "A Crusade for a Christian World." This title caught the feeling of renewed expectation of the immediate postwar era. Over the three-year period from 1947 to 1950 emphasis was given to the organization of 200 new congregations, the securing of new members, and recruitment for the ministry and mission fields. Tithers were encouraged to contribute to an overall financial goal of $14,-000,000 over and above regular offerings. The largest program ever attempted by the Disciples, the Crusade was incorporated and operated under its own bylaws. L. N. D. Wells (1876-1963) pastor of East Dallas Christian Church, Dallas, Texas, was made chairman and Paul G. Preston, executive secretary of the Pension Fund, was elected chairman of the administrative board. C. O. Hawley of Unified Promotion served as executive secretary of the Crusade. In June 1947 G. Gerald Sias (1906-), minister at Danville, Illinois, became general director of the Crusade.[2]

As A Crusade for a Christian World got under way, still another development took place which would greatly affect the future of the Disciples. Under the auspices of the Home and State Missions Planning Council, Orman L. Shelton (1895-1959), dean of the School of Religion, Butler University, wrote an important book entitled *The Church Functioning Effectively*. Published in 1946, it outlined an efficient reorganization of the local church board.[3] Most Disciples congregations still had a traditional board composed of elders and deacons. Shelton proposed seven "functional" committees: membership development, worship and devotional life, Christian education, missionary outreach, finance and

---

1. *Christian-Evangelist*, May 15, 1946, p. 484.
2. *Christian-Evangelist*, October 2, 1946. p. 984. See also, January 8, 1947, p. 32; January 15, 1947, p. 73; and April 16, 1947, p. 387.
3. Orman L. Shelton, *The Church Functioning Effectively* (St. Louis: Christian Board of Publication, 1946).

stewardship education, evangelism, and property. These committees would enlist the members of the congregation and would be responsible to an executive board made up of chairmen of the various committees. A general board composed of elders, deacons, and the executive board would meet from time to time to give general oversight to the work of the congregation. The Home and State Missions Planning Council later published manuals on each of the functional committees and their duties. Widely accepted from the first, the functional approach to church program was adopted within a short time by a large number of Disciples congregations.

By means of the promotional activity of the staff of A Crusade for a Christian World and aided by the popularity of Shelton's functional plan, many of the goals of the Crusade were reached. At a breakfast meeting at Indianapolis on April 5, 1951, attended by representatives of state, area, and national agencies, the conclusion of the Crusade was announced. Over $8,000,000 had been raised for the causes cooperating in Unified Promotion with an additional $2,000,-000 to come from "accepted goals." A Crusade for a Christian World, while not entirely successful in all its aims, had given a lift to the life of the denomination.[4] There was a resurgence of Christian life among the congregations. Out of the experience of the Crusade came the idea to plan programs for a decade at a time.

EXPANDED SERVICES

The work of the International Convention, meeting annually, became even more important after World War II. This body was advisory to the agencies and boards of the denomination and to the congregations. It provided inspiration and fellowship for ministers, leaders, and laypersons, and its work was increasingly heavy. With the retirement of Graham Frank in 1946 as part-time general secretary, the decision was made to create a full-time office for the convention. Assessments made against agencies, boards, and societies reporting to the International Convention assured adequate financing. Gaines M. Cook (1897-), state secretary

---

4. *Christian-Evangelist*, April 25, 1951. p. 399.

of Ohio was called as executive secretary; Harry B. Holloway (b. 1879) of Indianapolis became business manager and Gertrude Dimke was office secretary. Holloway had served as transportation secretary previously. Offices were opened at Indianapolis in September 1946,[5] and the new incorporation was approved at the Cincinnati convention in October 1949. From time to time attempts were made to have the convention meet biennially but the preference for an annual meeting continued. A Department of Public Relations was established in 1954 to assist in keeping the churches informed.

The convention, meeting at Des Moines in 1956, changed its name from International Convention of Disciples of Christ to the International Convention of Christian Churches (Disciples of Christ).[6] After 150 years the question of name was still before the Disciples. "Christian Churches" and "Disciples of Christ" had been used interchangeably for many years, and the new name was thought to "preserve our identity." The main function of the convention office was to plan and carry out the annual assembly, to represent the denomination in ecumenical concerns, and to supervise the publication of the annual Year Book. The public relations office regularly sent out information about activities of the Christian Churches (Disciples of Christ). The International Convention remained the one place where every area of church program and organization met.

During this period Disciples achieved a new level of congregational worship in comparison with earlier times. Most of the church buildings erected were architecturally respectable and aesthetically pleasing. Under the auspices of the Home and State Missions Planning Council, *Christian Worship: A Service Book* was published in 1953. Compiled by G. Edwin Osborn of the seminary faculty of Phillips University, this service book standardized a form of worship in hundreds of congregations. Ministers generally began to wear pulpit gowns and the ministerial cutaway coat (standard dress in city congregations as late as the 1940s) went into mothballs. Pastoral counseling became a major concern and ministers received clinical pastoral education.

---

5. *Christian-Evangelist*, October 2, 1946. p. 985.
6. *Christian-Evangelist*, October 24, 1956. p. 1068.

The Disciples had never developed an assembly ground such as the Presbyterians have at Montreat or the Baptists at Ridgecrest in North Carolina. Frank Dixon, Leslie T. New, and Hubert Jarvis, laymen of North Carolina, had such a dream for the Christian Churches (Disciples of Christ). The Southeastern Christian Assembly was incorporated in 1948, and in 1949 the International Convention voted to accept the assembly as an agency of the convention. A total of 649 acres of land was purchased in the mountains of North Carolina near the town of Black Mountain, and at the International Convention at Portland, Oregon, in 1953 the name "Christmount" was given the assembly. The first executive secretary of the Christmount Christian Assembly was Dr. Howard S. Hilley (1892-1963), retired president of Atlantic Christian College. Slowly and with care the site was developed to include a dining hall, cottages, private residences, a library and, later, a guest house. Roads, water, and sewerage developments were added as funds became available. A paper, *Christmount Voice,* was begun in 1953. Over the years the assembly has sponsored a varied program of spiritual development including an annual Christmount Week, church conventions, conferences, and a lay school.[7]

NEED FOR PROGRAM COORDINATION RECOGNIZED

A Crusade for a Christian World had revealed impingements between general agencies and state and area societies. Growing out of that experience came the desire of the denomination's leaders to find a way to deal with the overlapping of work between the agencies which the Crusade had made obvious. The International Convention, meeting at San Francisco in 1948, set up a committee to make recommendations for the consideration of the agencies regarding coordination of programs. The committee, reporting to the convention held at Cincinnati in October 1949, recommended the formation of a Council of Agencies to deal with these problems. The Council was to be responsible to the International Convention and to be composed of representatives of the various agencies reporting to the convention.

7. *History of Christmount Christian Assembly,* ed. by Christine W. Davis, n.p., 1973, pp. 5 ff.

Membership in the Council was mandatory upon agencies and institutions reporting directly or indirectly to the convention. The Council was formed. Its first task at its initial meeting in 1950 was the supervision and development of a Long-Range Program for the decade of 1950-1960. The Council met biennially and dealt with the many areas of tension between the various convention agencies. Slowly the societies and institutions of the Christian Churches (Disciples of Christ) became aware of the total program of the church.

A further move toward program coordination came with the formation of the National Church Program Coordinating Council. Created in 1949 and beginning operation in 1950, this council widened the scope of program planning. Christian education, higher education, women's organizations, and stewardship education were not included in the Home and State Missions Planning Council. Congregations were burdened with an overabundance of materials and coordination was needed, especially in the areas of calendar and leadership. The National Church Program Coordinating Council was composed of representatives from all groups planning programs for congregational use. For the first time Disciples had a means to review all program plans, to seek agreement for a combined effort of program development and to eliminate conflicts in program calendar.

Just as the Christian Woman's Board of Missions had challenged Disciples women to extraordinary accomplishments between 1874 and 1920, the United Christian Missionary Society developed their interest further. By the end of World War II many leaders saw that Disciples women were ready to take additional steps toward a unified program. Missionary organization was but one of the several types of service in which women were interested. Parallel in development with missionary organizations had been Ladies' Aid Societies, Business and Professional Women's Guilds, and, after 1912, Women's Councils. First developed by Mrs. Ralph S. Latshaw (1865?-1939) of Kansas City, Missouri, the Women's Council concept sought to unite all the women of a given congregation in six phases of study. They were devotional life, evangelism, social action, Christian family life, stewardship, and missions. Women's Councils grew out of the recognition that women desired to work in the church in a wider perspective than was possible in a missionary society alone.

By 1947 several of the state and area women's missionary societies were discussing the possibilities of a joint board composed of the missionary societies, departments of religious education, and the women's missionary societies. There was already cooperation in many instances between the boards in children's and in youth work. While unification of the boards was not to be considered for several years, this was further recognition of the desire of women to participate in the total life of the church. Another movement in the churches that was leading women to a new form of program participation was the adoption of the functional committee approach to local church organization which had been developed by Orman L. Shelton. In the functional committee approach, women were to be involved in all phases of the church's program. As increasing numbers of congregations adopted the functional organization, it was only natural that within a short time Disciples women would seek a new form of organization for their work.

The program for Disciples women which emerged took the name Christian Women's Fellowship. A committee composed of state and area secretaries and presidents of women's work from across the United States and Canada met at Turkey Run State Park, Indiana, in January 1949. Its purpose was to plan and work toward what they hoped would be a more effective organization of women. As their plan developed CWF was to help women in Christian living and was to have three emphases: worship, study, and service. All women of the church were considered to be a part of the organization. A constitution was adopted. A committee to write an organizational manual met early in 1950 and soon published guidance for local groups. CWF was warmly received nearly everywhere, and a favorable response was immediate in most congregations.

As with the creation of the UCMS in 1920, some women's groups had chosen not to participate in the new program. While the number of organized women's groups in the United States and Canada declined in this period, the strength of the women's program continued to grow. As state, provincial, and area CWF organizations were formed, the Department of

Missionary Organizations of the UCMS became the Department of Christian Women's Fellowship. Another consequence of the desire of women to move beyond missionary concern was that beginning July 1, 1957, the state and national CWF participated in the general support of all agencies of the church by their gifts to Unified Promotion. Regional goals for Unified Promotion were made and accepted, underwriting the total program of the church. In 1960 the women's organizations of the National Christian Missionary Convention became a part of the CWF.

As early as 1952, Jessie M. Trout proposed the idea of a world gathering of Disciples women.[8] A fellowship to include women of Great Britain, Australia, New Zealand, India, Thailand, the Philippines, and Japan would give encouragement and inspiration to all Disciples. In a called meeting at the International Convention at Portland, Oregon, in July 1953, an International CWF comprising women of the United States and Canada was launched with Freda Putnam of Ohio as president. Plans for a world gathering of women were discussed. At the World Convention held at Toronto in 1955, with women from twenty nations present, the World CWF was organized. Hilda Green of England was elected president and Juliana Banda of the Philippines, vice-president. A newsletter was begun and the use of common prayer topics agreed upon. This world organization of women meets regularly at the time of the World Convention of Churches of Christ.

The women's meeting at Portland in 1953 also proposed having an International Assembly of women from the United States and Canada every four years. The first International CWF Quadrennial Assembly was held on the campus of Purdue University, Lafayette, Indiana, in June 1957. Hazel Rudduck of Mishawaka, Indiana, international vice-president, served as general chairman. Women from everywhere in the United States and Canada, as well as many overseas countries, enjoyed the rich fellowship and learning experience. With three to four thousand women in attendance, such international assemblies are held every four years.

By 1948 a Department of Men's Work had been organized within the UCMS with William H. McKinney (1891-1971) as

---

8. *Christian-Evangelist*, July 2, 1952. p. 656. See also, November 19, 1952. p. 1149.

executive secretary. The first national laymen's retreat was held at Cane Ridge meetinghouse near Paris, Kentucky, August 11-14, 1949. The men were addressed by Alben W. Barkley, the Vice President of the United States.[9] A second national retreat for men was held in August 1951. Several thousand Disciples laymen from throughout the United States and Canada attended this gathering held at Bethany, West Virginia. Programs were planned by an advisory commission. In 1951 the general men's program and organizations in congregations of the Christian Churches (Disciples of Christ) were given the name Christian Men's Fellowship. An emblem was adopted in 1955. CMF seeks to foster fellowship, study, and service among the men of a congregation. Opportunity for wider fellowship is provided in area and general gatherings.

Christian Men's Fellowship rounded out a fellowship concept which began with Christian Youth Fellowship in 1944. The special interests of men, women, and young people were met by such programs. Implicit in the concept of "fellowship" programs was the recognition that the program and mission of the church were one. As the years passed a division between men's and women's fellowships seemed unnecessary. In January 1969, a meeting was held between the International CWF Advisory Council and the Central Committee of CMF. Together the two groups looked at the plans for the new Christian Life Curriculum for CWF/CMF, general programs, group studies, and retreat materials. Increasingly men and women worked together in Christian living and service.

UNIFICATION LEADS TO RESTRUCTURE

As Disciples sought to serve the needs of people and the churches better after World War II, a climate for change developed. After the war it was not possible to return to the same church program which had served an earlier generation. New demands were made upon the structures of the Disciples. The organizations, agencies, and institutions which had served the Disciples previously were inadequate for the new challenges facing the church. The Disciples

---

9. *Christian-Evangelist*, September 14, 1949. p. 892.

experience with A Crusade for a Christian World revealed the need for more intensive program coordination. As early as 1948, while the Crusade was still on, several Disciples leaders had recommended that a churchwide commission be set up to review organizational structure and program. More determined leaders favored a study conducted by the agencies themselves which led to the organization of the Council of Agencies.

For the next several years the Council of Agencies struggled fruitlessly with the problem of overlapping in program and personnel. Agency leaders ineffectually sought ways and means to eliminate tensions, impingements, and duplication of program among the many agencies and other societies. Finally, a Committee on Future Work formed by the Council during the biennium of 1954-1956 recommended the appointment of a Committee on Brotherhood Organization and Interagency Relationships. This committee, under the chairmanship of Wilbur H. Cramblet, held an important consultation at the Disciples Divinity House at Chicago in the summer of 1957. The question of whether the Disciples were organized in an efficient manner to fulfill their mission was central. It became clear that the structure of the International Convention must reflect more fully an inclusive and unified church program and organization. Dissatisfaction with state and area organization was widely discussed. Increasing involvement of women in all aspects of church life had underscored the overlapping at the regional level of programs serving the congregations. Many of the area missionary societies and women's organizations were talking merger and working on unification.

Following a "Conference on Unification" held at Indianapolis in the spring of 1958, attended by 250 national and area leaders, unification of state and area boards became a priority. A *Manual on Unification* was published in 1959 suggesting ways in which a single program might be developed. Guidelines were established for the unification of missionary societies, women's organizations, departments of religious education, and other such agencies so that a unified program might be presented to the congregations and one state, provincial, or area office could be maintained. There were tensions, fears, and concerns, but, in general, state and area unification was accomplished successfully in most areas. New constitutions and bylaws were written and adopted providing for a single state, provincial, or area board to plan and direct a total program.

During 1958 a series of "Listening Conferences" sponsored by the Council of Agencies was held throughout the United States and Canada. They revealed the intense interest in additional program and structural coordination. Unification and coordination of general program and staff were demanded. At the Council of Agencies, meeting at Culver-Stockton College in July 1958, complete restructure of Disciples organization and program was brought into focus. Willard M. Wickizer, executive secretary of the Division of Home Missions of the UCMS, presented a paper reflecting his views on possible plans based on his long experience in organizational work. The Council of Agencies after full consideration of the ideas presented in this paper requested the International Convention, meeting at St. Louis in October 1958, to create a committee to study how restructure might be accomplished. The convention approved and appointed such a committee.

Under the chairmanship of Wickizer, a Study Committee on Brotherhood Structure consisting of eleven persons met three times during 1959-1960 to explore the complex question of a reorganization of the agencies and program of the Christian Churches (Disciples of Christ). Two basic decisions were made by this committee in its several meetings. One called for the leadership in any program of restructure to be centered in the International Convention itself as the voice of all the churches. The second decision was that restructure would depend upon thorough cooperation between the churches and the agencies to create a total program for the church. Under such a plan all agencies were to hold themselves ready to change.

This study committee reported its findings to the International Convention which met at Louisville in October 1960. The committee report, adopted unanimously by the convention, recommended that plans for a new form of organization, henceforth known as "restructure," go forward through listening conferences, consultations, institutes, and lectures in seminaries. The task of restructuring, which was to involve all aspects of life of the Christian Churches (Disciples of Christ) throughout the decade of the 1960s, had begun.[10]

ECUMENICAL DEVELOPMENTS

Since the early days of the International Uniform Lesson Committee, the formation of the Federal Council of Churches and the World Missionary Conference at Edinburgh, the Christian Churches (Disciples of Christ) had been active in the ecumenical movement. Disciples representatives regularly attended national and world gatherings, contributing in thought and leadership to the development of the many ecumenical programs. With their historic emphasis on Christian unity it was only natural that the Christian Churches would take an interest in such gatherings. Disciples also contributed several outstanding executives to ecumenical organizations. Dr. Robert M. Hopkins served as executive secretary of the World Council of Christian Education from 1928 to 1938. Dr. Emory Ross served as executive secretary of the Foreign Missions Conference of North America after many years as a missionary in Africa. Dr. Samuel Guy Inman, a Disciples missionary to South America, became a specialist in Latin American affairs and served as secretary of the Committee on Cooperation in Latin America from 1915 to 1939.

After the World Missionary Conference at Edinburgh in 1910, a continuing committee was appointed. Growing from a movement initiated by Bishop Charles H. Brent and Peter Ainslie, a planning conference on Faith and Order was called for Geneva, Switzerland, in 1920. A full conference was held at Lausanne in 1927. A second conference was held at Edinburgh in 1937. Parallel to Faith and Order was the Universal Christian Council for Life and Work which held meetings at Stockholm in 1925 and at Oxford in 1937.[11] Disciples had representatives at all of these early ecumenical gatherings. Representatives of both Faith and Order and Life and Work

---

10. Loren E. Lair, *The Christian Churches and Their Work* (St. Louis: The Bethany Press, 1963), pp. 283 ff.
11. Disciples were also represented at the two conferences on World Christianity sponsored by the International Missionary Council at Jerusalem in 1928 and at Madras in 1938.

met at Utrecht, in the Netherlands, May 1938, to draft a constitution for a World Council of Churches. A provisional committee of thirty-four members was established and a staff organized for a World Council of Churches (In Process of Formation). Plans for the first assembly, to be held in the summer of 1941, were interrupted by World War II but the interim committee continued its existence in Geneva during the war and until the World Council of Churches was launched in 1948.

A World Conference of Christian Youth was held at Amsterdam, in the Netherlands, just before the outbreak of war in Europe in 1939. Immediately following the war, recognizing the importance of future leaders in the church, the provisional staff of the World Council of Churches organized a World Conference of Christian Youth at Oslo, Norway, for the summer of 1947. Disciples young people and their leaders attended the Amsterdam and Oslo meetings of youth. By the summer of 1948 Europe had sufficiently recovered from the devastation of war for the leaders of the church to consider the calling of the first assembly of the World Council of Churches to meet at Amsterdam.

The International Convention meeting at Buffalo, New York, in 1947 elected Disciples delegates to the first assembly of the World Council. They were George W. Buckner, Jr., (1893-) Gaines M. Cook, Harry B. McCormick, and Mrs. E. V. Pugh. Hampton Adams (1897-1965), Alfred T. DeGroot, Magruder E. Sadler (1896-1966), and Mrs. Mossie Wyker (1902-) were named as alternates.[12] These delegates along with other Disciples as visitors, attended the sessions of the first assembly held at Amsterdam from August 22 to September 5, 1948. Delegates represented 140 church bodies in forty countries at this gathering. Peter Ainslie was one of the ecumenical leaders recognized at this meeting. Disciples have been active participants on the committees and in the assemblies of the World Council of Churches in the years following Amsterdam.

In the meantime, a consensus was growing within the United States that there should be a unification of the various national ecumenical organizations and agencies into a single council. For nearly ten years, beginning with a con-

---

12. *Christian-Evangelist,* September 24, 1947. p. 957.

ference at Atlantic City in 1941, numerous meetings were held to discuss the bringing together of the Federal Council of Churches, the Home Missions Council of North America, the International Council of Religious Education, the Missionary Education Movement of the United States and Canada, the National Protestant Council of Higher Education, the United Council of Church Women, the United Stewardship Council, and the Foreign Missions Conference of North America. These negotiations culminated in the formation of the National Council of Churches of Christ in the late fall of 1950. Snow was deep on the ground on November 29 when delegates from twenty-nine Protestant and Eastern Orthodox churches moved in solemn procession into a church in downtown Cleveland, Ohio, to declare their solidarity in Christian faith.[13] Disciples delegates, including Gaines M. Cook and George W. Buckner, Jr., were part of this historic occasion.

In 1953 Dr. Roy G. Ross, a Disciples executive secretary of the International Council of Religious Education, was named the second general secretary of the National Council of Churches, succeeding Samuel McCrea Cavert. For many years another Disciples leader, Wilbur C. Parry (1900-), served as assistant general secretary. Jesse M. Bader served as secretary of the Department of Evangelism for the Federal Council, and later for the National Council of Churches, until his retirement in 1953.

Disciples have taken great interest in the support of the National Council of Churches and its predecessor organizations. They have contributed liberally in leadership and finance to that which they believe to be of primary importance, the unity of the church. Edgar DeWitt Jones, minister of Central-Woodward Christian Church, Detroit, Michigan, served as president of the Federal Council of Churches in 1936-1938. Mrs. Mossie Wyker was elected president of United Church Women (now Church Women United) in 1956. J. Irwin Miller (1909-), industrialist and layman from Columbus, Indiana, was president of the National Council of Churches in 1960-1963. Numerous Disciples have served on important committees and in various capacities on the staffs of ecumenical organizations at home and abroad.

---

13. *Christian-Evangelist,* May 10, 1950. p. 455. See also December 16, 1950. p. 1092.

THE OPTIMISTIC 1950s

By the 1950s economic recovery was all but complete. The United States had entered upon a period of almost full employment. In an unprecedented building boom in housing, public structures, and churches, the country tried to make up for the building lag of twenty previous years. For several years in the decade the combined church-building programs of Christian groups exceeded one billion dollars. There were problems and troubled areas, however. The possibility of universal destruction became real as other nations acquired nuclear capability. A great anticommunist crusade jeopardized the freedom of innocent persons in the "McCarthy era." American Negroes became increasingly resistant to discrimination and deprivation, and the Supreme Court sustained them in its historic decision outlawing inequality in education. Automation in industry concerned workers, and the conquest of space was begun. American churches, including the Christian Churches (Disciples of Christ), were concerned with all these developments as they reflected life in the United States. Most of these problems and concerns were met with a characteristically American optimism and belief in the future.

The prosperity of the 1950s led to many changes in church life. Staffs of national and area agencies were enlarged. Increased services were provided to congregations. Congregations enlarged their staffs, paid off debts, provided parsonages for their ministers, and contemplated the building of new sanctuaries and educational buildings. This was a time when downtown city congregations seriously considered moving to the suburbs where most of their members had moved. More land was available for building at the outskirts of the city, providing ample parking for an increased number of automobiles. New and larger buildings provided for an expanded program of activities.

The Korean War in 1951-1953 slowed, but did not halt, the development of new buildings and increased activity of the churches. The Korean conflict affected only a small percentage of church families. Some tension was felt as to whether there was justification of American participation in the war, but, on the whole, churches consented to the national involvement. Disciples reserve chaplains were called to active duty briefly. Hostilities came to a close with the signing of an armistice at Panmunjom in July 1953. Most of the American troops stationed in South Korea were withdrawn and returned home.

Toward the end of the 1950s the unprecedented growth of the economy and the nation began to slow. A national recession lasting for two years began in 1959. Church organizations local, area, and national felt the pinch of overexpansion and a mild inflation. The difficulties were felt by all agencies of the Christian Churches (Disciples of Christ) but especially by Unified Promotion and its largest agency, the United Christian Missionary Society. By 1960 it was clear that the Long-Range Program of the decade would not achieve all of its goals, but the challenge had brought forth considerable effort on the part of the churches. Much had been accomplished. All of this coincided with the growing interest in a more efficient and effective church structure. Program coordination and unification of boards and agencies became a practical as well as a theoretical concern.

SIGNIFICANT ETHNIC DEVELOPMENTS

World War II and the Korean War affected the Christian Churches (Disciples of Christ) in still other ways. American Negroes who had fought valiantly with their white brothers and sisters for freedom and the preservation of the nation were unwilling to accept the discrimination they had known previously. Determined efforts were made during and after these wars to integrate the armed forces and to eliminate the racial discrimination found here. A move toward integration followed throughout the fabric of American society. The Congress of Racial Equality (CORE) and other similar organizations became increasingly militant in support of integration and equal opportunity. This was the beginning of what the next decade would call the "civil rights" movement.

Disciples leaders in national organizations participated in these moves toward freedom and equality from the beginning. As early as 1945 the National Christian Missionary Convention requested the establishment of a biracial advisory committee to guide the work of black Disciples in which both the National Convention and the several Disciples agencies working with black congregations could share. This was a step more than had been taken when the National Convention was organized in 1917. Such a committee was approved and the United Christian Missionary Society further agreed to turn over to this committee the funds formerly used in supporting field workers of the UCMS.[14] Shortly thereafter a National Christian Missionary Convention office was established at Indianapolis for closer coordination of efforts of black Disciples with the church agencies located there.

As CORE and other organizations working for justice for American Negroes became more active, black Disciples found white leaders willing to stand beside them. Black Disciples were included as the various programs of the Disciples evolved following World War II. Newly formed churchwide organizations were assumed to be interracial as they came into being. The International CYF Commission, the International CWF Assembly, and Christian Men's Fellowship were racially inclusive. Encouragement was given to black Disciples leaders to assume responsibility and prepare for wider service. Rosa Page Welch (1900-) of Chicago had long been an "ambassador of goodwill," seeking to develop friendship between black and white Christians generally. Church school literature and other publications of the Christian Churches (Disciples of Christ) spoke out for racial justice.

Every effort was made to encourage black Disciples to attend the International Convention, and many did so, since there were never any racial restrictions. When Disciples conventions, national boards, and their committees refused to meet in segregated facilities, hotels in major cities were opened to all. National, state, and area leaders worked aggressively to integrate area conventions and conferences. While not fully effective, such moves throughout the middle 1940s and the 1950s made possible further gains in leadership and program for black Disciples.

---

14. *Disciples of Christ Year Book,* 1945, Indianapolis, Year Book Publication Committee, p. 9.

After World War II the Christian Churches (Disciples of Christ) became increasingly aware of the Spanish-speaking peoples in the United States. Actually, Disciples had included Spanish-speaking persons in their home missions outreach as early as June 1899 when the American Christian Missionary Society had approved the first appropriation to a Spanish-speaking congregation of Disciples. At that time there were fewer than 250,000 Spanish-speaking people in the entire United States living in towns and on ranches along the Mexican border. By the 1970s the number had increased to 6,000,000, and they had moved in great numbers to the cities and to all parts of the country, especially the North. In 1899 there was one Disciples congregation among them. In the 1970s there were more than twenty-three such congregations. Some of these congregations were financially independent while others received subsidies. In addition there were congregations with Spanish departments and several community centers serving Spanish-speaking Americans.

The first of the Spanish-speaking Disciples congregations met in San Antonio, Texas. Organized in 1899, it was later disbanded. In 1908 a month-long revival meeting under the leadership of Samuel Guy Inman and Felipe Jimenez resulted in the congregation's reorganization. The Mexican Christian Institute (now Inman Christian Center) was established at San Antonio in 1913 as a service and social center. During the early period the congregation held its services in the social center, but in 1925 a separate building for the congregation was built with funds raised by Texas women as a part of the "Jubilee Fund" of 1924. Growth was slow and support was meager, but the center and congregation survived. The second oldest Spanish-speaking congregation was organized as a mission at Robstown, Texas, in 1912. Soon there were congregations at San Benito and McAllen. Later congregations were established at Amarillo, Corpus Christi, Brownsville, and Dallas. There is an annual Spanish Convention of Christian Churches in Texas.

One early congregation of Spanish-speaking Disciples was formed at Kansas City, Missouri. The Kansas City Mexican Mission was begun in 1913 in the back room of a grocery store. It was sponsored by the combined women's organization of Jackson County, Missouri. Shortly thereafter the Alta

Vista Christian Church was organized as a congregation of Disciples.

Puerto Ricans began migrating to the continent immediately following the Spanish-American War. Their number was relatively small, however, for the next fifty years. Following World War II Puerto Rican immigration jumped from a few hundreds each year to several thousands. By the late 1950s nearly one million Puerto Ricans were living in the United States and over 650,000 of that number lived in New York City. Among the arrivals were members of the Christian Churches (Disciples of Christ) in Puerto Rico. During the 1930s a revival in Puerto Rico had added substantially to the numbers of Disciples. Theirs was a zealous and enthusiastic faith. Evangelism and Christian stewardship were important to Puerto Rican Disciples for whom the church was the center of life. Puerto Rican Disciples, arriving in New York with their boundless energy and their dynamic faith, were soon organizing their own congregations in New York City.

Sometime before 1940 a group of Puerto Rican Disciples met in an apartment on 111th Street in New York City and organized a congregation. As soon as they were financially able, they purchased a store-front building on a lot twenty feet wide to house their young church. Naming their congregation La Hermosa (The Beautiful), the church continued to grow and to expand its program. In 1943 the congregation related itself to the Christian Churches (Disciples of Christ) and became the mother congregation of the existing Puerto Rican Disciples churches in the city. Other congregations in the New York City area include Monte Hermon and Third Christian Church in Manhattan, the Evangelical Church of Disciples and Second Christian Church in the Bronx, Sinai Christian Church and First Spanish Church in Brooklyn. An annual Spanish Convention of Christian Churches in the northeastern area is held.

As Cuban refugees came to join Puerto Ricans and to add to the number of Spanish-speaking Americans, Disciples congregations have been formed in other parts of the United States. By the 1970s there were Spanish-speaking congregations in Miami, Florida; Chicago, Illinois; Gary, Indiana; and Lorain, Ohio. In the northeastern part of the

United States Spanish-speaking congregations were established at Rochester, New York; Bridgeport, Connecticut;
and Lawrence, Massachusetts. The Eastmont Community
Center was established at Los Angeles to serve Spanish-
speaking residents. While Spanish continued to be the basic
language of these churches, many congregations became
bilingual. A national office of program and service to Spanish
and bilingual congregations of the Christian Churches
(Disciples of Christ) was later established, and a directory of
ministers and congregations was published at regular intervals.[15]

RESURGENCE IN HIGHER EDUCATION AND THEOLOGICAL RENEWAL

One of the unanticipated outcomes of World War II was the
program of veterans' education which made it possible for
thousands of returning servicemen to attend college and university. The return of the G.I.'s to their homes and
their eventual enrollment on hundreds of campuses created a
resurgence in higher education throughout America. Church-
related colleges and universities received a large number of
students seeking an education by means of the "G.I. Bill."
Disciples colleges and universities expanded as rapidly as
possible to accommodate the influx of students, adding
faculty and buildings. Thanks to this program and the
general prosperity of the 1950s, the institutions of higher
education among the Christian Churches (Disciples of
Christ) became stronger and more secure than ever before.
Closely related to the growth in student population was an
upsurge in the number of men and women wishing to give
their lives in Christian service. Nearly all Disciples campuses
reported record numbers of students for the ministry.

By the early 1950s the theological renewal which had begun
prior to World War II reasserted itself. The experiences of war
raised basic philosophical and theological questions for a
large number of persons. The postwar theological renewal
found expression in no single theological system or school of
thought. The most influential theological viewpoints were

---

15. Byron Spice, *Discipulos Americanos.* (Indianapolis, UCMS, 1964), pp. 45-72.
See also *Directorio Ministerio De Habla Hispana,* Indianapolis, Division of
Homeland Ministries, 1974-1975 and succeeding years.

those derived from Europe where the shattered optimism of the immediate postwar years produced a deep interest in "existentialism."

Existential thought sought for an understanding of existence itself and was interested in immediate experience and in the paradoxes of existence. There were "theistic" existentialists such as Jacques Maritain and "nihilistic" existentialists such as Jean Paul Sartre and Albert Camus, all of France. Insights were borrowed from such sources as Martin Buber, an Israeli, and Nicolai Berdyaev, Russian refugee. The more traditional Reformation theology of Emil Brunner, Swiss theologian, sought to renew the earlier Christian heritage. The "existentialism" of Soren Kierkegaard, the "dour Dane," became known among American students. Paul Tillich, recently arrived in the United States from Germany, appropriated some of the existentialist concepts to explain Christian doctrine in contemporary terms.

Certain major themes in theological thinking in general can be identified even though it is impossible to see a common denominator among the tendencies that were manifest in the theological revival of the 1950s. One clearly identifiable theme was that of the sovereignty of God. With the reassertion of the idea of a transcendent God, there was a repudiation of the notion that man is master of his own destiny. The doctrine of "grace" was reasserted. A decisive reaction against any optimistic evaluation of the human situation became evident. Sin was accepted as a fact and was viewed as powerful and demonic. Biblical authority as a source for theology became increasingly recognized. Biblical revelation was newly appreciated. A belief in Jesus Christ as Lord and Savior as central to the faith was emphasized. An attempt was made to understand more fully the nature of the church. Finally, as theology sought more traditional roots it moved to a more radical position in regard to social issues and politics.[16] An influential interpreter of Disciples was William Robinson, longtime principal of Overdale College and editor of *The Christian Advocate* in England. He spent the last years of his active ministry as professor of Christian doctrine at the Butler School of Religion (now Christian

---

16. Ahlstrom, *A Religious History of the American People,* pp. 949 ff.

Theological Seminary) and lectured widely in America on theological topics. His best known book was *The Biblical Doctrine of the Church.*

By the late 1950s the reawakening of interest in biblical theology and in Christian doctrine had begun to permeate the churches. This interest was no longer restricted to the seminaries. Lay groups began to participate in serious theological inquiry. The church school curriculum of the Christian Churches (Disciples of Christ) was rewritten to give emphasis to biblical and doctrinal instruction. As postwar generations of seminary students were introduced to the various theological modes, were graduated, and began to advocate the theological renaissance, changes in emphasis in church life began to appear. The institutional and program aspects of the Christian Churches (Disciples of Christ) were affected in numerous ways.

The seminaries of the Christian Churches (Disciples of Christ) began to expand as greater numbers of students attended. Several new institutions were created to serve important areas of church life. While the nation was at war in 1942, the Disciples Divinity House came into being in association with Vanderbilt Divinity School at Nashville, Tennessee. It was at the height of the theological renewal, however, that most changes took place in seminary education. In 1958 the New Haven Disciples House and Center was organized with the help of the UCMS to serve Disciples students at Yale Divinity School and to encourage continuing education. The program did not flourish for long and was closed in 1972 after fourteen years of service. The Christian Churches (Disciples of Christ) in Southern California for many years had believed there was a need for a seminary in that area. When the Southern California School of Theology moved from Los Angeles to Claremont in 1959, the churches of Southern California organized the Disciples Seminary Foundation to serve Disciples students attending the School of Theology.

Theological renewal as much as other developments led to a change of emphasis at several Disciples seminaries. In 1958 Christian Theological Seminary at Indianapolis became a separate corporation to continue and add to the functions formerly performed by the School of Religion of Butler

University. Brite College of the Bible of Texas Christian University at Fort Worth in 1963 became Brite Divinity School. Lexington Theological Seminary in 1965 became the new name for The College of the Bible at Lexington, Kentucky. There were some casualties during this period. Drake Divinity School of Drake University at Des Moines, Iowa, closed in 1967 after many years of service. In 1972 the Missouri School of Religion returned exclusively to the teaching of undergraduate courses at the University of Missouri at Columbia after a number of years of experimentation as a seminary for rural pastors.

Further evidence of theological fermentation among the Christian Churches (Disciples of Christ) was the creation of the Panel of Scholars in 1957 in the midst of the religious revival then evident in the United States. A groundwork was being laid for a future reorganization. Created under the sponsorship of the United Christian Missionary Society and the Board of Higher Education, the panel was to prove a significant influence in a reinterpretation of the Disciples. As the panel was convened for its first meeting under the chairmanship of Howard E. Short in January 1957, it was asked

to restudy the doctrines of Disciples of Christ, justifying their conclusions on the basis of the best available scholarship. It was agreed that the Panel would have complete freedom, deciding for themselves the areas they would consider and how they would proceed with their studies, but it was hoped that the Panel would see fit to consider theologically some of the more practical issues and problems confronting Disciples of Christ.[17]

For nearly four years the Panel met to consider scholarly papers on all aspects of faith and life among the Christian Churches (Disciples of Christ). In 1963 these papers were published in a three-volume report under the general editorship of W. Barnett Blakemore (1912-1975) of the Disciples Divinity House in Chicago.[18] The expectations of the spon-

17. Ronald E. Osborn, *The Reformation of Tradition,* Vol. I., The Panel of Scholars Reports, 1963. p. 8.
18. Issued under the general title *The Renewal of Church, The Panel of Scholars Reports,* ed. by W. Barnett Blakemore (St. Louis, The Bethany Press, 1963), the three volumes were:
    Vol. I, *The Reformation of Tradition,* Ronald E. Osborn, editor.
    Vol. II, *The Reconstruction of Theology,* Ralph Wilburn, editor.
    Vol. III, *The Revival of the Churches,* W. Barnett Blakemore, editor.

soring agencies were more than fulfilled as the papers of the
Panel were widely read and studied. The reports were
published just as the work of the Commission on Restructure
was getting under way. There can be little doubt that the
work of the Panel of Scholars greatly influenced the discussions and decisions on structure and organization which
came later.[19]

Indirectly related to these developments, but important to
the intellectual life of the Disciples, was the organization of
an Association of Disciples for Theological Discussion in 1959
under the leadership of Walter W. Sikes (1896-1966). Composed of Disciples professors teaching in undergraduate institutions and seminaries and representing various dis-
ciplines, the association exists to read and discuss papers on a
variety of scholarly topics. Under its sponsorship several
theological studies came to publication.

The work of the Panel of Scholars and the resulting discussions among leaders, ministers, and laypersons revealed
that the theological doctrine most consistently concerning
Disciples at the time was the doctrine of the church. Along
with most other American Protestant denominations,
Disciples had talked about the church without having a very
clear understanding of its nature and function. They sought
to examine it biblically, historically, sociologically, and
theologically. With all the wide range of Disciples thought,
tradition, and practice, no one had ever stopped to consider
how it might all be brought into focus. Through the years
there had been the organization of congregations, state,
provincial, and area missionary societies, a variety of general
boards, agencies, and institutions to serve Christian needs,
but never had there been an understanding of how all these
organizations related to one another or to the universal
Church of Christ except as autonomous entities. The International Convention, the most representative of all the structures, was only a meeting place for representatives of the
churches, individuals, and numerous agencies. As the work
of the Commission on Restructure got under way in the
1960s, its deliberations were informed by the theological
revival of the 1950s.

---

19. Loren E. Lair, *The Christian Church (Disciples of Christ) and Its Future* (St.
Louis, The Bethany Press, 1971), p. 32 ff.

18

TOWARD A RESTRUCTURED CHURCH

The pendulum swung from the enthusiasm and interest in religion which marked the 1950s to disenchantment and a crisis of faith in the 1960s. Organized religion, particularly the mainline Protestant denominations, declined. The assassination of John F. Kennedy in November 1963 brought into office Lyndon B. Johnson (1908-1973) who served until 1968. Johnson was the second President of the United States to be a member of the Disciples. These years led to a complete realignment and restructure of the Disciples as the Commission on Restructure went about its task. At the same time there was a growing social consciousness as Disciples and the nation grappled with the issues of "civil rights" and an unpopular war in Vietnam. These were years when a consortium of nine denominations, including the Christian Church (Disciples of Christ), proposed "A Plan of Union" for member churches to consider.

PRELUDE TO RESTRUCTURE

The Study Committee on Brotherhood Structure between 1958 and 1960 became decisive in identifying issues and in raising important questions which needed consideration. Out of this committee's discussions and recommendations came suggestions that pointed the way for future work. The study committee went to the membership. It prepared and sent out a questionnaire to one thousand ministers, laypeople, and seminarians, seeking and securing information on what needed to be done to relieve tensions and solve problems in existing structures.

By 1960 a desire, readiness, and expectancy for structural change were apparent. Disciples leadership, including many of the prominent ministers, was aware that something more than conventions and agencies was needed. When the study committee made its report at the Louisville convention in October 1960, its recommendation for the creation of a Commission on Restructure was received with enthusiasm and adopted. The months following the adoption of the report were given to plans for a major restructure of the International Convention and its agencies.

The process proceeded under the enabling resolution. A Commission on Restructure was to be composed of not less than 120, and not more than 130, persons elected for a three-year term. The membership of the commission was to consist of representatives nominated by each state, province, and area board, eight state and area executives, the members of a central committee, six chief executives of national agencies not included on the central committee, ten college and seminary faculty members, the editor of *The Christian,* the editor of *World Call,* and thirty-nine to forty-nine persons to be nominated at large. The attempt was to be made to secure a commission as representative of all the churches as possible.[1] A central committee, consisting of fifteen to eighteen persons, was to be appointed from the membership of the commission to give direction.

The Board of Directors of the International Convention elected the members of the central committee, some of whom had been on the original study committee. As the central committee became organized, it set forth guidelines for the work of the commission. The central committee determined that it would meet twice each year and the full commission

---

1. Lair, *The Christian Church (Disciples of Christ) and Its Future,* pp. 45 ff. See this book for a detailed history of the Commission on Restructure and the development of the Provisional Design.

annually. A bibliography of materials to be read and studied by the members of the commission was prepared. The central committee supervised the preparation of a list of nominees for membership on the commission. These names were submitted to the Board of Directors of the International Convention for election. The central committee proposed a chart of existing structures of organization and interrelationships for the study of commission members.

Within a few months the International Convention staff and the Board of Directors had worked effectively with the central committee in setting up the commission. Granville T. Walker (1908-), minister of University Christian Church, Fort Worth, Texas, was chosen as chairman of the Commission on Restructure. He was a respected pastor with proven administrative ability. In the succeeding years his insight, general knowledge, tact, and sensitivity proved invaluable to the work of the commission. At Los Angeles in 1962 A. Dale Fiers (1906-), former pastor and from 1951 president of the UCMS, was chosen administrative secretary of the commission. Fiers brought to his work extensive administrative experience, but most of all a pastoral concern and spiritual depth. The Commission on Restructure held its first meeting from October 30 to November 1, 1962, at St. Louis. Its work over the next several years was to determine the future direction of the Disciples.

From the beginning it was realized that it would be important to keep members, ministers, and organizations informed as to what was happening. Furthermore, communication was to be two-way. Congregations, agencies, and state and area boards were to communicate their concerns to the commission as well as to be informed of the commission's actions. Disciples editors, Howard E. Short of *The Christian* and Samuel F. Pugh (1904-) of *World Call*, each agreed to use the pages of those publications to provide a forum for discussion of the many aspects of restructure. By means of articles, editorials, and question-and-answer columns, the issues were discussed freely from many viewpoints.

As the work of the Commission on Restructure got under way other developments ran a parallel course. In the late 1950s plans had been laid for a "Decade of Decision" program for 1960-1970. These plans were developed into a program of advance in Christian education, evangelism, and stewardship. The International Convention meeting at Los Angeles in 1962 pledged continued support to the Park Avenue Christian Church in New York City. Recognition was given to the importance of the Christian Churches (Disciples of Christ) having a strong congregation in America's largest city. Also the state and area secretaries for several years had been expressing the need for an association to give mutual support to state, provincial, and area programs. In 1962 the Conference of State and Area Secretaries and Board Chairmen was organized. Meeting annually, the conference considered those matters of concern to regional programs and strategy.

THE CHRISTIAN CHURCH FOUNDATION

In 1961 a charter was granted by the state of Indiana to the Christian Church Foundation. This unique organization came into being under the direction of Spencer P. Austin (1909-), D. Ervin Sheets (1903-), and Rolland H. Sheafor (1914-) and was sponsored by Unified Promotion. Its purpose was to form a trust and endowment for all the causes cooperating in Unified Promotion. The Christian Church Foundation became the instrument by which individuals and families wishing to give sums of money in their wills or by direct gifts to the church could preserve the principal. Only the income would be distributed to Christian causes. Endowments and trusts were held by various agencies, but there was no other place where money could be given for the benefit of all causes.

James R. Reed (1927-) became the first president of the Christian Church Foundation in 1964, under the board of Unified Promotion. In 1967 the board of Unified Promotion set up a study committee to examine the place of the foundation in a restructured church. The decision was made to create a board independent of Unified Promotion. At the Seattle Assembly in 1969 this decision was recognized and a separate board was elected. Theodore P. Beasley (1900-) of Dallas, Texas, gave the first large gift to the foundation in 1968. Since that time other substantial gifts and many smaller gifts have been received by the Foundation.

PRINCIPLES OF A PROVISIONAL DESIGN

During the years 1962 and 1963 the Commission on Restructure devoted itself to study, to conferences, and to planning by task committees. These working committees dealt with specific questions such as the rights and responsibilities of local congregations, the nature and authority of the International Convention, and the role of ecumenical relationships. Considerable progress in understanding three manifestations of the church had been made by the time the second meeting of the commission was held at Chicago on July 1-4, 1963. The three manifestations of the church were considered to be the congregation, the region (state, province, or area program and organization), and the general manifestation (churchwide program and agencies). Slowly a philosophical and theological basis for restructure emerged from these deliberations.

By the time of the third full meeting of the commission, at Louisville, June 29-July 1, 1964, general directions of restructure were discerned. Proposals were made at this meeting which later formed the foundation for the development of the Provisional Design. Four basic guidelines were agreed upon:

1. The structure will be designed so that the Christian Church (Disciples of Christ) in all its manifestations at all levels reflects its oneness and the unity of the church.

2. The Christian Church will follow the principles of representative government through the structuring of delegate bodies.

3. The Christian Church in its national manifestation will have representation from local congregations and from regions (states or areas).

4. The Christian Church will express its unity of purpose and mission through the adoption of declarations which express a covenantal relationship in the various manifestations of the church and all its separate parts.[2]

These guidelines were consistent with the traditions and historic practice of the Disciples. Furthermore, a firm theological understanding provided the foundation on which the commission wished to build a restructured church. There was solid agreement that the concept of "churches" and

---

2. *Ibid.*, p. 70.

Graham Frank

Gaines M. Cook

A. Dale Fiers

Kenneth L. Teegarden

The adoption of the Provisional Design for the Christian Church (Disciples of Christ) at the 1968 Kansas City, Missouri, General Assembly (pictured below) climaxed a half century of organizational development begun in 1917 with the origin of the International Convention of Disciples of Christ. During the transition from part-time operation to today's responsible structure, three men served as general secretary, executive secretary, or general minister and president.

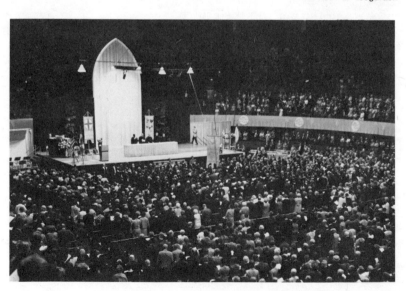

"agencies" must give way to recognition of the *one church*. Impetus for such a concept of the church came from the work of Ronald E. Osborn, one of the members of the commission. Osborn believed the following emphases should guide the commission:

1. The calling of the church is to fulfill the divine intention: the church is the servant of God.

2. The nature of the church is manifest in her essential being; a community of the spirit taking institutional form within the realities of history, a people of the covenant.

3. The building of the church is the divine-human process of her formation according to her constitution; it is edification, the spiritual and institutional building-up of the body of Christ.[3]

It was clear by now to the Commission on Restructure that it had moved beyond an International Convention of Christian Churches (Disciples of Christ) to a consideration of the Christian Church (Disciples of Christ). The Louisville meeting of the commission voted to establish a committee on a provisional design for the Christian Church (Disciples of Christ) and to work on such a design from the standpoint of every manifestation of the church: local, regional, and general.

THE PROVISIONAL DESIGN ADOPTED

At the International Convention meeting at Detroit in 1964 the principles developed by the Commission on Restructure were reported. General approval was given by the convention. During the next two years work on a Provisional Design for the Christian Church (Disciples of Christ) went forward. When Gaines M. Cook retired as executive secretary of the International Convention in 1964, A. Dale Fiers was chosen to succeed him. At this time Fiers left his position as administrative secretary of the Commission on Restructure. Shortly thereafter Kenneth L. Teegarden (1921-) was called to serve the commission as administrative secretary. Meetings to consider restructure developments were held in every state and area during 1965. A series of thirteen regional assemblies was also held. They were attended by over 15,000

---

3. Ronald E. Osborn, *Toward the Christian Church* (St. Louis, Bethany Press, 1964). p. 10

individuals representing congregations throughout the United States and Canada. In these meetings thorough discussions concerning the directions of restructure took place.

Anticipating the next International Convention, the Commission on Restructure met at Cincinnati July 5-8, 1966. At the International Convention (now called Assembly) meeting at Dallas in 1966 the commission presented its first proposals for the Provisional Design. It recommended that the International Convention call a delegate assembly to consider the design. Authorization was asked to call a provisional General Assembly of the Christian Church (Disciples of Christ) to meet at St. Louis in 1967. It proposed that the General Assembly meet biennially. Each of these proposals aroused spirited debate, but after much discussion the recommendations passed. Stephen J. England (1895-) of Enid, Oklahoma, presided with patience and skill during the sometimes difficult business sessions of the assembly. But the assembly at Dallas gave every indication of favoring the directions of the commission.

The first delegate assembly, meeting under revised bylaws of the convention, was held at St. Louis in 1967. This assembly made several modifications and amendments to the proposals of the commission in regard to the Provisional Design. Various elements of the proposed possible form and structure were scrutinized in freewheeling debate, but, in general, the assembly gave approval to the directions for a Provisional Design as outlined by the Commission on Restructure. Forrest L. Richeson (1908-) of Minneapolis, Minnesota, was president. Between this meeting and an assembly planned for Kansas City in 1968, the states, areas, and agencies were to give their approval to a revised Provisional Design. It would be necessary for two-thirds of the churchwide agencies to act favorably on the proposals during this period if restructure were to proceed.

Delegates gathered in keen anticipation for the crucial assembly meeting at Kansas City in 1968. In the same city the International Convention had been organized in 1917. Now, fifty-one years later, action was to be taken to replace the convention and its agencies with a correlated structure as proposed in A Provisional Design for the Christian Church (Disciples of Christ). Favorable authorization had been voted by the necessary bodies. At Kansas City by nearly unanimous vote, the International Convention of the Christian Churches (Disciples of Christ) and its related agencies was reconstituted in accordance with the Provisional Design. There the first Provisional Assembly of the Christian Church (Disciples of Christ) was convened with Ronald E. Osborn as the presiding moderator.

It was a move of great significance for the heirs of the Stone-Campbell movement. The enthusiasm for the action was such that the assembled delegates spontaneously broke into the Doxology after the vote approving the motion. The approved design was the result of eight years of effort led by a hard-working Commission on Restructure and participated in by thousands of Disciples. The action shifted the Disciples into a new concept of what it meant to be the church. The Christian Church (Disciples of Christ) would spend many years implementing this action.

OPPOSITION TO RESTRUCTURE AND THE PROVISIONAL DESIGN

With the action of the Kansas City Assembly, the Christian Churches (Disciples of Christ) had begun the process of becoming the Christian Church (Disciples of Christ). They had resolved the question of identity. No longer were they to be a movement of individuals, congregations, and agencies working together in an annual convention. They were now to become church. Based on a solid theological foundation the way was prepared for a renewal of the church and a deepening of its commitment to its Lord and its mission.

From the beginning there had been responsible differences of opinion on various proposals of the commission. Within the commission itself there was vigorous debate on specific principles and issues. Open discussion and eventual compromise made possible the creative procedure which led to the Provisional Design. Always, however, there was a willingness to accept the will of the majority. From time to time suggestions and criticisms were received from individuals and congregations and from state and area meetings. All these suggestions were carefully considered by the commission and where possible they were written into the plan.

Other opposition to restructure and, later, to the design, was of a different sort. For many years a large number of individuals and congregations had not been willing to accept the will of the majority in matters concerning the direction of the Disciples. Some of those individuals and congregations had withdrawn their support from the International Convention and its agencies. A sizable number of such persons and congregations, however, although they had not withdrawn, had not given support to the program of the Christian Churches (Disciples of Christ.) Soon after the Commission on Restructure began its work an "anonymous" Committee for the Preservation of the Brotherhood appeared. This group published and distributed two documents anonymously in the form of "open letters" to Christian Churches and Churches of Christ. They were entitled "Freedom or Restructure?" and "The Truth About Restructure." Four copies of each pamphlet were mailed to every congregation listed in the Year Book of the Christian Churches (Disciples of Christ).

The "anonymous" committee was later revealed to have been organized in the First Christian Church, Canton, Ohio, at the instigation of James DeForest Murch. Murch was the author of both pamphlets. Their printing and distribution had been financed by B. D. Phillips of Butler, Pennsylvania, who had long been a critic of organized efforts. The main thrust of the committee's opposition had to do with what its members considered a threat to the freedom of the congregation and to property rights. In 1965 Murch wrote and published *The Free Church,* an entire book on the subject. A later book notes that over 2,000 copies of this book were distributed to key churches free of charge.[4]

Little harm was done to the progress of restructure among those congregations which were well informed about plans for reorganization and had closely cooperated with the International Convention and its agencies. Congregations which were not well informed and which had little contact with Disciples programs experienced no little confusion. A widespread effort was made to answer the points raised by the

---

4. James DeForest Murch, *Adventuring for Christ in Changing Times* (Louisville: Restoration Press, 1973). pp. 288 ff.

pamphlets and to identify the pertinent issues. Unfortunately the attacks on restructure made the major question one of property rights, whereas the Provisional Design was concerned with the mission of the church. The right of congregations to hold and control their property was not jeopardized, but claims that they were jeopardized made an effective red herring to mislead the suspicious.

Answers to the basic questions raised about restructure were given in the various publications. The entire issue of *The Christian* for January 30, 1966, was devoted to explaining the proposal. *World Call* carried a number of articles on the subject. One positive result of the pamphlets was that the members of the Commission on Restructure worked even harder to point out the rights of congregations in the Provisional Design. The commission made certain that what it proposed did not do violence to Disciples belief and practice, but found that some people could not be convinced.

A few concerns and fears were expressed as early as 1964 among those persons with definite loyalties to the International Convention. The widely respected and venerable Winfred E. Garrison, speaking at a breakfast meeting for ministers at the time of the Detroit International Convention, questioned the wisdom of some of the directions in which restructure seemed to be going. His address, entitled "A Fork in the Road," suggested that the Christian Churches (Disciples of Christ) were at a point of deciding between two directions. Garrison implied that if they were not careful the Disciples would choose the wrong "fork in the road." He later indicated he believed the wrong fork had been taken.

Opposition to the policies proposed by the Commission on Restructure was later organized by some of those who had regularly supported the International Convention. Following the Dallas assembly in 1966, the Commission on Restructure held a short meeting to make plans for its work in anticipation of the 1967 assembly scheduled for St. Louis. There Robert W. Burns (1904-) of Atlanta, Georgia, a past president of the International Convention and a member of the Commission on Restructure, raised serious questions about the rights of congregations under restructure. The commission had made it clear that its work in this area was tentative, but Burns wanted further guarantees written into the draft. The commission was not able or willing to do this. No further action was possible until the assembly in 1967. Some months after this brief commission meeting in Dallas, Burns and others formed the Atlanta Declaration Committee. Its purpose was to arouse as much opposition as possible to restructure at the point of property rights and congregational autonomy. The Atlanta Declaration Committee existed for some time but received support from only a small circle. It was Burns, however, who made the motion in the final meeting of the Commission on Restructure that the Provisional Design be adopted.

Another form of "loyal opposition" was given leadership by Charles H. Bayer (1927-), minister of University Disciples of Christ Church at Chicago. Under his guidance a fellowship of concerned individuals known as "Disciples for Mission and Renewal" was formed. A significant number of younger ministers and laypersons were disturbed that restructure was concerned almost exclusively with organizational matters. Members of Disciples for Mission and Renewal wanted to emphasize the mission of the church and its renewal. For several years a publication known as *Bread and Wine* was issued and distributed to members and to persons attending the General Assembly. In time the fellowship dissolved its formal organization, but those persons favoring this position continued to make their viewpoint known.

After the nearly unanimous approval of the Provisional Design at Kansas City in 1968, more than 2,300 congregations asked that their listing be removed from the *Year Book,* leaving 4,046 participating congregations by 1970. (Many more congregations withdrew over the next three years.) A widespread and well-financed campaign was conducted by opponents, the main argument of which was the assertion that unless the congregation withdrew by a certain time they would place themselves in jeopardy of losing control of their church property. In reality these withdrawals represented a completion of a process which had begun much earlier.

A majority of these congregations had not supported the work of the Disciples financially for many years, so their withdrawal cost the denominational budget less than $100,000 a year. They had not cooperated with the International Convention of Christian Churches (Disciples of Christ), and

of American Churches listed the "Christian Churches and Churches of Christ" as a separate religious grouping in addition to the Christian Church (Disciples of Christ) and the Churches of Christ. This was a formal acknowledgment of a division which had been in process since the formation of the North American Christian Convention in 1927.

IMPLEMENTING THE PROVISIONAL DESIGN

The Provisional Design for the Christian Church (Disciples of Christ) called for a representative General Board of approximately 225 persons to meet annually to care for the work of the church between assemblies. An elected Administrative Committee, smaller in size than the General Board, was to care for urgent matters and to prepare for the General Board meetings. When the Provisional Design was adopted at Kansas City in 1968, it made provision for interim plenary structures. This facilitated the development of the life and work of the Christian Church. A provisional General Board met in brief session at Kansas City and authorized the continuation of committees and commissions of the International Convention until such time as they were modified or replaced. A calendar of dates for future meetings of the General Board and its Administrative Committee was approved. A tentative understanding was reached for a reorganization of general administrative units. All that was done would be considered experimental and subject to further analysis and review. A. Dale Fiers became the first general minister and president of the restructured church.

The first biennial General Assembly of the Christian Church (Disciples of Christ) was held at Seattle, Washington, in 1969. Myron C. Cole (1909-), minister of Hollywood-Beverly Christian Church, Los Angeles, served as moderator. Steps were taken to institute the new plenary structures of the church according to the Provisional Design. Provision was made for a continuing Committee on Structure and Function. The purpose of this committee was to work for an indefinite period of time on a permanent constitution for the Christian Church (Disciples of Christ). It was recognized that this undoubtedly would require many years. In the meantime, state, provincial, and area conventions became

there was no reason to believe that they would support a restructured church. By their request, in 1971 the *Year Book* delegate regional assemblies to meet usually on alternate years with the General Assembly.

In 1969 at Lexington, Kentucky, the last National Christian Missionary Convention was held. At that convention the black Disciples voted overwhelmingly in favor of merging with the General Assembly of the Christian Church (Disciples of Christ). A National Convocation of the Christian Church was to continue as trustee for the National Christian Missionary Convention Corporation and was to meet usually on alternate years with the General Assembly. John R. Compton became the administrative secretary of the convocation. After Compton's return to a pastorate in 1973, William K. Fox (1917-) became administrative secretary with assignment in the General Office as assistant to the general minister and president of the Christian Churches (Disciples of Christ).

At the second biennial General Assembly at Louisville in 1971 an important Committee on Black Church Work was voted into existence. This committee worked to expand and to improve the witness among black people of the Christian Church (Disciples of Christ). The committee consisted of approximately twenty persons appointed from various church units by the general minister and president after consultation. The National Convocation provided sufficient representation to assure a black majority on the committee and the administrative secretary of the National Convocation was to serve as chairman.[5]

The new name, Christian Church (Disciples of Christ), had so far meant relatively little in the actual functioning of the various agencies of the church. There were significant implications, however, from the standpoint of theology and philosophy. A new way of viewing the interrelatedness of the various manifestations of the church had been shown. In accepting a covenantal relationship, as well as a structured one, Disciples were more than ever bound to one another in their commitment to Christ and the mission of the church. What had formerly been the agencies of the International

---

5. *1974 Year Book and Directory of the Christian Church (Disciples of Christ)*, Indianapolis, General Office of the Christian Church (*Disciples* of Christ), p. 70.

Convention now became divisions, councils, and administrative units of the Christian Church (Disciples of Christ). Seven divisions, four councils, and several auxiliary units were created within the new structure to care for aspects of the program of the church.

The largest agency of the Disciples had been the United Christian Missionary Society. This organization moved in 1971 to implement the Provisional Design by forming itself into two major divisions of the church. A Division of Homeland Ministries was organized to care for the program and concerns of the church in the United States and Canada. A Division of Overseas Ministries was organized to care for the worldwide concerns of the Christian Church (Disciples of Christ). Each of these divisions was incorporated. Each had its own board of trustees or directors. The United Christian Missionary Society became a holding company, distributing its income to the two divisions. Virgil A. Sly (1901-), who had become president of the UCMS in 1964, served until his retirement in October 1968. Thomas J. Liggett (1919-) was president during the process of restructure. He served from October 1968 until February 1974. After 1974 the president of the Division of Overseas Ministries became the nominal president of the UCMS.

In recent years other agencies have restructured themselves into responsible units of the Christian Church (Disciples of Christ). As of 1975 the church and its responsible units are:[6]

Board of Church Extension of Disciples of Christ

Board of Higher Education

Christian Board of Publication

Christian Church Foundation

Christian Church Services, Inc.

Christmount Christian Assembly, Inc.

Church Finance Council (Unified Promotion)

Conference of Regional Ministers and Board Chairmen of the Christian Church (Disciples of Christ) in the United States and Canada.

Council on Christian Unity

---

6. *1975 Year Book and Directory of the Christian Church (Disciples of Christ)*, pp. 19-40.

Discipledata, Inc.

Disciples of Christ Historical Society

The Disciples Peace Fellowship

Division of Homeland Ministries

Division of Overseas Ministeries

European Evangelistic Society

The National Benevolent Association (Division of Social and Health Services)

The National City Christian Church Corporation

The National Evangelistic Association of the Christian Church (Disciples of Christ)

Pension Fund of the Christian Church (Disciples of Christ)

The United Christian Missionary Society

Among the units of the church listed above two are newer than the others and a description of them follows:

Discipledata, Inc. was formed in 1971 to provide computer and budgetary services to the various units and congregations of the Christian Church (Disciples of Christ). While financially independent, it shares certain personnel as well as some directors with the Board of Church Extension.

Christian Church Services, Inc., a subsidiary corporation was formed in 1973 to provide all other organizations support services in communication, accounting and financial reporting, personnel, purchasing, printing and mailing, and property management.

The General Assembly at Seattle approved appointment of a Committee on 1970 and Beyond. At the General Assembly meeting at Louisville this committee recommended quadrennial program planning and proposed five mission imperatives for special emphasis between 1971 and 1975. The recommended imperatives were: Leadership; Evangelism and Renewal; World Order, Justice and Peace; Ecumenical Involvement; Reconciliation in the Urban Crisis. Over the years emphasis was given to each of these special areas.[7] New emphases were to be selected in each future quadrennial period. James M. Moudy (1916-), chancellor of Texas Christian University, was elected moderator at Seattle to serve through the General Assembly of 1971. The General

---

7. *1970-71 Year Book and Directory of the Christian Church (Disciples of Christ),* p. 51.

Assembly at Louisville in 1971 elected Walter D. Bingham (1921-), minister of Third Christian Church, Louisville, Kentucky, as moderator. He was the first black Disciple to hold the office. Jean Woolfolk (1921-), an insurance executive from Little Rock, Arkansas, was elected moderator at Cincinnati in 1973. She was the first woman Disciple to serve in this office.

By 1973 the rising inflation in the nation's economy was reflected in the increased cost of publishing. An earlier decline in subscriptions to *World Call* and *The Christian* had caused concern. Plans were now laid to combine these two magazines into a biweekly publication representing all of the concerns of the Christian Church (Disciples of Christ). Known as *The Disciple,* the first issue of the new magazine came from the press in January 1974. In 1975 it became a semimonthly publication.

Unified Promotion became the Church Finance Council in 1974. Some people had thought the name "Unified Promotion" was unclear to everybody except headquarters promoters. Others believed it lacked stewardship emphasis. The new name sought to emphasize this church unit's responsibility for adequately financing the whole mission of the church.

The Commission on Brotherhood Finance became the Commission on Budget Evaluation and continued its function of allocating budgets for the general units and educational and regional institutions of the church. Under the commission's leadership, educational and negotiating conferences are regularly held in each region of the church.

A. Dale Fiers served as general minister and president of the church until October 1973, at which time Kenneth L. Teegarden was formally installed in the office.

CONTINUING SOCIAL AWARENESS

Martin Luther King, Jr., became the first president of the Southern Christian Leadership Conference in February 1957. By 1960 the SCLC, along with other groups, was leading a movement of nonviolent resistance to segregation which spread throughout the South. Students active in the Committee on Racial Equality (CORE) joined with a newly organized Student Nonviolent Coordinating Committee (SNCC) to eliminate segregated public transportation facilities. Later in the 1960s came the voter registration drive which, despite resistance and violence, was continued until a larger number of blacks was enfranchised than ever before. In 1963 the long-remembered march was made on Washington. Many Disciples were among the 250,000 persons who marched for equality and justice. From the steps of the Lincoln Memorial, Martin Luther King, Jr., spoke of his "dream" to this vast audience.

Events in 1965 determined that there would be an increased social awareness among the churches. First, the burning of the Watts district of Los Angeles made the nation more aware of discontent. Next the march from Selma to Montgomery, Alabama, brought over 25,000 persons together in the cause of racial justice. Congress enacted civil rights legislation largely because the churches were openly involved, and, all over the South, Negroes began to vote and to gain election to public office. After the assassination of Martin Luther King, Jr., at Memphis in April, some of the activists' energy was diverted to the growing concern over the war in Vietnam.[8]

As American military involvement increased, the issue became ever more divisive within the country and among the churches. Many years were to pass before the scars of Vietnam would begin to heal. All of these developments were of importance to the Christian Church (Disciples of Christ). At first, mainly young people and seminarians were involved in the rising tide of events connected with the "black revolution" and Vietnam. Shortly thereafter, national Disciples leaders and local pastors shared in the sit-ins, demonstrations, and marches.

At the St. Louis assembly in October 1967 an early response to the urban crisis was urged upon congregations and the various units of the Christian church. The Division of Church Life and Work of the United Christian Missionary Society was requested to consider ways in which priority could be given to urban needs and to make specific suggestions on ways in which the churches could respond to

---

8. Ahlstrom, *A Religious History of the American People*, pp. 1073 ff.

the crisis of the cities. The Council of Agencies at a meeting in Indianapolis in March 1968 issued "A Call for the Response of the Christian Churches." Martin Luther King, Jr.'s assassination a month later gave an added urgency for action. At this time the Division of Church Life and Work of the UCMS created and activated the Urban Emergency Action Committee. A new program called Reconciliation emerged as a direct result of this committee's efforts. Staff members were assigned to devote a major portion of their time to Reconciliation concerns.

The urban emergency program was designed to be many faceted. Funds for Reconciliation became a prime goal. Reconciliation was planned to focus on programs and projects which would help people to help themselves. Areas of special concern such as employment and economic opportunity, housing, educational programs for children, youth and adults were identified. Reconciliation funds in the amount of $2 million over and above the regular budget over a two-year period were sought from congregations, foundations, and special gifts. A number of general and regional units of the church advanced funds so that projects might get under way more quickly. Reconciliation-supported projects included community centers, organizations seeking to provide equal employment opportunities and community organization programs aimed at helping black citizens achieve equality.

The General Assembly at Kansas City in October 1968 commended the progress of the Reconciliation Steering Committee. Even in the midst of the adoption of the Provisional Design, the General Assembly approved a resolution which endorsed the efforts to mobilize the church's resources to confront the urban emergency. The General Assembly at Seattle approved a continued program for the biennial 1969-1971. One interesting development involved the Steering Committee's appointment of an "investment committee." The purpose of this committee was to encourage the units of the Christian Church to invest endowments and surplus monies in minority-controlled banks and businesses in order to generate investment power as a means of meeting some of the urban crisis problems.[9]

---

9. *1969 Year Book and Directory of the Christian Church (Disciples of Christ)*, pp. 42 ff.

In the spring of 1969 the churches of America were startled by the demands of James Forman and the Black Economic Development Conference for "reparations." By "taking over" worship services and other church gatherings at selected places about the country, Forman and his followers called attention to their needs. A "Black Manifesto" was read in Riverside Church at New York City, demanding financial remuneration for black people who had been exploited for many years. The white community, in general, reacted with a certain amount of shock to these demands. The General Board of the Christian Church (Disciples of Christ) wrote a widely praised response, including recommendations for action. The Reconciliation program was extended from two to four years and the financial goal increased from $2,000,000 to $4,000,000. Local, regional, and general manifestations of the church were to allocate increased funds for crisis-related ministries. Directed by a Steering Committee on Reconciliation Beyond 1972 reconciliation programs continued. In this and other ways, the Christian Church (Disciples of Christ) sought to express social responsibility in the 1970s.

CONTINUING ECUMENICAL CONCERNS

A little-noticed event of 1910 proved to be of great importance. Peter Ainslie formed an organization to carry on a program of activities aimed at stimulating an interest in Christian unity among Disciples. Disciples responded by using it more adequately to participate in activities related to Christian unity. This organization continued its program after 1913 as the Association for the Promotion of Christian Unity. In October 1954 its name became the Council on Christian Unity. As such it has continued to serve as an administrative council of the Christian Church (Disciples of Christ). Ainslie remained president of the association until 1925 when he resigned. He was followed in the presidency by Levi G. Bateman, Edgar DeWitt Jones, Herbert L. Willett, Homer W. Carpenter, G. Edwin Osborn, and Hampton Adams. Executive secretaries have been H. C. Armstrong (1877-), until 1941; George Walker Buckner, Jr., from 1941 to 1958; Robert Tobias (1919-), from 1958 to 1960, and George G. Beazley, Jr., from 1960 to 1973. During Beazley's tenure the title executive secretary was changed to president. Paul A. Crow, Jr., (1931-)

became president in September 1974.

From its beginning the Council on Christian Unity sought to promote Christian union by means of conferences of various types. Shortly after its organization in 1910 the council sponsored a conference of Congregationalists, Disciples, Episcopalians, and Presbyterians in New York City. Other conferences were held from time to time through the years seeking to present the principles and progress of the ecumenical movement. It was early recognized that the conduct of formal negotiations for union between the Disciples and other denominations was the proper function of the International Convention. The General Assembly was similarly empowered by the Provisional Design. The Council on Christian Unity through the years, however, sought to encourage conversations leading to more formal negotiations. In this manner conversations were arranged between the Disciples and the American Baptists in the first half of the twentieth century.

Discussions between Disciples and Baptists had actually been held within ten years after the separation from the Baptists in 1830. In 1841 a conference sponsored by the Disciples on possible union had been held at Lexington, Kentucky. Alexander Campbell himself attended this meeting. Little was accomplished because the Baptists practically boycotted it.[10] Under the leadership of Baptists a conference was held between Baptists and Disciples in 1866.[11] Again in the 1890s discussions were held on the possibility of a Baptist-Disciples union but to no avail.

The widespread interest in the developing ecumenical movement within the first decade of the twentieth century rekindled interest in cooperation between Baptists and Disciples. Since the practice of immersion of adult believers was held in common by both denominations, it was assumed union was possible and desirable. The possibilities of union between the two groups became a live issue between 1903 and 1910. There were many local conferences and an exchange of editorial opinion.[12] Similar meetings, exchanges, and over-

10. *Millennial Harbinger,* 1841, p. 259. Winfred E. Garrison, *Christian Unity and Disciples of Christ,* St. Louis: Bethany Press, 1955. See pp. 165 ff. for a fuller account of Baptist-Disciples relations.
11. *Millennial Harbinger,* 1866, p. 224.
12. *Christian-Evangelist,* July 23, 1903. pp. 102 ff.

tures continued until the Northern (American) Baptist Convention of 1930 rejected the recommendations of its committee that closer cooperation in program and projects be developed with the Disciples. Thereafter formal consultation between the two denominations ceased for a time.

The Association for the Promotion of Christian Unity decided not to let the matter drop. It quietly developed informal conversations and continued friendship between the leaders. When the time again seemed ready, the International Convention was asked to undertake more formal negotiations. In the 1940s the two conventions appointed a joint commission to organize conversations and conferences which would lead to better understanding. A committee of Baptist and Disciples leaders prepared a historical and a theological statement which was given wide circulation. A new hymnal was prepared and published jointly in 1940. Such was the interest that it was thought possible that the two denominations could take immediate steps toward union. Simultaneous conventions were held at Chicago in May 1952 but once again all the effort came to naught. At the last minute the Baptists withdrew from the plan. There the matter has rested.

During World War I a proposal was made by the Presbyterian Church U.S.A. for a union of denominations. The first such proposal in America, a Conference on Organic Union was held at Philadelphia in 1918 with representatives from nineteen communions, including the Disciples, in attendance. What came to be known as "The Philadelphia Plan" was prepared and submitted for adoption by a second conference in 1920. This plan of union was based upon a concept of close cooperation between autonomous denominations looking toward full corporate union at a later date. Probably because of its emphasis upon federation rather than organic union, no church approved the plan. The Disciples had only a marginal participation in the American Council on Organic Union but some Disciples did regularly attend its meetings.[13]

Another proposal which involved the possibility of the union of several denominations was officially designated the

---

13. Paul A. Crow, Jr. in *The Christian Church (Disciples of Christ): An Interpretative Examination in the Cultural Context,* pp. 275 ff. Crow's essay is an excellent and comprehensive treatment of the experience of the Christian Church (Disciples of Christ) in the ecumenical movement.

Conference on Church Union. Initiated by the General Council of the Congregational Christian Churches, a proposal was publicized by the Federal Council of Churches calling for a conference on organic union of denominations "recognizing one another's ministries and sacraments." A resolution was presented and approved by the International Convention meeting at Columbus, Ohio, in 1946 calling for Disciples participation in the conference.

The initial meeting of the conference, held at Greenwich, Connecticut, in December 1949, was the first of a series of meetings which led to the "Greenwich Plan." Nine denominations were represented in the conference. The International Convention appointed as its delegates George Walker Buckner, Jr., Gaines M. Cook, A. Dale Fiers, Riley B. Montgomery, Charles Clayton Morrison, and Roy G. Ross. Gaines Cook served as secretary of the conference. Charles Clayton Morrison, editor of *The Christian Century* and a leading Disciples ecumenical leader, presented the draft of a plan of union which got the conference under way. Later a committee was appointed to draft a specific plan of union to be presented to a larger meeting held at Cincinnati in 1951. Other conferences were held, but little progress was made before the meetings came to an end in 1958.

After the formation in 1957 of the United Church of Christ (a union of the Congregational Christian Churches and the Evangelical and Reformed Church) tentative agreements were reached for a series of meetings between the Christian Churches (Disciples of Christ) and the newly formed United Church of Christ. Before such conversations got under way, however, an event transpired which was to absorb the interest and resources of several of the denominations for many years.

The Sunday before the triennial meeting of the National Council of Churches began at San Francisco in December 1960, Eugene Carson Blake, stated clerk of the United Presbyterian Church, preached at Grace Episcopal cathedral. In his sermon Blake proposed a consultation between representatives of the Episcopal, Methodist, and Presbyterian churches, and the United Church of Christ looking toward an organic union that would be "both catholic and reformed." His sermon electrified all persons committed to the ecumenical movement and especially those longing for organic union of churches.

Following this sermon steps were taken to form what came to be known as the "Consultation on Church Union" (COCU). In addition to the four denominations mentioned in Blake's sermon, ultimately six other denominations joined the consultation. The Christian Churches (Disciples of Christ), joined the other churches involved in a series of meetings which began in 1962. Paul A. Crow, Jr., served as the first general secretary of COCU from 1968 to 1974. After years of discussion and drafting, "A Plan of Union" was presented in 1970 to the member churches for their study and reaction. By means of papers, discussions, and hard work it was possible for the Consultation on Church Union to come to tentative agreement on several elements in the plan, especially on basic biblical and theological questions. These agreements were generally approved by COCU's constituency. In the two-year study between 1970 and 1972 it became clear there was no unanimity on the questions of structure and organization, which matters were referred back to COCU's plenary sessions for further development.

George G. Beazley, Jr., as president of the Council on Church Unity, gave creative leadership to the Disciples participation in the work of the Consultation on Christian Union. Along with the promising developments within the consultation, Beazley was able to develop the council's journal, *Midstream,* into a major ecumenical publication.

After the Second Vatican Council of the Roman Catholic Church which ended in 1965, it became possible for Disciples to enter into bilateral conversations with the Roman Catholic Church in the United States. Under the Council on Christian Unity's leadership, two dialogue sessions a year were held in the 1970s. While nothing definitive came from these meetings, a good understanding of position was achieved. Thus, in its ecumenical involvements, the Christian Church (Disciples of Christ) continued its concern for and emphasis on Christian unity.

FACING THE FUTURE

The challenge of the future is before the Christian Church (Disciples of Christ). Those who take up the task and carry it forward will find ways to give creative leadership to the church and its mission. It is unfortunate, in a way, that so much of history has to be written in terms of organizational structure and institutional development. Much of the real story, always elusive, lies in the lives of the thousands of men and women who have given their time and treasure in dedicated service to the proclamation of the Gospel and to the carrying forward of the mission of the church.

In the beginning, members of the Disciples thought of themselves as a part of the American frontier. As such they cherished the rugged individualism and supposed freedom of the frontier. They soon found that their very existence as a body of Christian people was seriously threatened by this position. Their concern for evangelism and missionary expansion was jeopardized by lack of means to accomplish their purpose. Through bitter experience they learned that undisciplined freedom often led to fragmentation and separation.

Except for occasional conferences on "internal" unity or Christian unity "forums," the three main groups deriving from the Stone-Campbell movement are seldom in contact with one another. The Christian Church (Disciples of Christ) functions as a part of American Christianity as one denomination among many denominations. Its future history and development will be closely related to that of all American Christianity.

In the light of biblical and theological understanding Christian unity will be realized ultimately. Disciples would do well to remember the words of Peter Ainslie, prophet of Christian unity, "If this movement is of God, He will not forget us; if it is not of Him, we desire it to be forgotten; but, believing that it is of the Lord, we are students of the problem of Christian union above all other issues in the Church."[14] Until there is unity in the church the Christian Church (Disciples of Christ) will continue its witness to the necessity for a united church based on the scriptures, so that the world may believe.

---

14. Peter Ainslie, *The Message of the Disciples for the Union of the Church* (New York: Fleming H. Revell, 1913), p. 34.

BIBLIOGRAPHY

A GUIDE TO THE LITERATURE OF THE CHRISTIAN CHURCH (DISCIPLES OF CHRIST)

Although the Christian Church (Disciples of Christ) did not originate until the early nineteenth century, there is a wealth of material concerning the history and thought of the movement. Following the example of Alexander Campbell, a prolific writer as well as an enterprising publisher, Disciples have relied heavily upon the printed word. The printing press has figured decisively in their development from the beginning to the present. This bibliography is designed to be selective and suggestive but not exhaustive in any sense. In spite of omissions and gaps, it aims to make students of Disciples history aware of the significant literature so that they may be able to pursue particular subjects of special interest in greater depth and detail.

I. *American Religious History*

To understand the past and present of the Christian Church (Disciples of Christ) without falling into the trap of denominational parochialism, it is essential to take into full account the sweep and complexity of American religious history together with church antecedents especially in Europe. Sydney E. Ahlstrom's comprehensive and insightful *A Religious History of the American People* (New Haven: Yale University Press, 1972) is the best one-volume treatment of the subject. In their *American Christianity: An Historical Interpretation with Representative Documents*, 2 vols. (New York: Charles Scribner's Sons, 1960 and 1963) H.

Shelton Smith, Robert T. Handy, and Lefferts A. Loetscher enrich their narrative with the extensive use of sources and helpful bibliographical suggestions. Widely read for many years, William W. Sweet's *The Story of Religion in America* (New York: Harper and Row, 2d rev. ed., 1950) remains useful but needs to be balanced by more recent surveys such as Winthrop S. Hudson's *Religion in America* (New York: Charles Scribner's Sons, 1965) and Edwin S. Gaustad's *A Religious History of America* (New York: Harper and Row, 1966). Among the excellent studies of Protestantism in America are Winthrop S. Hudson's *American Protestantism* (Chicago: University of Chicago Press, 1961) and Martin E. Marty's *Righteous Empire: The Protestant Experience in America* (New York: Dial Press, 1970). H. Richard Niebuhr's *The Kingdom of God in America* (New York: Willett, Clark and Co., 1937) provides a corrective to his earlier *Social Sources of Denominationalism* (New York: H. Holt and Co., 1929) and is a classic interpretation of the central theological motifs in American Protestantism. No single work on Christianity in the United States is more suggestive and seminal than Sidney E. Mead's *The Lively Experiment: The Shaping of Christianity in America* (New York: Harper and Row, 1963). This slim volume of 211 pages is nothing less than essential reading for anyone seriously interested in the course of American Christianity.

For an account of the varied and numerous religious groups in the United States, one should consult either Frank S. Mead's *Handbook of Denominations in the United States* (Nashville: Abingdon Press, 5th ed., 1970) or the older compendium by Frederick E. Mayer entitled *The Religious Bodies of America* (St. Louis: Concordia Publishing House, 2d ed., 1956). Edwin S. Gaustad's *Historical Atlas of Religion in America* (New York: Harper and Row, 1962) is a valuable reference work. By far the most exhaustive guide to the literature on the history of religion in America is Nelson R. Burr's *Critical Bibliography of Religion in America,* 2 vols. (Princeton: Princeton University Press, 1961). The *Harvard Guide to American History,* 2 vols. (Cambridge, Mass.: Belknap Press of Harvard University Press, rev. ed., 1974), edited by Frank Freidel, is the most useful bibliography of American history.

II. *Bibliographies and Indexes of Disciples Literature*

A number of Disciples bibliographies have been published and are available in almost any library which maintains a sizable collection of Discipliana. This fortunate circumstance is due primarily to the sustained and invaluable work of Claude E. Spencer, for many years curator of the Disciples of Christ Historical Society in Nashville, Tennessee. Spencer's *An Author*

Catalog of Disciples of Christ and Related Religious Groups (Canton, Mo.: Disciples of Christ Historical Society, 1946) needs to be updated but is indispensable. He also has compiled *Theses Concerning Disciples of Christ and Related Religious Groups* (Nashville: Disciples of Christ Historical Society, 1964) and *Periodicals of the Disciples of Christ* (Canton, Mo.: Disciples of Christ Historical Society, 1943). Two vastly important and long-lived journals, *The Christian-Evangelist* and the *Christian Standard,* have been indexed. Both indexes—*The Christian-Evangelist Index, 1863-1958,* 3 vols. (St. Louis and Nashville: Christian Board of Publication and Disciples of Christ Historical Society, 1962) and the massive *Christian Standard Index, 1866-1966,* 6 vols. (Nashville: Disciples of Christ Historical Society, 1972)—were prepared under the close supervision of Spencer. Archivist Marvin D. Williams, Jr. headed the team which developed a *Preliminary Guide to Black Materials in the Disciples of Christ Historical Society* (Nashville: Disciples of Christ Historical Society, 1971).

Two excellent bibliographical essays deserve to be mentioned. Roscoe M. Pierson's "The Literature of the Disciples of Christ and Closely Related Groups" appeared first in *Religion in Life* (Spring 1957) and was reprinted promptly in *The College of the Bible Quarterly* (July 1957). More recently Howard E. Short contributed a chapter on "the literature of the Christian Church (Disciples of Christ)" to *The Christian Church (Disciples of Christ): An Interpretative Examination in the Cultural Context* (St. Louis: Bethany Press, 1973) edited by George G. Beazley, Jr. In addition to Spencer's works, a few bibliographical aids paved the way for the essays by Pierson and Short. The earliest, no doubt, was John W. Monser's *The Literature of the Disciples, a Study* (St. Louis: Christian Publishing Co., 1906). Winfred E. Garrison followed with "The Literature of the Disciples of Christ," an eighteen-page list of books and periodicals in the *Bulletin of the Disciples Divinity House* (April 1923). Retaining Garrison's title, Alfred T. DeGroot and Enos E. Dowling expanded his bibliography to seventy-eight pages and published it in pamphlet form (Advance, Ind.: Hustler Printing Co., 1933). Subsequently, DeGroot also compiled "a design for a catalog" on *Literature of the Churches of Christ in Great Britain and Ireland* (Fort Worth: Privately printed, 1950).

Many studies in Disciples history provide solid bibliographies. David E. Harrell, Jr.'s *Quest for a Christian America: The Disciples of Christ and American Society to 1866* (Nashville: Disciples of Christ Historical Society, 1966) and *The Social Sources of Division in the Disciples of Christ, 1865-1900* (Atlanta and Athens, Ga.: Publishing Systems, Inc., 1973) are especially recommended. Also helpful is the selective bibliography in *The Disciples of Christ: A History* (St. Louis: Christian Board of Publication, 1948; revised ed., 1958) by Winfred E. Garrison and Alfred T. DeGroot. More specialized is the list of books and pamphlets by Disciples on the subject of Christian unity in Winfred E. Garrison's *Christian Unity and Disciples of Christ* (St. Louis: Bethany Press, 1955). Indeed an enormous amount of work is yet to be done, but it is clear that Disciples have made substantial progress in developing guides to their literature.

III. *Selected Sources*

Of all the documents in the entire course of Disciples history, the most important ones are *The Last Will and Testament of the Springfield Presbytery* (1804) and Thomas Campbell's *Declaration and Address of the Christian Association of Washington County, Washington, Pa.* (Washington, Pa.: Printed by Brown and Sample, 1809). No first edition copy of *The Last Will and Testament* is known to exist, but it is available in numerous volumes, sometimes with the *Declaration and Address*. See, for example, the reprint by Bethany Press in 1955. The full text of *An Apology for Renouncing the Jurisdiction of the Synod of Kentucky. To Which Is Added a Compendious View of the Gospel and a Few Remarks on the Confession of Faith* (Lexington, Ky.: Printed by Joseph Charless, 1804), written by Barton W. Stone and others, appears in the *Biography of Eld. Barton Warren Stone, Written by Himself: With Additions and Reflections* by John Rogers (Cincinnati: Published for the author by J. A. and U. P. James, 1847). This work is included in *The Cane Ridge Reader* (Cane Ridge Preservation Project, 1972) edited by Hoke S. Dickinson. Charles A. Young provided easy access to five *Historical Documents Advocating Christian Union* (Chicago: Christian Century Co., 1904). In addition to *The Last Will and Testament* and the *Declaration and Address*, Young's collection includes Alexander Campbell's *Sermon on the Law*, Isaac Errett's *Our Position* and James H. Garrison's *The World's Need of Our Plea*.

The best source for the study of Barton W. Stone's life is his autobiography with additions by John Rogers. Stone's *An Address to the Christian Churches in Kentucky, Tennessee, and Ohio, on Several Important Doctrines of Religion* (Nashville: M. and J. Nowell, 1814) is reprinted with the exception of his section on the Shakers in James M. Mathes's *Works of Elder B. W. Stone to Which Is Added a Few Discourses and Sermons* (Cincinnati: Moore, Wilstach, Keys and Co., 2d ed., 1859). For insight into Stone's theological perspective, one should read his treatise on the doctrine of the trinity entitled *Letters to James Blythe, D. D., Designed as a*

Reply to the Arguments of Thomas Cleland, D. D. (Lexington, Ky.: Printed by William Tanner, 1824) and his *Atonement. The Substance of Two Letters Written to a Friend* (Lexington: Printed by Joseph Charless, 1805). Stone's *History of the Christian Church in the West,* a series of articles in the *Christian Messenger* in 1827, was republished by Roscoe M. Pierson in *The College of the Bible Quarterly* (January 1956).

Unlike his father, Alexander Campbell was an unusually productive writer and frequently served as his own publisher. To provide a comprehensive view of biblical doctrine, Campbell wrote *A Connected View of the Principles and Rules by Which the Living Oracles May Be Intelligibly and Certainly Interpreted . . .* (Bethany, Va.: M'Vay and Ewing, 1835). Revised and published as *The Christian System, in Reference to the Union of Christians and a Restoration of Primitive Christianity, as Plead in the Current Reformation* (Bethany, Va.: Printed by A. Campbell, 1839), this volume figured decisively in shaping the theology of Disciples and has remained in print to the present. Singling out baptism for special attention, Campbell wrote *Christian Baptism: With Its Antecedents and Consequences* (Bethany, Va.: A. Campbell, 1851). Some of his most significant addresses are gathered together in *Popular Lectures and Addresses* (Philadelphia: James Challen and Son, 1863). Finding no New Testament in English which squared precisely with the original Greek text, he added prefaces, various emendations, and an appendix to the translation by George Campbell, James Macknight and Philip Doddridge and published it as *The Sacred Writings of the Apostles and Evangelists of Jesus Christ, Commonly Styled the New Testament* (Buffalo, Va.: A. Campbell, 1826).

Campbell engaged in several public debates. "A very numerous and respectable congregation" weighed the arguments presented by John Walker and Campbell on *Infant Sprinkling Proved to Be a Human Tradition; Being the Substance of a Debate on Christian Baptism* (Steubenville, Ohio: Printed by James Wilson, 1820). Three years later W. L. Maccalla and Campbell opposed each other in *A Debate on Christian Baptism . . .* (Buffalo, Va.: Campbell and Sala, 1824). Campbell's *Debate on the Evidences of Christianity . . .* with Robert Owen (Bethany, Va.: A. Campbell, 1829) attracted widespread attention as did his *A Debate on the Roman Catholic Religion . . .* with John B. Purcell (Cincinnati: J. A. James and Co., 1837). In 1843 Nathan L. Rice provided Campbell's opposition in *A Debate . . . on the Action, Subject, Design and Administrator of Christian Baptism . . .* (Pittsburgh: Thomas Carter, 1844). Moderated by Henry Clay, the Campbell-

Rice debate lasted for eighteen days and filled a volume of 912 pages. Not to be overlooked is Campbell's series of six articles entitled "Anecdotes, Incidents and Facts Connected with the Origin and Progress of the Current Reformation," which appeared in *The Millennial Harbinger* during 1848 and was published again in 1954 by the Disciples of Christ Historical Society in the *Harbinger and Discipliana.* A judicious selection of Campbell's theological writings is arranged topically in Royal Humbert's *A Compend of Alexander Campbell's Theology* (St. Louis: Bethany Press, 1961).

Walter Scott joined Alexander Campbell, Barton W. Stone and John T. Johnson in editing *Psalms, Hymns, and Spiritual Songs, Original and Selected* . . . (Bethany, Va.: Printed by A. Campbell, 1834). A later edition, revised and expanded, appeared under the cover title, *Christian Hymn Book.* Scott explained his basic theological message in *The Gospel Restored, a Discourse of the True Gospel of Jesus Christ* . . . (Cincinnati: Printed by O. H. Donogh, 1836). More than two decades later he wrote *The Messiahship; or, Great Demonstration* . . . (Cincinnati: H. S. Bosworth, 1859).

Following the death of Alexander Campbell in 1866, new leadership provided a continuing stream of literature for second- and third-generation Disciples. Robert Milligan's systematic treatment of biblical doctrine, *An Exposition and Defense of the Scheme of Redemption as It Is Revealed and Taught in the Holy Scriptures* (Cincinnati: R. W. Carroll, 1869), was extremely influential among Disciples for decades. A number of important addresses by thoughtful Disciples in the 1880s, including Isaac Errett's "The Grounds of Christian Fellowship," are preserved in the multi-volume *Missouri Christian Lectures.* See, for example, *The Missouri Christian Lectures, Selected from the Courses of 1886, 1887, and 1888* (Cincinnati: Standard Publishing Co., 1888). To make available a careful restatement of the Disciples theological position for his time, James H. Garrison edited and published *The Old Faith Restated: Being a Restatement by Representative Men, of the Fundamental Truths and Essential Doctrines of Christianity, as Held and Advocated by the Disciples of Christ* . . . (St. Louis: Christian Publishing Co., 1891). One of Garrison's contemporaries, William T. Moore, had selected a representative group of the best Disciples preachers and included a sermon from each of them in his *The Living Pulpit of the Christian Church* . . . (Cincinnati: R. W. Carroll, 1868). He lived to compile *The New Living Pulpit of the Christian Church* (St. Louis: Christian Board of Publication, 1918) fifty years later. Calling to mind the two Moore volumes published fifty years apart, P. Hunter

Beckelhymer edited *The Vital Pulpit of the Christian Church* (St. Louis: Bethany Press, 1968).

As Disciples moved through the post-Civil War era and into the twentieth century, they became embroiled in the controversy between conservatives and liberals that troubled much of mainstream Protestantism in the United States. The most influential biblical scholar among Disciples conservatives, John W. McGarvey completed his *A Commentary on Acts of Apostles, with a Revised Version of the Text* (Cincinnati: Wrighton and Co., 1863) while the Civil War raged. Later works of his include the still useful *Lands of the Bible; A Geographical and Topographical Description of Palestine . . .* (Philadelphia: Lippincott, 1881) and the two-volume *Evidences of Christianity* (Cincinnati: Guide Printing and Publishing Co., 1886, 1891). For an understanding of a pioneering liberal preacher in the Disciples, see *Life, Letters and Addresses of Dr. Lewis L. Pinkerton* (Cincinnati: Chase and Hall, 1871) edited by John Shackleford, Jr. Liberalism among the Disciples reached its zenith at Disciples Divinity House in Chicago under the leadership of Herbert L. Willett and Edward Scribner Ames. *The Bible Through the Centuries* (Chicago: Willett, Clark and Colby, 1929) and *Our Bible: Its Origin, Character, and Value* (Chicago: Christian Century Press, 1917) are but two of Willett's many works. Ames's *The Psychology of Religious Experience* (Boston: Houghton, 1910) and *Religion* (New York: H. Holt and Co., 1929) helped him gain high visibility outside the circle of his own communion. Peter Ainslie, the most ardent and respected ecumenist in the full sweep of Disciples history, gave his *The Message of the Disciples for the Union of the Church, Including Their Origin and History* (New York: Revell, 1913) as lectures at Yale Divinity School and later called church division *The Scandal of Christianity* (Chicago: Willett, Clark and Colby, 1929).

Organized for the purpose of reexamining the thought and witness of Disciples in the light of their historic position and modern scholarship, the Panel of Scholars worked for several years beginning in 1957. W. Barnett Blakemore served as general editor of the panel reports, *The Renewal of Church* (St. Louis: Bethany Press, 1963), which appeared in three volumes: *The Reformation of Tradition* edited by Ronald E. Osborn; *The Reconstruction of Theology* edited by Ralph G. Wilburn; and *The Revival of the Churches* edited by W. Barnett Blakemore. Two essays in the first volume—Blakemore's "Reasonable, Empirical, Pragmatic: The Mind of Disciples of Christ" and Osborn's "Dogmatically Absolute, Historically Relative"—are especially important. Equally suggestive and perceptive is Osborn's "Formula in Flux: Reformation for the Disciples of Christ?" in *What's Ahead for the Churches?* (New York: Sheed and Ward, 1964) edited by Kyle Haselden and Martin E. Marty. In the 1960s Disciples also reexamined their church structure and reconstituted themselves into the Christian Church (Disciples of Christ) on the basis of "A Provisional Design for the Christian Church (Disciples of Christ)." For the text of the document, as submitted by the Commission on Brotherhood Restructure, see the 1966 *Year Book of the Christian Churches (Disciples of Christ)* (Indianapolis: International Convention of Christian Churches).

The *Year Book,* first issued in 1885, is the official compendium of information on Disciples. The series of volumes entitled *Proceedings of the General Christian Missionary Convention* is a useful source of Discipliana prior to the publication of yearbooks. Printed minutes of the American Christian Missionary Society (1897-1917) and of the Foreign Christian Missionary Society (1897-1917) also may be consulted. The first *A Directory of the Ministry of the undenominational fellowship of Christian Churches and Churches of Christ* (Pattonville, Mo.: n. p., 1955) was compiled by Vernon M. Newland. Ministers of Churches of Christ were listed annually in *A Church Directory and List of Preachers of Churches of Christ* (Austin, Tex.: Firm Foundation Publishing Co.) until 1950. Each year since 1957 the same publisher has issued *Where the Saints Meet: A Directory of the Congregations of the Churches of Christ.*

The periodical literature of Disciples is so massive as to be overwhelming. Because of their great impact on the Stone-Campbell movement, a few journals deserve special attention. Alexander Campbell's *Christian Baptist* (1823-1830) and *The Millennial Harbinger* (1830-1870) together with Barton W. Stone's *The Christian Messenger* (1826-1845) and Walter Scott's *The Evangelist* (1832-1844) are clearly the most important sources for understanding pre-Civil War Disciples life and thought. Following the Civil War, Benjamin Franklin's ultraconservative *American Christian Review* (1856-1887) attracted a large following and wielded vast influence into the late 1870s. The *Gospel Advocate* (1855-), edited by David Lipscomb and Elisha G. Sewell for many years, gave strong support to rigid restorationism and became a dominant voice in the Churches of Christ. Isaac Errett's powerful *Christian Standard* (1866-) shifted from a progressive to an increasingly reactionary editorial policy after his death in 1888; it backed dissident Disciples who founded the North American Christian Convention which emerged into the "undenominational fellowship" known as Christian Churches and Churches of Christ. Errett's friend and ally, James H. Garrison, saw his *The Christian-Evangelist*, established as the *Gospel Echo* in 1863, gain acceptance as the representative paper of Disciples of Christ. Shortly after 1900 *The Christian-Evangelist* eclipsed the *Standard* in power and influence. Having been renamed *The Christian*, it merged with *World Call* (1919-1973) in 1974 to form *The Disciple*, the biweekly and in 1975 the semimonthly journal of the Christian Church (Disciples of Christ).

Additional Sources: A Sample

Books and Pamphlets

Adams, Hampton. *Why I Am a Disciple of Christ*. New York: Thomas Nelson and Sons, 1957.

Ames, Van Meter, ed. *Beyond Theology: The Autobiography of Edward Scribner Ames*. Chicago: University of Chicago Press, 1959.

Athearn, Walter S. *Religious Education and American Democracy*. Boston: Pilgrim Press, 1917.

Bower, William C. *The Curriculum of Religious Education*. New York: Charles Scribner, 1925.

_____ . *The Living Bible*. New York: Harper, 1936.

_____ . *Through the Years: Personal Memoirs*. Lexington, Ky.: Transylvania College Press, 1957.

Brents, Thomas W. *The Gospel Plan of Salvation*. Nashville: J. T. S. Fall, 1868.

Burnham, Frederick W. *Unification; The How, What and Why of the United Christian Missionary Society*. St. Louis: United Christian Missionary Society, 1927.

Butler, Pardee. *Personal Recollections with Reminiscences by His Daughter, Mrs. Rosetta B. Hastings . . . .* Cincinnati: Standard Publishing Co., 1889.

Campbell, Alexander. *Familiar Lectures on the Pentateuch; Delivered Before the Morning Class of Bethany College, During the Session of 1859-1860*. Cincinnati: H. S. Bosworth, 1867.

Centennial Convention Report. Cincinnati: Standard Publishing Co., n.d.

Cotten, Carroll C. *The Imperative Is Leadership: A Report on Ministerial Development in the Christian Church (Disciples of Christ)*. St. Louis: Bethany Press, 1973.

Cowden, John B. *Thinking Toward Christian Unity*. West Nashville, Tenn.: Published by the author, 1928.

Directorio Ministerio De Habla Hispana. Indianapolis: Division of Homeland Ministries, Christian Church (Disciples of Christ).

Dunlavy, John. *The Manifesto, or a Declaration of the Doctrines and Practice of the Church of Christ*. Pleasant Hill, Ky.: P. Bertrand, 1818.

Errett, Isaac. *First Principles: or, the Elements of the Gospel Analyzed and Discussed in Letters to an Inquirer.* Cincinnati: H. S. Bosworth, 1868.

————. *Linsey-Woolsey and Other Addresses.* Cincinnati: Standard Publishing Co., 1893.

————. *Talks to Bereans.* Cincinnati: R. W. Carroll and Co., 1872.

Fiers, A. Dale. *This Is Missions.* St. Louis: Christian Board of Publication, 1953.

Franklin, Benjamin. *The Gospel Preacher,* 2 vols. Cincinnati: Franklin and Rice, 1869.

Garrison, James H. *Memories and Experiences.* St. Louis: Christian Board of Publication, 1926.

————, ed. *Our First Congress.* St. Louis: Christian Publishing Co., 1900.

————, ed. *The Witness of Jesus and Other Sermons by Alexander Procter.* St. Louis: Christian Publishing Co., 1901.

Garrison, Winfred E. *Variations on a Theme.* St. Louis: Bethany Press, 1964.

Haggard, Rice. *An Address to the Different Religious Societies, on the Sacred Import of the Christian Name.* Reprinted in Footnotes to Disciple History, no. 4. Nashville: Disciples of Christ Historical Society, 1954.

Headington, Joel A. and Franklin, Joseph, eds. *Choice Selections from the Writings of Benjamin Franklin.* St. Louis: John Burns, 1879.

Hinsdale, Mary L., ed. *Garfield-Hinsdale Letters.* Ann Arbor: University of Michigan Press, 1949.

Jenkins, Burris A. *Where My Caravan Has Rested.* Chicago: Willett, Clark and Co., 1939.

Jones, Edgar D. *Blundering into Paradise.* New York: Harper and Row Publishers, Inc., 1933.

————. *A Man Stood Up to Preach and Fifteen Other Sermons.* St. Louis: Bethany Press, 1943.

McAllister, Lester G., ed. *Alexander Campbell at Glasgow University, 1808-1809.* Nashville: Disciples of Christ Historical Society, 1971.

McGarvey, John W. *The Autobiography of J. W. McGarvey.* Lexington, Ky.: The College of the Bible, 1960.

McLean, Archibald. *A Circuit of the Globe.* St. Louis: Christian Publishing Co., 1897.

McNemar, Richard. *The Kentucky Revival, or, a Short History of the Late Extraordinary Outpouring of the Spirit of God, in the Western States of America . . . .* Cincinnati: John W. Browne, 1807.

Manire, B. F., ed. *Thomas W. Caskey's Last Book Containing an Autobiographical Sketch of His Ministerial Life, with Essays and Sermons.* Nashville: Messenger Publishing Co., 1896.

Maus, Cynthia P. *Time to Remember.* New York: Exposition Press, 1964.

Milligan, Robert. *Reason and Revelation* . . . . Cincinnati: R. W. Carroll and Co., 1868.

Moore, William T. *The Plea of the Disciples of Christ* . . . . Chicago: Christian Century Co., 1906.

Morrison, Charles C. *The Meaning of Baptism.* Chicago: Disciples Publication Society, 1914.

————. *What Is Christianity?* Chicago: Willett, Clark and Co., 1940.

Mullins, George G., ed. *Caskey's Book: Lectures on Great Subjects* . . . . St. Louis: John Burns, 1884.

————. *My Life Is an Open Book.* St. Louis: John Burns, 1883.

O'Kelly, James. *Divine Oracles Consulted.* Hillsboro, N. C.: n.p.: 1800.

Osborn, G. Edwin, ed. *Christian Worship: A Service Book.* St. Louis: Christian Board of Publication, 1953; 2d ed., 1958.

Osborn, Ronald E. *In Christ's Place: Christian Ministry in Today's World.* St. Louis: Bethany Press, 1967.

Purviance, Levi, ed. *The Biography of Elder David Purviance, with His Memoirs* . . . . Dayton, Ohio: Published for the author by B. F. and G. W. Ells, 1848.

Richardson, Robert. *The Principles and Objects of the Religious Reformation Urged by A. Campbell and Others, Briefly Stated and Explained.* Bethany, Va.: A. Campbell, 2d ed., 1853.

Robinson, William. *The Biblical Doctrine of the Church.* St. Louis: Bethany Press, 1948; rev. ed., 1955.

Rogers, John I., ed. *Autobiography of Elder Samuel Rogers.* Cincinnati: Standard Publishing Co., 1880.

Scoville, Charles R. *Evangelistic Sermons Delivered During the Great Meetings at Pittsburgh and Des Moines.* Des Moines: Christian Union Publishing Co., 1902.

Shelton, Albert L. *Pioneering in Tibet: A Personal Record of Life and Experience in Mission Fields.* New York: Revell, 1921.

Shelton, Orman L. *The Church Functioning Effectively.* St. Louis: Christian Board of Publication, 1946.

Srygley, Fletcher D. *Seventy Years in Dixie.* Nashville: Gospel Advocate Publishing Co., 1891.

Stone, Barton W. *A Reply to John P. Campbell's Strictures on Atonement.* Lexington, Ky.: Joseph Charless, 1805.

Sweeney, Zachary T., ed. *New Testament Christianity,* 3 vols. Columbus, Ind.: Printed for the editor, 1923, 1926, 1930.

Updike, Jacob V. *Updike's Sermons* . . . . Cincinnati: Standard
Publishing Co., 1891.
Zollars, Ely V. *A Creed That Needs No Revision,* Cincinnati: Standard Publishing Co., 1900.
————. *The Great Salvation.* Cincinnati: Standard Publishing Co., 1895.

Periodicals

Apostolic Times (Lexington, Ky.) 1869-1885.
Christian Century; originally named *Christian Oracle* (Des Moines, Iowa; Chicago, Ill.) 1884-
Christian Plea; originally named *Gospel Plea* (Edwards, Miss.; Nashville, Tenn.) 1896-1965 (?).
Christian Preacher (Cincinnati, Ohio; Georgetown, Ky.) 1836-1840.
Christian Quarterly (Cincinnati, Ohio) 1869-1876.
The College of the Bible Quarterly; renamed *Lexington Theological Quarterly* (Lexington, Ky.) 1910- ; suspended 1926-1937.
Encounter (Indianapolis, Ind.) 1955-; superseded *Shane Quarterly,* 1940-1955.
Lard's Quarterly (Georgetown and Frankfort, Ky.) 1863-1868.
Mid-Stream (Indianapolis, Ind.) 1961- .
Missionary Tidings (Indianapolis, Ind.) 1883-1918.
New Christian Quarterly (St. Louis, Mo.) 1892-1896.
Octographic Review (Indianapolis, Ind.) 1887-1939.
Restoration Herald (Cincinnati, Ohio) 1922- .
Scroll; originally named *Quarterly Bulletin of the Campbell Institute* (Chicago, Ill.) 1903- .
Touchstone; originally named *Spotlight* (Cincinnati, Ohio) 1925-1927.
United Society News (St. Louis, Mo.) 1925-1926.
Up-Date on the Black Church (Indianapolis, Ind.) 1973- .

IV. *Secondary Literature: General Histories and Interpretations*

Historical surveys detailing the origin and development of the Disciples have been available for many years. Before the turn of the last century, Benjamin B. Tyler contributed *A History of the Disciples of Christ* (New York: Christian Literature Co., 1894) to the series of denominational histories published under the auspices of the American Society of Church History. The scholarly Errett Gates, having completed his still useful *The Early Relation and Separation of Baptists and Disciples* (Chicago: Christian Century Co., 1904), broadened the scope of his work in *The Disciples of Christ* (New York: Baker and Taylor Co., 1905). Interest among Disciples in their past mounted as they prepared to celebrate the centennial observance of Thomas Campbell's *Declaration and Address*. Editor of *The Reformation of the Nineteenth Century* (St. Louis: Christian Publishing Co., 1901), James H. Garrison entitled his centennial history of Disciples *The Story of a Century* (St. Louis: Christian Publishing Co., 1909). Also published in the centennial year, William T. Moore's massive (830 pp.) *A Comprehensive History of the Disciples of Christ* (New York: Revell, 1909) is more enduring in value and continues to be read and cited by students of Disciples history. In the next decade Morrison M. Davis condensed his *The Restoration Movement of the Nineteenth Century* (Cincinnati: Standard Publishing Co., 1913) into *How the Disciples Began and Grew* (Cincinnati: Standard Publishing Co., 1915); and Walter W. Jennings traced the *Origin and Early History of the Disciples of Christ* (Cincinnati: Standard Publishing Co., 1919) from James O'Kelly through Alexander Campbell.

If Disciples have a substantive appreciation for their history without exaggerating its significance on the American scene, the credit belongs to Winfred E. Garrison more than to any other historian, past or present. Following his *Religion Follows the Frontier: A History of the Disciples of Christ* (New York: Harper and Row, 1931), he wrote the succinct *An American Religious Movement: A Brief History of the Disciples of Christ* (St. Louis: Christian Board of Publication, 1945) and a study guide, *Whence and Whither the Disciples of Christ* (St. Louis: Christian Board of Publication, 1948). Then he collaborated with Alfred T. DeGroot on *The Disciples of Christ: A History* which for a solid generation served mainstream Disciples as their definitive history. More recently *The Christian Church (Disciples of Christ): An Interpretative Examination in the Cultural Context*, edited by George G. Beazley, Jr., placed Disciples within the context of world Christianity and took seriously the tumultuous shifts in the intellectual climate of the 1960s. Less satisfying in terms of perspective but highly readable is Louis and Bess White Cochran's *Captives of the Word* (Garden City, New York: Doubleday, 1969), a narrative history of Disciples emphasizing the life and work of Alexander Campbell.

The Search for the Ancient Order (2 vols.) by Earl I. West is regarded as the standard historical treatment of the Stone-Campbell movement among members of Churches of Christ. The first volume (Nashville: Gospel Advocate Co., 1949) concludes with a discussion of the church during the Civil War; Volume 2 (Indianapolis: Religious Book Service, 1950) covers the period from 1866 to 1906 at which time Churches of Christ were listed officially as a group of congregations separate and distinct from Disciples. Still another history, James D. Murch's *Christians Only: A History of the Restoration Movement* (Cincinnati: Standard Publishing Co., 1962), is based on the conviction that only the "undenominational fellowship" of Christian Churches and Churches of Christ faithfully interprets the basic witness of the Disciples fathers. Describing his own fellowship as "the great center" and Churches of Christ as the "right wing" of the Restoration Movement, Murch labeled mainstream Disciples as "leftists." In his helpful discussion of *The Grounds of Divisions Among the Disciples of Christ* (Chicago: Privately printed, 1940), Alfred T. DeGroot marshaled strong evidence to support the thesis that restorationism is divisive rather than unitive. Subsequently, Stephen J. Corey traced in meticulous detail the disruptions among Disciples from 1900 to 1950 in his *Fifty Years of Attack and Controversy: The Consequences among Disciples of Christ* (Published by The Committee on Publication of the Corey Manuscript, 1953). Regardless of theological orientation and cultural outlook, all students of the Stone-Campbell tradition will find *Churches of Christ: A Historical, Biographical, and Pictorial History of Churches of Christ in the United States, Australasia, England and Canada* (Louisville: John P. Morton and Co., 1904), edited by John T. Brown, to be an extremely useful collection.

The social history of Disciples has not been overlooked or treated superficially. Especially recommended are David E. Harrell, Jr.'s carefully researched and heavily documented *Quest for a Christian America: The Disciples of Christ and American Society to 1866* and *The Social Sources of Division in the Disciples of Christ, 1865-1900*. Harrell's works are thoroughgoing reappraisals of nineteenth-century Disciples and major contributions to the historiography of the movement. Also worthy of mention are James A. Crain's *The Development of Social Ideas Among the Disciples of Christ* (St. Louis: Bethany Press, 1969) and *Trumpet Call of Reformation* (St. Louis: Bethany Press, 1959), a socio-cultural study of Disciples by Oliver R. Whitley.

In his solid and brief *Doctrine and Thought of the Disciples of Christ* (St. Louis: Christian Board of Publication, 1951), Howard E. Short provided an admirable guide to Disciples thought. It has been read and studied widely as has his *Christian Unity Is Our Business: Disciples of Christ within the Ecumenical Movement* (St. Louis: Bethany Press, 1953). Other concise summaries of Disciples beliefs and practices include *What We Believe* (St. Louis: Bethany Press, 1960), edited by James M. Flanagan, and a pamphlet entitled *Who Are the Christian Churches and What Do We Believe?* (Published by the authors, 1954), co-written by R. Frederick West and William G. West. A much fuller treatment can be found in Alfred T. DeGroot's *Disciple Thought: A History* (Fort

Worth, Texas: Published by the author, 1965) with an overview by
Winfred E. Garrison. Ronald E. Osborn's essay, "Theology among
the Disciples," in Beazley's *The Christian Church (Disciples of
Christ)* is an excellent statement on the principal themes and basic
shifts in Disciples theology over the years. Winfred E. Garrison
added significantly to the self-understanding of Disciples with his
perceptive *Heritage and Destiny: An American Religious Movement Looks Ahead* (St. Louis: Bethany Press, 1961).

Additional Histories and Interpretations

Abbott, Byrdine A. *The Disciples, an Interpretation.* St. Louis:
Christian Board of Publication, 1924.

Ames, E. Scribner. *The Disciples of Christ: Their Growth, Their
Heritage, Their Timeliness.* A pamphlet published by the
author, 1943.

————. *Whither Disciples?* A pamphlet published by University
Church of Disciples of Christ in Chicago, 1939.

Blakemore, W. Barnett. *The Discovery of the Church: A History of
Disciple Ecclesiology* (The Reed Lectures for 1965). Nashville:
Disciples of Christ Historical Society, 1966.

DeGroot, Alfred T. *Church of Christ Number Two.* Published by
the author, 1956.

————. *New Possibilities for Disciples and Independents.* St.
Louis: Bethany Press, 1963.

England, Stephen J. *We Disciples: A Brief View of History and
Doctrine.* St. Louis: Christian Board of Publication, 1946.

Fife, Robert O.; Harrell, David E., Jr. and Osborn, Ronald E.
Disciples and the Church Universal (The Reed Lectures for
1966). Nashville: Disciples of Christ Historical Society, 1967.

Ford, Harold W. *A History of the Restoration Plea.* Oklahoma City:
Semco Color Press, 1952.

Fortune, Alonzo W. *Origin and Development of the Disciples.* St.
Louis: Christian Board of Publication, 1924.

Garrison, Winfred E. *Christian Unity and Disciples of Christ.* St.
Louis: Bethany Press, 1955.

Hailey, Homer. *Attitudes and Consequences in the Restoration
Movement.* Rosemead, Calif.: Old Paths Book Club, 2d ed., 1952.

Jordan, Robert L. *Two Races in One Fellowship.* Detroit: United
Christian Church, 1944.

Kershner, Frederick D. "Stars" in *Christian Standard.* A serial
from March 9, 1940 to Dec. 7, 1940.

Lair, Loren E. *The Christian Churches and Their Work.* St. Louis:
Bethany Press, 1963.

Longan, George W. *Origin of the Disciples of Christ*. St. Louis: Christian Publishing Co., 1889.

Lowber, James W. *The Who and the What of the Disciples of Christ*. Nashville: Gospel Advocate Co., 1892.

Lyda, Hap. *A History of Black Christian Churches (Disciples of Christ) in the United States through 1899*. Ann Arbor: University Microfilms, 1973.

Major, James B. "The Role of Periodicals in the Development of the Disciples of Christ, 1850-1910." Unpublished Ph.D. thesis, Vanderbilt University, 1966.

Murrell, Arthur V. *The Effects of Exclusivism in the Separation of the Churches of Christ from the Christian Church*. Ann Arbor: University Microfilms, 1972.

Phillips, Thomas W. *The Church of Christ*. New York: Funk and Wagnalls, 1905.

Pugh, Samuel F., ed. *Primer for New Disciples*. St. Louis: Bethany Press, 1963.

Robinson, William. *What Churches of Christ Stand For: The Origin, Growth, and Message of a Nineteenth Century Religious Movement*. Birmingham, England: Churches of Christ Publication Committee, 1926.

Van Kirk, Hiram. *The Rise of the Current Reformation, or a Study in the History of Theology of the Disciples of Christ*. St. Louis: Christian Publishing Co., 1907.

Walker, Dean E. *Adventuring for Christian Unity: A Survey of the History of Churches of Christ (Disciples)*. Birmingham, England: Berean Press, 1935.

Welshimer, Pearl H. *Concerning the Disciples: A Brief Resumé of the Movement to Restore the New Testament Church*. Cincinnati: Standard Publishing Co., 1935.

V. *Secondary Literature: Specialized Studies*

Much of the secondary literature concerning the history and thought of Disciples and related religious movements is biographical. No recent collections of biographies have been published, but several older volumes are useful. These include Thomas W. Grafton's *Men of Yesterday, a Series of Character Sketches of Prominent Men Among the Disciples of Christ* (St. Louis: Christian Publishing Co., 1899), Jesse J. Haley's *Makers and Molders of the Reformation Movement: A Study of Leading Men among the Disciples of Christ* (St. Louis: Christian Board of Publication, 1914), Frederick D. Power's study guide entitled *Sketches of Our Pioneers* (New York: Revell, 1898), William C. Rogers's *Recollections of Men of Faith, Containing Conversations* with Pioneers of the Current Reformation (St. Louis: Christian Publishing Co., 1889) and The Christian Portrait Gallery; Consisting of Historical and Biographical Sketches and Photographic Portraits of Christian Preachers and Others (Cincinnati: Published by the author, 1864) by M. C. Tiers. William T. Moore's The Living Pulpit of the Christian Church and The New Living Pulpit of the Christian Church have been mentioned earlier as has John T. Brown's Churches of Christ. Brown confined his Who's Who in Churches of Christ (Cincinnati: Standard Publishing Co., 1929) mainly to Disciples recognized for their conservatism. For vignettes of leaders among the Churches of Christ up to 1932, see Henry L. Boles's Biographical Sketches of Gospel Preachers, Including the Pioneeer Preachers of the Restoration Movement (Nashville: Gospel Advocate Co., 1932). The Dictionary of American Biography contains essays on a number of influential Disciples ranging in time from Stone and the Campbells to Herbert L. Willett.

Several biographies and other monographs have helped to bring the pre-Civil War period of Disciples history into reasonably clear focus. William G. West's Barton Warren Stone: Early American Advocate of Christian Unity (Nashville: Disciples of Christ Historical Society, 1954) explores theological issues in much greater depth than Charles C. Ware's meticulous Barton Warren Stone, Pathfinder of Christian Union (St. Louis: Bethany Press, 1932). Walter Scott: Voice of the Golden Oracle (St. Louis: Christian Board of Publication, 1946), a very readable biography by Dwight E. Stevenson, is based in part on sources not consulted by William Baxter in preparing his older Life of Elder Walter Scott, with Sketches of His Fellow Laborers, William Hayden, Adamson Bentley, John Henry, and Others (Cincinnati: Bosworth, Chase and Hall, 1874). Lester G. McAllister's Thomas Campbell: Man of the Book (St. Louis: Bethany Press, 1954) is a solid and scholarly work in contrast to Alexander Campbell's Memoirs of Elder Thomas Campbell, Together with a Brief Memoir of Mrs. Jane Campbell (Cincinnati: H. S. Bosworth, 1861). William H. Hanna uncovered the minutes of the Chartiers Presbytery detailing the trial of the elder Campbell and reprinted them in his Thomas Campbell, Seceder and Christian Union Advocate (Cincinnati: Standard Publishing Co., 1935).

Although Alexander Campbell has received far more attention than any other figure in Disciples history, the best biography of him in print is still Robert Richardson's classic Memoirs of Alexander Campbell, Embracing a View of the Origin, Progress and Principles of the Religious Reformation which He Advocated, 2 vols. (Philadelphia: J. Lippincott, 1868, 1870). Reprinted as two volumes in one as early as 1871, it has appeared in many editions. The definitive biography of Campbell has been written by Eva Jean Wrather. Her massive (3,000 pages) and exhaustive two-volume typescript entitled "Alexander Campbell: Adventurer in Freedom" is on deposit in the archives of the Disciples of Christ Historical Society. *The Fool of God* (New York: Duell, Sloan and Pearce, 1958) by Louis Cochran is an engaging historical novel portraying the life of Campbell. Winfred E. Garrison's investigation of *Alexander Campbell's Theology, Its Sources and Historical Setting* (St. Louis: Christian Publishing Co., 1900) was submitted as his Ph.D. thesis at the University of Chicago in 1897. Important aspects of Campbell's thought and work have been treated in D. Ray Lindley's *Apostle of Freedom* (St. Louis: Bethany Press, 1957), Harold L. Lunger's *The Political Ethics of Alexander Campbell* (St. Louis: Bethany Press, 1954), Cecil K. Thomas's *Alexander Campbell and His New Version* (St. Louis: Bethany Press, 1958), Granville T. Walker's *Preaching in the Thought of Alexander Campbell* (St. Louis: Bethany Press, 1954) and R. Frederick West's *Alexander Campbell and Natural Religion* (New Haven: Yale University Press, 1948). More recently Perry E. Gresham, editor of *The Sage of Bethany: A Pioneer in Broadcloth* (St. Louis: Bethany Press, 1960), reflected on *Campbell and the Colleges* (Nashville: Disciples of Christ Historical Society, 1973) in his Reed Lectures for 1971.

Alexander Campbell's biographer and close friend, Robert Richardson, is the subject of *Home to Bethphage: A Biography of Robert Richardson* (St. Louis: Christian Board of Publication, 1949) by Cloyd Goodnight and Dwight E. Stevenson. Another Bethany College associate, Campbell's son-in-law, is treated at length in Frederick D. Power's *Life of William Kimbrough Pendleton* (St. Louis: Christian Publishing Co., 1902). In *The Story of D. S. Burnet: Undeserved Obscurity* (St. Louis: Bethany Press, 1954), Noel L. Keith highlighted the individual who led Disciples into cooperative programs and structures at the national level. No Disciple of the first generation was more colorful and outspoken than the central character in Louis Cochran's historical novel, *Raccoon John Smith* (New York: Duell, Sloan and Pearce, 1963). The *Life of Elder John Smith with Some Account of the Rise and Progress of the Current Reformation* (Cincinnati: R. W. Carroll, 1870) by John A. Williams is a fascinating account of religion and society in backwoods America. John Rogers's *Biography of Elder J. T. Johnson* (Cincinnati: Published by the author, 2d ed., 1861) and Peter Donan's *Memoir Of Jacob Creath, Jr.* (Cincinnati: R. W. Carroll, 1872) also are interesting older works.

It is clear that the middle period of Disciples history, unlike the pre-Civil War decades, has been neglected. Even so, some biographical studies shed light on this exceedingly complex and transitional era. For insight into pivotal post-Civil War figures, see William C. Morro's *"Brother McGarvey": The Life of President J. W. McGarvey of The College of the Bible* (St. Louis: Bethany Press, 1940), William E. Tucker's *J. H. Garrison and Disciples of Christ* (St. Louis: Bethany Press, 1964), and Earl I. West's *The Life and Times of David Lipscomb* (Henderson, Tenn.: Religious Book Service, 1954). No published work on Isaac Errett has appeared since James S. Lamar's *Memoirs of Isaac Errett,* 2 vols. (Cincinnati: Standard Publishing Co., 1893). In his study of the first Disciple to become President of the United States, Woodrow W. Wasson explored the religion and education of *James A. Garfield* (Nashville: Tennessee Book Co., 1952). Ronald E. Osborn's engaging *Ely Vaughn Zollars: Teacher of Preachers, Builder of Colleges* (St. Louis: Christian Board of Publication, 1947) and Lester G. McAllister's *Z. T. Sweeney: Preacher and Peacemaker* (St. Louis: Christian Board of Publication, 1968) call attention to the manifold contributions of two prominent leaders. *Thinking Things Through with E. E. Snoddy* (St. Louis: Bethany Press, 1940) by Alonzo W. Fortune is an intellectual biography of a gifted Disciples teacher. Francis M. Arant in *"P. H."—The Welshimer Story* (Cincinnati: Standard Publishing Foundation, 1958) recounted the life and work of an extraordinary pastor who found himself in serious disagreement with mainstream Disciples and played a major role in forming the undenominational fellowship of Christian Churches and Churches of Christ. One of the most effective and admired leaders among Disciples women was memorialized in *Helen E. Moses, of the Christian Woman's Board of Missions* (New York: Revell, 1909) edited by Jasper T. Moses. See also Bertha M. Fuller's *Sarah Lue Bostick, Minister and Missionary* (Little Rock, Ark.: Private printing, 1949). Among the accounts of overseas missionaries are Flora B. Shelton's *Shelton of Tibet* (New York: Doran, 1923) and Clayton C. Smith's *The Life and Work of Jacob Kenoly* (Cincinnati: Privately printed, 1912).

Beginning with Amos S. Hayden's *Early History of the Disciples in the Western Reserve, Ohio* . . . (Cincinnati: Chase and Hall, 1875), Disciples have produced a sizable collection of volumes which treat the development of their movement in particular regions. Alonzo W. Fortune's *The Disciples in Kentucky* (Published by the Convention of the Christian Churches in Kentucky, 1932) and *North Carolina Disciples of Christ* (St. Louis: Christian Board of Publication, 1927) by Charles C. Ware are good older works. In addition to Henry K. Shaw's excellent *Buckeye*

Disciples: A History of the Disciples of Christ in Ohio (St. Louis: Published by the Christian Board of Publication for the Ohio Christian Missionary Society, 1952) and *Hoosier Disciples: A Comprehensive History of the Christian Churches (Disciples of Christ) in Indiana* (St. Louis: Published by Bethany Press for the Association of the Christian Churches in Indiana, 1966), the best of the more recent state histories include Clifford A. Cole's *The Christian Churches of Southern California* (St. Louis: Christian Board of Publication, 1959), Wilbur H. Cramblet's *The Christian Church (Disciples of Christ) in West Virginia* (St. Louis: Bethany Press, 1971), Stephen J. England's *Oklahoma Christians* (Oklahoma City: The Christian Church in Oklahoma, 1975), Colby D. Hall's *Texas Disciples* (Fort Worth: Texas Christian University Press, 1953), J. Edward Moseley's *Disciples of Christ in Georgia* (St. Louis: Bethany Press, 1954) and *Tennessee Christians* (Nashville: Reed and Company, 1971) by Herman A. Norton. Reuben Butchart wrote the standard history of *The Disciples of Christ in Canada since 1830* (Toronto: Canadian Headquarters' Publications, Churches of Christ [Disciples], 1949), while Archibald C. Watters surveyed the history of Disciples in Great Britain in his *History of British Churches of Christ* (Indianapolis: Butler University School of Religion, 1948). H. R. Taylor's *The History of Churches of Christ in South Australia, 1846-1959* (Published by the Churches of Christ Evangelistic Union Inc. in South Australia, n. d.) supplements A. W. Stephenson's *One Hundred Years: A Statement of the Development and Accomplishments of Churches of Christ in Australia* (Melbourne: Austral Printing and Publishing Co., 1946) and Aaron B. Maston's older *Jubilee Pictorial History of Churches of Christ in Australia* (Melbourne: Austral Publishing Co., 1903). Fretwell Godfry edited *Centennial Souvenir: Being a Brief History of the Associated Churches of Christ in New Zealand, 1844-1944* (Wellington: G. Deslandes, 1944) to provide an account of Disciples in that land. Particular fields of missionary endeavor receive thorough treatment in Robert G. Nelson's *Disciples of Christ in Jamaica, 1858-1958* (St. Louis: Bethany Press, 1958) and in John D. Montgomery's *Disciples of Christ in Argentina, 1906-1956* (St. Louis: Bethany Press, 1956).

An exceptionally helpful review of the total work and witness of Disciples at home and abroad in the late 1920s can be found in *Survey of Service: Organizations Represented in International Convention of Disciples of Christ* (St. Louis: Christian Board of Publication, 1928). It was prepared for publication under the general editorship of William R. Warren, biographer of *The Life and Labors of Archibald McLean* (St. Louis: Bethany Press, 1923). A pioneering missionary executive of the first rank, McLean himself wrote *The History of the Foreign Christian Missionary Society* (New York: Revell, 1919). *The American Christian Missionary Society and the Disciples of Christ* (St. Louis: Christian Board of Publication, 1937) by Grant K. Lewis appeared more than a half-century after Francis M. Green's *Christian Missions, and Historical Sketches of Missionary Societies Among the Disciples of Christ* . . . (St. Louis: John Burns, 1884). The most complete *History of the Christian Woman's Board of Missions* (n. p., 1920) was written by Ida W. Harrison. *The Shape of Adam's Rib* (St. Louis: Bethany Press, 1970) by Lorraine Lollis is a lively history of women's work in the Christian Church from 1874 to 1969. William M. Smith's *For the Support of the Ministry* (Indianapolis: Pension Fund of Disciples of Christ, 1956) reviews the birth and growth of the Board of Ministerial Relief and its successor, the Pension Fund of Disciples of Christ. Of the histories of educational institutions related to the Christian Church (Disciples of Christ), the best is Dwight E. Stevenson's *Lexington Theological Seminary, 1865-1965* (St. Louis: Bethany Press, 1964). Other excellent recent works include W. Barnett Blakemore's monograph on the first seventy-five years of the Disciples Divinity House of the University of Chicago, *Quest for Intelligence in Ministry* (Chicago: Disciples Divinity House, 1970); *Texas Christian University: A Hundred Years of History* (Fort Worth: Texas Christian University Press, 1973) by Jerome A. Moore; and *Transylvania: Tutor to the West*, John D. Wright, Jr. Transylvania University, 1975.

Additional Specialized Studies: A Brief List

Athearn, Clarence R. *The Religious Education of Alexander Campbell.* St. Louis: Bethany Press, 1928.

Azlein, Arthur A. *A History of the Disciples of Christ in the National Capital Area.* Washington, D. C.: mimeographed, 1963.

Barber, William J. *Disciple Assemblies of Eastern North Carolina.* St. Louis: Private edition by Bethany Press, 1966.

Baxter, William. *Life of Knowles Shaw, the Singing Evangelist.* Cincinnati: Central Book Concern, 1879.

Belcastro, Joseph. *The Relationship of Baptism to Church Membership.* St. Louis: Bethany Press, 1963.

Black, Robert E. *The Story of Johnson Bible College.* Kimberlin Heights, Tenn.: Tennessee Valley Printing Co., 1951.

Boren, Carter E. *Religion on the Texas Frontier.* San Antonio: Naylor Co., 1968.

Bower, William C. and Ross, Roy, eds. *The Disciples and Religious Education.* St. Louis: Christian Board of Publication, 1936.

Campbell, Selina H. *Home Life and Reminiscences of Alexander Campbell by His Wife.* St. Louis: John Burns, 1882.

Caruthers, E. W. *A Sketch of the Life and Character of the Rev. David Caldwell, D.D.* Greensborough, N. C.: Printed by Swaim and Sherwood, 1842.

Castleberry, Otis L. *They Heard Him Gladly: A Critical Study on Benjamin Franklin's Preaching,* Rosemont, Calif. Old Paths, 1913.

Castleman, William J. *Samuel Guy Inman, 1905-1916.* Indianapolis: Christian Communications Reporter, 1969.

Dahlberg, Edwin T., ed. *Herald of the Evangel.* St. Louis: Bethany Press, 1965.

Darst, H. Jackson. *Ante-Bellum Virginia Disciples.* Richmond, Va.: Virginia Christian Missionary Society, 1959.

Dickinson, Elmira J. *A History of Eureka College.* St. Louis: Christian Publishing Co., 1894.

Dye, Eva N. *Bolenge: A Story of Gospel Triumphs on the Congo.* Cincinnati: Foreign Christian Missionary Society, 1909.

Egbert, James. *Alexander Campbell and Christian Liberty.* St. Louis: Christian Publishing Co., 1909.

Flowers, Ronald B. "The Bible Chair Movement in the Disciples of Christ Tradition: Attempts to Teach Religion in State Universities." Unpublished Ph.D. thesis, University of Iowa, 1967.

Forster, Ada L. *A History of the Christian Church and Church of Christ in Minnesota.* St. Louis: Christian Board of Publication, 1953.

Fortune, Alonzo W. *Adventuring with Disciple Pioneers.* St. Louis: Bethany Press, 1942.

Four Faces of Christian Ministry: Essays in Honor of A. Dale Fiers. St. Louis: Bethany Press, 1973.

Gates, Robert W. "Samuel Davies to Barton W. Stone: A Study of Antecedents." Unpublished B.D. thesis, Lexington Theological Seminary, 1964.

Giovannoli, Harry. *Kentucky Female Orphan School, a History.* Midway, Ky.: n. p., 1930.

Green, Francis M. *Hiram College and Western Reserve Eclectic Institute; Fifty Years of History, 1850-1900.* Cleveland: O. S. Hubbell Printing Co., 1901.

————. *The Life and Times of John Franklin Rowe.* Cincinnati: F. L. Rowe, 1899.

Haldane, Alexander. *Memoirs of the Lives of Robert Haldane of Airthrey, and of His Brother, James Alexander Haldane.* New York: Carter and Brothers, 1857.

Hale, Allean L. *Petticoat Pioneer: The Story of Christian College.* Columbia, Mo.: Christian College, 1956; revised ed., 1968.

Haley, Jesse J. *Debates that Made History: the Story of Alexander Campbell's Debates with Rev. John Walker, Rev. W. L. Maccalla, Mr. Robert Owen, Bishop Purcell, and Rev. Nathan L. Rice.* St. Louis: Christian Board of Publication, 1920.

Haley, Thomas P. *Dawn of the Reformation in Missouri.* St. Louis: Christian Publishing Co., 1888.

Hall, Colby D. *Rice Haggard: The American Frontier Evangelist Who Revived the Name Christian.* Fort Worth: University Christian Church, 1957.

Hamlin, Griffith A. *The Life and Influence of Dr. John Tomline Walsh.* Wilson, N. C.: Published by the author, 1942.

_____ . "The Origin and Development of the Board of Higher Education of the Christian Church (Disciples of Christ), 1894-1968." Unpublished M.S.E. thesis, Southern Illinois University, 1968.

Harmon, Marion F. *A History of the Christian Churches in Mississippi.* Aberdeen, Miss.: n. p., 1929.

Haynes, Nathaniel S. *History of the Disciples of Christ in Illinois, 1819-1914.* Cincinnati: Standard Publishing Co., 1915.

Hodge, Frederick A. *The Plea and the Pioneers in Virginia.* Richmond, Va.: Everett Waddey Co., 1905.

Hopson, Ella L. *Memoirs of Dr. Winthrop Hartly Hopson.* Cincinnati: Standard Publishing Co., 1887.

Humble, Bill J. *Campbell and Controversy.* Rosemead, Calif.: Old Paths Book Club, 1952.

Idleman, Finis S. *Peter Ainslie, Ambassador of Good Will.* Chicago: Willett, Clark and Co., 1941.

Jennings, Walter W. *Transylvania, Pioneer University of the West.* New York: Pageant Press, 1955.

Johnson, Charles M. *The Frontier Camp Meeting: Religion's Harvest Time.* Dallas: Southern Methodist University Press, 1955.

Kellems, Jesse R. *Alexander Campbell and the Disciples.* New York: R. R. Smith, 1930.

Lair, Loren E. *The Christian Church (Disciples of Christ) and Its Future.* St. Louis: Bethany Press, 1971.

Leslie, Ruth R. and Wilson, May E. *Historia de la Iglesia Cristiana (Discípulos) en Mexico.* n. p., 1971.

Lipscomb, David. *Life and Sermons of Jesse L. Sewell.* Nashville: Gospel Advocate Publishing Co., 1891.

MacLean, John P. *A Sketch of the Life and Labors of Richard McNemar.* Franklin, Ohio: Published by the author, 1905.

Marshall, Frank H. *Phillips University's First Fifty Years.* Enid, Okla.: Phillips University, 1957.

Mathes, James M. *Life of Elijah Goodwin.* St. Louis: John Burns, 1880.

Miller, Raphael H., ed. *Charles S. Medbury, Preacher and Master Workman for Christ.* St. Louis: Christian Board of Publication, 1932.

Montgomery, Riley B. *The Education of Ministers of Disciples of Christ.* St. Louis: Bethany Press, 1931.

Moore, William T. *The Life of Timothy Coop.* Cincinnati: Standard Publishing Co., 1889.

Morton, C. Manly. *Kingdom Building in Puerto Rico, a Story of Fifty Years of Christian Service.* Indianapolis: United Christian Missionary Society, 1949.

Moseley, J. Edward. *The Concern for Benevolence Among Disciples of Christ.* St. Louis: National Benevolent Association of the Christian Churches [1957].

Muir, Shirley L. and others. *Disciples in Canada, 1867-1967.* n. p.

Nance, Ellwood C. *Florida Christians.* Winter Park, Fla.: College Press, 1941.

Osborn, Ronald E. "The Eldership Among Disciples of Christ; a Historical Case Study in a 'Tent-Making Ministry,' " *Mid-Stream,* Winter, 1967.

Page, Emma, ed. *The Life Work of Mrs. Charlotte Fanning.* Nashville: McQuiddy Printing Co., 1907.

Paulsell, William O. "The Disciples of Christ and the Great Depression." Unpublished Ph.D. thesis, Vanderbilt University, 1965.

Peters, George L. *The Disciples of Christ in Missouri.* Columbia, Mo.: Published by the Centennial Commission of the Missouri Convention of Christian Churches, 1937.

————. *Dreams Come True: A History of Culver-Stockton College.* Canton, Mo.: Board of Trustees, Culver-Stockton College, 1941.

Peters, Harry H. *Charles Reign Scoville, the Man and His Message.* St. Louis: Bethany Press, 1924.

Peterson, Orval D. *Washington-Northern Idaho Disciples.* St. Louis: Christian Board of Publication, 1945.

Powell, Anna D. *Edward Lindsay Powell.* Louisville: Herald Press, 1949.

Rains, Paul B. *Francis Marion Rains.* St. Louis: Christian Board of Publication, 1922.

Rice, Perry J. *Disciples of Christ in Chicago and Northeastern Illinois.* n. p.

Ritchey, Charles J. *Drake University through Seventy-five Years, 1881-1956.* Des Moines: Drake University, 1956.

Rogers, James R. *The Cane Ridge Meeting House* . . . . Cincinnati: Standard Publishing Co., 1910.

Savage, Murray J. *Haddon of Glen Leith: An Ecumenical Pilgrimage.* Glen Leith, Dunedin: Associated Churches of Christ in New Zealand, 1970.

Shaw, Henry K. "The Founding of Butler University, 1847-1855." n. p., 1962. Reprinted from the *Indiana Magazine of History,* Sept. 1962.

Smith, Benjamin L. *Alexander Campbell.* St. Louis: Bethany Press, 1930.

Spice, Byron. *Discipulos Americanos: Sixty-five Years of Christian Churches' Ministry to Spanish-Speaking Persons.* Indianapolis: United Christian Missionary Society, 1964.

Stanger, Allen B. *The Virginia Christian Missionary Society: One Hundred Years, 1875-1975.* Richmond, Va.: The Christian Church (Disciples of Christ) in Virginia, [1975].

Stevenson, Dwight E. *The Bacon College Story: 1836-1865.* Lexington, Ky.: The College of the Bible, 1962.

————. *Disciple Preaching in the First Generation.* Nashville: Disciples of Christ Historical Society, 1969.

Swander, Clarence F. *Making Disciples in Oregon.* Portland: n. p., 1928.

Thompson, Ernest T. *Presbyterians in the South, 1607-1861.* Richmond, Va.: John Knox Press, 1963.

Tyler, J. Z. *Disciples of Christ in Virginia.* Richmond, Va.: n. p., 1879.

The Untold Story: A Short History of Black Disciples, St. Louis: Christian Board of Publication, 1976.

Ware, Charles C. *A History of Atlantic Christian College.* Wilson, N. C.: Atlantic Christian College, 1956.

————. *South Carolina Disciples of Christ: A History.* Charleston, S. C.: Christian Churches of South Carolina, 1967.

Ware, Elias B. *History of the Disciples of Christ in California.* Healdsburg, Calif.: F. W. Cooke, 1916.

Watson, George H. and Mildred B. *History of the Christian Church in the Alabama Area.* St. Louis: Bethany Press, 1965.

Wilburn, James R. *The Hazard of the Die: Tolbert Fanning and the Restoration Movement.* Austin, Tex.: Sweet Publishing Co., 1969.

Wilcox, Alanson. *History of the Disciples of Christ in Ohio.* Cincinnati: Standard Publishing Co., 1918.

Willett, Herbert L.; Jordan, Orvis F. and Sharpe, Charles M., eds. *Progress: Anniversary Volume of the Campbell Institute on the Completion of Twenty Years of History.* Chicago: Christian Century Press, 1917.

Willis, Cecil. *W. W. Otey: Contender for the Faith; a History of Controversies in the Church of Christ, 1860-1960.* Akron, Ohio, 1964.

Woolery, W. Kirk. *Bethany Years, the Story of Old Bethany . . . .* Huntington, West Va.: Standard Printing and Publishing Co., 1941.

Young, M. Norvel. *A History of Colleges Established and Controlled by Members of the Churches of Christ.* Kansas City: Old Paths Book Club, 1949.

Zimmerman, John D. *Sunflower Disciples: Kansas Christian Church History.* n. p. Published as a series of articles in the *Kansas Messenger.*

INDEX